WHALING AND INTERNATI

Whales are regarded as a totemic symbol by some nations and as a natural marine resource by others. This book presents a complex picture of legal problems surrounding the interpretation of the International Convention for the Regulation of Whaling and the role of its regulatory body, the International Whaling Commission. Contemporary whaling is about the competing interests of whaling nations (which are in the minority), non-whaling nations (which are in the majority) and indigenous peoples. Whales are covered by many international conventions, which has led to a very fragmented legal situation and does not necessarily ensure that whales are protected. This is one of the paradoxes of the contemporary international legal regime that are explored in this book. The book also examines the contentious issue of the right of indigenous peoples to whaling and questions whether indigenous whaling is very different from commercial practices.

MALGOSIA FITZMAURICE is a Professor of Public International Law at Department of Law, Queen Mary University of London. She has published on the subjects of environmental law, the law of treaties, indigenous peoples and whaling.

WHALING AND INTERNATIONAL LAW

MALGOSIA FITZMAURICE

CAMBRIDGE
UNIVERSITY PRESS

CAMBRIDGE
UNIVERSITY PRESS

University Printing House, Cambridge CB2 8BS, United Kingdom

One Liberty Plaza, 20th Floor, New York, NY 10006, USA

477 Williamstown Road, Port Melbourne, VIC 3207, Australia

314-321, 3rd Floor, Plot 3, Splendor Forum, Jasola District Centre, New Delhi - 110025, India

79 Anson Road, #06-04/06, Singapore 079906

Cambridge University Press is part of the University of Cambridge.

It furthers the University's mission by disseminating knowledge in the pursuit of education, learning and research at the highest international levels of excellence.

www.cambridge.org
Information on this title: www.cambridge.org/9781108735230

© Cambridge University Press 2015

First published 2015
First paperback edition 2018

A catalogue record for this publication is available from the British Library

Library of Congress Cataloging in Publication data
Fitzmaurice, M., author.
Whaling and international law / Malgosia Fitzmaurice.
pages cm
ISBN 978-1-107-02109-9 (Hardback)
1. Whaling–Law and legislation.   2. Wildlife conservation (International law)
3. International Convention for the Regulation of Whaling (1946 December 2)   I. Title.
K3900.W57.F58 2015
343.07'6928–dc23   2015022168

ISBN 978-1-107-02109-9 Hardback
ISBN 978-1-108-73523-0 Paperback

CONTENTS

ABBREVIATIONS

ACCOBAMS	Agreement on the Conservation of Cetaceans of the Black Sea, Mediterranean Sea and Contiguous Atlantic Area
ACS	American Cetacean Society
AJIL	American Journal of International Law
ART	Animal Rights Theory
ASC	Antarctic Seals Convention
ASCOBANS	Agreement on the Conservation of Small Cetaceans of the Baltic, North East Atlantic, Irish and North Seas
ASIL	American Society of International Law
ASM	Age at Sexual Maturity
ASR	International Law Commission Articles on State Responsibility
ASW	Aboriginal Subsistence Whaling
ASWS	Aboriginal Subsistence Whaling Sub-Committee
AWI	Animal Welfare Institute
AWMP	Aboriginal Whaling Management Procedure
AWMS	Aboriginal Whaling Management Scheme
AYBIL	Australian Yearbook of International Law
BFSP	British and Foreign State Papers
BWU	Blue Whale Unit
BYIL	British Yearbook of International Law
CBD	Convention on Biological Diversity
CC	Conservation Committee
CCAMLR	Commission for the Conservation of Antarctic Marine Living Resources; Convention on the Conservation of Antarctic Marine Living Resources
CERD	International Convention on the Elimination of All Forms of Racial Discrimination
CESCR	Committee on Economic, Social and Cultural Rights
CITES	Convention on International Trade in Endangered Species of Fauna and Flora
CLA	Catch Limit Algorithm
CMS	Convention on the Conservation of Migratory Species of Wild Animals

CoE	Council of Europe
COP	Conference of the Parties
CPUE	catch per unit of effort
CRC	Convention on the Right of the Child
DFO	Department of Fisheries and Oceans
DOC	US Department of Commerce
EA	Environmental Assessment
ECHR	European Convention on Human Rights
ECOSOC	UN Economic and Social Council
ECtHR	European Court of Human Rights
EEZ	exclusive economic zone
EJIL	European Journal of International Law
EIS	Environment Impact Statement
ENGO	environmental non-governmental organisation
EPBC Act	Environment Protection and Biodiversity Conservation Act
ESA	Endangered Species Act
EU	European Union
FAC	Finance and Administration Committee
FAO	Food and Agriculture Organization
GATT	General Agreement on Tariffs and Trade
GYIL	German Yearbook of International Law
HRC	Human Rights Committee
HSI	Humane Society International
HTO	Hunters and Trappers Organisation
ICCPR	International Covenant on Civil and Political Rights
ICES	International Council for the Exploration of the Sea
ICESCR	International Covenant on Economic, Social and Cultural Rights
ICJ	International Court of Justice
ICR	Institute of Cetacean Research
ICRW	International Convention for the Regulation of Whaling
IGO	intergovernmental organisation
ILC	International Law Commission
ILM	International Legal Materials
ILO	International Labour Organization
IMO	International Maritime Organization
IOS	International Observer Scheme
ISC	Infractions Sub-Committee
ITLOS	International Tribunal for the Law of the Sea
IUCN	International Union for the Conservation of Nature
IWC	International Whaling Commission
JARPA	Japanese Research Programme in the Antarctic
JARPN	Japanese Research Programme in the North West Pacific

JCNB	Joint Commission on the Conservation and Management of Narwhal and Beluga
JSCW	Japanese Small Coastal Whaling
JWG	Joint Working Group
KANUKOKA	Greenland Association of Municipalities
KNAPK	Organisation of Fishermen and Hunters
LNTS	League of Nations Treaty Series
MARPOL	1973 Convention on Prevention of Pollution from Ships
MEA	Multilateral Environmental Agreement
MMAP	Global Plan of Action for the Conservation, Management and Utilisation of Marine Mammals
MMPA	Marine Mammal Protection Act
MOU	Memorandum of Understanding
MqJICEL	Macquarie Journal of International and Comparative Environmental Law
MSY	maximum sustainable yield
MSYR	maximum sustainable yield rate
NAC	North Atlantic Committee for Coordination of Marine Mammals Research
NAMMCO	North Atlantic Marine Mammal Commission
NEPA	National Environmental Policy Act
NEWREP-A	New Scientific Research Programme in the Antarctic Ocean
NGO	non-governmental organisation
NMP	New Management Procedure
NOAA	National Oceanic and Atmospheric Administration
NWMB	Nunavut Wildlife Management Board
ODIL	Ocean Development & International Law
PCES	Permanent Council for the Exploration of the Sea
RCADI	Recueil des Cours de Droit International
RECIEL	Review of European Community and International Environmental Law
RMP	Revised Management Procedure
RMS	Revised Management Scheme
RST	Review of Significant Trade
SAC	Special Areas of Conservation
SC	Scientific Committee
SLA	Strike Limit Algorithm
SOS	Southern Ocean Sanctuary
TAC	Total Allowable Catch
TEK	traditional ecological knowledge
TPAK	Organisation of Leisure Hunters
UDHR	Universal Declaration of Human Rights

UNCLOS	United Nations Convention on the Law of the Sea
UNDRIP	United Nations Declaration on the Rights of Indigenous Peoples
UNEP	United Nations Environmental Programme
UNESCO	United Nations Educational, Scientific and Cultural Organization
UNTS	United Nations Treaty Series
VCLT	Vienna Convention on the Law of Treaties
WDCS	Whale and Dolphin Conservation Society
WGWKM	Working Group on Whale Killing Methods and Associated Welfare Issues
WTO	World Trade Organization
WWF	World Wildlife Fund

ACKNOWLEDGEMENTS

The author would like to express her thanks to Mr Andrew Filis for his excellent comments on the first draft of this book, to the anonymous reviewer for very constructive comments on the structure of the book and to Ms Elizabeth Spicer and Ms Gillian Dadd from Cambridge University Press for their support during the work on the manuscript.

The author would also like to express her thanks to Brill–Nijhoff for giving her permission to include in this book Chapter 8 ('A case study of the protection of the narwhal whale'), which is an updated and extended version of the article 'So Much Law, So Little Protection! A Case Study of the Protection of the Narwhal' published in the *Yearbook of Polar Law* (2009), 21–54.

The author also wishes to thank Professor Donald Rothwell for kindly making available articles from the *Australian Yearbook of International Law*.

TABLE OF CASES

International courts and tribunals

Inter-American Court of Human Rights

Àngela Poma Poma v. Peru, Communication 1457/2006, 27 March 2009, UN Doc. CCPR/C/95/D/1457/2006 (2009)

International arbitration tribunal

Pacific Fur Seal Arbitration, Moore's International Arbitration, 755 (1893)

International Court of Justice

Barcelona Traction, Light and Power Company Limited, Judgment, ICJ Reports 1970, p. 3

Continental Shelf (Libyan Arab Jamahiriya v. Malta), Judgment, ICJ Reports 1995, p. 13

East Timor (Portugal v. Australia), Judgment, ICJ Reports 1995, p. 90

Gabčíkovo–Nagymaros Project (Hungary v. Slovakia), Case Concerning, 1997 ICJ Reports, p. 7

Legality of the Threat or Use of Nuclear Weapons, Advisory Opinion, ICJ Reports 1996, p. 226

Oil Platforms (Islamic Republic of Iran v. United States of America), Case Concerning, Judgment, ICJ Reports 2003, p. 16

Pulp Mills on the River Uruguay (Argentina v. Uruguay), Case Concerning, Judgment, ICJ Reports 2010, p. 14

Questions Relating to the Obligation to Prosecute or Extradite (Belgium v. Senegal), Judgment, ICJ Reports 2012, p. 422

Request for an Examination of the Situation in Accordance with paragraph 63 of the Court's Judgment of 20 December 1974 in the Nuclear Tests (New Zealand v. France) Case, Order of 22 September 1995

South West Africa, Second Phase, Judgment, ICJ Reports 1966, p. 6

Whaling in the Antarctic (Australia v. Japan, New Zealand intervening), Judgment, www.icj-cij.org/docket/files/148/18136.pdf

International Tribunal for the Law of the Sea

United Nations Human Rights Committee

World Trade Organization

National courts

Bangladesh

The Philippines

United States of America

TABLE OF TREATIES, DECLARATIONS AND GENERAL COMMENTS

Treaties

xiv

Declarations

General Comments

~

Introduction

Whaling is a source of issues of great interest not only for lawyers (both national and international) but also for philosophers and anthropologists. It is a topic that has been covered by numerous publications, undoubtedly excellent; however, some, while covering whaling holistically, were published before the latest important developments took place (such as the *Whaling in the Antarctic* case), while others have mainly focused on discrete legal aspects of whaling. More than a few questions of international law have been looked at from very diverse viewpoints, and, on occasion, have been the cause of highly emotional reactions. The history of whaling is certainly not short of examples where whaling emerges as a complex, conflict-ridden and divisive field.

The complexity of whaling became patently clear in the 2014 *Whaling in the Antarctic* case before the International Court of Justice (ICJ), analysis of which is contained in a subsequent chapter of the present publication. Whaling engages a plethora of legal issues, ranging from biodiversity considerations to those relating to trade and the environment, to questions of, among other things, interpretation within the context of the law of treaties. Furthermore, whaling is an example of the close link between, and the dynamic interplay of, science and law.

From a philosophical and, more specifically, ethical point of view, one could query whether animals in general (and whales in particular) have rights, and, if so, what might be the interplay of such rights with those of other rights holders. To be more precise, how might animal rights engage with the right to cultural identity not only of, say, indigenous peoples, but also of other peoples who, although not indigenous in the traditional sense, are peoples whose history is not unrelated to whaling: for instance, the Japanese, the Icelanders, the Faroese and the Norwegians. Therefore, the matters that whaling engages are certainly not limited to the field of environmental law (or the notion of biodiversity).

This collection of thematically self-standing chapters does not aim to present whaling in an all-encompassing and exhaustive manner; rather it seeks to highlight particular issues that, for the most part, are complex and contentious in legal and ethical senses. It also provides some historical background that points towards the presence of contentious issues from the early stages of interstate whaling regulation and that are still very much present. The historical background demonstrates not only that the complexity of the issues connected to whaling is not new (but has had a rather continuous character), but also that these issues are not exclusively confined to the International Whaling Commission phenomenon.[1] From a historical perspective, the conflict between utilisation and conservation was already present during the negotiations of the first whaling conventions, and some of the main actors that were engaged in a (contentious) dialogue still play a prominent role in the whaling conflict.

The book covers contemporary issues of whaling, and includes an analysis of the 1946 Whaling Convention and its Commission. It also explores issues of whaling for commercial, aboriginal and scientific purposes.

The book provides analyses of the ethical questions relating to whaling, and introduces the doctrine of intergenerational equity as it may apply to whaling. It includes observations on the relationship between the International Whaling Convention and other multilateral environmental agreements – both global (such as the Bonn Convention on Migratory Species) and regional (such as the Agreement on Conservation of Small Cetaceans of the Baltic, North East Atlantic, Irish and North Seas and the Agreement on the Conservation of Cetaceans of the Black Sea, Mediterranean Sea and Contiguous Atlantic Area). It analyses the relationship of the Whaling Convention with trade (regarding the Convention on International Trade in Endangered Species of Wild Fauna and Flora). Furthermore, the book also deals with whaling outside the framework of the Whaling Convention.

Finally, it contains certain suggestions for the future, particularly in relation to methods of conflict resolution within the International Whaling Commission with regard to whaling for commercial, aboriginal and scientific purposes.

---

[1] This is well evidenced in the excellent book of Kurkpatrick Dorsey, *Whales and Nations: Environmental Diplomacy on the High Seas* (University of Washington Press, 2014).

1

The history of whaling

Introduction

The present chapter is devoted to outlining, albeit only briefly, the historical aspects of whaling, since, as was stated in the Introduction, this book focuses principally on current issues concerning whaling. This chapter will be primarily focused on whaling and its development throughout the centuries, with special attention to the pre-conventional and early conventional regulation. A substantial part of this chapter will be devoted to analysis of the two pre-Second World War Conventions, the 1931 Geneva Convention and the 1937 London Agreement. The main purpose of this chapter is to show that the contemporary problems concerning whaling are to some extent a continuation of the issues that existed earlier and which prompted States to conclude the above-mentioned treaties.

The 1931 and 1937 Conventions formed the basis for the 1946 Convention for the Regulation of Whaling (which will be discussed in Chapter 2). In order to fully appreciate the 1946 Convention and its role in relation to whales and whaling, it is necessary to present an analysis of previous international instruments. As will be seen, neither of the two preceding Conventions can be hailed as a success. The 1946 Convention is considered by many not to be the most effective international treaty, the reasons for which are complex and are not confined only to legal issues but also extend to scientific and political issues. However, this Convention is still operational after almost seventy years since its signing; therefore, despite the serious problems, it exhibits a certain resilience and longevity.

1.1 Pre-conventional whaling

Modern whaling began in 1868. Until that year,

> the capture of whales was as crude as it was daring: men from rowing boats would hurl hand-harpoons or bomb-lances at the swiftly moving

whale, limiting the catch to those species, such as the Right, Greenland, and Sperm Whales, which floated when dead.[1]

Whaling appears to have begun thousands of years ago, possibly as early as 2200 BC.[2] It is believed that the first organised hunt was conducted by the Basques in 700 AD, followed by the Flemish and the Normans, and then the British and the Dutch, surpassing the whaling activities of the Basques. Spain, Norway and France started whale hunting in the ninth century AD. The British, the Dutch and the Germans expanded their whaling activities to the North Atlantic. Japan and Russia are considered to have started coastal whaling in the twelfth century and the US in the sixteenth century.[3] The early period of whaling was characterised by whaling from land stations as the main method, with the use of hand-thrown harpoons and nets from rowing boats. After that, the captured whales were processed in coastal waters. Subsequent to the depletion of coastal whale resources, the period of pelagic – that is to say, in the open ocean away from the coast – whaling began.[4] Pelagic whaling also resulted in the following: the expansion of whaling techniques; Russia establishing stations in Korea; and land stations opening in many other littoral States, such as Australia and Canada.[5] With the development of new technology relating to vessels, however, land stations lost their importance. Whales were processed entirely on-board factory ships, which resulted in States expanding their operations beyond territorial waters. Whale catches also increased due to new technology, such as shell harpoons with an explosive head which detonated inside the whale, shortening the time of dying for the whale, and sonar devices and helicopters to

---

[1] On the history of whaling, see in particular: Richard Ellis, *Men and Whales* (New York: Knopf, 1991); L. Larry Leonard, 'Recent Negotiations Toward the International Regulation of Whaling', AJIL 35 (1941), 90–113, 91. See also: James M. Savelle and Nobuhiro Kishigami, 'Anthropological Research on Whaling: Prehistoric, Historic and Current Contexts', *Senri Ethnological Studies, No. 84, Anthropological Studies of Whaling* (Osaka: National Museum of Ethnology, 2013), pp. 1–48.

[2] Lisa Kobayashi, 'Lifting the International Whaling Commission's Moratorium on Commercial Whaling as the Most Effective Global Regulation of Whaling', *Environs* 29 (2006), 177–219.

[3] Ibid., p. 181.

[4] www.britannica.com/EBchecked/topic/449062/pelagic-zone, last accessed 27 December 2014.

[5.] Kobayashi, above n. 2, 181.

track whales. In the end, the main commercial whaling concentrated on the Antarctic.[6]

Tønnessen and Johnsen have observed that old and modern whaling differ biologically, technically and economically.[7] They explain that the baleen whales caught in the past were right whales (mostly the Nordkaper), and, from about 1600 onwards, the Greenland whale.[8] In contrast, modern whaling is based on hunting rorquals, due to the fact that the stocks of right whales were in effect decimated in the nineteenth century, and so were no longer profitable. Rorquals' physical characteristics (such as their speed) required different hunting methods to right whales. This was the beginning of modern whaling.[9] The modern method (first introduced by the Norwegian Sven Foyn, off the coast of Finnmark) involved steam- or diesel-driven boats; a harpoon fired from a canon, positioned on the bow of the boat; a grenade attached to the harpoon, which exploded inside the whale; and a line attached to the harpoon, in order to haul the whale to the surface and tow it to the shore station or to a floating factory. Commercially, this method was almost exclusively aimed at the extraction of oil, demand for which played a crucial role in the development of whaling.[10] Tønnessen and Johnsen describe in great detail the rapid development of various non-humane methods of killing whales by many whaling countries, including Great Britain and the United States, but also by others such as Germany. Two such methods, developed in Great Britain, were the use of 'bomb-lances', that is to say whale shell, and exploding harpoons (invented in 1831), which were a combination of shell and a harpoon in a single projectile equipped with a line.[11]

Unlimited and unregulated whaling commenced in 1883 and lasted for twenty-one years that 'proved more than stocks of whales could stand'.[12] The whale catchers had to find new grounds, as, for instance, stocks around Northern Finnmark became entirely depleted. However, the technique of killing whales by the grenade harpoon, introduced by Foyn, remained unchanged for another hundred years.[13] Until 1883, there are no reliable data on the number and type of species caught. Tønnessen

---

[6] Ibid., 182–3.
[7] J. N. Tønnessen and A. O. Johnsen, *The History of Modern Whaling*, trans. R. I. Christophersen (Canberra: Australian National University Press, 1982), p. 6.
[8] Ibid., p. 5.　　[9] Ibid., p. 6.　　[10] Ibid., pp. 6–7.　　[11] Ibid., p. 18.　　[12] Ibid., p. 35.
[13] Ibid., p. 35. See also Savelle and Kishigami, above n. 1, 7.

and Johnsen are of the view that, despite the lack of data, it is without doubt that all species of whales were caught, not only blue whales.[14]

Another invention contributing to an increase in the number of whale species hunted occurred in 1921 when Peter Sørlle patented a 'slip-way' for factory ships (it was a vent through which whales could be hauled onto the deck to be flensed). This invention rendered unnecessary the presence of whalers in harbours and shores.[15] Ships whaling in waters off South Georgia and the South Shetland Islands, west of the Antarctic Archipelago, and using their harbours and shores, which were under British sovereignty, had required permits from the British Colonial Office for such activity. Therefore, the permits system could be seen as providing a degree of regulation in the pre-conventional era, given that such permits were a means of limiting whaling and controlling the industry. However, the introduction of 'slip-way' vessels made permits from the British Colonial Office redundant, thus leading to whaling reverting to its formerly unregulated state. From 1925, due to 'slip-way' use, 'pelagic whaling became the order of the day; expeditions made of catchers and factory ships could remain at sea for long periods of time, following the whale migrations, catching fresher whales, and thereby obtaining larger quantities of oil'.[16]

1.2   The history of whaling immediately before and during conventional regulation

The largest expansion in the entire history of whaling occurred in two separate periods: 1927–31 relating to Norwegian–British whaling and 1934 relating to Japanese–German whaling.

The most important factor for this expansion was the improvement in world markets following the world economic crisis of the interwar period that had affected whale oil sales and therefore production.[17] Tønnessen and Johnsen have produced figures relating to the scope of the expansion of whaling. For instance, for the period 1927–8, 13,775 whales were caught, resulting in 1,037,393 barrels of oil. During that period, there were 6 shore stations, 18 floating stations and 84 catchers. For the period 1930–1 the figures were: 40,201 whales caught; 3,608,348 barrels of oil; 6 shore stations, 41 floating factories; and 238 catchers. In relation to pelagic Antarctic whaling, in 1927–8 10,138 whales were caught,

---

[14] Tønnessen and Johnsen, above n. 7, p. 36.   [15] Leonard, above n. 1, 91.
[16] Ibid., 92.   [17] Tønnessen and Johnsen, above n. 7, p. 367.

resulting in 733,912 barrels of oil, and there were 17 floating factories and 61 catchers. In 1930–1, 37,438 whales were caught, resulting in the production of 3,384,048 barrels of oil, and there were 41 floating stations and 200 catchers.[18] These numbers clearly indicate that most whaling was conducted as Antarctic pelagic whaling; it quadrupled in the course of three successive periods. However, over-production and over-expansion coincided with the world crisis and a decrease in the price of all raw materials, which resulted in the collapse of the excess capacity (that is to say, the production capacity that was not being absorbed by market demand) in the whaling industry.[19]

Certain changes in numbers of caught whales occurred after the 1931 Geneva Convention.[20] However, the United Kingdom only ratified this Convention four and a half years after its signing, and, in the meantime, continued with its unrestricted whaling. Eighteen nations, including Norway, ratified before the United Kingdom did. 'In Norwegian quarters it was stated that Norway may be forced to abolish all restrictions, given that unrestrained British catching had created so much bitterness among Norwegian whalers that the situation was untenable.'[21] After the 1931 Convention entered into force, for the first time in the history of whaling the term 'quotas' was used in the production agreement between Norway and Unilever (the consumer goods company).[22] However, the Convention did not result in any great success, largely due to the reluctance of States and companies to adhere to a system of private quota agreements.[23]

The 1937 London Agreement on Whaling was no more successful than the 1931 Convention. Suffice it to note at this point that the primary object of the London Conference – namely, to restrict catches in order to preserve whale stocks – proved a total fiasco.[24] It failed to prevent 11,519 more baleen whales being killed and 683,815 more barrels of oil being produced than in the previous season. Antarctic pelagic whaling never

---

[18] Ibid., p. 385. There are some discrepancies in these numbers. For example, for the season 1930–1 the number of killed whales was, according to International Whaling Statistics, even higher at 42,874. International Whaling Statistics, vol. 13 (1939), 3–4.

[19] Tønnessen and Johnsen, above n. 7, p. 385.

[20] Convention for the Regulation of Whaling, 24 September 1931, 155 LNTS 349.

[21] Tønnessen and Johnsen, above n. 7, p. 401.

[22] Unilever is an Anglo-Dutch multinational consumer goods company co-headquartered in London and Rotterdam. Its products include food, beverages, cleaning agents and personal care products.

[23] Tønnessen and Johnsen, above n. 7, p. 406.   [24] Ibid., p. 453.

8   THE HISTORY OF WHALING

recovered after the excessive whaling of the 1930s (partly due to the increased number of whale catchers). Japan and Germany accounted for 84 per cent of the production increase in the 1937–8 period.[25] World production in the 1936–7 period totalled 3 million barrels of oil.

The London Agreement also failed to restrict the number of catchers. Between 1936 and 1937, 19 catchers were built in Norway, 20 in the United Kingdom, 40 in Germany and 28 in Japan, thus bringing the world total to 107. Out of the total number, 23 were for Norwegian companies, 30 for British, 24 for German, 28 for Japanese and 2 for Panamanian companies. The talks during the London Conference on restricting the number of whale catchers failed.[26] The late 1930s resulted in a slaughter of fin whales, due to a decrease in numbers of caught blue and humpback whales, which had been over-fished. The 1938 amendment to the London Agreement also failed.

Generally, the late 1930s were characterised by a decrease in the production of whale oil but this was due only to over-fishing, not to conservation efforts. During the Second World War, there was a slump in catches. For the 1940–1 period the figures for pelagic whaling were as follows: the Norwegians caught 2,387 whales and produced 203,317 barrels of oil; the British caught 3,116 whales and produced 229,780 barrels of oil; the Japanese (over the course of six expeditions) caught 9,992 whales and produced 622,413 barrels of oil.[27] An additional cause of concern was the number of immature whales killed. The percentage of immature blue whales killed more than doubled from 8.14 per cent in 1930–1 to 20.83 per cent in 1938–9.[28]

1.3   The 1931 Geneva Convention on Whaling: circumstances leading to its conclusion

The need for the regulation of whaling was brought to the attention of the League of Nations in 1925 by M. José Suarez in his report on Codification, Questionnaire No. 7, 'Exploitation of the Products of the Sea',[29] in which he observed that the modern whaling industry was 'rapidly exterminating the whale' and added further that:

---

[25] Ibid., p. 454.   [26] Ibid., pp. 455–6.   [27] Ibid., p. 483.
[28] International Whaling Statistics, vol. 14 (1940), 10, cited in Leonard, above n. 1, 93–4.
[29] Report of M. José Suarez, 'Exploitation of the Products of the Sea'. The Committee of Experts, convened by the Council of the League of Nations (in accordance with the Assembly Resolution of 22 September 1924), was authorised after sending a

[t]oday [whaling] is carried out with the help of a perfected form of weapon and special craft; but the increase in its scope is due to the manner in which the animal is treated once it has been killed. The extraction of the *oil*, which previously had to be done ashore, is now done in floating factories, which accelerates the process ten- or twenty-fold and renders national control impossible.[30]

Early efforts to regulate whaling were not aimed at the protection of whales but, rather, at securing a high price for whale oil. During the 1932–3 period, Norwegian whaling companies concluded production agreements for this purpose, and later secured a decision of the *Storting* (the Norwegian Parliament) to that effect. The whaling companies had limits on the absolute number of whales they could kill but the number of barrels of oil that these companies were allowed to produce could be increased by more efficient processing of the whale.[31] The minimum production was calculated per blue whale and was fixed at 100 barrels. These production agreements also concerned closed seasons; no hunting was to take place before 20 October, with the exception of South Georgia, for which there was an early start date (10 October).[32] However, British and Japanese companies did not enter into any such agreements, and continued with their activities without being subjected

questionnaire to various governments to draw up a list of questions which were 'ripe' for codification. On 7 April 1927, the Committee submitted seven questions that were ready to be codified. The question of exploitation of the products of the sea was no. 7 on the list. Report to the Council of the League of Nations on the Questions Which Appear Ripe for Codification, League of Nations Doc. C.196.M.70.1927.V, p. 122, cited in Leonard, above n. 1, 97. See also Philip Jessup, 'L'exploitation des richesses de la mer', RCADI 29 (1929), 401–514; Arnold Raestad, 'La chasse à la baleine en mer libre', *Revue de Droit International* 2 (1928), 595–642.

[30] In his Report Suarez adopted a very modern approach to the protection of natural resources of the sea and referred to the wealth of the sea as the patrimony of the whole human race, therefore: '[t]o save this wealth, which, being today the uncontrolled property of all, belongs to nobody, the only thing to be done is to discard the obsolete rules of the existing treaties, which were drawn up with other objects, to take a wider view, and to base a new jurisprudence ... on the scientific and economic considerations which ... may be put forward, compared and discussed at a technical conference by the countries concerned'. Reproduced in Shabtai Rosenne (ed.), *The Law of Treaties: A Guide to the Legislative History of the Vienna Convention* (1970); League of Nations, *Committee of Experts on the Progressive Codification of International Law (1925–1928)*, 2 vols. (1972); League of Nations, *Conference on the Codification of International Law* (1930), 4 vols. (1975), at 146.

[31] Leonard, above n. 1, 96.

[32] International Whaling Statistics, vol. 5 (1934), 2, cited in Leonard, above n. 1, 96.

to any regulation. Soon, this resulted in Norwegian companies returning to unrestricted whaling.

There were certain oddities in the League of Nations' timid attempts at regulating the whaling industry.[33] For example, leadership on the work on whaling under the auspices of the League of Nations (in conjunction with ICES)[34] was provided by Johan Hjort, a Norwegian who also on occasion (and unofficially) represented whale oil industrial interests, including at the meeting in Geneva that had led to the first treaty on the conservation of whales. It appeared to be a daunting task to reconcile the interests of the expanding whaling industry (in the 1920s) with the welfare of whales. The United Kingdom made diplomatic efforts to head off 'ill-conceived and embarrassing proposals, which seemed to be anything coming from the League of Nations'.[35] These 'embarrassing' proposals related to the attempts to regulate whaling, including closed seasons, a cap on whaling, sanctuaries and generally concluding an international convention.[36] However, in the years leading to the conclusion of the 1931 Convention two leaderships emerged: Norway with regard to legal matters; and the United Kingdom with regard to scientific research. These two leading whaling nations were not always in agreement, and had very different ideas relating to one of the most basic questions: how and when whale migration took place. However, the expansion of whaling was so great that Hjort was of

---

[33] See excellent monographs on the history of whaling, including contemporary issues, by Kurkpatrick Dorsey, *Whales and Nations: Environmental Diplomacy on the High Seas* (University of Washington Press, 2014), p. 36; and Graham Burnett, *The Sounding of a Whale. Science and Cetaceans in the Twentieth Century* (University of Chicago Press, 2012), in particular chapters 1–3.

[34] The International Council for the Exploration of the Sea (ICES) is a global organisation that develops science and advice to support the sustainable use of the oceans. Established in 1902, originally for the purpose of setting up a forum to discuss aspects of marine research, ICES evolved into a leading collector of marine information, bringing together scientific experts from a broad range of specialties: www.britannica.com/EBchecked/topic/290834/International-Council-for-the-Exploration-of-the-Sea-ICES, last accessed 27 December 2014. ICES is a network of more than 4,000 scientists from over 350 marine institutes in 20 member countries and beyond. 1,600 scientists participate in ICES activities annually. Through strategic partnerships its work is also extended into the Arctic, the Mediterranean Sea, the Black Sea and the North Pacific Ocean. ICES advances this through the coordination of oceanic and coastal monitoring and research, and advises international commissions and governments on marine policy and management issues: www.ices.dk/Pages/default.aspx, last accessed 27 December 2014.

[35] Cited in Dorsey, above n. 33, p. 36.   [36] Ibid., p. 36.

the view that science would not be able to answer fundamental questions in time.[37]

The Whaling Committee at the Copenhagen Council presented a
Report in 1934 that clearly indicated that leaving the control of whaling
dependent on a voluntary agreement – which might at any time cease
to operate – was unsatisfactory. The Whaling Committee concluded its
findings by stating that: '[a]ny measures of control in order to be
effective would need to be applied by international agreement'.[38]
Suarez, in his Report, presented a deplorable state of the whaling industry, and recommended a new system of justice/legal regime construed
on the basis of scientific and economic considerations. In order to
conceive such a system, he recommended convening a technical conference of interested States to discuss it. Suarez expressed the need for
immediate action in order to protect whales, and singled out Norwegian
companies for unsustainable killing of whales to achieve very high
profits.[39]

The questionnaire sent to States included the question whether an
international agreement should be concluded 'regarding the exploitation
of the products of the sea'. The view of the United Kingdom was that
international rules governing the exploitation of the products of the sea
were best established by concluding bilateral and multilateral agreements
by concerned States. It also stated that it would not be advisable to
conclude one general convention governing all products of the sea,
but rather to enter into particular conventions, relating to particular
products and particular areas.[40] Japan supported the conclusion of bilateral and plurilateral agreements between States directly concerned in the
exploitation of sea resources.[41] This was also the preferred position of
France.[42] There was a group of States – the Netherlands, Germany and
Norway – that would have preferred to refer the matter to the Economic
Committee of the League of Nations, to examine it in conjunction with
the Permanent Council for the Exploration of the Sea (PCES) in
Copenhagen.[43] In fact, the regulation of the exploitation of the living
resources of the sea, of which whaling was merely a subset, garnered

[37] Ibid., p. 37.
[38] *Rapports et procès-verbaux des réunions*, 84 (1934), 42, cited in Leonard, above n. 1, 96.
[39] Suarez, above n. 29, 123–4, cited in Leonard, above n. 1, 97.
[40] Ibid., 146, cited in Leonard, above n. 1, 97.
[41] Ibid., 172, cited in Leonard, above n. 1, 97.
[42] Ibid., 164, cited in Leonard, above n. 1, 97.
[43] Ibid., 181, cited in Leonard, above n. 1, 97.

significant support. Denmark was of the view that such a matter was of practical importance, and Romania supported the inclusion of Questionnaire No. 7 as a matter of 'the highest importance for the future of mankind', a stance which, in fact, is the modern approach adopted towards whaling and has found its expression in the Preamble to the 1946 Whaling Convention (discussed in Chapter 2).

There were also different views, such as those of Portugal, which held that the general question of the conservation of the living resources of the sea could be solved through the extension of the territorial sea up to twelve or fifteen nautical miles. Regarding the particular issue of whaling, Portugal supported the concluding of an international agreement to prevent the killing of pregnant females and young whales, and to restrict the use of floating factories.[44] Sweden was particularly concerned about whaling in the Antarctic waters.[45] The United States supported the idea of convening an international conference to solve the problem of excessive and unregulated whaling in the high seas.[46] Eventually, the matter of the desirability of the regulation of whaling was submitted for consideration to the Economic Committee of the League of Nations to act in collaboration with other organisations, in particular with the PCES.[47]

In 1928, the Report of the Economic Committee was submitted to the League Council.[48] The Committee made several observations. First, the PCES recommended that it was advisable to convene a body of experts to study the problem of international protection of whales. It further stated that at the time, although there was no danger of complete extermination of certain species of whales, there was real danger of commercial extermination. Due to the very high costs of modern whaling, companies had to kill a large number of whales in order to turn over a profit, 'and if hunting becomes unprofitable it will stop by itself, long before the whales are exterminated', the Committee stated.[49] At that time stocks of bowhead whales and right whales were considered to be almost entirely depleted due to the considerable value of their oil and the ease with which they were killed. However,

---

[44] Ibid., 193, cited in Leonard, above n. 1, 97.
[45] Ibid., 240, cited in Leonard, above n. 1, 97.
[46] Ibid., 161, cited in Leonard, above n. 1, 97.
[47] Ibid., League of Nations Doc. A.18.1927.V, p. 7, cited in Leonard, above n. 1, 97.
[48] *Rapports et procès-verbaux des réunions*, 49 (1928), 112, cited in Leonard, above n. 1, 98.
[49] *League of Nations Official Journal* (1929), 1594, cited in Leonard, above n. 1, 99.

stocks of blue, fin, sperm and humpback whales were estimated at the time as plentiful.[50]

Also in 1928, the Whaling Committee of the PCES recommended international regulation for extensively migrating species of whale, and also called upon governments to promulgate regulation preventing 'wasteful exploitation of whales', which would involve protection of immature whales and full utilisation of carcasses of whales.[51] The Economic Committee of the League of Nations advised that the Committee of Experts should prepare the text of an agreement to be submitted to governments. The Committee of Experts convened in 1930 and submitted a draft convention which was based on the 1929 Norwegian Whaling Act, which required complete protection of right whales, provided for the utilisation of the whole carcass of a whale, and required the submission of detailed statistical data on hunting activities for the purposes of collecting accurate statistical data for the future. The Economic Committee made some changes to the draft, and the League Council, which was in favour of the Convention, submitted it to the members and non-members of the League of Nations for comments.[52] The Committee of Experts submitted a final Report, drafted by Mr Birger Braadland, and the draft Convention to the Assembly.[53] The Report emphasised that the purpose of the Convention was to lay down rules to protect the interests of the whaling industry, by preserving this 'source of wealth available to all'. The Report also expressed concern that should the provisions of the Convention not extend to all States (including non-parties), then the entire whaling industry would be at risk, as, 'under the protection of the flag of States not parties to the Convention, vessels may engage in operations contrary to the rules adopted by common accord with a view of safeguarding industry the very existence [of which] is seriously imperilled'.[54]

The Special Committee of the United States Senate on Conservation of Wildlife Resources also examined the draft Convention from the perspective of the interests of the United States (with regard to the whaling

---

[50] R. Kellogg, 'What is Known of the Migration of Some of the Whalebone Whales', *Annual Report of the Smithsonian Institution* (1928), 467–94. See on Kellogg, Burnett, above n. 33, pp. 191–325 (chapter 3: 'The Prince of Whales').
[51] *League of Nations Official Journal* (1929), 1596, cited in Leonard, above n. 1, 99.
[52] Leonard, above n. 1, 99.
[53] League of Nations Doc. A.64.1931.II.B, cited in Leonard, above n. 1, 100.
[54] Agreement, Final Act, para. 9.

industry of the United States).[55] The Report of the Special Committee, in a manner similar to Braadland's Report, outlined the purpose of the draft Convention to be to preserve the interests of the whaling States, including the United States. It read as follows:

> The steady growth of this [whaling] industry in the last few years, thanks to the improvements in equipment and technique, has resulted in an ever-larger increase in the number of *baleanoptera* killed. Estimates obtained from various sources show that, for several years past, the number taken has varied from 25,000 to 30,000 each season! For the season which has just closed, the enormous figure of 40,000 has been mentioned. Past experience shows the necessity of making an effort to prevent the extinction of the species that are chiefly hunted by modern whalers.[56]

The Convention for the Regulation of Whaling was opened for signature in Geneva on 24 September 1931 and was ratified by twenty-eight States.[57] It came into force on 16 January 1935.

The ratification of the 1931 Convention by the United Kingdom was quite a complex affair. The United Kingdom was unable to pass the necessary domestic legislation on whaling and 'much less engineer a powerful international organisation'.[58] Having heavily influenced several governments to sign the 1931 Convention, the British government was itself in the rather embarrassing position of failing to ratify it in due course.[59] Eventually, the 1931 Whaling Convention was given effect in the United Kingdom by means of primary legislation. Prior to the deposit of the act of ratification, the British Parliament enacted legislation giving effect to the 1931 Convention, namely, the Whaling Industry (Regulation) Act 1934, which had received royal assent in 1934.[60] One of the provisions of the 1934 Act was the establishment of Whale Fishery Inspectors authorised to board or enter for inspection any ship or factory believed to be used for hunting or treating whales, and to ask for any documents from the master of the ship. This Act also provided for

---

[55] Senate Committee Print, 73rd Cong., 2nd Sess. Incorporating report pursuant to Senate Resolution 246, 71st Congress, 'Economics of the Whaling Industry with Relationship to the Convention for the Regulation of Whaling', cited in William Roy Vallance, 'The International Convention for Regulation of Whaling and the Act of Congress Giving Effect to its Provisions', AJIL 31 (1937), 112–19, 114.

[56] Ibid., 115.

[57] 1931 Convention for the Regulation of Whaling, 155 LNTS 349, www.ecolex.org/ecolex/ledge/view/RecordDetails?id=TRE-000073&index=treaties/, last accessed 19 June 2015.

[58] Dorsey, above n. 33, p. 54.   [59] Ibid., p. 54.   [60] 1934 c. 49, 24 and 25 Geo 5.

the imposition of a fine of £100 in case of obstruction or refusal to facilitate the Inspectors in the discharge of their duties.[61]

Other States also enacted legislation to introduce the Convention in their domestic legal order where the constitutional settings in question required it. In the United States the relevant Bill was approved by the President of the United States in 1936.[62] The Bill was partly based on the 1918 Migratory Bird Treaty (United States and Canada) and the 1936 Act giving effect to the 1911 Convention for the Preservation and Protection of Fur Seals and Sea Otters of the North Pacific Ocean (United States, Great Britain, Japan and Russia).[63] Regulations under the 1911 Convention were issued by the Secretary of Commerce and the Secretary of the Treasury and approved by the President in 1936.[64] These Regulations stated that all whaling operations should be 'deemed compatible' with the terms of the Convention and the Regulations (Article 4). The Regulations included two exceptions from prohibited whaling: whaling for 'scientific purposes' and native Eskimo whaling, the description of which reflected the provisions of the Convention. It should be noted that dolphin and porpoise stocks were exempted from the Regulations (Article 6).

Japan did not sign the 1931 Convention. The requests on the part of the British and Norwegian governments for Japan to sign were met with the reply that such action would be premature, as the Japanese whaling industry was in its infancy and, thus, the situation was not one of parity between the parties – in other words, Japan would need time to further develop its whaling industry before subjecting it to international regulation. A further argument on the part of Japan was that whaling conventions were very complex and required further study before accession.

---

[61] Statutory Rules and Orders, 1935, No. 885. See also the 1934 Board of Trade Whaling Industry (Ship) Regulations, Statutory Rules and Orders, 1935, No. 885, cited in Vallance, above n. 55, pp. 116–18.

[62] 47 Stat., Pt 2, p. 1872, cited in Vallance, above n. 55, p. 118.

[63] Text available at http://iea.uoregon.edu/pages/view_treaty.php?t=1897-FurSealSeaOtter NorthPacificOceanBeringSea.EN.txt&par=view_treaty_html, last accessed 27 December 2014.

[64] Federal Register, 17 October 1936, Vol. I, p. 1871. Regulations were issued by other States, such as Norway (Act of 14 June 1935, published in Legal Gazette 1936); Denmark (*Lovtidende for Kongeriget* Denmark 1934), 578–80; Mexico (*Dario Official*, 15 March 1927); Finland (Law of 13 March 1936 and Decree of 3 April 1936); Scotland (Whale Fisheries (Scotland) Act 1907; and Whaling Industry (Factory) (Scotland), Regulations, 19 July 1935), cited in Vallance, above n. 55, p. 118.

Dorsey observed: '[it] was a refrain that Western diplomats would hear right to the outbreak of war'.[65]

1.4 The provisions of the 1931 Convention

Article 1 of the Convention laid down the general obligation of the State Parties to the Convention, namely, that they take, within the limits of their jurisdiction, 'appropriate measures to ensure the application' of its provisions and 'the punishment of infractions'. In other words, the general obligation regarding compliance with the Convention rested on the Parties themselves. While the Convention had a very limited scope in terms of the species over which it extended (as it only applied to baleens and whalebone whales (Article 2)), it nonetheless had wide jurisdictional scope over the marine territories to which it applied (namely, it extended over not just the territorial sea/national waters of State Parties but also over the high seas (Article 9)).

Article 3 of the Convention stated that '[t]he present Convention does not apply to aborigines dwelling on the coasts of the territories of the High Contracting Parties', thus acknowledging that certain departures might be justifiable. However, this exclusion was conditioned. Aboriginal whaling enjoyed exclusion only if it was conducted in canoes, pirogues or other exclusively native craft propelled by oars and sails; without the use of firearms; by aboriginal peoples who were not in the employment of persons other than aboriginals; and, finally, aboriginal peoples must not be under contract to deliver products of their whaling to any third person. This is a clear indication of how cultural identity featured as a forceful consideration so as to exclude aboriginal subsistence whaling from the scope of the Convention.

Articles 4 and 5 introduced the prohibited categories of whale hunting: namely, the killing or hunting of right whales including North Cape whales, Greenland whales, southern right whales, Pacific right whales and southern pygmy whales; and the taking or killing of calves, suckling whales or immature whales which are accompanied by calves or suckling whales.

The 1931 Convention also imposed an obligation that the fullest possible use of carcasses of whales be made. Furthermore, the Convention included a provision concerning the remuneration of gunners and

---

[65] Dorsey, above n. 33, p. 58.

crews of whaling vessels, providing that it depended to a 'considerable extent' upon such factors as the size, species, value and yield of oil to whales taken – not merely upon the number of whales killed – in so far as payment was made dependent on results (Article 7).

Article 8 introduced an obligation of licensing of whaling vessels on the part of the State Party whose flag the vessel flew. What is more, under Article 8, any State Party in whose waters or territory a vessel already licensed by another Contracting State engaged in whaling might also request that a licence be sought by that vessel.

Article 10 imposed an obligation on State Parties to obtain 'the most complete biological information practicable with regard to each whale taken'. The Convention also required reports from factories (on land and afloat) under the jurisdiction of a State Party 'on the number of whales of each species treated in each factory and of the amounts of oil of each grade and the quantities of meat, guano and other products derived from them' (Article 11).

Furthermore, State Parties had the duty of submitting to the International Bureau of Whaling Statistics in Sandefjord statistical information, at convenient intervals (but not longer than a year), regarding all whaling operations within their jurisdiction (Article 12).[66]

1.5 Evaluation of the 1931 Convention

The 1931 Whaling Convention did not prove to be particularly effective. It was assessed as having done 'little more than rally the support of nations to the cause of conservation' and as having just 'in that way started the proverbial ball on its journey'.[67] It was also considered that, due to the participation in the Convention of non-whaling nations (such as Poland, Switzerland and Czechoslovakia), 'the group had become large and unwieldy, and the conservation programme, accordingly, was left for the interested nations to work out at successive conferences conducted on a much smaller scale',[68] which may be said in the view of many to be a continuing problem with the 1946 Whaling Convention. Indeed the

---

[66] Such information had to include the following: the date of taking; place of taking; species; sex; length; when fetus was present, length, sex, if possible; when practicable the contents of the stomach; the name and tonnage of each floating factory; the number and aggregate tonnage of the whale catchers; and a list of the land stations which were in operation during the period concerned.

[67] Leonard, above n. 1, 100.   [68] Ibid., 100–1.

1931 Convention was rather basic, considering the complexity of the issues involved, and its contents were rather succinct, barely covering all relevant issues. According to the majority of States, the Convention was concluded to protect the interests of whaling States by stopping unsustainable slaughter of whales. Conservation of whales was only a means of securing more species to hunt. It was only a strong statement on the part of the United States Secretary of State that mentioned the plight of whales. However, it must be mentioned that from a contemporary perspective, this Convention introduced certain conservation measures, as well as reporting and statistical requirements. It also included exemptions on the basis of aboriginal subsistence whaling. It must also be mentioned that United States legislation provided for whaling for scientific purposes, thus laying down the framework for contemporary whaling regulation that relates to commercial, scientific and aboriginal whaling. 'The 1931 Convention ... was "a small step" toward a conservation regime that might control whaling. The emphasis has to be on the word *small*, because the limits were, indeed, not much compared to the power of the whaling industry.'[69] Dorsey is correct in saying that London had settled for an 'elemental standard of conduct' as the basis for the more effective action. Any stronger action on the part of the United Kingdom would have meant the undermining of its own interests or creating a system that would not have been accepted by the Norwegians. However, by agreeing on a restricted Convention, the founding fathers of the 1931 instrument 'began a long tradition of recognizing that the problem was greater than any feasible solution and of settling for minor progress'.[70]

1.6   Events leading to the 1937 Agreement

It became clear from the beginning that the 1931 Convention did not meet the expectations of managing whaling in a more orderly manner than had hitherto been the case. Therefore bilateral agreements were concluded, such as that between the United Kingdom and Norway concerning hunting south of 40 degrees south latitude in order to restrict whaling to a certain period (December 1936–March 1937) and limit the number of vessels per expedition. However, whaling conducted by other States was unrestricted.[71]

---

[69] Dorsey, above n. 33, p. 47.   [70] Ibid., p. 48.   [71] Leonard, above n. 1, 101.

The differences between whaling States were irreconcilable. The Norwegians were desirous of retaining their national hold on the whaling industry (aided by British cooperation). Meanwhile, however, Germany and Japan in particular were driving for roles that would reflect their perceived national status; therefore, 'the old whalers were not about to yield their positions, but the new whalers obviously would not accept the *status quo*'.[72] Increased interest in whale oil on the part of Germany formed part of the national policy of a mercantilist *Drang nach Autarkie* ('drive to autarky'). The established whaling nations were prejudiced against the Japanese whaling efforts; a fact driven in part by racism on the part of the former.[73] However, there was also some resentment towards Japanese whaling due to what was perceived as inefficient processing of whales. The Japanese were producing very little oil, thus not extracting 'every last drop of oil'.[74] The Japanese defence was that they were more interested in meat than in oil. Europeans were, however, of the view that the Japanese were simply stripping off the best parts of whales and throwing the carcasses overboard, against the principles of the 1931 Convention (which, however, was not binding on Japan which was not a Party to it). It may be said that the general consensus was that the Japanese did not follow conservation practices 'and for the lack of a better term, cheated'.[75]

Having recognised that the 1931 Convention failed to achieve its purpose, and also that bilateral agreements were not successful, in 1937 the British government convened a meeting in London to discuss the problems of whaling.[76] The British Minister of Agriculture and Fisheries, William Morrison, said as follows:

> The path of conservation is beset by many difficulties, but as we are all gathered to pursue a common object, I hope that your united efforts will find a way through or over those difficulties, and that we may reach an Agreement which will be beneficial for all of us, and which because of its reasonableness and its practical character, may induce those who are not with us today to work with us in the near future.[77]

The new 1937 Agreement for the Regulation of Whaling and the Final Act was signed on 8 June 1937.[78] Paragraph 5 of the Final Act addressed

---

[72] Dorsey, above n. 33, p. 61.   [73] Ibid., p. 62.   [74] Ibid., p. 62.   [75] Ibid., p. 62.

[76] The following States were invited: Norway, New Zealand, Republic of Ireland (Eire), Germany, Australia, Argentina, the Union of South Africa and the United States.

[77] Ex.Doc.C, p. 20, cited in Leonard, above n. 1, 101.

[78] International Agreement for the Regulation of Whaling, 8 June 1937, 190 LNTS 79. The initial Contracting Parties to the Convention were: Union of South Africa, United States,

the problems of reconciling two very different interests: those of land
stations and those of factory ships.[79] Other factors preventing a full
agreement on the text included the divergent interests of States, the
disparity of terms regarding the various methods of whaling, and protectionism on the part of various States. The United Kingdom, Norway,
Japan and Germany conducted their whaling operations in the Antarctic,
and thus depended on pelagic whaling; and Australia, Canada, Madagas-
car, Newfoundland, New Zealand and South Africa had interests in land
stations operating in their territories. Japan and the Faroe Islands primarily utilised the whale meat for human foodstuff and animal feed, and
treated oil as a secondary product. Therefore, as it was stated, '[a]ny
regulations which tend to favour one group of states as against another,
even though the regulations be scientifically sound, are bound to receive
little consideration in a general convention'.[80] However, it was observed
that Powers 'interested in the whaling industry' were absent at the
Convention conference.[81]

1.7   The provisions of the 1937 Agreement

The main objectives of the 1937 Agreement were to regulate factory ships
and land stations, and to protect whales, through certain conservation
measures and the prohibition of wastage, in order to preserve whale
hunting and the industry. On the basis of this Agreement its Parties
undertook an obligation 'to take appropriate measures to ensure the
application of the provisions of the ... agreement and the punishment
of infractions against the said provisions, and, in particular, [to] maintain
at least one inspector of whaling on each factory ship under their
jurisdiction' (Article 1(1)). The scope of the application of the Agreement
was defined in Article 2: it applied to factory ships and whale catchers

Australia, Germany, United Kingdom, Ireland, New Zealand and Norway. Canada and
Mexico acceded afterwards.
[79] 'It has been urged that whaling as hitherto prosecuted from some land stations, especially
near the equatorial zone, has been wasteful and harmful because [the] physiological
condition of the whales taken was such that their oil yield was low and because whales
[were] taken at those stations when they were about to throw their calves. Against this
may be argued that the raising of the size limits for various species under the agreement
will greatly restrict the catch brought to the land stations, that the land stations, not
enjoying mobility of the factory ships, are already handicapped in the pursuit of whales,
and that whatever catch they take is a comparatively insignificant fraction of the total
catch', cited in Leonard, above n. 1, 101–2.
[80] Ibid., 102   [81] Ibid., 102.

and to land stations (as defined under Article 18). According to the same Article, the Agreement applied to all waters in which whaling was conducted. Under this Agreement, it was national governments – rather than some intergovernmental organisation – that were required to promulgate regulations and to prosecute infractions or contraventions of the Agreement.

Article 4 prohibited the killing or taking of grey and/or right whales. Article 5 specified the depths from the surface of the sea below which the killing of blue whales, fin whales, humpback whales and sperm whales was to be prohibited. Article 6 imposed further prohibitions on killing calves or suckling whales or female whales that were accompanied by calves or suckling whales.

This Agreement too introduced some conservation measures by setting closed seasons (Articles 7 and 8). Article 8 forbade the use of factory ships, or whale catchers attached thereto, for the purpose of taking or treating baleen whales in any waters south of 40 degrees south latitude, except during the period 8 December–7 May. Article 8 prohibited the use of land stations, or whale catchers attached thereto, for the purpose of taking or treating whales in any area or in any waters for more than six continuous months in any period of twelve months.

What is more, the Agreement set the areas in which the use of factory ships or whale catchers was forbidden. These areas were the following: in the Atlantic Ocean north of 40 degrees south latitude and in the Davis Strait, Baffin Bay and Greenland Sea; in the Pacific Ocean east of 150 degrees west longitude between 40 degrees south latitude and 35 degrees north latitude; in the Pacific Ocean west of 150 degrees west longitude between 40 degrees south latitude and 20 degrees north latitude; and in the Indian Ocean north of 40 degrees south latitude (Article 9).

Scientific whaling was introduced in this Agreement, that is to say, whaling for purposes that advance scientific understanding. Article 10 provided that any Party to the Agreement might grant to any of its nationals a special permit authorising the national to kill, take or treat whales for this purpose, subject to restrictions as to number and such other conditions as the Contracting Party deemed fit. The killing of whales for scientific purposes was exempted from the operation of the Agreement.

The remuneration of gunners and factory ship and land station crews depended to a considerable extent on the following factors: the size, yield of whales taken and their number. However, bonus payments to the gunners and crews of whale catchers in respect of any whale the taking of which was prohibited were also prohibited (Article 13). All whaling operations under the jurisdiction of the Parties to the Agreement were to be recorded and communicated to the International Bureau for Whaling Statistics in Norway (Articles 16 and 17). These provisions mirrored those of the 1931 Convention.

The 1937 Agreement was first intended to remain in force until 30 June 1938, that is to say, for only a year. However, it was provided that should, before the expiry date, a majority of governments (which had to include those of the United Kingdom, Germany and Norway) agree to extend its duration, the Agreement could be extended and remain in force perpetually unless the Contracting Parties agreed to modify it. Any Contracting Party, however, could, at any time after 30 June 1938, withdraw from it, provided that it gave notice before 1 January of any year to the government of the United Kingdom, which was the Depository of the Agreement. Consequent to any such notice, the Agreement was to cease to be binding in respect to that Contracting Party after the thirtieth day of June following notification. Any other Party might, by giving notice within one month after the receipt of communication of withdrawal by any other Party, withdraw from the Agreement, 'so that it cease to be in force respecting it after the same date' (Article 21).

The Final Act emphasised that this Agreement was to contribute to maintaining whale stocks and to securing the 'prosperity of the whaling industry'. The Act also noted that further measures of conservation might be necessary. The most important conservation measures prescribed by the Agreement, according to the Final Act, were the stipulation of closed seasons; the prohibition on the taking of certain species of whales already threatened with extinction; the prohibition on the taking of female whales with calves and suckling whales; the restriction of the taking of whales that were below a certain size; and the requirement that all parts of a whale be commercially exploited. The Final Act particularly addressed the issue of land stations and the taking of whales by means that caused unnecessary stress to whales. However, such stressful methods might have increased given that the Agreement introduced limitations on pelagic whaling. In general, the Final Act made several recommendations to the Parties to the Convention in order to limit the catching of whales and regulate the methods of killing them, to avoid wastage.

One of the real risks contemplated in the Act was the possible tactical re-registration of ships to States which were not Parties to the Agreement in order for the whaling industry operatives to evade regulation under the Agreement. State Parties were called upon to try to stop any such practice, by, for instance, permitting such a transfer 'only under licence of the government'. Finally, the Act urged that a conference be held in London the following year, in order to study the results of the forthcoming season, and to consider the question of the modification or extension of the Agreement.

1.8 The circumstances leading to the extension of the 1937 Agreement and the 1938 Protocol to the Agreement

In June 1938, the British Foreign Office notified the Parties to the Agreement that notice had been received about the wish to extend its duration. In accordance with the wishes of the Parties to the Agreement, an International Whaling Conference was convened in June 1938 in London. In addition to the Parties to the Agreement, Denmark, France and Japan were represented at the Conference, and Portugal was an observer.[82] The British Minister of Agriculture and Fisheries, Mr Morrison, addressing the Conference, stated that despite the Agreement, over 8,000 more whales had been killed in 1937 and about 120,000 more tonnes of oil sold, which constituted an increase of more than 25 per cent. This resulted in the decrease of oil prices from £20 to £12 per tonne, which was too low a price to sustain the costly Antarctic whaling expeditions. Further, he conceded that two major errors were made in the whaling industry: overproduction that rendered whaling uneconomic; and overexploitation. Regarding the latter, he stated:

> [it] reduced the stock to the level at which not only over-production, but economic exploitation becomes impossible. The past history of whaling throughout the world, and recent statistics, show that we are dealing with an exhaustible stock, and that, unless we take measures to conserve it, we shall within measurable time have no whaling industry at all.[83]

He stated bluntly that nobody could plead ignorance as to the effects of unrestricted exploitation of whaling stocks and observed the utmost necessity of adopting urgent conservation measures to maintain the whaling industry.[84]

---

[82] Leonard, above n. 1, 102.   [83] Ex.Doc.C, 10–21, cited in Leonard, above n. 1, 103.
[84] Ibid., 103.

One of the loopholes which States introduced in order to circumvent restrictions on the use of factory ships was to moor them in territorial waters of a State as a 'land station'. However, this practice was rejected by the majority of States at the Conference as 'a factory ship does not lose its character of being a ship until at least it loses its power of independent movement, and that a factory ship moored in territorial waters is no less a ship than any other ship which drops its anchor or is moored in a port'.[85] This issue prompted the French government to enter reservations concerning land stations at the time of acceding to the Protocol.[86] The question of Faroe Islands land stations was also brought to the attention of the Conference. (It may be noted that little has changed, as at the present time Faroese whaling is still raising questions as to its sustainability and methods.) The Danish government, on behalf of the Faroe Islands, claimed that hunting conducted there was mainly for food in the form of whale meat and therefore the restrictions on hunting from two land stations should not apply.[87] The Whaling Committee of the Copenhagen Council was also alarmed by the decline of blue whale stocks which, considering their unrestricted exploitation, might soon reach the point of economic exhaustion.[88]

The Conference considered seven methods of regulating the whaling industry:[89] (1) a further reduction of the open season; (2) a limitation of the number of catchers which might be used in connection with each expedition; (3) an overall limitation of output during the Antarctic whaling season, by which was meant that a limit of output should be fixed, after which all whaling should cease, though the limit might be reached before the end of the open season; (4) the fixing of a maximum oil production which no expedition should exceed in any Antarctic season; (5) the introduction of special measures for humpback whales; (6) the establishment of a sanctuary in waters of 40 degrees south

---

[85] Final Act, International Whaling Conference, London, June 1938, para. 17. 196 LNTS 131.

[86] 'First, the term "land station" employed in the Principal Agreement means a factory on and/or anchored at the same spot during the whole of [the] hunting season, and one which cannot be subsequently employed as a factory ship fishing in the deep sea. Secondly, should any regulations be introduced regulating the number of land stations as thus defined, France reserves the right to establish [and] maintain three of such stations in her possessions in the southern hemisphere.' Final Act, para. 17, cited in Leonard above n. 1, 103.

[87] Final Act, para. 18, cited in Leonard, above n. 1, 103.

[88] *Rapports et procès-verbaux des réunions*, 107 (1938), 120, cited in Leonard, above n. 1, 103, para. 6.

[89] Protocol, Final Act, para. 7, AJIL 34 (1940), 120, cited in Leonard, above n. 1, 103.

latitude; and (7) the closure of additional areas against pelagic whaling.[90] States felt that the further curtailment of the open season would increase the temptation to evade certain provisions of the 1937 Agreement (namely, Articles 11 and 12). In fact, all other suggestions aimed at limiting the number of whales killed were also rejected. The means of preventing the extinction of humpback whales were not fully agreed upon; only partial measures were adopted in the Protocol. The suggestion of the establishment of a whale sanctuary was adopted for at least two years. However, the area of the Arctic Ocean north of the Pacific Ocean, between 66 degrees north latitude and 72 degrees north latitude, on a request of the Japanese delegation, was exempted.

1.9   The Protocol on Whaling

The Protocol[91] itself is an international agreement amending the 1937 Agreement. It clarified many provisions of the Agreement. Article 1 specified that with reference to Articles 5 and 7 of the Agreement, 'it is forbidden to use a factory ship or a whale catcher attached thereto for the purpose of taking or treating humpback whales in any waters south of 40 degrees latitude during the period from 1st October, 1938, to the 30th September, 1939'. It also modified certain provisions of the Principal Agreement. It prohibited 'the use of a factory ship or a whale catcher attached thereto for the purpose of taking or treating baleen whales in the waters south of 40 degrees south latitude from 70 degrees west longitude westwards as far as 160 degrees west longitude for a period of two years from 8th December 1938'. There is also a clarification in Article 4 relating to Article 5 of the Principal Agreement, which concerns the request by Denmark on behalf of the Faroe Islands, which states that:

> [t]o Article 5 of the Principal Agreement shall be added the following: except that blue whales of not less than 65 feet, fin whales of not less than 50 feet and sperm whales of not less than 30 feet in length may be taken for delivery to land stations provided that the meat of such whales is to be used for local consumption as human or animal food.

The Protocol was in force for one year, with the possibility of extension. In 1939, a new Conference for the Regulation of Whaling was convened

---

[90] Ibid., para. 7, 120, cited in Leonard, above n. 1, 103.
[91] 1938 Protocol to the Agreement, 196 LNTS 131.

in London in order to review the whaling seasons in 1938 and 1939 and to discuss the desirability of extending, for a further period of time, the prohibition on the killing of humpback whales.

1.10 Evaluation of the 1937 Agreement and the Protocol

Reactions to the 1937 Agreement were mixed. In general, the Norwegians were of the view that it was a good start towards effective conservation. However, Norwegian whalers had been very critical of their government as they felt betrayed overall by this Agreement, arguing that the 'Japanese are going to benefit by the abstentions of others'.[92] The main problem with both the Agreement and the Protocol was (similarly to the 1931 Convention, under the new regime of the International Convention for the Regulation of Whaling) their enforcement.

In the whaling season 1937–8, no less than fifteen right whales were killed (some with foetuses). There were also excessive killings by whaling vessels belonging to non-parties to both instruments. The US government had prosecuted illegal whaling.[93] The United Kingdom replaced Norway as the leading whaling nation. However, there was a decline in whale catches by the United Kingdom and Norway in proportion to other nations (about 40 per cent). It was stated that in 1937–8, the purpose of the 1937 Agreement was defeated by the actions of States which were not Parties to it. That said, it would appear that the 1937 Agreement had been a step forward in the protection of those whale species that had hitherto been threatened with extinction, given that a certain degree of protection was granted to, among other things, females and calves. The Agreement had also stipulated periods of protection, and land and vessel factories were regulated, thus providing further degrees of protection for whale stocks. It should also be noted that the provisions of the Agreement in relation to the collection of statistical data and the exchange of information led to improvements in data gathering

---

[92] Dorsey, above n. 33, p. 68.

[93] In 1939–40 there were two cases pending before the Second District Court of the United States. The first was *United States* v. *Western Operating Corporation*, where the respondent faced trial for having killed nineteen blue whales under seventy feet in length and one whale under fifty-five feet, in violation of the 1936 Whaling Treaty Act and the Agreement. In the second case, the American Whaling Company was charged with having killed thirty-one humpback whales under thirty-five feet in length and twenty-seven female whales accompanied by calves. Leonard, above n. 1, 109–10.

and so on.[94] In general the above agreements (namely, the 1931 Convention, the 1937 Agreement and the 1938 Protocol) imposed on the whaling industry conservation measures that may sensibly be divided into four categories:

(1) the prohibition on the capture of species of whales which are fast reaching extinction;
(2) the regulation over species of whales which may be captured by (i) setting closed and open seasons; (ii) reserve areas in which there is prohibition of taking whales; (iii) the stipulation of restrictions relating to the size and character of those whales that are taken (for instance, suckling whales);
(3) the regulation of activities of whale catchers and floating factories in how they process whales;
(4) the obligations of the governments (i) to enforce the regulations; (ii) to collect and share data and information in order to facilitate the further studying of the problem.[95]

Dorsey observed, from the point of view of a historian, that:

With an unavoidable war just over the horizon, it is hard to call the 1937 and 1938 meetings missed opportunities in whaling conservation ... without Japanese acquiescence, the world's powerful whaling companies and some governments were not about to accept strict conservation rules. In the face of obvious Japanese intransigence the diplomats, scientists, whalers and bureaucrats who met in 1937 and 1938 created a set of rules and floated interesting ideas, many of which were infeasible at the time.[96]

Concluding remarks

There is no doubt that from a historical perspective hunting of whales was excessive and utterly unsustainable, driven by greed. Although the general assessment of both the pre-Second World War Conventions has not been very positive, in the view of the present author they are not entirely without merit. It is a fact that their effectiveness was not very impressive; but they have provided a legal framework for the future regulation of whaling, which is not perfect but is still in existence. Issues such as the complete protection of certain species, the establishment of whale sanctuaries and the organisation of aboriginal whaling are inherited from these Conventions.

---

[94] Leonard, above n. 1, 110–12.   [95] Ibid., 106.   [96] Dorsey, above n. 33, p. 82.

Interestingly, some subjects that caused a certain degree of disagreement during the negotiations of the 1931 and 1937 Conventions (and the 1938 Protocol), such as whaling in the Faroe Islands and, in particular, the establishment of sanctuaries and whaling therein, have remained very much disputed areas. The whale products (such as oil) are no longer of interest to States, but nevertheless whaling is still a great cause of tensions, disagreements and dissatisfaction between States. Whaling is an issue that is politicised and contentious. The main difference between historical tensions concerning whaling and contemporary ones is that in the past the underlying tensions were caused by the desire of achieving the utmost financial gain that led to the extinction of whale species; whilst at present they have to do to a greater degree with cultural diversity on the one hand and animal rights and environmental ethics on the other. Such a change in attitudes to whaling has also resulted in a change of stage-setting in the world of whaling. Many States that were the main actors in the exploitation of whales in the previous period have changed their policy towards whaling. The United Kingdom has become a very anti-whaling State and supports the general policy of the European Union in this respect.

It is without doubt that a very interesting phenomenon has occurred. Some of the States have remained among the main pro-whaling actors, albeit that their underlying policy and objectives regarding continuation of whaling have changed and acquired a different dimension; that is to say, that they have moved from mostly commercial objectives to being based, at least to a certain degree, on the right to cultural diversity (for instance, in Norway and Japan).

2

The International Convention for the Regulation of Whaling

Introduction

This chapter will deal with the main provisions of the International Convention for the Regulation of Whaling (ICRW) and provide critical analysis of recent developments regarding whaling within the legal framework of the ICRW. The diverse and critical views of scholars and practitioners will be presented in relation to the contemporary functioning of the Convention. The functioning of the ICRW will also be discussed from the historical perspective.

Some of the questions relating to the Convention are well known and have been the subject of numerous excellent publications. Nevertheless it is necessary to address them, not only in order fully to understand new developments, but also for reasons of completeness of the presentation. Issues such as aboriginal whaling will only be outlined in this chapter, and fully analysed in later chapters of the book.

2.1 The background to the 1946 ICRW

In 1946, when States gathered to regulate whaling, 'they found themselves creating a new institution that was simultaneously very conservative and somehow radical'.[1] Relying on using scientific expertise, the drafters of the Convention followed the more progressive tradition of the US in trying to reconcile the needs of industry with those of the conservation of whale stocks (as exemplified in the Preamble to the Convention by the reference to sustainable use).[2] Acting United States Secretary of State Dean Acheson declared that whales were 'the wards of the entire world', a 'common resource' that must be conserved.[3]

---

[1] Kurkpatrick Dorsey, *Whales and Nations: Environmental Diplomacy on the High Seas* (University of Washington Press, 2014).
[2] Ibid., p. 114.   [3] Ibid., p. 115.

He emphasised the need for cooperation in the use of the world's resources, arguing that the conference illustrated 'increasing cooperation among the nations in the solution of international conservation problems'. Against this background, the Convention's objective appears to have been to serve as a means towards achieving such cooperation aimed at the conservation of whale stocks.[4] The approach of the United Kingdom was not so much focused on conservation of the world's whales as on preservation of the whaling industry. This attitude was by and large dictated by the postwar conditions prevailing in the United Kingdom, namely, scarcity, hunger and want.[5] It is also worth mentioning a remark made by Davidson, the United States Assistant Secretary of the US Interior Department, that science was the key to sustainable use.[6] He also explained his vision for the International Whaling Commission, the central body of the Convention, to be a body of scientific excellence, the vocation of which would be the careful management of resources belonging to the whole world, thus contributing to 'a more peaceful and happy future for mankind'.[7]

The negotiations of the ICRW were eventful. Delegates agreed to two clauses from the US progressive-era laws: protection of aboriginal whaling and authorisation for collecting whales for scientific purposes, with both of these grounds for whaling being outside the stipulated quotas. There were some unexpected events concerning the arrival of the Soviet delegation, which, to ensure their participation in the Convention, gained some concessions, such as an extended season in 1946–7, from the other delegates.

Two issues in particular caused a certain degree of disagreement among the delegates: the tacit acceptance system of operation of the Convention (which involved an opting-out procedure) and the two-thirds majority voting procedure for any amendment to the agreed schedule of regulations. The former survived, while the latter was changed to three-quarters of the Convention Parties in order to make an amendment, thus ensuring that the agreement of a greater proportion of the Contracting Parties was necessary to effect any change. The Norwegian delegation advocated that the International Whaling Commission (IWC) be afforded competence to adopt binding decisions. The United Kingdom also favoured a stronger IWC. However, there were delegations which were fully satisfied with the IWC not being granted the competence to take binding decisions, such as the French and Dutch delegations, both of which were

---

[4] Acheson cited in ibid., p. 115.   [5] Ibid., p. 115.   [6] Ibid., p. 116.   [7] Ibid., p. 117.

against a stronger IWC given that such a development would have been to the detriment of their own interests, which were best served by their governments. The opting-out system was necessary as the proposed model of the IWC created a new agency that would have curtailed the freedom of action of States on the high seas and, therefore, would have had negative implications on the ability of States to pursue their particular economic benefit unfettered.[8] Without the inclusion of the opting-out procedure, the United States, the Netherlands, France and the Soviet Union would not sign the ICRW. Dorsey observed that, in retrospect, the failure to reject the opting-out system had been the greatest mistake of the 1946 meeting. It is not a surprise to note how opting-out mechanisms often led to the undermining of the collective efforts of a group of States. For instance, it is not unknown for States to resort to the opting-out mechanism in order to avoid implementing decisions detrimental to their interests. Still, Dorsey's reflections aside, the refusal to include any such mechanism could have reasonably led to the alienation of some States, thus undermining whatever chances for interstate cooperation and action may have existed at the time. The Norwegian and British position vis-à-vis the opting-out procedure was based on inaccurate projections with regard to future developments, such as the expansion of Soviet whaling. Having miscalculated in their outlook, they adhered to a vision of the future of the whaling industry in which Norway and the United Kingdom dominated, to the exclusion of other serious whaling nations. The proposal to subject the IWC to the oversight of the Food and Agriculture Organization (FAO) also did not gain acceptance.[9]

The delegates broke the negotiations into two parts: the first part was to agree on a new Protocol modelled on the 1945 Protocol to regulate the whaling season 1947–8; and the second part was to negotiate a more complex convention – namely, the 1946 ICRW – to establish the IWC. Such an approach would give more time to the signatories of the ICRW to ratify it. Most importantly, the Convention retained the annual limit, established in 1944, of 16,000 blue whale units (BWU) in Antarctic waters. The US, Norwegian and United Kingdom delegates were of the view that such quota should be based on continuity, so that they could establish a statistical basis on which to be able to determine the number of whales. In addition, Kellogg, the US delegate, argued that the quota of

---

[8] Ibid., p. 120; see also p. 119.   [9] Ibid., pp. 120–1.

16,000 BWU was meant to set the limit that constituted two-thirds of the annual catch in the last seven peaceful seasons, which had been too intensive. The quota did not satisfy delegates who considered it to be too high.[10] The BWU was later criticised and abandoned.

The ICRW remains to this day the principal international vehicle for the regulation of whaling; it is a treaty regime which has set up a treaty body, namely, the IWC (or the 'Commission'), aimed at the implementation of the ICRW. The ICRW was signed by the major whaling nations at the time of adoption.[11] The text of the ICRW was largely based on the draft provided by the United States, which followed fisheries conventions in force at that time.[12]

The ICRW consists of the Convention itself, as well as a Schedule that is an integral part of the Convention text. The Convention sets out the general regulatory scheme for the management of whale stocks. The Schedule, according to Article V(1), introduces standards to be followed regarding 'conservation and utilization' of whale species. It deals with the specific issues relating to conservation, such as: open and closed seasons; whaling methods; size limits for each whale; and inspection. Article III(2) sets out the procedure for the amendment of the Schedule, which, as referred to earlier, must be effected by a three-quarters majority of voting members.[13] There were several subsequent amendments to the Schedule (including the imposition of the Moratorium), such as the establishment of the Indian Ocean Sanctuary and the Southern Ocean Sanctuary.[14]

---

[10] Ibid., p. 122.

[11] International Convention for the Regulation of Whaling, 2 December 1946, 161 UNTS 72. The original signatories were: Argentina, Australia, Canada, Chile, Denmark, France, the Netherlands, New Zealand, Norway, Peru, South Africa, the Soviet Union, the United Kingdom and the United States.

[12] Steven Freeland and Julie Drysdale, 'Co-operation or Chaos? Article 65 of the United Nations Convention on the Law of the Sea and the Future of the International Whaling Commission', MqJICEL 2 (2005), 1–36, 5.

[13] Article V(2) explains the nature of the amendments to the Schedule to: '(a) . . . be such as are necessary to carry out the objectives and purposes [of the Convention] and to provide conservation, development, and optimum utilization of the whale resources; (b) . . . be based on scientific findings; (c) . . . not involve restrictions on the number or nationality of factory ships or land stations . . .; (d) . . . take into consideration the interests of the consumers of whale and the whaling industry'.

[14] See William T. Burke, 'Legal Aspects of the IWC Decision on the Southern Ocean Sanctuary', ODIL 28 (1997), 313–27, 313; Patricia W. W. Birnie, 'Opinion on the Legality of the Development of the Southern Ocean Whale Sanctuary by the International Whaling Commission' (High North Alliance, 1995).

Against this historical backdrop of considerable interstate cooperation, contemporary conflict around whaling matters seems patently at odds with the past. Nowadays, one witnesses conflict at the Annual Meetings of the Commission; conflict between States outside the Commission (concerning the whaling activities of Japan in the Southern Ocean, which resulted in an important Judgment of the International Court of Justice);[15] and conflicts between whalers and environmental activists of such regularity and extent that they are frequently referred to as 'whale wars'.[16] There is no obvious or imminent solution to these conflicts appearing on the horizon.[17]

---

[15] *Whaling in the Antarctic (Australia v. Japan: New Zealand intervening)*, Judgment of 31 March 2014, www.icj-cij.org/docket/files/148/18136.pdf, last accessed 22 December 2014.

[16] There have been numerous incidents of clashes between anti-whalers and Japanese boats. For example, in January 2010, according to news agencies, 'anti-whaling activists accused Japanese whalers of ramming and sinking a high-tech protest boat in the frigid Southern Ocean ... but Japan said that its ship could not avoid the collision': available at www.reuters.com/article/2010/01/06/us-whaling-australia-idUSTRE60509820100106, last accessed 24 December 2014. See also, for example, 'Fact finding report into the collision involving the New Zealand registered craft *Ady Gil* and the Japan registered whaling ship *Shonan Maru No. 2* in the Southern Ocean on 6 January 2010 of the Australian Maritime Safety Authority 2010', http://pw2.netcom.com/~horse/prophecy.htm, last accessed 22 December 2014.

[17] The problems concerning whaling and the protection of whales have been the subject of a great number of excellent publications, such as those that take a comprehensive approach to the issues: Alexander Gillespie, *Whaling Diplomacy: Defining Issues in International Environmental Law* (Cheltenham: Edward Elgar Publishing, 2005); Gerry J. Nagtzaam, 'The International Whaling Commission and the Elusive Great White Whale of Preservationism', http://works.bepress.com/gerry_nagtzaam/2, last accessed 24 December 2014; Gerry J. Nagtzaam, *The Making of International Environmental Treaties. Neoliberal and Constructivist Analyses of Normative Evolution* (Cheltenham: Edward Elgar Publishing, 2009); Maria C. Maffei, 'The International Convention for the Regulation of Whaling', *International Journal of Marine and Estuarine (Coastal Law)* 12 (1997), 287–305; Patricia W. W. Birnie, 'Are Twentieth-Century Marine Conservation Conventions Adaptable to Twenty-First-Century Goals and Principles?' *International Journal of Marine and Estuarine (Coastal) Law* 12 (1997), Part I, 307–39; Part II, 488–532; Freeland and Drysdale, above n. 12; Robert L. Friedheim (ed.), *Toward a Sustainable Whaling Regime* (Washington University Press, 2001); Ed Couzens, *Whales and Elephants in International Conservation Law and Politics: A Comparative Study* (Abingdon: Routledge, 2014); William C. G. Burns, 'The International Whaling Commission and the Regulation of the Consumptive and Non-Consumptive Uses of Small Cetaceans: The Critical Agenda for the 1990s', *Wisconsin International Law Journal* 13 (1994), 105–44; Peter Davies, 'Cetaceans', in Michael Bowman, Peter Davies and Catherine Redgwell, *Lyster's International Wildlife Law* (2nd edn, Cambridge University Press, 2010), pp. 150–98.

The Preamble to the ICRW includes among its aims 'the proper conservation of whale stocks and ... the orderly development of the whaling industry', thus preserving these historical binary objectives of conserving whale stocks and preserving the industry. However, even in terms of these fairly contained objectives, the IWC never really successfully 'delivered'. Stocks were inadequately monitored, and depletion continued. As a result (but against the backdrop of a very much changed membership and a fundamentally different concept as to what the purpose of control should be), in 1982, the IWC introduced a complete ban on commercial whaling (known generally as the Moratorium or 'zero quotas'), which came into effect in the season 1985–6. It was intended, however, only to be temporary. It was anticipated that stocks would recover and that, in due course, safe and sustainable levels of stocks of at least some species would have been reached in order to allow the resumption of commercial whaling. However, all attempts at finding an acceptable basis for a properly controlled resumption of whaling have so far failed, and the Moratorium is still in effect. Nonetheless, substantial levels of whaling continue, on the alleged basis of other provisions of the ICRW, and to some extent outside the direct purview of the IWC. While there are also other points of contention (including the validity of sanctuaries introduced or proposed by the IWC, and other aspects of IWC terms such as 'aboriginal whaling'), above all it is 'scientific whaling' and the issue of a resumption of commercial whaling that underlie the state of conflict that currently exists. There are a number of interrelated reasons for this state of conflict, the nature of which will be reviewed in more detail elsewhere in the present publication.

2.2 Changes relating to whaling and to the international environment

The first of the series of fundamental changes has taken place in the field of whaling itself, and, equally importantly, in what might be considered the general attitude of the world towards whaling. These changes include, in the first place, a substantial reduction in the economic importance of whaling. After all, energy resources – as whale oil once was – come from other, chiefly hydrocarbon-related, sources. For instance, since kerosene replaced whale oil as a source of lighting in lamps, and vegetable oils replaced it as the basis for manufacture of margarine, the market for whale oil has almost completely vanished. Furthermore, with a brief resurgence to meet shortages after the end of the Second World War, demand for whale meat, outside the special case of certain indigenous populations, has become limited to only a very small number of nations, in which demand seems to be diminishing.

The second fundamental change that has come about relates to the emergence of environmental awareness on the part of scientists, industry, governments, populations, international organisations and so forth. This awareness includes concern for the welfare of the global ecosystem and concern for the heritage of nature and the preservation of species. The growth of these attitudes reached a focal point in the holding of the 1972 Stockholm Conference on the Human Environment and the issuing of the Stockholm Declaration on the Human Environment. On the basis of this, one witnesses the advent of a whole raft of multilateral environmental agreements (MEAs) which were concluded in the latter part of the twentieth century, as well as the appearance of legal principles, or other notions with degrees of legal effect, such as sustainable development, sustainability, intergenerational equity and the precautionary principle.

Whaling might well have been the subject of just such an agreement, framed on a global basis and with preservation of the species as its overriding objective. But whaling was, of course, already the subject of the ICRW – in that sense, the subject of some specialist existing body of law – and the ICRW, neither in terms of its original membership, nor, more importantly, in terms of its original purpose, amounted to such an agreement. On the other hand, it certainly cannot be said that the development of international law and of international cooperation since the contracting of the ICRW has been of no consequence to whaling.[18] While during the initial decades of the IWC, whaling was relatively unaffected by regulation, the advent of global MEAs has meant that whaling could sensibly engage with other legal regimes set up by such international conventions as the United Nations Convention on the Law of the Sea (UNCLOS)[19] and the Convention on International

---

[18] Casey Watkins, 'Whaling in the Antarctic: Case Analysis and Suggestions for the Future of Antarctic Whaling and Stock Management', *New York International Law Review* 25 (2012), http://ssrn.com/abstract=2035631, at p. 4, last accessed 20 December 2014; Duncan Currie, 'Whales, Sustainability and International Environmental Governance', RECIEL 16 (2007), 45–57.

[19] United Nations Convention on the Law of the Sea, Montego Bay, 10 December 1982, 1833 UNTS 3.

Trade in Endangered Species of Wild Fauna and Flora (CITES).[20] It has also become plausible that whaling could be subject to the effects of developing general principles such as the precautionary principle. As a result, partly due to changes in whaling and the market for whale products, and partly due to changes in attitudes, there has also been a fundamental change in the players involved in the issue of whaling generally, and in the membership of the IWC in particular.

Thus, first, the number of so-called 'whaling nations' has greatly decreased. On the other hand, the number of States professing to be concerned about whaling has increased. As a result, despite this reduction in the number of States engaged in whaling on any significant scale, membership of the IWC has increased from the fifteen original signatories in 1946 to the current eighty-nine. Furthermore, one also witnesses the advent of another type of actor: namely, global environmental non-governmental organisations (NGOs) which are often responsible for, or otherwise influential in shaping, public consciousness about whaling. Their influence could also extend to States and international organisations, towards which their heavy presence at meetings of the IWC and its Scientific Committee testifies. A limited number of these have even become involved in direct action against whaling. Thus, it has been said that, '[t]he virtual explosion of public concern over the fate of the whales, which became the symbol of the emerging environmental movement, is best illustrated by the participation of environmental NGOs in IWC meetings. The number of NGOs increased from six in 1972 to more than 50 at the beginning of the 1980s.'[21] Notwithstanding these changes, however, there are still a few States which passionately uphold what they see as an almost inalienable right to continue commercial whaling, and there has thus developed a fundamental difference of attitude among the Member States of the ICRW towards whaling and, indeed, towards the very underlying objectives of the Convention and the Commission. For this limited number of remaining 'whaling nations', whaling – albeit these days in a properly controlled and sustainable manner – remains a

---

[20] Convention on International Trade in Endangered Species of Wild Fauna and Flora, Washington, 3 March 1973, 993 UNTS 243.

[21] Sebastian Oberthür, 'The International Convention for the Regulation of Whaling: From Over-Exploitation to Total Prohibition', *Yearbook of International Co-operation on Environment and Development* (1998–9), 29–37. See an excellent overview of the ICRW and the IWC: Tara Jordan, 'Revising the International Convention on the Regulation of Whaling: A Proposal to End Stalemate within the International Whaling Commission', *Wisconsin International Law Journal* 29 (2012), 833–68.

legitimate activity along with other sustainable forms of exploitation of marine resources.[22] However, for the largely non-whaling nations, vociferously backed by the powerful lobby of environmental and preservationist NGOs – as well as by much general public opinion – whaling in any form is seen as an unnecessary and, indeed, immoral activity which should, at least as an eventual objective, be permanently banned altogether.[23] The view was expressed that in fact, at present, notwithstanding the duality of the purposes and objectives of the ICRW (the regulation of the whaling industry and preserving of whale stocks), the second of these objectives has overtaken the first one, and that the Convention is now distinctly preservationist, evidence of which is the imposition of the Moratorium; and that without a formal amendment, the objective of the Convention has been altered.[24]

So much did these remaining whaling nations feel that they were being swamped, in the IWC, by the preservationists, that, at the 2006 Annual Meeting of the IWC, they felt it necessary to make what has come to be known as the 'St Kitts and Nevis Declaration'. In it, they restated what they saw as the real and fundamental purpose of the ICRW and the Commission as being to 'implement a management regime to regulate commercial whaling', but noted 'the position of some members that are opposed to the resumption of commercial whaling on a sustainable basis irrespective of the status of whale stocks'.

2.3   Weaknesses in the ICRW

The second major cause of the present state of affairs arises from the provisions of the ICRW itself which are both, in some respects, inherently weak and, in others, simply inappropriate to take account of the

---

[22] In relation to the continued whaling aspirations of Japan, which is the most important of these remaining whaling nations in relation to present conflicts, see Keiko Hirata, 'Why Japan Supports Whaling', *Journal of International Wildlife Law and Policy* 8 (2005), 129–49. Hirata points to deep-seated cultural and political factors in Japan, as a result of which Japan's present attitude to whaling is unlikely to change in the near future.

[23] Perhaps the high point of the development of an ethical dimension in the world's attitude to whaling was reached in the formation in 2010 of the 'Helsinki Group' which involves a group of scientists and philosophers whose motto is 'We affirm that all cetaceans as persons have the right to life, liberty and wellbeing', and who issued the so-called 'Declaration of Rights for Cetaceans: Whales and Dolphins', see at www.cetaceanrights.org, last accessed 20 December 2014.

[24] Duncan French, *International Law and Policy of Sustainable Development* (Manchester University Press, 2005), p. 126.

massive changes in the modern context, outlined above, in which they are supposed to operate. A number of these aspects or provisions are fundamental to the current issues. There are also a number of aspects that, although peripheral, contribute to the overall dysfunctional state of the IWC, and, therefore, ought not sensibly to be ignored in any assessment of how to remedy the present impasse. Having thus looked at the provisions of the ICRW, we now turn to how these might have influenced events since 1972, and will finally consider the legal aspects of the possibilities for resolution of the conflict.

One of the major weaknesses of the ICRW is its very rudimentary international enforcement mechanism. The main responsibility for the enforcement of the provisions of the Convention remains with the Parties to the Convention. According to Article IX(1), the State Parties to the ICRW are in charge of its enforcement in respect to actions of 'persons under [their] jurisdiction', as for the prosecution of its violations. As Freeland and Drysdale observe, this provision does not address the situation where breaches of the Convention are committed beyond the limits of national jurisdiction of any State Party to the ICRW. They also observe that there is no enforcement in relation to breaches of this Convention by a State, as, under the present regime, in such situations the IWC has no jurisdiction.[25] This lack of an enforcement mechanism, according to those authors, is one of the major weaknesses of the ICRW.[26]

Freeland and Drysdale explain that, in the absence of an internal enforcement mechanism, two forms of ad hoc external enforcement procedures seem to have been developed. The first of these external procedures was developed by the United States through the introduction of certain statutory amendments, which, in effect, have established the United States as some sort of international 'policeman' over whaling matters even in cases relating to States that are not Parties to the ICRW.[27] The authors refer to the 1971 Pelly Amendment to the Fishermen's Protective Act of 1967 (the 'Pelly Amendment') and the 1979 Packwood–Magnuson Amendment, which apply in cases where the actions of foreign nationals have a negative impact on the effectiveness of the ICRW and the IWC.[28] In

---

[25] Freeland and Drysdale, above n. 12, 10.   [26] Ibid., 11.   [27] Ibid., 11.
[28] 22 USC para. 1978 (2000); 16 USC para. 1821 (2000). Under the Pelly Amendment, once it is determined by the Secretary of Commerce that the standard has been breached, he/she has to certify that to the United States President, who then has discretion to impose sanctions against the certified State. The failure of the President to impose sanctions

practice, however, the impact of both of these Acts has been insignificant, as there is reluctance to impose sanctions, and also the quotas allocated to Japan in the waters of the United States were very low or even zero. The United States also used these Acts to react against Japanese scientific whaling, in particular in 2000. After Japan announced that its fishermen had harvested one sperm whale, four Bryde's whales and six minke whales for scientific purposes, the United States State Department reacted by adopting diplomatic action aimed at pressuring Japan to abandon the programme. United States measures involved the cancelling of a bilateral fisheries consultation meeting in 2000; the United States not participating in two ministerial meetings held in Japan on environmental matters; and the United States' opposition to the IWC 2001 meeting taking place in Japan. The United States State Department also considered all other options as a reaction to Japanese lethal scientific whaling, such as potential trade measures under the Pelly Amendment. On 13 September 2001, the Secretary of Commerce certified Japan under both the Pelly and Packwood–Magnuson Amendments. The result of this was President Clinton's action not to negotiate a new Governing International Fisheries Agreement with Japan, thus preventing Japan from being allocated any amounts of various types of fish in the exclusive economic zone (EEZ) of the United States during the period of certification. Although Japanese fishermen had not fished in the United States' fishery conservation zone for a long time, Clinton's action deprived Japan of future opportunities for fishing in this zone. Japan protested but pledged to reduce its total whale catch for the 2000 season.[29]

An example of the rather weak impact of the Pelly Amendment is the reaction to commercial whaling of Iceland. It appears that, in this instance, political factors featured heavily in the decision of the United States President. In a Memorandum Regarding Pelly Certification and Icelandic Whaling, the United States President outlined what action was taking place. On 11 July 2011, Secretary of Commerce Gary Locke certified under section 8 of the Pelly Amendment that nationals of Iceland were conducting whaling activities that diminished the effectiveness of

under the Pelly Amendment leads to review of the matter by the United States Congress. The Packwood–Magnuson Amendment was concerned exclusively with the ICRW. According to this provision, the President, having received a certification under the Pelly Amendment, has the duty to reduce fishing rights of the certified State's fishing quotas in United States waters by at least 50 per cent. Freeland and Drysdale, above n. 12, 11–12.

[29] Sean P. Murphy, 'US Sanctions Against Japan for Whaling', AJIL 95 (2001), 151–2.

the IWC's conservation programme. In his letter of 19 July 2011, Secretary Locke expressed his concern about these actions, which was shared by the President. The general reaction was rather weak, as the President directed 'the Secretaries of State and Commerce to continue to keep the situation under review and to continue to urge Iceland to cease its commercial whaling activities', and, '[t]o this end, within 6 months, or immediately upon the resumption of fin whaling by Icelandic nationals, I direct departments and agencies to report to me on their actions through the Departments of State and Commerce'.[30] Another example is the reaction to the certification of Norway, resulting from its opting out of the 1986 Moratorium and continuing with commercial whaling, which was not followed by the imposition of trade sanctions.[31]

The second form that ad hoc enforcement takes relates to the presence of NGOs, as discussed earlier. According to Freeland and Drysdale, the actions of various environmental non-governmental organisations (including Greenpeace, Humane Society International and Sea Shepherd) could provide a degree of enforcement.[32] They are observers accredited to the IWC; therefore, to a certain extent, they could have some influence on the decision-making process of the IWC by, among other things, drawing to the attention of the IWC anything untoward. However, their actions outside the IWC are at times perceived as very controversial even by the anti-whaling movement.

The question of enforcement is closely related to the review of compliance of State Parties with an MEA, in our case with the ICRW.[33] Compliance techniques can have various manifestations, such as: the inclusion of observers; the existence of an international inspection panel; autonomous tracking systems, and so on. The establishment of any system of compliance by the IWC met with objections by State Parties, and the existing International Observer Scheme (IOS) was not followed by States, as becomes clear by the fact that the most recent international observers' appointments took place in 1986. Vessel identification schemes have been only partly observed by the State Parties.[34] One of

[30] Memorandum Regarding Pelly Certification and Icelandic Whaling, www.whitehouse. gov/the-press-office/2011/09/15/memorandum-regarding-pelly-certification-and-icelandic-whaling, last accessed 20 December 2014.
[31] www.whitehouse.gov/the-press-office/2011/09/15/message-president-congress, last accessed 12 January 2015.
[32] Freeland and Drysdale, above n. 12, 14.
[33] See in depth on this subject, Gillespie, above n. 17, pp. 357–83 (chapter on 'Compliance').
[34] Ibid., pp. 359–60.

the obstacles to the implementation of the Revised Management Procedure is also the question of international observers. A significant weakness
of the mechanism is the fact that whaling States have the right to veto
inspectors of whom they do not approve (see on that Chapter 3).[35]

It may be added that a large number of MEAs have bodies with
jurisdiction to ensure that there is compliance and the mechanisms to
ensure implementation on the part of State Parties of the provisions of
particular treaties. There are numerous examples of such compliance
(implementation) bodies established by various MEAs, such as: the
Basle Convention on the Management of Hazardous Wastes; the Kyoto
Protocol;[36] and the UNECE Convention on Access to Information,
Public Participation in Decision-Making and Access to Justice in Environmental Matters (the 'Aarhus Convention').[37] The powers and structure
of these bodies vary but it may be said that the description in the Basle
Convention captures quite aptly the general nature of such a mechanism:
'[t]he objective of the mechanism is to assist Parties to comply with their
obligations under the Convention and to facilitate, promote, monitor and
aim to secure the implementation of and compliance with the obligations
under the Convention' (Article 1: Objectives); and

> [t]he mechanism shall be non-confrontational, transparent, cost-effective
> and preventive in nature, simple, flexible, non-binding and oriented in the
> direction of helping parties to implement the provisions of the Basle
> Convention. It will pay particular attention to the special needs of
> developing countries and countries with economies in transition, and is
> intended to promote cooperation between all Parties ...
>
> (Article 2: Nature of the Mechanism).

The ICRW is one of a few exceptions to MEAs developing such a
mechanism. As Gillespie has noted, a proposal to remedy this was tabled
by the United States government at the 2000 IWC Meeting in Adelaide.
The general lack of a spirit of cooperation pervading the work of the
IWC was also quite obvious during the debates concerning the possible
establishment of a committee. Despite support from States such as
New Zealand, the proposal of the United States met with several objections concerning the extent of the role of the NGOs and also the

---

[35] Ibid., pp. 67–8.
[36] Basle Convention on the Control of Transboundary Movements of Hazardous Wastes
    and Their Disposal, 22 March 1989, 1673 UNTS 126.
[37] UNECE Convention on Access to Information, Public Participation in Decision-making
    and Access to Justice in Environmental Matters, 25 June 1998, 2161 UNTS 447.

composition of the proposed compliance/implementation/review Committee. Norway likened the Committee to a 'kangaroo Court' resulting in 'unfair Judgments'.[38] Such negative and contentious attitudes are very much a feature of the IWC. It may be noted that the role of NGOs is very pronounced in the Aarhus Convention Compliance Committee (far more extensive than as suggested in the case of the ICRW Review Committee, as they not only participate in the Committee but also have jurisdiction to bring a case to its attention).

2.4 Major aspects and provisions of the ICRW

As suggested earlier, the present section relates to those provisions of the ICRW which are directly relevant to the main thrust of the present conflicts. In this respect, the present author has already outlined the conflict which has developed concerning the very purpose of control of whaling, and the first major aspect of the ICRW which thus calls for consideration is its 'object and purpose'. There are a number of other provisions which also directly relate to the present situation and which will be outlined in this section, namely, in particular, provisions relating to so-called 'scientific' whaling and 'aboriginal' whaling, as well as others which are less directly related, such as membership of the Convention and its so-called 'opting-out' procedure. The years between the 1937 London Agreement[39] and the 1946 Convention (in effect, the years of the Second World War)[40] did see a reduction in whaling activity due to a reduced number of operating factories; but after the war, increased demand for edible fat was reflected in increased whaling and further depletion of whale stocks,[41] and it was in response to this that in 1946 the ICRW was concluded with the intention of establishing more comprehensive control over whaling.

The provisions of the ICRW, indeed, showed substantial development over those of the two earlier Conventions; however, in certain fundamental respects – the nature of its participation and its objectives – it remained substantially similar to them. Furthermore, it inherited certain provisions – in particular in relation to 'aboriginal' and 'scientific' whaling – that are also much involved in the present disputes.

---

[38] Gillespie, above n. 17, p. 374.
[39] International Agreement for the Regulation of Whaling, 8 June 1937, 190 LNTS 79.
[40] International Convention for the Regulation of Whaling, 2 December 1946, 161 UNTS 72.
[41] Oberthür, above n. 21, 31.

2.5   The form of the Convention

The ICRW consists of the Convention itself, to which is appended, as an integral part, the Schedule.[42] It is in the Schedule, which has been constantly amended, that detailed regulatory provisions are set out; and, as we shall see, the most important mode of operation of the IWC is by way of amendment of the Schedule.

2.6   Participation in the ICRW

In common with its two predecessor Conventions, the ICRW was originally an agreement between whaling nations – that is to say, nations having a substantial interest in whaling, many with significant whaling industries. There were originally no more than fifteen signatories. All of these were, as had been the case with the two predecessor Conventions, to a greater or lesser extent 'whaling nations'. On this occasion, however, all the major whaling nations were either original parties to the Convention or (as was the case with Japan) joined shortly after the Convention had come into force. But despite this limited original participation (which accorded with the nature and purpose of the Convention), it was open to accession by all States (Article X(2)) and allowed the great increase in membership by largely non-whaling nations from the early 1970s onwards and the ensuing change in the balance between whaling and non-whaling States on the IWC, which was to have far-reaching results.

It was also expressly provided (in Article XI) that Member States could withdraw from the Convention on the simple giving of notice, a facility that was to be made use of by more than one State faced with unwelcome developments in the IWC. Thus, for instance, a number of States threatened withdrawal during the 1950s, resulting in the abandonment of proposed reductions in catches; and in 1982 Canada withdrew, leaving it free to set its own limits for aboriginal whaling. In the context of the present disputes, the ease, from a purely legal point of view, with which Japan in particular could (were it to be so disposed) withdraw from the Convention is a factor to be taken into account. Most recently, Denmark has threatened to withdraw from the Convention unless the

---

[42] Article I(1): 'This Convention includes the Schedule attached thereto which forms an integral part thereof. All references to "Convention" shall be understood as including the said Schedule either in its present terms or as amended in accordance with the provisions of Article V.'

Commission satisfactorily sets limits for the aboriginal subsistence whaling of Greenland.[43]

It may be remembered that, apart from this possibility of total withdrawal, the Convention also provided for an opting-out system, enabling States to avoid being bound by unwelcome decisions of the IWC.

2.7 Object and purpose

The origin of the concern about whaling at the League of Nations in 1925 was the potential adverse effect on the industry caused by the depletion of whale stocks. This was not expressly reflected in the 1931 Convention, which lacked a Preamble, and did not contain any statement as to its underlying purpose. But it is accepted that the 1931 Convention was, in effect, conservationist, in the interests of the whaling industry, rather than in relation to whale stocks per se; and, indeed, it has been criticised on that very ground. Its successor, the 1937 International Agreement for the Regulation of Whaling (the 'London Agreement'), on the other hand, did have a Preamble which clearly stated the underlying object and purpose as being to further the desire of the State Parties 'to secure the prosperity of the whaling industry and, for that purpose, to maintain the stock of whales'. In that sense, the objective of maintaining whale stocks was subservient to the objective of protecting the whaling industry. Apart from its own statements of purpose, the ICRW's Preamble in effect extends the effect of this statement of purpose by its express endorsement of 'the principles embodied in the provisions' of the London Agreement. The ICRW contains a more detailed statement of object and purpose in its Preamble than had the preceding convention, and these are supplemented to some extent by other provisions within the body of the Convention. Overall, the better view is that, on balance, these support the contention that the object and purpose of the ICRW is the regulation of whaling in order to conserve stocks for the purpose of their continued exploitation. Thus, the Preamble notes that the signatories, *inter alia*, desire:

> to establish a system of international regulation for the whale fisheries to ensure proper and effective conservation and development of whale stocks on the basis of the principles embodied in the provisions of the

---

[43] See Chris Wold and Michael S. Kearney, 'The Legal Effects of Greenland's Unilateral Aboriginal Subsistence Whale Hunt', *American University International Law Review* 30 (2015), 561–609, 598.

International Agreement for the Regulation of Whaling, signed in London on 8th June, 1937,

in consequence of which they have:

decided to conclude a convention to provide for the proper conservation of whale stocks and thus make possible the orderly development of the whaling industry.

And in earlier paragraphs, the Preamble notes that the signatories recognise

that the whale stocks are susceptible of natural increases if whaling is properly regulated, and that increases in the size of whale stocks will permit increases in the number of whales which may be captured without endangering these natural resources

and

that it is in the common interest to achieve the optimum level of whale stocks as rapidly as possible without causing widespread economic and nutritional distress.

We may also refer to the existence of provisions within the body of the 1946 Convention that are only really compatible with an intention to support continued exploitation of whale stocks. Thus, for instance, Article V(2) of the Convention, which deals with amendments to the regulatory provisions of the Schedule, states that amendments to the Schedule:

(a) shall be such as are necessary to carry out the objectives and purposes of this Convention and to provide for the conservation, development, and optimum utilization of the whale resources.

and

(d) shall take into consideration the interests of the consumers of whale products and the whaling industry.

Furthermore, Article VIII(4) (in relation to the collection of scientific data) refers to this as being 'indispensable to sound and constructive management of the whale fisheries'.

All that said, however, it is effectively the standpoint of the current majority of non-whaling States forming the majority on the IWC that the proper purpose of that body is the permanent banning, at least, of commercial whaling (and in the absence of a change of stance by preservationists, it seems likely that calls for the banning of aboriginal whaling may well follow). It is exactly against that stance that the whaling nations produced the above-mentioned St Kitts and Nevis Declaration.

On the other hand, notwithstanding the above commentary on the object and purpose of the ICRW on the basis of its express terms, its Preamble does, however, contain some wording which could sensibly be held to support a more 'preservationist' stance. To be more precise, according to the very first paragraph, the signatories recognise 'the interest of the nations of the world in safeguarding for future generations the great natural resources represented by the whale stocks'. This wording introduces the notion of intergenerational equity (see Chapter 5). It also amounts to some recognition that whale stocks constitute world resources for the benefit even of future generations, and this is an issue that was already emphasised by some States at an early stage of the work of the IWC. Thus, for instance, Gillespie notes that when in 1955 objections were made by a group of States to a proposed reduction in catches, this caused the United States to suggest: 'The whales are a world resource and not the property of any one individual nation, or group of nations.' Likewise, New Zealand added: '[T]he stocks of whales are ... a general trust and ... no country is free to neglect this consideration, nor is the commission free to neglect it ... in the limits it is setting.'[44]

In conclusion, therefore, one may reasonably argue that the objects of the ICRW – in effect inherited from, and restated in more detail than, the 1937 London Agreement – if not exactly 'dual' (as is sometimes said), at least embody the tension between, or the binary of, on the one hand, the expressly commercial objective of conserving and managing whale stocks in order to provide for the 'orderly development of the whaling industry', and, on the other, recognition that whales are a 'general trust' to be safeguarded for 'future generations'. It is true that, wherever the concepts of 'sustainability' and 'utilisation' are linked, an inherent tension arises between the two, though not necessarily one that is insoluble. Particularly since the 1972 Stockholm Conference, concerns regarding all forms of natural preservation, and, more specifically, regarding animal welfare and the preservation of wild species of fauna, have become more commonly shared, and thus, have led to changes in attitudes towards, among other things, whaling. In the contemporary world there is a widespread perception of real, and indeed sharp, conflict between the objectives of

---

[44] Gillespie, above n. 17, p. 5.

animal welfare and industry protection. In the case of whales, some would even argue that this goes as far as to question the very validity and morality of any degree of exploitation of such species at all. In any event, reconciliation of the two forms of objective has proved highly problematic.[45] The issues concerning the 'object and purpose' of the Whaling Convention are still very much unresolved and were the subject of a very heated discussion during the *Whaling in the Antarctic* case (which will be discussed in Chapter 3).

2.8 Provisions relating to 'aboriginal' and 'scientific' whaling: general outline

This section presents a general outline of the legal issues relating to scientific[46] and aboriginal – that is to say, indigenous – whaling. As discussed earlier, these two bases of whaling have historically been exempted from outright bans at different stages of whaling regulation. Present contentions also relate to two particular forms of whaling which have long been recognised as distinct from general commercial whaling, namely, aboriginal whaling and, more importantly in relation to the present disputes, scientific whaling. These forms of whaling have acquired special significance because they are excluded from the Moratorium on commercial whaling, and thus have provided the possibility for certain nations to continue some whaling activity despite the banning of commercial whaling.

2.9 Scientific whaling

Article VIII(1) of the ICRW recognises a special category of so-called 'scientific' whaling, which is excluded from the operation of the Convention. It provides that:

> Notwithstanding anything contained in this Convention any Contracting Government may grant to any of its nationals a special permit authorizing that national to kill, take and treat whales for purposes of scientific

---

[45] Gregory Rose and George Paleokrassis, 'Compliance with International Environmental Obligations: A Case Study of the International Whaling Commission', in James Cameron, Jacob Werksman and Peter Roderick (eds.), *Improving Compliance with International Environmental Law* (London: Earthscan, 1996), pp. 147–74, 147.

[46] 'Scientific whaling' is often also referred to as 'Scientific Permit' or 'Special Permit' whaling: see, for example, IWC website: http://iwc.int/permits, last accessed 20 December 2014.

research subject to such restrictions as to number and subject to such other conditions as the Contracting Government thinks fit, and the killing, taking, and treating of whales in accordance with the provisions of this Article shall be exempt from the operation of this Convention.

This provision substantially reproduces the equivalent Article 10 from the 1937 Agreement. The notable characteristic of this provision, which was an important issue in the litigation before the ICJ, is that it leaves the granting of 'special permits', and the whole question of what may properly constitute scientific whaling, in the hands of the granting State to determine. This freedom is extended by Article VIII(2) to the manner of processing and disposal of whales caught in the course of 'special permit' whaling. On the other hand, Articles VIII(3) and (4) do impose certain obligations in relation to the gathering of scientific data from such whaling, and their transmission to the IWC by the granting State.[47]

2.10   Aboriginal whaling

Whaling by indigenous or aboriginal peoples for their own subsistence purposes has always been recognised as a special case within the field of whaling generally. Thus, the 1931 Convention contained a clause excluding aboriginal whaling from its provisions.[48] The ICRW does not contain any equivalent provision in relation to aboriginal subsistence whaling in the body of the Convention, but the Schedule did already recognise its special position in Article 2, as originally appended to the Convention, which stated that: 'It is forbidden to take or kill grey whales or right

---

[47] Article VIII: '3. Each Contracting Government shall transmit to such body as may be designated by the Commission, in so far as practicable, and at intervals of not more than one year, scientific information available to that Government with respect to whales and whaling, including the results of research conducted pursuant to paragraph 1 of this Article and to Article IV. 4. Recognizing that continuous collection and analysis of biological data in connection with the operations of factory ships and land stations are indispensable to sound and constructive management of the whale fisheries, the Contracting Governments will take all practicable measures to obtain such data.'

[48] Article 3 of the 1931 Convention provides as follows: 'The present Convention does not apply to aborigines dwelling on the coasts of the territories of the High Contracting Parties provided that (1) They only use canoes, pirogues or other exclusively native craft propelled by oars or sails; (2) They do not carry firearms; (3) They are not in the employment of persons other than aborigines; (4) They are not under contract to deliver the products of their whaling to any third person.'

whales, except when the meat and products of such whales are to be used exclusively for local consumption by the aborigines.'

In practice, the Commission has continued this recognition by setting quotas for aboriginal catches of species which were already banned from commercial whaling.[49]

Most importantly, the special position of aboriginal subsistence whaling was recognised through its exclusion from the Moratorium. The absence of express positive provisions relating to aboriginal whaling generally is reflected in the absence of any definition of what it comprises in the current treaty provisions. This ambiguity and lack of clarity constitute a yet further weakness in the provisions of the ICRW that, in turn, has led to disputes as to the meaning of aboriginal whaling. However, the IWC has developed a definition of aboriginal subsistence whaling so that it must be conducted under the condition of 'needs' and that meat and other whale products are to be used exclusively for the purpose of local consumption by the aboriginal people. The definition states that the objectives of such whaling are to:

- ensure that risks of extinction are not seriously increased by whaling;
- enable native people to hunt whales at levels appropriate to their cultural and nutritional requirements (also called 'needs'); and
- move populations towards and then maintain them at healthy levels.[50]

It is the responsibility of national governments to provide the IWC with evidence of the cultural and subsistence needs of their people. The role of the Scientific Committee in relation to this whaling is to provide scientific advice on safe catch limits for such stocks.[51]

---

[49] See WDC (Whaling and Dolphin Conservation), www.wdcs.org/submissions_bin/Abor iginal_Subsistence_Whaling.pdf, last accessed 21 January 2015. See further on aboriginal whaling, Chapter 7.

[50] IWC website, http://iwc.int/aboriginal, last accessed 15 October 2014.

[51] See, on this subject, Leena Heinämäki, 'Protecting the Rights of Indigenous Peoples – Promoting the Sustainability of the Global Environment?', *International Community Law Review* 11 (2009), 3–68; Kamrul Hossain, 'Hunting by Indigenous Peoples of Charismatic Mega-Fauna: Does the Human Rights Approach Challenge the Way Hunting by Indigenous Peoples is Regulated?', *International Community Law Review* 10 (2008), 295–318; Benjamin J. Richardson, 'Indigenous Peoples, International Law and Sustainability', RECIEL 10 (2001), 1–12; Alexander Gillespie, 'Aboriginal Subsistence Whaling: A Critique of the Inter-relationship Between International Law and the International Whaling Commission', *Colorado J. Int. Env'l Law & Policy* 12 (2001), 77–139; Stephen M. Hankins, 'The United States' Abuse of the Aboriginal Whaling Exception: A Contradiction in United States Policy and a Dangerous Precedent for the Whale', *UC Davis Law Review* 24 (1990), 489–530.

2.11   Other relevant provisions of the ICRW

Apart from the major problems outlined in the foregoing sections, one may also note a number of less fundamental, though not insignificant, weaknesses in the provisions of the ICRW, which, as already suggested, may add to the difficulties of arriving at a satisfactory solution to the present impasse within the terms of the ICRW.

In the first place, one may mention the use of the term 'whale fisheries'. This has tended to give rise to an assumption of similarity in nature and equivalence between whaling and commercial fisheries. From the point of view of preservationists, this has had the unfortunate effect of encouraging the view that whales, like fish, mature quickly and so can readily be harvested.[52] As Nagtzaam said, '[i]n treating whaling like any other fishery agreements, the drafters of the agreement placed too great an emphasis on short-term economic considerations in overcoming shortage of whale fats and oils at the expense of legitimate scientific concerns about the effects of over-exploitation of existing stocks'.[53]

2.12   The definition of whale: a general outline

A second weakness in the drafting of the ICRW that has given grounds for continuous dispute within the IWC is the inadequacy of the definition of a whale, which has created much confusion as to exactly which cetaceans fall within its scope – in particular whether its provisions cover so-called 'small' as well as 'large' cetaceans.[54] The Convention does not provide a formal definition of the term 'whale'; but it does, in an Annex to the Convention, provide a list of names that have historically been applied to whales. Thus, it has been said that, while 'some governments take the view that the IWC has the legal competence to regulate catches only of these named ... whales (which are all "great whales")', '[o]thers believe that all cetaceans, including the smaller dolphins and porpoises, also fall within IWC jurisdiction'.[55] In the intervening years the ongoing debate in the IWC on which cetaceans

---

[52] Nagtzaam, *Whaling Diplomacy*, above n. 17, 167.   [53] Ibid.

[54] The term 'cetaceans' comprises two groups: 'large' and 'small' (or 'toothed' and 'baleen'). www.iwcoffi ce.org/conservation/smallcetacean.htm, last accessed 16 October 2014. (See also Appendix A to this publication.)

[55] Gillespie, above n. 17, p. 278.

were under its mandate became more of a political issue than one based on a biological definition. As Gillespie phrased it, '[w]ithin the broader debate, the answer whether a species is "small" or not, and the inter-linking question of whether this grants the IWC jurisdiction over them, will often depend on which side of the jurisdictional debate the protag-onists fall'.[56]

The thirty-second meeting of the IWC debated the issue of the jurisdiction of the IWC over small cetaceans. Some States remained adamant that their initial exclusion from the Annex to the Schedule should place them outside the IWC jurisdiction. Only by unanimous agreement of all members of the IWC could this be reversed. Other States, however, adopted the view that what would have amounted to the 'creeping jurisdiction' of the IWC could in the circumstances be acceptable. The ongoing contentious debates on this issue resulted during some periods in the exclusion of the transmission of infor-mation on small cetaceans submitted by States to the IWC. This issue has still not been satisfactorily resolved. However, the IWC does acknowledge the need for further international cooperation to conserve and rebuild depleted stocks of these cetaceans. In order to do so, it has encouraged countries to seek scientific advice on small cetaceans from the IWC, and has invited IWC Member States to provide technical or financial assistance to countries with threatened species. The Commis-sion has agreed that the Scientific Committee can study and provide advice on small cetaceans and the Committee has established a sub-committee on small cetaceans which has operated since 1979. Like the great whales, small cetaceans are potentially vulnerable to a number of anthropic threats, including bycatch in fishing gear, hunting, pollution, habitat degradation, coastal and offshore developments and climate change. There is a very successful voluntary fund established by the IWC on conservation of small cetaceans, in order to encourage research projects with a special emphasis on capacity building within developing countries. One of the functions of the Scientific Committee (through its sub-committee on small cetaceans) is to identify priority species/regions for review, their distribution, stock structure, abun-dance, seasonal movements, life history, ecology, status and potential threats.[57]

---

[56] Ibid., p. 278.
[57] International Whaling Commission, https://iwc.int/smallcetacean, last accessed 4 March 2015.

2.13 The precautionary principle and the ICRW

The ICRW does not expressly embody the precautionary principle per se.[58] In broad brushstrokes, this principle relates to scientific uncertainty. As is well known, the most frequently cited and the most authoritative formulation of this principle is contained in the 1992 Rio Declaration on Environment and Development:

> In order to protect the environment, the precautionary approach shall be widely applied by States according to their capabilities. Where there are threats of serious or irreversible damage, lack of full scientific certainty shall not be used as a reason for postponing cost-effective measures to prevent environmental degradation.

Voigt succinctly describes the precautionary principle in the following way: '[i]n essence it means that where there is less than clear scientific evidence, decision-makers should take extra precaution and not use the lack of evidence as a pretext to advance'; and that 'once a risk – not necessarily the actual threat itself – has been identified, the lack of scientific proof of cause and effect shall not be used as a reason for not taking action to protect the environment'.[59]

The majority of modern international treaties have adopted it as a founding principle, as for example in global treaties, such as the 1996 London Protocol to the 1972 Convention on the Prevention of Marine Pollution by Dumping of Wastes and Other Matter,[60] and in many regional treaties, such as the 1992 Convention on the Protection

---

[58] There are a great number of publications on the precautionary principle. See Alexander Gillespie, 'The Precautionary Principle and the 21st Century: A Case Study of Noise Pollution in the Ocean', http://workspace.ascobans.org/sites/ascobans/files/the%20precautionary%20principle%20and%20noise%20pollution2.pdf, last accessed 24 March 2015; for the most comprehensive analysis, see: A. Trouwborst, *Precautionary Rights and Duties of States* (Leiden: Martinus Nijhoff Publishers, 2006); A. Trouwborst, *Evolution and Status of the Precautionary Principle in International Law* (The Hague: Kluwer Law International, 2002); David Freestone and Ellen Hey (eds.), *The Precautionary Principle: The Challenge of Implementation* (The Hague: Kluwer Law International, 1996); Rosie Cooney, 'The Precautionary Principle in Biodiversity Conservation and Natural Resource Management. An issues paper for policy-makers, researchers and practitioners' (Cambridge: International Union for Conservation of Nature, 2004).

[59] Christina Voigt, 'A Precautionary Approach to the Whaling Convention: Will the ICJ Challenge the Legality of Scientific Whaling?', in I. L. Backer, O. K. Fauchald and C. Voigt (eds.), *Pro Natura – Festskrift til Hans Christian Bugge* (Oslo: Universitetsforlaget, 2012), pp. 557–84, 572, 573.

[60] 1996 London Protocol, 1046 UNTS 120.

of the Environment of the Baltic Sea Area.[61] It may be said that it has acquired the status of a norm of customary international law, although this is not a view shared by all scholars, practitioners and dispute settlement bodies.[62]

In relation to whales, Voigt gives several reasons why the precautionary principle will have to be applied in many areas regulated by the ICRW: data acquisition; the risks to the population; and repercussions of these uncertainties on the conservation and management of whale stocks. There are several environmental risks to whales, such as climate change, chemical pollution, ozone depletion and UV-B radiation and degradation of habitats.[63] She postulates, therefore, that the interpretation of the Whaling Convention and its Article VIII (scientific whaling) to restrict lethal methods should be based on, and informed by, the precautionary principle.[64] It is considered by some authors that to some extent the practice of the IWC in the period from 1974 to the present, no doubt partly due to the increasing NGO influence within the IWC, is an example of the active use of the precautionary principle – after all, there is a Moratorium on commercial whaling in place, which is often put forward as an example of the application of this precautionary principle.[65]

However, a very different view was expressed by Andresen et al., who argue that the imposition of the Moratorium was effected mainly for

---

[61] 1992 Convention on the Protection of the Environment of the Baltic Sea Area, 1507 UNTS 167.

[62] See, on both approaches, Gillespie, above n. 58.   [63] Voigt, above n. 59, pp. 574–81.

[64] Ibid., p. 582.

[65] Freestone and Hey, above n. 58, p. 10; Cooney, above n. 58, p. 22, who is also of the view that the RMP and the establishment of sanctuaries are an expression of the application of the precautionary principle by the IWC. The Japanese Commissioner to the IWC (Morishita) and Dr Dan Goodman in strong terms condemn the application of the precautionary principle by the IWC (for example, to the establishment of sanctuaries, which according to these authors are an 'abuse' of the precautionary principle, since they are created irrespective of the status of the whaling stocks). Joji Morishita and Dan Goodman, 'Role and Problems of the Scientific Committee of the International Whaling Commission in Terms of Conservation and Sustainable Utilisation of Whale Stocks', *Global Environmental Research* 9 (2005), 157–66, 162. See also the very critical approach of Milton Freeman, who is of the view that the precautionary principle disregards the advice of the IWC Scientific Committee, which has concluded that some whale stocks could be harvested: Milton M. R. Freeman, 'Science and Trans-Science in the Whaling Debate', in Milton M. R. Freeman and Urs Kreuter (eds.), *Elephants and Whales. Resources for Whom?* (Basle: Gordon and Breach Science Publishers, 1994), pp. 143–57, 146.

political purposes. They claim that there was scientific evidence that whaling for some species, such as minke and baleen whales, could have been implemented in 'a sustainable manner'. In conclusion, these authors stated that 'from 1998 to the present day it is hard to escape the conclusion that there has been a continuous abuse of the precautionary principle, to some extent in the SC [Scientific Committee] and especially in the Commission'.[66] Similarly, William Burke evaluated the application (or non-application) of the precautionary principle by the IWC very unfavourably, in particular regarding the continuation of the Moratorium on whaling, against the evidence of the recovery of certain stocks, a situation that he calls 'an abuse of the precautionary approach as well as a violation of the ICRW and the UNCLOS'.[67]

Voigt assumes that the application of the precautionary principle within the IWC 'may prove to provide a valid and practicable way to overcome the dichotomy of the ICRW's objectives and the differences in the ICRW between the position of those of its members which want to continue whaling and those which do not'.[68] Taking into consideration the significantly divergent views on the application of the precautionary principle within the IWC, regrettably the present author does not share this view. Unfortunately, the application of this principle in relation to the ICRW can be added as one more item on the list of the divisive issues.

Concluding remarks

This overview of the provisions of the ICRW clearly indicates that most of the issues in relation to the Convention are contentious, starting with its binary object and purpose: on the one hand, the conservation and management of whale stocks in order to provide for the 'orderly development of the whaling industry', and, on the other, recognition that whales are a 'general trust', to be safeguarded for 'future generations'.

---

[66] Steinar Andresen, Lars Walløe and G. Kristin Rosendal, 'The Precautionary Principle: Knowledge Counts but Power Decides', in Rosie Cooney and Barney Dickson (eds.), *Biodiversity and the Precautionary Principle: Risk and Uncertainty in Conservation and Sustainable Use* (London: Earthscan, 2005), pp. 39–55, 50.

[67] William T. Burke, 'A New Whaling Agreement and International Law', in Friedheim, above n. 17, p. 69.

[68] Voigt, above n. 59, p. 572. A pragmatic view was expressed by Michael Heazle, who explains that uncertainty is inherent in science. However, the IWC never made an effort about how to manage current uncertainty in terms of facilitating a political agreement among its members as to how much scientific uncertainty is acceptable: Michael Heazle, *Scientific Uncertainty and the Politics of Whaling* (Seattle and London: University of Washington Press, 2006), 186.

Indeed, this 'dual' object and purpose of the Convention was one of the most argued and disputed areas during the pleadings (written and oral) in the *Whaling in the Antarctic* case and it has been interpreted and analysed by the Court in its Judgment.[69] There is no conclusive interpretation of the object and purpose of the ICRW and neither the Judgment in this case nor the pleadings of the Parties have shed much light on this issue. However, the most important statement regarding the object and purpose of the Convention by the Court was, in broad brushstrokes, that the object and purpose of the ICRW cannot be changed but the emphasis regarding certain provisions relating to its object and purpose may evolve. This statement of the Court, although very important, is far from clear, as the question of the change of the focus on certain provisions of a treaty can also be subject to various, and frequently irreconcilable, interpretations. The current, it may be said undesirable, state of affairs regarding the functioning of the Whaling Convention cannot be easily remedied or even improved, as there are many different factors that impair the effectiveness of this instrument.

One of the factors that has been suggested as detrimental to the effectiveness of the Whaling Convention is its advanced age. The ICRW was negotiated and structured almost seventy years ago and its main provisions were based on two pre-war treaties from 1931 and 1937. The basic structure of the Convention reflects the approaches to environmental matters of the period when it was negotiated and, of course, it was not based on principles that characterise the contemporary approach to environmental protection, such as the precautionary principle (approach) or polluter-pays principle. In reality (although such an argument might be considered debatable), it was only in the 1990s that global environmental conventions and regional environmental treaties embraced these principles. Global conventions of the 1970s concluded just before or after the 1972 Stockholm Conference on the Human Environment did not include such principles, examples being the 1972 London (Dumping) Convention[70] and the 1973 Convention on Prevention of Pollution from Ships (MARPOL).[71] However, these Conventions, through resolutions of their organs and their practice, embraced the precautionary principle in their

---

[69] See, in depth, Malgosia Fitzmaurice, 'The Whaling Convention and Thorny Issues of Interpretation', in Malgosia Fitzmaurice and Dai Tamada (eds.), *Whaling in the Antarctic: The Judgment and Its Implications* (to be published by Brill–Nijhoff, 2016). On file with the author.
[70] Convention on Prevention of Marine Pollution by Dumping, 1046 UNTS 120.
[71] Convention on Prevention of Pollution from Ships, 340 UNTS 184.

functioning.[72] Both the above-mentioned Conventions are considered to be very successful and, in many ways, may even be regarded as exemplary regarding their effectiveness. The case of the ICRW is no different, and it may be argued that, through the practice of the International Whaling Commission, the precautionary principle was implemented (see above, section 2.13). Therefore, in the view of the present author, the lack of success and the diminished effectiveness of the Whaling Convention is probably not a result of this instrument's age. This state of affairs may be ascribed in part to extra-legal factors, such as the attitudes of the parties to the ICRW, which will be analysed in detail in the next chapter. The lack of common understanding, and the acrimonious atmosphere between the members of the Whaling Commission, has had a paralysing effect on the functioning of the Commission. The Convention has evolved into a political tool. It is regrettable that there is no immediate solution to be offered to overcome the impasse. Unfortunately, the Judgment of the Court has not changed strained relationships between members of the Commission, as was very clearly evidenced by its very tense sixty-fifth Meeting in Slovenia, held after the rendering of the Judgment by the Court.

---

[72] For example, it is considered that the ban on dumping of all nuclear waste in the London Convention is due to the application of the precautionary principle: Bénédicte Sage-Fuller, *The Precautionary Principle in Marine Environmental Law. With Special Reference to High Risk Vessels* (Abingdon: Routledge, 2013), p. 71. The same author considers that the designation of special areas under MARPOL also indicates the application of the precautionary principle: p. 225. It may also be mentioned that the International Maritime Organization adopted in 1995 Guidelines on Incorporation of the Precautionary Approach in the Context of Specific IMO Activities, which expressly refer to Principle 15 of the Rio Declaration on Environment and Development on the precautionary approach: www.imo.org/blast/blastDa taHelper.asp?data_id=15641&filename=67%2837%29.pdf, last accessed 6 March 2015.

3

The International Whaling Commission

Introduction

This chapter will describe and analyse the structure, development and functioning of the International Whaling Commission (IWC). It is organically linked to the previous chapter, which focused on the International Convention for the Regulation of Whaling (ICRW). The IWC is a regulatory body of the Whaling Convention. Much has been written about it: but as the present author has observed, for reason of completeness and also of a better understanding of current developments, it is necessary to outline the fundamental issues regarding this international body. In broad brushstrokes, it may be said that the structure and decision-taking procedure of the IWC do not differ greatly from those of such bodies as the fisheries commissions or the bodies of the Conventions adopted under the auspices of the International Maritime Organization, the majority of which take their decisions on the basis of the opting-out system (or tacit acceptance). In this chapter the Judgment in the *Whaling in the Antarctic* case, in which the International Court of Justice made important statements regarding not only scientific whaling but also interpretation of the ICRW and its Article VIII (scientific whaling), will be analysed as well.

3.1 General overview and structure of the International Whaling Commission

3.1.1 Introduction

As noted in Chapter 2, concerns over the oceans' stocks of whales first arose in the initial decades of the twentieth century due to serious depletion resulting from the development of the whaling industry, and, in particular, modern methods of whaling such as the use of boats with steam engines, harpoon guns and factory ships, in the latter half of the nineteenth century. These developments arose to meet the growing demand for whaling products, particularly whale meat, whale oil and baleen, which existed during the nineteenth century and the first half of the twentieth century. These products constituted a lucrative resource; and a number of major States had mature commercial whaling industries. It was against this backdrop that international legal regulation of whaling was introduced through a series of conventions culminating in the conclusion in 1946 of the ICRW, which remains to this day the main international vehicle for the interstate regulation of whaling, and which operates, as discussed in Chapter 2, a treaty regime that includes the IWC set up pursuant to the Convention. The IWC regulates whaling through the Schedule to the ICRW in order to adopt measures specifying (1) protected and unprotected species; (2) open and closed seasons; (3) open and closed waters; (4) size limits for each species; (5) time, methods and intensity of whaling; and (6) gear restrictions (ICRW Article V(1)).

The IWC has been disparaged for bringing 'disorder', rather than 'order', to the issue of the protection of whales.[1] Certain authors, such as Birnie, believe that the role and functioning of the IWC would be much more effective if it was seen as part of a general 'proper and effective system'. For instance, according to Birnie, a more harmonious system could include closer integration/cooperation between the IWC and other international agreements, such as the UN Convention on the Law of the Sea (UNCLOS) and especially the Convention on Biological Diversity (CBD).[2] As an aside, within the area of normative interpretation, this view is neither new nor ground-breaking. Irrespective of whether practice reflects this, the whole body of international law contains the important principle of systemic integration which acts as a vehicle to reconcile norms that are relevant to State Parties but that are found in different instruments, so long as such norms are legally relevant to the parties in question. Birnie has noted that such an approach would be beneficial to whales, as the IWC has a limited jurisdiction and the reliance on general treaties would strengthen their protection. It can be argued that although such a

[1] See Steinar Andresen, 'The International Whaling Regime: Order at the Turn of the Century?', in D. Vidas and W. Oestreng (eds.), *Order for the Oceans at the Turn of the Century* (Lysaker: Nansen Institute, 1999), pp. 215–28. Andresen is of the view that 'it would be a tall order for anyone to claim that this regime is characterised by order'.

[2] Patricia Birnie, 'Framework for Cooperation', in William C. G. Burns and Alexander Gillespie (eds.), *The Future of Cetaceans in a Changing World* (Ardsley, NY: Transnational Publishers, 2003), p. 114. One of the arguments for such a broader approach, according to Birnie, was an initial US proposal to subjugate the IWC to the FAO, a suggestion which did not survive the negotiations of the ICRW.

view has some merit, the provisions of the CBD are vague and general to the point that, as a consequence, they would probably amount to protection that was rather ineffective. What is more, the implementation of the CBD provisions would be down to its State Parties, which, again, brings us to the issue of effective enforcement. (Concerning the relationship between the IWC and other Convention, see Chapter 6.)

As at present, and as discussed earlier in this publication, despite the evident history of interstate cooperation regarding whaling regulation, the state of whaling nowadays appears to be one of conflict: conflict at the Annual Meetings of the IWC; conflict between States; and conflicts between whalers and environmental activists of such regularity and extent that they are frequently referred to as 'whale wars'. There is at present no obvious or imminent solution to these conflicts.

3.1.2 The structure of the IWC

Unlike the two earlier whaling conventions, the ICRW, in Article III, provided for the establishment of a permanent treaty body, the IWC. Membership of the Commission is open to all State Parties to the ICRW, irrespective of whether they are whaling or non-whaling nations. It is not surprising that this open membership structure of the IWC has resulted in accusations that State Parties which practise whaling were attempting de facto sponsorship of a number of a non-whaling State Parties in order to manipulate the balance of power in the IWC.[3]

---

[3] There are at present eighty-nine Parties to the ICRW; all Parties have Commissioners at the IWC. Most Parties are non-whaling nations. Peter J. Stoett, *The International Politics of Whaling* (Vancouver: UBC Press, 1997), p. 64. The Technical Committee of the IWC is effectively the meeting of the Commission during which all major matters are discussed and, if necessary, can be recommended to the IWC by simple majority: see Ray Gambell, 'The International Whaling Commission and the Contemporary Whaling Debate', in John R. Twiss Jr and Randall R. Reeves (eds.), *Conservation and Management of Marine Mammals* (Washington: Smithsonian Institution Press, 1999). The Commission is supported by the work of the following Committees, Sub-committees and Working Groups: *The Scientific Committee (SC)*. An important feature of the Convention is the emphasis it places on scientific advice. The SC comprises around 200 leading cetacean scientists from many countries, and its main meeting is held annually. In addition, each year a number of intersessional workshops and working groups deal with specific issues. *The Conservation Committee (CC)* was established through Commission Resolution 2003-1. Its work includes initiatives to reduce the frequency of ship strikes, measures to allow the strategic development of the whale-watching industry, and the development of Conservation Management Plans. It also receives sanctuary proposals and national reports on cetacean conservation. *The Finance and Administration Committee (FAC)* advises the Commission

The IWC is the main organ of the ICRW, having as its most important function the keeping under review and the revising, so far as is deemed necessary, of the measures laid down in the ICRW Schedule which govern the conduct of whaling throughout the world. It acts by means

on expenditure, budgets, scale of contributions, financial regulations and staff questions. In 2011–12 the FAC reviewed the Commission's overall governance arrangements and introduced new measures to increase transparency, ensure cost savings and establish other efficiencies in the way the Commission works. *The Aboriginal Subsistence Whaling Sub-Committee (ASWS)* considers relevant information and documentation from the Scientific Committee and examines the nutritional, subsistence and cultural needs relating to aboriginal subsistence whaling and the use of whales for such purposes. The ASWS provides advice on the dependence of aboriginal communities on specific whale stocks to the Commission for its consideration and determination of appropriate management measures. *The Infractions Sub-Committee (ISC)* considers matters and documents relating to the International Observer Scheme and infractions in so far as they involve monitoring and compliance with the Schedule to the 1946 Convention, as well as penalties for infractions (http://iwc.int/commission-sub-groups, last accessed 20 December 2014). *The Working Group on Whale Killing Methods and Associated Welfare Issues (WGWKM)* was established in 2000 to review information and documentation available so as to advise the Commission on whale-killing methods and associated welfare issues. The links between the IWC and other organisations in civil society can be maintained through the medium of observers. As shown in this publication, the voice of civil society is very important and many of the accredited non-governmental organisations (NGOs) make pertinent state-ments and clarify issues under discussion in the IWC. As a general rule, observation at IWC meetings is limited to the following: representatives of non-party States; intergovern-mental organisations (IGOs); and *accredited* NGOs. Any international organisation and any State that is not a party to the ICRW may be represented at meetings of the IWC by an observer or observers in the following cases: if it has previously attended any IWC meeting; if it submits its request in writing to the IWC sixty days prior to the start of the meeting; or if it has been invited by the IWC. Observers may attend – but have no voting rights at – all meetings of the IWC and the Technical Committee, and any meetings of subsidiary groups of the IWC and the Technical Committee, with the exception of the IWC meetings that are open only to Commissioners (of the IWC Member States) and the FAC. IGO representatives with particular relevance to the work of the SC may participate as non-voting members, subject to the agreement of the Chair of the Committee acting according to such policy as the IWC may decide. Non-party States may be represented by observers at meetings of the SC. The requirements for NGOs to obtain observer status are as follows: any NGO expressing an interest in matters covered by the ICRW may be accredited as an observer. Requests for accreditation must be submitted in writing to the IWC sixty days prior to the start of the meeting and the IWC may issue an invitation with respect to any such request. Applications from NGOs are open to the ICRW State Parties to review. Once accredited, an NGO remains so until the IWC decides otherwise. Obser-vers from each NGO are allowed to attend whichever meetings are open to non-members; however, the number of representatives that an NGO may send may be limited in order that all non-members interested in observing an IWC meeting be allowed to attend. The IWC determines the level of the registration fee, and the rules of conduct, and may define other conditions for the attendance of NGO observers. Any NGO which has an accredited

of amendment of the Schedule, as provided in Article V(1). Measures contained in the Schedule, among other things: provide for the complete protection of certain cetacean species; designate specified areas as whale sanctuaries; set limits on the numbers and size of whales which may be taken; prescribe open and closed seasons and areas for whaling; and prohibit the capture of suckling calves and female whales accompanied by calves. The IWC also coordinates the compilation of catch reports and other statistical and biological records. However, there are important limitations on these powers which play a significant part in the present impasse.

In the first place, though decisions of the IWC may normally be arrived at by simple majority, Article III(2), provides that 'a three-fourths majority of those members voting shall be required for action in pursuance of Article V'; that is, for all amendments to the Schedule, and, consequently, generally for the imposition of further regulations on whaling. We shall look further at the impact of this provision, initially, on the imposition of the Moratorium and at the core of the present disputes on the protracted problems of having the Moratorium lifted.

In relation to amendments to the Schedule under Article V, such as the imposition of the Moratorium, Article V(2) further provides that these:

> (a) shall be such as are necessary to carry out the objectives and purposes of this Convention and to provide for the conservation, development, and optimum utilization of the whale resources; (b) shall be based on scientific findings; ... and (d) shall take into consideration the interests of the consumers of whale products and the whaling industry.

We have already noted above the importance, in the current situation, of the provisions under (a) and (d) of this paragraph. We shall see below that the provision under (b), requiring decisions in relation to

---

observer to an IWC meeting may nominate a scientifically qualified observer to be present at meetings of the SC. Any such nomination must reach the IWC Secretary not less than sixty days before the start of the meeting in question, and must specify the scientific qualifications and relevant experience of the nominee. The SC Chair decides upon the acceptability of any nomination; however, rejection requires consultation with the Chair and Vice-Chair of the IWC. Observers admitted under this rule shall not participate in discussions, but the papers and documents of the SC shall be made available to them at the same time as to members of the Committee. NGOs may also make opening statements. Observers from NGOs must also pay the fee. For example, in 2011 the IWC set the following fees for accredited NGOs: £520 for the first observer and £260 for any additional observer (https://iwc.int/observers_ngo, last accessed 20 April 2015).

amendment of the Schedule to be 'based on scientific findings', is also crucial. In fact this reflects a trend towards evidence-based policy-making, which, effectively, disciplines unfettered policy development in that it restricts it to that which is scientifically sound. In other words, it is part of the wider efforts to place politics and diplomacy on more disciplined – in certain cases, technocratic – bases.

Another important capacity of the IWC is set out in Article III(4), which provides that: '[t]he Commission may set up, from among its own members and experts or advisers, such committees as it considers desirable to perform such functions as it may authorise'. Pursuant to this provision, in 1950, the IWC set up a Scientific Committee (SC).[4] This, as the IWC itself puts it, in part reflected the general references in the Convention to the need for scientific research, but, more importantly, related to the requirements of Article V(2)(b), referred to above, pursuant to which amendments to the Schedule must be based on scientific findings. It might be thought that there would arise from these provisions a definite relationship between the findings of the SC and the subsequent decisions of the IWC concerning whaling regulations requiring amendment to the Schedule. But this has not necessarily been the case, and the relationship, or the lack of it, has been a source of concern and controversy, as, indeed, has the working of the SC in itself. But it may be noted at this stage that the potential for politics to trump science in the working of the SC, as is often alleged by some to be the case, has some foundation in its wide composition. The divisive atmosphere in the SC is very clearly illustrated by Aron, Burke and Freeman, who observed that scientific uncertainty regarding whaling led to some statements adverse to Japanese scientific whaling which were not based on facts but were examples of 'imprudence and irresponsibility'.[5]

---

[4] The functions of the SC are listed in Article IV of the ICRW, which provides that: 'The Commission may either in collaboration with or through independent agencies of the Contracting Governments or other public or private agencies, establishments, or organizations, or independently (a) encourage, recommend, or if necessary, organize studies and investigations relating to whales and whaling; (b) collect and analyse statistical information concerning the current condition and trend of the whale stocks and the effects of whaling activities thereon; (c) study, appraise, and disseminate information concerning methods of maintaining and increasing the populations of whale stocks.'

[5] William Aron, William T. Burke and Milton M. R. Freeman, 'Science and Advocacy: A Cautionary Tale from the International Whaling Debate', in Burns and Gillespie, above n. 2, p. 91.

Be this as it may, in the final and purely legal analysis, the SC is a supportive body to, and set up by, the IWC; and it may be said that reports and submissions by the SC are not binding on the IWC. The (advisory) position of the SC vis-à-vis the IWC might lead to disregard of SC Recommendations, including the IWC's potential departure from a science-based approach. Therefore, it would appear that such a situation would be neither *ultra vires* nor otherwise legally inappropriate in and of itself (although lending itself to criticism, as shown by the practice of the IWC). It may be noted, however, that in recognition of the ICJ Judgment in the *Whaling in the Antarctic* case, the IWC strengthened the role of the SC in the granting of special permits for scientific whaling by States, which is a far-reaching development.[6]

We have referred above to the possibility for State Parties to withdraw from the ICRW altogether, and thereby avoid being bound by any forms of regulation under its provisions. For States that do not wish to be bound by a particular regulation that is being proposed, but do not want to take the drastic step of full withdrawal, there is also the possibility of avoiding being bound by new regulations simply by objecting to them under the provisions of Article V(3) of the Convention, which provides, broadly, that any regulation introduced by the IWC by way of amendment of the Schedule (in effect all new regulations or amendments to existing regulations introduced since the adoption of the original Schedule) shall not be binding on any party which, in proper form and in sufficient time, objects to being bound by it. This provision is an example of the so-called 'opting-out'

---

[6] 'Now, therefore, the Commission: ... 2. Instructs the Scientific Committee to consider and revise how it reviews special permit research programmes, including in relation to the Annex P: Process for the Review of Special Permit Proposals and Research Results from Existing and Completed Permits, in light of the matters set out in paragraph 1 above, for consideration by the Commission. 3. Requests that no further special permits for the take of whales are issued under existing research programmes or any new programme of whale research until: (a) the Scientific Committee has reviewed the research programme to enable it to provide advice to the Commission in accordance with the instructions above; and (b) the Commission has considered the report of the Scientific Committee and assessed whether the proponent of the special permit programme has acted in accordance with the review process described above; (c) the Commission has, in accordance with Article VI, made such recommendations on the merits or otherwise of the special permit programme as it sees fit': http://uk.whales.org/blog/chrisbutler-stroud/2014/09/iwc-passes-resolution-to-implement-icj-ruling-and-control-future, last accessed 11 January 2015.

procedure or 'tacit acceptance' (as mentioned in Chapter 2), according to which each relevant act taken by an international organisation becomes automatically binding on each Member State unless a State expressly takes steps to exempt itself from being bound by it: in other words, a State must 'opt out' of it to evade the legal effects of such an act. The opposite of this procedure, as may be seen in other international agreements that contain such provisions, is the 'opting-in' procedure, under which a State is only bound by a decision when it expressly agrees to be so bound: in other words, where a State 'opts in' to its effect. When first developed, both these procedures were deemed useful in that they were instrumental in ensuring buy-in on the part of States to legal regimes. The alternative might have been that States that were reticent to subject themselves to interstate regulation would avoid accession altogether, thus generally making interstate cooperation less effective. Arguably, opt-out procedures have encouraged States to sign up to conventions which they might otherwise have been reluctant to join because of the possibility of finding themselves bound by onerous provisions on the basis of majority decisions in the convention's organs.

However, in relation to the IWC, the opting-out procedure has been the subject of much criticism from the time of its negotiation, for rendering the IWC toothless and ineffective. Indeed, in the first decades of the functioning of the IWC, objections were so frequent that they were seen as considerably undermining its efficiency. Opting-out procedures may provide 'rogue' States with an opportunity for capriciously manipulating the procedure in order to evade international obligations. Be that as it may, these are the risks of introducing into regimes such procedures: to further restrict their use would require highly nuanced language potentially rendering opt-out procedures redundant. Again, this is the cost of ensuring wide participation in regimes which, had there been no opt-out procedure included, would have otherwise had smaller memberships. For instance, a regime lacking such a procedure leaves State Parties with few options, with the most ostensible one being that of withdrawal from the Convention altogether. This would have been an outcome that would have undercut the effectiveness of the whole regime. For instance, the withdrawal of Norway from the ICRW would have tolled the death knell of the entire regulation regime. On the other hand, it can be seen as providing a ready opportunity for States to avoid being bound by decisions they dislike without incurring the international hostility that might follow from their complete withdrawal. This inherent weakness has become particularly destructive in its effect when the attitudes and objectives of the Parties have become so polarised. Indeed, we shall see that States have not limited themselves to using the opting-out procedure in the IWC when faced with decisions they do not like, but have, in fact, been willing to avoid being bound by such decisions through the more drastic, though procedurally simple, means of withdrawing from the Convention altogether.

It may be noted here that, while the provisions of Article V(3)(c) of the Convention make provision for the subsequent withdrawal of an objection – whereupon a party would become bound by the provision to which it had initially objected – there is no provision for a subsequent objection. Thus, should a State fail to object to a provision being introduced by way of an amendment to the Schedule, and as a consequence become bound by it, it would not be open to it to make a later objection so as to cease to be bound by that amendment. As we shall see below, this is an important factor in relation to the present impasse in the IWC, in that States which had not originally objected to the Moratorium now find themselves unable to avoid being bound by it unless they withdraw from the entire regime, or unless the IWC overturns, or otherwise sets aside, the amendment in question.

This situation has resulted in one case wherein a State Party (namely Iceland) withdrew altogether from the ICRW in order not to be bound by its Moratorium, only later to attempt to rejoin, albeit by submitting a formal reservation to the offending provisions (namely, those in the Schedule relating to the Moratorium).

3.1.3   The territorial and substantive extents of IWC jurisdiction

A further issue that has been contested in the IWC is the precise extent of the IWC's mandate over marine zones within the jurisdiction of State Parties. This has been particularly important in relation to medium and small cetaceans, which are predominantly coastal species. A further factor that complicates the question of the IWC's jurisdiction is the fact that State Parties' conceptions of what are the limits of their territorial sea and exclusive economic zone (EEZ) are not necessarily coextensive. The ICRW may state in Article I(2) that it applies to 'all waters'; however, many States objected to the jurisdiction of the IWC in their territorial sea and their EEZs on the basis that it would be *ultra vires* the IWC. This has called into question the interplay with other international legal instruments. For instance, the issue arose regarding how Article I(2) of the ICRW relates to certain provisions in UNCLOS.[7]

Thus, UNCLOS Article 311(2) ('Relation to other conventions and international agreements'), Article 61(2) ('Stocks occurring within the exclusive economic zones of two or more coastal states or both within the exclusive economic zone and in an area beyond and adjacent to it'), Article 64(1) ('Highly migratory species') and Article 65 ('Marine mammals') all relate to the EEZ of littoral States. Gillespie poses two questions regarding the relationship between the IWC and UNCLOS: do signatories agree to cede their own sovereignty to the IWC on the issue of whaling; and is the ICRW compatible with UNCLOS? Further questions arose in this context in relation to the leading role of the IWC regarding small cetaceans. Canada, although not a member of the IWC, argued that the relevant UNCLOS provisions referred to 'competent international organisations' (in the plural), thus admitting the possibility that other whaling bodies beyond the IWC may also be involved, rather than that there ought to be deference towards the IWC. Gillespie has also expressed the view that the role of the IWC in relation to whales is reinforced by Section 17.61 of Agenda 21 of the 1992 Rio Conference on the Environment and Development, which expressly refers to the IWC as being competent on questions relating to great whales and other cetaceans.[8]

3.1.4   The 1982 Moratorium

After the 1972 Stockholm Conference on the Human Environment, and in the context of the over-exploitation of whale stocks (which has been

---

[7] United Nations Convention on the Law of the Sea, Montego Bay, 10 December 1982, 1833 UNTS 3.

[8] Section 17.61 states that States recognize: 'a. The responsibility of the International Whaling Commission for the conservation and management of whale stocks and the regulation of whaling pursuant to the 1946 International Convention for the Regulation of Whaling; b. The work of the International Whaling Commission Scientific Committee in carrying out studies of large whales in particular, as well as of other cetaceans; c. The work of other organisations, such as the Inter-American Tropical Tuna Commission and the Agreement on Small Cetaceans in the Baltic and North Sea under the Bonn Convention, in the conservation, management and study of cetaceans and other marine mammals' (http://sustainabledevelopment.un.org/content/documents/Agenda21.pdf, last accessed 22 December 2014). See also Alexander Gillespie, 'Small Cetaceans, International Law and the International Whaling Commission', *Melbourne Journal of International Law* 2 (2001), 257–303 and Alexander Gillespie, *Whaling Diplomacy: Defining Issues in International Environmental Law* (Cheltenham: Edward Elgar Publishing, 2005), p. 289.

referred to as amounting to 'whaling Olympics'),[9] and of all the changes mentioned above, proposals were submitted, in particular prompted by NGOs, to introduce a global Moratorium on whaling. This idea was also supported by the United States and Australia. The idea of the Moratorium first came under consideration in 1973 in the aftermath of the Stockholm Conference, when the US suggested a ten-year Moratorium before the IWC's Technical Committee. This idea was rejected, since the Scientific Committee was of the view that 'such a blanket Moratorium on whaling could not be justified scientifically'.[10] The SC rather suggested that 'a decade of intensified research on cetaceans should be conducted in parallel with further development of the policy of bringing catch restrictions into line with the best available knowledge of the state of stocks'.[11] The late 1970s were characterised by a significant number of inconclusive discussions regarding the suggested Moratorium. However, due to the enlarged membership of the IWC, its structure was changing and there was a shift towards the policy which has been referred to as 'protectionism, mainly motivated by uncertainty over abundance'.[12] The Moratorium was finally enacted in 1982 (effective in the season 1985/86), when the IWC imposed a zero-catch limit for commercial whaling of all stocks of whale, which effectively constituted a Moratorium on commercial whaling. This amounted to a major victory for the preservationists. It also marked the start, effectively, of a new era in the history of the IWC in which the dichotomy between the opposing views on the object and purpose of the Convention, to which we referred above, became ever more pronounced. This, again, is unsurprising given that the duality of objectives enshrined in the ICRW effectively armed one camp – the preservationists – against the other – the conservationists – thus allowing this conflict to express itself in the promotion of one single objective, namely whale conservation, over the other, namely the longevity of the commercial whaling industry through, among other things, the conservation of whale stocks.

The Moratorium was embodied in an amended paragraph 10(e) of the Schedule, which reads as follows:

[9] Robert L. Friedheim, 'Moderation in the Pursuit: Explaining Japan's Failure in the International Whaling Negotiations', ODIL 27 (1996), 349–78, 355.

[10] Chairman's Report of the Twenty-Fourth Meeting, 24 *Rep. Int'l Whaling Comm'n*, cited in A. W. Harris, 'The Best Scientific Evidence Available: The Whaling Moratorium and Divergent Interpretations of Science', *Wm & Mary Env'l L. & Pol'y Rev.* 29 (2005), 375–450, 377.

[11] Ibid., 377.   [12] Ibid., 379.

> Notwithstanding the other provisions of paragraph 10, catch limits for the
> killing for commercial purposes of whales from all stocks for 1986 coastal
> and the 1985/86 pelagic seasons and thereafter will be zero. This provision
> will be kept under review, based upon the best scientific advice, and by
> 1990 at the latest the Commission will undertake a comprehensive assess-
> ment of the effects of these decisions on whale stocks and consider
> modification of this provision and the establishment of other catch
> limits.[13]

It is worth noting that, before the full Moratorium was agreed, more or
less all commercial whaling (excluding minke whales), as well as whaling
from factory ships, had been banned under earlier amendments to the
Schedule. In any event, the United States had ceased commercial whale
hunting as early as 1924; the United Kingdom in 1963; New Zealand in
1964; the Netherlands in 1964; Canada in 1972; Australia in 1978; and
South Africa in 1979.[14]

The idea of a global Moratorium in the 1980s had, unsurprisingly,
been opposed by the whaling industry, which had favoured the conservationist approach, giving rise to disagreement within the IWC as to the
extent of the Moratorium. This resulted in three proposals being tabled,
namely, a complete or general Moratorium, a Moratorium on commercial whaling and a Moratorium on the hunting of sperm whales. The
problem was how to reconcile the conflicting approaches of the conservationists and the preservationists. Many States, as well as NGOs, supported a firmly preservationist approach (in effect the banning of all
whaling). The whaling industry and whaling States, on the other hand,
continued to hold the view that whales remained a harvestable resource
and that certain conservationist measures aimed at their continued
sustainable exploitation could be tolerated on the part of non-whaling
States. However, as mentioned above, the structure of the IWC had
changed and a substantial number of members were now non-whaling

---

[13] Paragraph 10(e), IWC Schedule, February 1983; for a very detailed study of the circum-
stances preceding the Moratorium and the Moratorium itself see Gerry J. Nagtzaam, *The
Making of International Environmental Treaties. Neoliberal and Constructivist Analyses of
Normative Evolution* (Cheltenham: Edward Elgar Publishing, 2009), pp. 181–94.

[14] James M. Savelle and Nobuhiro Kishigami, 'Anthropological Research on Whaling:
Prehistoric, Historic and Current Contexts', in Nobuhiro Kishigami, Hisashi Hamaguchi
and James M. Savelle (eds.), *Senri Ethnological Studies, No. 84, Anthropological Studies on
Whaling* (Osaka: National Museum of Ethnology, 2013), p. 7. Just after the introduction
of the Moratorium on commercial whaling the following States still continued whaling:
Russia, Korea, Peru and Chile, Denmark (Greenland). At present Norway and Iceland
continue whaling.

nations with no whaling industry of their own and thus likely to take an anti-whaling approach. At the 1982 IWC meeting in Brighton, various States represented different views concerning the Moratorium. Japan opposed the blanket Moratorium, and Norway, Iceland and South Korea opposed any ban on whaling relating to scientific grounds. A group of States supported the Moratorium but expressed concern regarding the encroachment on sovereign rights of coastal States within their 200 nautical mile EEZ. Finally, the amendment to paragraph 10(e) of the Schedule was passed by twenty-five votes to seven, with five abstentions.[15]

The Moratorium that was eventually adopted involved an unequivocal ban on commercial whaling relating to all whale species. However, the exemptions to the ban on whaling (on aboriginal whaling and scientific whaling grounds under Article VIII of the ICRW) remained unaffected. Also, the Moratorium was imposed initially for a limited period of five years, to be reviewed in 1990. The Moratorium included: the obligation to respect zero-catch limits for the killing for commercial purposes of whales from all stocks (para. 10(e)); the Moratorium on the use of factory ships (para. 10(d)); and the prohibition of commercial whaling in the Southern Ocean Sanctuary (para. 7(b) of the Schedule).[16]

---

[15] Nagtzaam, above n. 13, pp. 181–94.

[16] The Moratorium on commercial whaling, paragraph 10(e), provides: 'Notwithstanding the other provisions of paragraph 10, catch limits for the killing for commercial purposes of whales from all stocks for the 1986 coastal and the 1985/86 pelagic seasons and thereafter shall be zero. This provision will be kept under review, based upon the best scientific advice, and by 1990 at the latest the Commission will undertake a comprehensive assessment of the effects of this decision on whale stocks and consider modification of this provision and the establishment of other catch limits.' The factory ship Moratorium, paragraph 10(d), provides: 'Notwithstanding the other provisions of paragraph 10, there shall be a Moratorium on the taking, killing or treating of whales, except minke whales, by factory ships or whale catchers attached to factory ships. This Moratorium applies to sperm whales, killer whales and baleen whales, except minke whales.' The Convention defines a 'factory ship' as a ship 'in which or on which whales are treated either wholly or in part' and defines a 'whale catcher' as a ship 'used for the purpose of hunting, taking, towing, holding on to, or scouting for whales' (Art. II(1) and (3)). The vessel *Nisshin Maru*, which has been used in JARPA II, is a factory ship, and other JARPA II vessels have served as whale catchers. As stated above, the ICJ (see paragraphs 229–30 of the *Whaling in the Antarctic* case) considers that all whaling that does not fit within Article VIII of the Convention (other than aboriginal subsistence whaling) is subject to paragraph 10(d) of the Schedule. It follows that Japan has not acted in conformity with its obligations under paragraph 10(d) in each of the seasons during which fin whales were taken, killed and treated in JARPA II. Paragraph 7(b), which establishes the Southern Ocean Sanctuary, provides in part: 'In accordance with Article V(1)(c) of the Convention,

There were many reasons why commercial whaling was eventually banned in 1982. As Nagtzaam explains, there were both economic and non-economic factors involved. Economic factors included the fact that whaling had already become a non-profitable activity. Also, threats from the United States government to impose sanctions through the extraterritorial effect of the United States' Pelly Amendment to the Fishermen's Protective Act also played an important role.[17] One of the most important non-economic factors was that in many States, and generally in their civil societies, greater awareness about whaling, no doubt due to the agitation of environmental NGOs, had led to whaling increasingly appearing as an ethical issue; thus giving rise to the notion that whales have an intrinsic right to life that is or ought to be legally enforceable. Nagtzaam states that:

> [t]his altered their identity within global society. For these states and most of the ENGOs, whaling was a barbaric practice and the taking even of one whale was anathema. These states have been at the forefront of strengthening the commercial Moratorium in the hope of stopping the taking of any whales. By voting for the Moratorium, the preservationist states internalised a new moral reality, played out on the global stage of the IWC, that killing whales was wrong and was to be opposed.[18]

The development of this view – according to which the banning of commercial whaling is justified not only by biological considerations but also on ethical grounds, emphasising the special character of these species, such as their intelligence – has been of critical importance in relation to the current situation concerning whaling (on this see Chapters 4 and 5). As we shall see below, it underlies, in particular, the major conflict that now exists as to the real objectives of control measures relating to whaling, and the extent to which, as they have now developed, they are still within the object and purpose of the ICRW.

Another reason for the imposition of the Moratorium was scientific uncertainty relating to the so-called New Management Procedure (NMP) (see Section 3.2), as a result of which, as observed by Morishita and Goodman, the SC could not reach a consensus on recommendations

---

commercial whaling, whether by pelagic operations or from land stations, is prohibited in a region designated as the Southern Ocean Sanctuary.'

[17] www.fws.gov/international/laws-treaties-agreements/us-conservation-laws/pelly-amend ment.html, last accessed 20 December 2014.

[18] Nagtzaam, above n. 13, p. 193.

relating to classification and catch limits of stock subject to commercial whaling. Morishita and Goodman argue that:

> This uncertainty in the science related to application of the NMP was the primary reason quoted by those who supported the adoption of the moratorium on commercial whaling in 1982. In other words, the Commission's main reason for introducing the moratorium on commercial whaling was the argued inadequacy of the scientific database for harvesting whale populations without exposing them to undue risks.[19]

Several States (Norway, Japan (initially) and the USSR) lodged objections to the imposition of the Moratorium, and one of the main whaling nations, Canada, withdrew from the ICRW altogether. Furthermore, after much discussion Norway and the USSR utilised the opt-out mechanism in relation to the Moratorium, and Japan initially intended to. Subsequently, however, the USSR did cease engaging in commercial whaling.

3.1.5 Events and attitudes since the conclusion of the Moratorium

The general scene

As stated above, whilst the Moratorium was originally intended to last for five years after its adoption, all attempts so far on the part of whaling nations to have it lifted have been unsuccessful, partly due to the inability of the IWC to arrive at a satisfactory science-based system of whale stock management. However, the main reason has been that the configuration of such forces at the IWC is such that, due to the majority voting system, the wishes of anti-whaling nations have eventually dominated. The result is that whaling nations now regard the IWC as having turned into an instrument for the abolition, as opposed to the regulation, of whaling. From their point of view, particularly that of Japan which continues to push for the eventual restoration of some commercial whaling in the Southern Ocean, this situation was exacerbated by the setting up, in 1994, of a Southern Ocean Sanctuary (SOS) which further affected Japan's whaling interests in maritime areas by amendment to the Schedule to

---

[19] Joji Morishita and Dan Goodman, 'Role and Problems of the Scientific Committee of the International Whaling Commission in Terms of Conservation and Sustainable Utilisation of Whale Stocks', *Global Environmental Research* 9 (2005), 157–66, citing G. P. Kirkwood, 'Background to the Development of Revised Management Procedures, Annex I, Report of the Scientific Committee', 42nd Report of the International Whaling Commission, p. 160.

the ICRW. Thus, paragraph 7(b) of the Schedule now provides, *inter alia*: '[i]n accordance with Article V(1)(c) of the Convention, commercial whaling, whether by pelagic operations or from land stations, is prohibited in a region designated as the Southern Ocean Sanctuary'. Having then defined the extent of the area, the provision continues: '[t]his prohibition applies irrespective of the conservation status of whale stocks in this Sanctuary'. Japan has opted out of its establishment.

According to Morishita, Japan's Commissioner to the IWC, the commercial whaling Moratorium became a symbol of the anti-whaling movement as it is 'a sacred cause, symbol, stereotype, and fortress'.[20] He also argued that even the IWC website only lists as endangered two species of whales, namely, the North Pacific right whale and the North Atlantic right whale (however, admitting that the levels of certain species, such as blue whales in the Atlantic Ocean, remain low and have not recovered from over-harvesting).[21]

Paragraph 7(b) of the Schedule also provides for ten-yearly reviews. In a sense, the creation of the SOS has had little practical effect, as all commercial whaling at all times has been subject to the total ban of the Moratorium. Notwithstanding that the SOS is often seen as a 'flagship' achievement by the preservationist lobby, it has received much criticism by some States on the ground that the decision behind it is insufficiently science-based. The whaling nations, however, initiated a number of moves to circumvent what they saw as a subversion of the whole object of the ICRW. The Moratorium has in fact left them some leeway, which they have not hesitated to use. As was mentioned above, the Moratorium has left an exception regarding aboriginal subsistence whaling and has not affected scientific whaling, which continues. It is argued that although aboriginal whaling, within the terms of the ICRW, by its definition cannot be commercial, it nevertheless has some commercial elements which appear to be tolerated by States. The policy of the Commission is considered to be inconsistent and illogical in respect of continuing the Moratorium while tolerating whaling which exhibits some features of being commercial.

Morishita stated as follows: 'the term "commercial whaling" is convenient jargon to differentiate some whaling activities from indigenous whaling. In reality it is not possible to separate clearly commercial

---

[20] Joji Morishita, 'The Truth about the Commercial Whaling Moratorium', in *Senri Ethnological Studies*, above n. 14, p. 337. See also Nagtzaam, above n. 13, p. 226.
[21] Morishita, above n. 14, p. 340.

whaling from indigenous whaling based on either the presence or absence of commercial activities.'[22]

Therefore, in sum, arguments submitted by Japanese scholars and practitioners in connection with the continuation of the Moratorium rely broadly on two grounds: that certain whale species are not actually endangered; and that there is a degree of overlap between commercial whaling and whaling for aboriginal subsistence purposes, and therefore the ambiguity concerning aboriginal whaling ought not to be interpreted in a manner that is more onerous for, or injurious to, whaling nations' interests. The use of these exemptions to the whaling ban, therefore, is highly contentious; far from ending conflicts, the Moratorium may have exacerbated them. Some States (thus, for instance, Iceland), disappointed by the continuation of the Moratorium on commercial whaling without sound scientific evidence, resumed commercial whaling in addition to carrying out a scientific programme, and, in 2000, Norway raised its quota of minke whales to 1,286 a year. Japan, meanwhile, continues its controversial scientific whaling programmes.

Iceland's 1990 withdrawal and 2002 re-accession subject to reservation

Unlike Norway, Iceland did not opt out of the 1982 Moratorium on commercial whaling. However, as a response to the Moratorium, Iceland intensified its controversial scientific whaling programme. Subsequently, in 1990, when the IWC decided to renew the Moratorium, Iceland withdrew from the ICRW, observing that the IWC was no longer a proper forum for the management of whales. One consequence of the departure of Iceland from the IWC was the establishment, in 1992, of the North Atlantic Marine Mammal Commission (NAMMCO, discussed in Chapter 6). In 2001–2, however, Iceland attempted to rejoin the ICRW, this time though with a formal reservation aimed at excluding it from being bound by the Moratorium. Iceland's otherwise perfectly legal attempt to rejoin the ICRW in this way caused quite some uproar, and met with considerable opposition in an already conflict-ridden IWC. Eventually, however, in 2002, Iceland's accession to the ICRW (and its formal reservation to paragraph 10(e) of the Schedule thereto) was accepted.[23]

---

[22] Ibid., p. 340.

[23] Alexander Gillespie, 'Iceland's Reservation at the International Whaling Commission', EJIL 14 (2003), 977–98; International Whaling Commission, https://iwc.int/_iceland, last accessed 5 April 2015.

Instruments of adherence were deposited on 8 June 2001, 10 May 2002 and 10 October 2002. All three instruments stated that Iceland 'adheres to the aforesaid Convention and Protocol with a reservation to paragraph 10(e) of the Schedule attached to the Convention'. The reservation contained in the instrument of adherence of 10 October 2002 was somewhat different in that it included a time limit before which commercial whaling would not resume. At the fifty-third Annual Meeting of the IWC in July 2001 in London, Iceland's status was determined by the following rulings from the Chair: (1) the IWC has the competence to determine the legal status of Iceland's reservation; (2) the IWC does not accept Iceland's reservation regarding paragraph 10(e) of the Schedule; (3) Iceland is invited to assist as an observer. Interestingly, Iceland had been treated as a member (that is to say, it was allowed to vote) until after the vote on the third ruling, after which it was treated as an observer. At the fifty-fourth Annual Meeting in May 2002 in Shimonoseki, the Chair observed that since the new instrument of adherence contained an identical reservation to that of the previous year – in other words, it had not changed – the IWC's decision on Iceland's membership from the previous year remained in force up to such time when the IWC decided otherwise. In the event, the Chair ruled that the status of Iceland's membership remained as had been agreed by the IWC the previous year. Consequently, Iceland was not allowed to vote. At the fifth Special Meeting in October 2002 in Cambridge, the Chair took the view that since the reservation attached to Iceland's most recent instrument of adherence appeared different, the IWC faced a new instrument of adherence and therefore the previous IWC decision was no longer applicable. Consequently, Iceland was allowed to vote. Due to disagreement in the IWC as to whether Iceland's reservation ought to be accepted, the Chair ruled that the IWC should follow the procedure adopted previously in London – namely, initially to establish the competence of the IWC to determine the legal status of Iceland's reservation. The Chair's ruling was upheld by a favourable vote of the IWC following an unsuccessful challenge. That vote had been preceded by a debate on whether Iceland should also be allowed to vote on whether the IWC had competence to review the former's reservation. According to the Chair, Iceland should be allowed to participate. This was upheld when put to the vote (despite a prior challenge).

The following countries subsequently formally objected to Iceland's reservation by notifying the depository government (namely, the United States): Argentina, Australia, Brazil, Chile, Finland, France, Germany,

Monaco, the Netherlands, Peru, Portugal, San Marino, Spain, Sweden, the United Kingdom and the United States. Italy, Mexico and New Zealand also objected to the reservation and noted that they did not consider the ICRW as being in force between their countries, and Iceland no longer considered itself to be a member of the IWC. Iceland argued, however, that its reservation to the Schedule ought to have been treated differently from a reservation to the actual Convention.

St Kitts and Nevis Declaration

The very strong sense of dissatisfaction of the whaling nations with what they perceived as the anti-whaling policy of the IWC lying behind the adoption of the Moratorium led to the adoption of the St Kitts and Nevis Declaration.[24] Among other things, it stated that:

> Concerned that after 14 years of discussion and negotiation, the IWC has failed to complete and implement a management regime to regulate commercial whaling;
>
> . . .
>
> Rejecting as unacceptable that a number of international NGOs with self-interest campaigns should use threats in an attempt to direct government policy on matters of sovereign rights related to the use of resources for food security and national development;
>
> Noting that the position of some members that are opposed to the resumption of commercial whaling on a sustainable basis irrespective of the status of whale stocks is contrary to the object and purpose of the International Convention for the Regulation of Whaling;
>
> Understanding that the IWC can be saved from collapse only by implementing conservation and management measures which will allow

---

[24] St Kitts and Nevis Declaration, www.unesco.org/csi/smis/siv/Forum/SKNdeclaration06. pdf, last accessed 11 January 2015. On 16–20 June 2006, during the meeting of the IWC, St Kitts and Nevis, Antigua and Barbuda, Benin, Cambodia, Cameroon, Côte d'Ivoire, Dominica, Gabon, Gambia, Grenada, Republic of Guinea, Iceland, Japan, Kiribati, Mali, Republic of the Marshall Islands, Mauritania, Mongolia, Morocco, Nauru, Nicaragua, Norway, Republic of Palau, Russian Federation, St Lucia, St Vincent and the Grenadines, Solomon Islands, Suriname, Togo and Tuvalu adopted this Declaration in order to express a vote of non-confidence in the IWC for the continuing Moratorium. Japan suggested a meeting to discuss the 'normalisation' of the IWC. Pro-whaling countries unsuccessfully challenged the 1982 Moratorium, and shifted the IWC focus from whale conservation to the management of commercial whaling. The St Kitts and Nevis Declaration was discussed and voted upon, and adopted by 33 votes in favour, 32 against and 1 abstention. It was the first time in more than 20 years that the Whaling Commission had expressed support for commercial whaling. The Declaration declared that the Moratorium on whaling was 'no longer necessary'. Other Japanese proposals during this meeting of the IWC were defeated but only by a small majority.

controlled and sustainable whaling which would not mean a return to historic over-harvesting and that continuing failure to do so serves neither the interests of whale conservation nor management;

. . .

Commissioners express their concern that the IWC has failed to meet its obligations under the terms of the ICRW and,

Declare our commitment to normalizing the functions of the IWC based on the terms of the ICRW and other relevant international law, respect for cultural diversity and traditions of coastal peoples and the fundamental principles of sustainable use of resources, and the need for science-based policy and rulemaking that are accepted as the world standard for the management of marine resources.

The Declaration embodies the reaction on the part of whaling States towards what they perceived as a fundamental deviation in the IWC's majority understanding of the purpose of whaling management that had led to these intractable conflicts within the IWC and that it was in urgent need of normalisation.

3.2   Conservation and management

For over twenty years the IWC used the so-called 'blue whale unit' (BWU) as its basis for annual catch limits, for setting the total amount of whales which could be taken in a year by States pursuing whaling. The unit was based on the amount of oil this species would typically produce. One blue whale unit equalled the oil produced from either one blue whale or two fin whales or two and a half humpbacks or six sei whales (para. 8(b) of the 1949 Schedule). In the mid-sixties, when the main product obtained from a whale changed from oil to meat, the system of blue whale units acceler-ated the decline of blue and fin whales, since the whalers chose to hunt larger species of oil-rich whales, despite the possibility of catching larger numbers of smaller whales. It is opined that the new era in the scientific approach to whaling was reached with the appointment of the 'Committee of Four' to review whale population dynamics in the Antarctic. They recommended a complete cessation of hunting of blue and humpback whales, decreased quotas for fin whales, as well as the abandonment of the BWU. These recommendations were met with partial success (humpback and blue whales were given total protection; sei whale hunting was not decreased; and the BWU remained).[25]

---

[25] Charlotte Epstein, *The Power of Words in International Relations. Birth of an Anti-Whaling Discourse* (Cambridge, Mass.: MIT Press, 2008), pp. 125–6.

The BWU was rejected in 1972 in favour of quotas on a species-by-species basis. In 1974, the IWC adopted a new system, the so-called New Management Procedure (NMP), which was eventually introduced in 1976. Under this procedure, each species was divided into up to twenty different stocks, with quotas set on a stock-by-stock basis. Each stock was classified as an 'initial management stock', a 'sustained management stock' or a 'protection stock' depending upon the relationship between the population level of the stock and the level of its 'maximum sustainable yield' (MSY), based on a principle that the taking of whales of a particular species should not exceed the ability of that stock to replenish itself at a rate which would maintain abundance at a commercially viable level.[26]

Theory indicated that if the original stock size can be calculated, it should be possible to take whales when they are at 50–60% of their original abundance. This rate of predation should be sustainable over time, presuming the stocks to be exploited can be brought back to their original numbers. Stocks falling 10% below MSY were to be exempt from exploitation and treated as protection stocks. Stocks at 10–20% above MSY could be exploited – but not too extensively, so they could recover and therefore be treated as sustained management stocks. Whale stocks more than 20% above MSY were treated as sufficiently abundant to be taken at a higher rate and treated as initial management stocks. The scheme, however, proved to be unworkable.[27]

The adoption of the NMP did not lead to effective protection of whales. There were several stumbling blocks: in particular, problems with establishing the maximum sustainable yield and stock sizes. Knowledge of the biological and recruitment features of whale species was insufficient and too imprecise to facilitate a reliable calculation of sustainable yields. The data which was available to the IWC consisted of a wide range of values for possible harvesting quotas. This state of affairs resulted in protracted debates between representatives of the industry and ecologists, who were calling for quota reduction due to uncertainties and lack of knowledge of stocks. Concerns relating to the protection of whales led to the imposition of the Moratorium on commercial whaling.

One of the controversial and divisive issues in the IWC was the lack of a scientifically reliable system either to estimate the levels of multiple stocks of whales within particular species, or to provide for the adequate

[26] Harris, above n. 10, 390.   [27] Friedheim, above n. 9, 356.

management of whaling.[28] Following the imposition of the Moratorium on commercial whaling, the IWC commenced work on the development of a more reliable system (known as the Revised Management Procedure on Baleen Whales (RMP)) which was intended, as the IWC put it, to be 'a scientifically robust method of setting safe catch limits for certain stocks (groups of whales of the same species living in a particular area) where the numbers are plentiful'.[29] The review of whale stocks which was undertaken by the IWC Scientific Committee included an examination of current stock sizes, recent population trends and productivity – this was known as a 'comprehensive assessment', and was part of the imposition of the Moratorium. At the time of the establishment of the Moratorium the meaning of this phrase had been unclear. The aims of the assessment were to provide in-depth evaluation of the status and trends of all whale stocks and to facilitate research-based management objectives and procedures. The Scientific Committee completed the assessment of whale species and stocks that related to aboriginal subsistence whaling, including those which could be subject to hunting in the event of a resumption of commercial whaling. (The stocks of whales which were researched included the following: grey whales in the North Pacific, bowhead whales off Alaska, minke whales in the Southern Hemisphere, North Atlantic and western Pacific, and fin whales in the North Atlantic.)

According to Gambell, an important aspect of this comprehensive assessment programme was the development and use of rigorous sighting surveys and photo-identification techniques, accompanied by more sophisticated data analysis, which all contributed to the credibility of the Scientific Committee and its estimates regarding whale stocks.[30] The SC spent over eight years developing the RMP, a method of setting safe catch limits of certain stocks (groups of whales of the same species living in a particular area) where the numbers were abundant. The RMP, however, even after its terms had been agreed by the SC, gave rise to much argument and was rejected twice by the IWC before, finally, being adopted in 1994,

[28] Alexander Gillespie, 'The Ethical Question in the Whaling Dispute', *Georgetown Int'l Env'l Law Review* 9 (1997), 355–87, 355, 357. André E. Punt and Greg P. Donovan, 'Developing Management Procedures that are Robust to Uncertainty: Lessons from the International Whaling Commission', *ICES Journal of Marine Science* 64 (2007), 603–12.

[29] Punt and Donovan, above n. 28, 603–12.

[30] Ray Gambell, 'World Whale Stocks', *Mammal Review* 6 (1976), 41–53; Gambell, above n. 3, p. 179; Ray Gambell, 'International Management of Whales and Whaling: An Historical Review of the Regulation of Commercial and Aboriginal Subsistence Whaling', *Arctic* 46 (1993), 97–107.

with concessions forced by the fact that certain issues were scientifically uncertain and therefore had become politicised. However, as Punt and Donovan state, the RMP 'is considered final' but has not been used due to the fact that the Moratorium on commercial whaling is still in force and no requests for advice on catch limits have been received by the IWC.

These authors admit that taking cetaceans for aboriginal and commercial purposes is a very politically sensitive issue. Even considering that the SC does not address issues regarding the political and ethical acceptability of whaling, transparency of development and evaluation of management procedures is of paramount importance. This also means that the Chair responsible for the development and management of this procedure has to be objective and independent, as does the computing manager at the IWC Secretariat.[31] The SC used computer simulation to set up a framework for the testing of a number of candidate single-stock management procedures. The aim of this procedure was to develop a generic system of management for application to a single stock of any baleen whale species being harvested on its feeding grounds rather than a specific approach to each and every species/stock being exploited. The RMP was developed on the basis of the following principles: that it have explicitly stated and prioritised objectives; that it be based on realistic data requirements; that it incorporate uncertainty explicitly; that it include a feedback mechanism; and that it be rigorously tested. The IWC described the management objectives in the following manner: to ensure that a stock would not be depleted below 54 per cent of its carrying capacity, in order that the risk of extinction of the stock would not be gravely increased by exploitation; to ensure the highest possible continuing yield from the stock; and to ensure stability of catch limits which were suitable for the orderly development of the whaling industry. The IWC accorded the highest priority to the first objective. After eight years the IWC designed the so-called single stock Catch Limit Algorithm (CLA) of the RMP, which appeared to cover all plausible uncertainties. The existence of an effective international inspectorate was also considered to be one of the essential elements of the NMP.[32]

---

[31] International Whaling Commission, https://iwc.int/rmpbw, last accessed 9 March 2015.
[32] Ray Gambell, 'The International Whaling Commission Today', in Gudrun Perturstdottir (ed.), *Whaling in the North Atlantic: Economic and Political Perspectives* (Reykjavik: University of Iceland Press, 1997). These elements are co-dependent: William C. G. Burns, 'The International Whaling Commission and the Future of Cetaceans', *Colo. J. Int'l Env'l L. & Pol'y* 8 (1997), 31, 58.

In real life situations, the IWC must manage multiple stocks of species. In order to cover uncertainty in its understanding of stock structure and mixing of stock, the RMP spreads catches over space (and time) by setting catch limits for areas that are small relative to the area inhabited by a stock (a so-called Small Area). The size of this Small Area has to be adjusted by further simulation tests specific to a particular species in a particular area and subject to a particular harvesting strategy. These simulations (which can be an onerous task), specified to cover the plausible range of uncertainty in stocks, are called Implementation Simulation Trials, and include the requirement for an Implementation Review to be conducted every five years. The specific implementation has been much more complex than the single stock trials used for developing the CLA. This procedure focuses primarily on uncertainties about stock structure, in particular temporal and spatial variation in the mixing of stocks in areas where whaling is conducted.[33]

The main underlying principle concerning the RMP was that this procedure must be based on data that is easily available in terms of quality and quantity. Available data was limited to the following: any historical and all ongoing catches; absolute abundance estimates available prior to management and periodically thereafter; and catch-relative abundance data such as catch per unit of effort (CPUE) data. However, subsequently the CPUE was dropped from the CLA due to problems with interpretation. The CLA at the heart of the RMP was based on setting safe catch limits for single stock only, and was therefore unsuitable for setting safe multi-stock catch limits. Robustness trials were conducted in relation to typical coastal whaling operations, pelagic operations and a combination of the two. Trials proved that catch limits should be set for Small Areas, defined as areas small enough to contain whales from only one biological stock or to be such that if whales from more than one biological stock were present, 'catching operations would be unable to harvest them in proportions different to their relative abundance in this area'. The basic way to apply the RMP was to use the CLA to set catch limits for a species in each Small Area. (There are two additional variants of this: Catch-cascading and Catch-capping.) From a scientist's point of view, the failure of the NMP was due to two main reasons: (1) the NMP proved to be unable to fulfil its intended role of facilitating scientific agreement on catch-limit recommendations (due to the fact that the

---

[33] See, in depth, Punt and Donovan, above n. 28, 607–10.

debate moved from what might be an appropriate catch control law to arguments about parameter values, such as the MSY, when implementing the law in relation to a particular case); and (2) even if agreement could have been reached about the best estimates of these parameters, arguments then developed about the scientific uncertainty within these values.[34] Apart from criticism of the NMP itself, there were problems with the reporting that is the basis for the CLA. It has been argued that reports from the former Soviet Union were deliberately falsified for a very long period of time, in order to cover violations of the international regulations.[35] The combination of scientific (the RMP) and non-scientific elements (inspection and observation schemes) gave rise to the Revised Management Scheme (RMS). In 1994, the RMS Working Group was established to work on: an effective inspection and observation scheme; arrangements to ensure that total catches over time are within the limits set under the RMS; incorporation into the RMS of the specification of the RMP and all other elements of the RMS, which is one of its objectives.[36] The other two objectives are as follows: arrangements to ensure that total catches over time are within limits set under the RMS; and incorporation into the Schedule of the specification of the RMP and all other elements of the RMS. Finally, in 2003 the Special Working Groups on RMP agreed that there were four main elements to the costs of the RMS: national inspectors; international observers; vessel monitoring systems; and catch verification.

The RMS therefore has as an objective of combining science and politics under a single *chapeau*. The RMS will not be put into operation before an inspection and observation scheme has been established. According to the IWC, this procedure is a robust method of setting safe limits for certain stocks where the numbers are plentiful.[37] The inspection and observation schemes being considered by the IWC are of

---

[34] Doug S. Butterworth, 'Why a Management Procedure Approach? Some Positives and Negatives', *ICES Journal of Marine Science* 63 (2006), 613–17, 613.

[35] Yulia V. Ivashchenko and Philip J. Clapham, 'Too Much Is Never Enough: The Cautionary Tale of Soviet Illegal Whaling', *Marine Fisheries Review* 76 (2014), 1–21, who say that '[w]ith the exception of occasional over-reporting of catches of certain "legal" species, most catches were greatly under-reported in the USSR's official submissions to the IWC', at 5. See also Yulia Ivashchenko, *Soviet Whaling: Past History and Present Impacts*, PhD, Southern Cross University e Publications@SC, 2013. Last accessed 17 April 2015.

[36] Punt and Donovan, above n. 28, 608–9; Harris, above n. 10, 412–16.

[37] Revised Management Scheme, International Whaling Commission, www.iwcoffice.org/conservation/rms.htm, last visited 8 March 2015.

two types: national inspectors to be appointed and paid by the Parties to the ICRW and to have jurisdiction over commercial whaling operations; and international observers who are selected from a list of suitable candidates. The list is established by the IWC's Secretariat. Such a list is subject to a scrutiny procedure by the Parties to the Convention, who may veto any candidate. The placement of the observers (after consultation with a party to the Convention) is decided by the Secretariat. The observers' tasks relate purely to monitoring functions, i.e. whether the whaling operations adhere to the ICRW's provisions; checking licences, equipment and logbooks, and also whether information on whaling operations is kept. The objectives of this inspection and observation scheme are, in particular, to ascertain that the rules and regulations of the ICRW and the IWC are adhered to; and to report any infractions of these rules to the Parties to the Convention and the IWC.[38] At the 2006 meeting 'the Commission accepted that an impasse had been reached at the Commission level on RMS discussions'.[39] Notwithstanding this impasse regarding the RMS, some State Parties to the ICRW were of the view that '[g]iven this scientific advance [the RMP] which has been accepted by the Commission, there has been pressure from some countries to remove the Moratorium for certain stocks of minke whales'.[40]

3.3   Attempts to solve the impasse

The impasse concerning the functioning of the IWC may be very generally summarised by the following two main reasons: the scientific (the failure to adopt the RMS), including the lack of reliable data as to the size of various whale stocks (which was one of the factors preventing the adoption of an 'informed' decision on whether to continue with the Moratorium); and the political, relating to the lack of agreement regarding the appointment of inspectors and international observers. There have been certain attempts to remedy the impasse within the IWC.

At the forty-ninth IWC Meeting in 1997, Michael Canny, Ireland's Commissioner, made several proposals, in order to break the deadlock at

---

[38] Report of the Revised Management Scheme, Expert Drafting Group, 53 Report of the IWC, Appendix IV (2002), at 5, 4.
[39] International Whaling Commission, https://iwc.int/rmp, last accessed 11 January 2015.
[40] Ibid.

the IWC. The so-called 'Irish Proposal'[41] was based on the premise that some of the whale stocks were recovering and some were in abundance. In the view of Ireland, it was still premature to resume commercial whaling, but, in principle, there was a basis for reaching a compromise between the preservationist and the conservationist factions within the IWC. The Irish Proposal was to the effect that the RMS should be completed and adopted (with the observers and inspection scheme in place), and that quotas under the RMS should be limited to the coastal areas of the States which were currently engaged in whaling operations. Such a solution would create a de facto whale sanctuary in the greater part of the world's oceans. What is more, it would require the following: whale products were to be used only for local consumption (no commercial trade in them would be permitted); the killing of whales for scientific purposes was not to be permitted; and strict regulations for whale watching were to be put in place in order to minimise the possible disturbance of whales. There were some reservations between the States concerning the Irish Proposal, but the general view was that it was a solid basis for discussion, which States conducted in the years that followed.

The RMS has yet to be adopted, as work on it has been suspended since 2007. The IWC noted at the 2007 Commission Meeting that 'an *impasse* had been reached' and observed that:

> individual governments or groups of governments could work towards the development of an RMS during the intersessional period. This item was retained on the agenda in Anchorage to provide an opportunity for governments to report on any intersessional activities and/or to propose further work. No such reports were received and no further work on the RMS was identified.[42]

Furthermore, apart from this particular issue, attempts to reach a compromise on the more general issues of disagreement, in particular whether there should be a resumption of commercial whaling in accordance with the provisions of the Moratorium as originally framed, continue to elude the IWC. In an important statement contained in the Introduction to the 'Proposed Consensus Decision', the Chair and Vice-Chair of the IWC stated as follows:

---

[41] Robert L. Friedheim, 'Introduction: The IWC as a Contested Regime', in Robert L. Friedheim (ed.), *Toward a Sustainable Whaling Regime* (Washington University Press, 2001), pp. 36–7; Nagtzaam, above n. 13, pp. 213–14.

[42] IWC/59, 2007.

> Very different views exist among the members regarding whales and
> whaling. For example, some seek to eliminate all whaling other than
> indigenous subsistence whaling, and some support whaling provided it
> is sustainable. This difference has come to dominate the time and
> resources of the Commission at the expense of effective whale conser-
> vation and management. The prevalent atmosphere of confrontation and
> mistrust among member governments has led to little progress being
> made on key practical matters of conservation and management since
> the early 1990s despite advances at a scientific level. This has created
> concerns among some members over the possible collapse of the IWC.
> The *status quo* is not an option for an effective multilateral organisation.[43]

This proposal had been the subject of discussions prior to the June
2010 IWC Annual Meeting in Agadir (Morocco). Talks were held on a
package deal regarding the resumption of limited commercial hunting
for the first time in twenty-four years under a draft plan drawn up by
an IWC Working Group (regulating whaling for the next ten years).
The draft aimed at a reduction of the number of whales hunted under
scientific whaling permits in return for strict limits on the number of
mammals killed. The basic provisions of the deal were that Japan
would reduce or phase out its whaling operations in the Southern
Ocean: its annual minke whale quota was to fall from 935 to 400 in
2010 and then to 200 in 2015. The proposal also suggested bringing
scientific whaling under the mandate of the IWC, that is to say,
removing it from the individual State's jurisdiction and, as a consequence, banning unilateral whaling. In exchange, Japan would be
assigned a quota for hunting whales in its coastal waters. Iceland
and Norway would receive quotas set by the IWC that could be
smaller than the quotas they currently awarded themselves. No other
countries would be permitted to begin hunting. In order to prevent
illegal hunting, observers on whaling boats and a DNA register for
meat would be introduced. Subsistence hunting by indigenous groups
would remain unaffected.

The proposal was aimed at the prevention of the collapse of the
IWC due to the stalemate in which groups of State Parties found
themselves owing to their irreconcilable differences of opinion on
the future of whaling. The plan to resume commercial whaling was

---

[43] Proposed Consensus Decision to improve the Conservation of Whales (from the Chair
and Vice-Chair of the Commission (62.rev.)), Annex E to the Report of the IWC,
2010, International Whaling Commission, www.iwc.int/futuredocs, last accessed 11
January 2015.

met with strong protests by NGOs and was ardently opposed by the European Union (EU). In the event, no decision was reached on the Consensus Decision, which was tabled by the Chair and Vice-Chair as a 'proposed' decision for further consideration. However, as Davies notes, significant stumbling blocks remain, preventing the implementation of the RMP/RMS, in particular, the establishment of an inspection and observation programme to ensure that commercial whaling operations are in compliance with the IWC's requirements.[44] A number of States put in individual written comments on the Proposed Consensus Decision. In particular, the Australian government spelt out with great clarity the standpoint of opponents of the lifting of the Moratorium, which is, essentially, an 'abolitionist' one. Thus, they stated that 'Australia will continue to argue vigorously that whaling should be phased down to zero, with total and permanent elimination of all whaling, other than aboriginal subsistence whaling, within a reasonable timeframe',[45] thereby expressing a new, ecological approach to the implementation of the ICRW.[46]

The 'Future of the IWC' process was introduced at the IWC's fifty-ninth Annual Meeting in 2007. It was aimed at addressing the most fundamental issues faced by the Commission. The main body of this work was completed in the period between 2007 and the sixty-second Annual Meeting in 2010. The main product was a document on 'A Proposed Consensus Decision to Improve the Conservation of Whales'. The 'Future of the IWC' was a process in which compromise was sought through a 'package deal' which would comprise, *inter alia*, Aboriginal Subsistence Whaling (ASW), Japanese Small Coastal Whaling (JSCW),

---

[44] Peter Davies, 'Cetaceans', in Michael Bowman, Peter Davies and Catherine Redgwell, *Lyster's International Wildlife Law* (2nd edn, Cambridge University Press, 2010), p. 168. See also Burns and Wandesforde-Smith, who argue that one of the most contentious issues is the observers whose establishment is provided for by the Revised Management Scheme (RMS) (International Observer Scheme (IOS)). The most complex issues are: who is going to pay for them?; whether the Parties may object to such observers; and how often infractions should be reported. 'A highly transparent and effective observer scheme is a critical issue for many parties given massive under-reporting of catches in the past by commercial whaling interests'. C. G. Burns and Geoffrey Wandesforde-Smith, 'The International Whaling Commission and the Future of Cetaceans in a Changing World', RECIEL 11 (2002), 199–210, 200.

[45] Richard Black, 'Petition calls for whaling Moratorium to remain', BBC News, 22 June 2010, www.bbc.co.uk/news/19384336, last accessed 11 January 2015.

[46] Jennifer L. Bailey, 'Arrested Development: The Fight to End Commercial Whaling as a Case of a Failed Norm Change', *European Journal of International Relations* 14 (2008), 289–318, 290.

the lifting of the 1982 Moratorium, the management of small cetaceans and the creation of whale sanctuaries.[47]

In 2011 the Commission stated its desire to maintain the progress achieved through the Future of the IWC process and agreed to:

> Encourage continuing dialogue amongst Contracting Governments regarding the future of the International Whaling Commission;
>
> Continue to build trust by encouraging Contracting Governments to coordinate proposals or initiatives as widely as possible prior to their submission to the Commission;
>
> Encourage Contracting Governments to continue to co-operate in taking forward the work of the Commission, notwithstanding their different views regarding the conservation of whales and the management of whaling.[48]

This document was discussed at the sixty-second Annual Meeting, but the Chair concluded that the Commission was not in a position to come to a consensus agreement on the measures proposed.[49] Thus this initiative was yet another unsuccessful attempt to overcome the impasse in the IWC.

In the meantime, attempts by other whaling nations to evade the restrictions of the Moratorium (such as the commercial sale of whale meat obtained through aboriginal whaling) continue – and this continues to cause outrage on the part of preservationist States, NGOs and civil society groups more generally.[50] At the Agadir Meeting of the IWC in July 2012, there was a degree of consternation at an announcement by South Korea that it intended to follow Japan by commencing scientific whaling, which it claimed was necessary to assess stocks. Many delegations voted against the proposal, and, to date, South Korea has not put it into effect; and in fact, by letter dated 4 January 2013, it announced that it had changed its position on the initial plan of scientific research whaling to non-lethal research methods.[51]

In conclusion, it may be said that, as Goodman observes, there are two factions at the IWC, relying on the following arguments. The basic premise of the pro-whaling faction is that whale stocks should be

---

[47] See, in depth on this, Ed Couzens, *Whales and Elephants in International Conservation Law and Politics: A Comparative Study* (Abingdon: Routledge, 2014), pp. 96–114.
[48] International Whaling Commission, https://iwc.int/future, last accessed 5 April 2015.
[49] Ibid.
[50] Alleged sale of whale meat by Inuit in Greenland: International Whaling Commission, https://iwc.int/meeting2012, last accessed 5 April 2015.
[51] Ibid.

managed as for any other marine resource, and that, therefore, to keep in place a Moratorium on whaling, despite scientific findings, would be contrary to the ICRW.[52] The anti-whaling faction includes the so-called 'Buenos Aires Group' of thirteen States from Central and South America; the EU Member States; Australia; New Zealand; and the United States. These States oppose the resumption of commercial whaling 'irrespective of the purpose of the ICRW or the status of whale stocks'.[53] They also oppose lethal research – in other words, scientific whaling – as not being necessary for management purposes. They argue that the ICRW requires modernisation by way of removing Article VIII, that is to say, the provision which provides that State Parties (rather than the IWC) may unilaterally grant scientific research permits. Alternatively, they suggest the removal of the opting-out (or tacit acceptance) procedure of Article V of the ICRW, which is not a realistic suggestion. According to these States, the focus of whaling-related activities should be on whale watching and the establishment of more whale sanctuaries.[54] However, as observed above, scientists such as Punt and Donovan are of the view that the RMP is final and ready to use. Most of these issues were debated during the *Whaling in the Antarctic* case.[55]

3.4   Japanese Whale Research Program under Special Permit in the Antarctic (JARPA II)

In 2005, Japan presented its Research Plan known as JARPA II to the IWC, and began Special Permit Whaling under JARPA II in the 2005–6 austral whaling season. The JARPA II Research Plan was finalised at a workshop in January 2005. The IWC Scientific Committee review of JARPA II was held in December 2006 after the commencement of the programme. The methodologies and kinds of data collected in JARPA II were very similar to those of a preceding research programme completed by Japan and known as JARPA. The JARPA II Research Plan objectives were as follows:

---

[52] Dan Goodman, 'Japanese Whaling and International Politics', in *Senri Ethnological Studies*, above n. 14, pp. 327–8.

[53] Ibid., 328.   [54] Ibid.

[55] *Whaling in the Antarctic (Australia v. Japan, New Zealand Intervening)*, Judgment, 31 March 2014, www.icj-cij.org/docket/files/148/18136.pdf, last accessed 24 March 2015. Total number of whales caught in scientific whaling (including Japan, Iceland and Korea), in the period 1985–2012: 15,563, http://iwc.int/table_permit, last accessed 24 October 2014.

(1) Monitoring of the Antarctic ecosystem, including:
   (i) whale abundance trends and biological parameters;
   (ii) krill abundance and the feeding ecology of whales;
   (iii) the effects of contaminants on cetaceans; and
   (iv) cetacean habitats;
(2) Modelling competition among whale species and future management objectives:
   (i) constructing a model of competition among whale species; and
   (ii) new management objectives including the restoration of the cetacean ecosystem;
(3) Elucidation of temporal and spatial changes in stock structure;
(4) Improving the management procedure for Antarctic minke whale stocks and improvement of MSYR (maximum sustainable yield rate) estimates for Antarctic minke whales; redefinition of appropriate management areas; and incorporation of effects arising from the inter-species relationships among the whale species.

As initially formulated, JARPA II was designed to sample, through lethal take, 850 +/–10% (maximum of 935 per season) Antarctic minke whales, 50 humpback whales and 50 fin whales. It was designed to run indefinitely, and to be reviewed every six years (six-year 'phases'). The actual lethal take of whales under JARPA II was 3,364 Antarctic minke whales, no humpback whales and 17 fin whales between 2005–6 and 2010–11. The Court noted that there was a discrepancy between the targets and the actual take and the lack of transparency in setting of targets (paras. 157–212 of the judgment).

3.5   The *Whaling in the Antarctic* case and its significance (scientific whaling (*Australia* v. *Japan, New Zealand, intervening*))

On 31 March 2014, the ICJ rendered its long-awaited Judgment on the issue of scientific whaling in the Antarctic on the part of Japan concerning the JARPA II programme.[56] As has been emphasised many times, the

---

[56] See above n. 55. The present section deals only with the most important aspects of the case. An in-depth analysis of all aspects of the Judgment in this case (substantive and procedural) will be published in Malgosia Fitzmaurice and Dai Tamada (eds.), *Whaling in the Antarctic: The Judgment and its Implications* (Leiden: Brill–Nijhoff, 2016). The book will be a result of the symposium devoted to the *Whaling* case organised at the University of Kobe from 31 May to 1 June 2014, www.edu.kobe-u.ac.jp/ilaw/en/whaling_programme_sympo.html, last accessed 22 December 2014. See, for some comments on the case: Marko Milanovic, 'ICJ Decides in the Antarctic Case: Australia Wins', *EJIL: Talk!* www.ejiltalk.org/icj-decides-the-whaling-in-the-antarctic-case-australia-wins/, last accessed 20 September 2014; Julian Arato, 'Subsequent Practice in the Whaling Case,

question of Japanese scientific whaling is highly incendiary. Not only were the proceedings before the Court evidence of it, but it has been a constant theme of the functioning of the IWC, with the detractors and defenders of this whaling exchanging quite strongly worded arguments.[57]

The Judgment contains numerous observations concerning the nature of scientific whaling in the context of the ICRW alongside observations relevant to the law of treaties. The jurisdiction of the ICJ in this case was based on Optional Clauses that establish the ICJ's compulsory jurisdiction. The contentious jurisdictional issue was the question of the interpretation of Australia's declaration. Japan submitted in its Counter-Memorial, and during oral argument, that the ICJ lacked jurisdiction to hear the case based on its interpretation of Australia's Optional Clause

and What the ICJ Implies about Treaty Interpretation in International Organizations', *EJIL: Talk!* www.ejiltalk.org/subsequent-practice-in-the-whaling-case-and-what-the-icj-implies-about-treaty-interpretation-in-international-organizations/, last accessed 22 December 2014. See also on the Judgment, Gerry J. Nagtzaam, 'Righting the Ship? Australia, New Zealand and Japan at the ICJ and the Barbed Issue of "Scientific Whaling"', *Australian Journal of Environmental Law* 1 (2014), 71–92; Richard Caddell, 'Science Fiction: Antarctic Research Whaling and the International Court of Justice', *Journal of International Law* 26 (2014), 331–40; Diane Desierto, 'Evidence in Environmental/Scientific Exceptions: Some Contrasts between the WTO Panel Report in *China–Rare Earths* and the ICJ Judgment in *Whaling in the Antarctic*', *EJIL: Talk!* www.ejiltalk.org/evidence-in-environmentalscienti fic-exceptions-some-contrasts-between-the-wto-panel-report-in-china-rare-earths-and-the-icj-Judgment-in-whaling-in-the-antarctic/, last accessed 19 June 2014; Cymie R. Payne, '*Australia v. Japan*: ICJ Halts Antarctic Whaling', *ASIL Insights*, www.asil.org/insights/volume/18/ issue/9/australia-v-japan-icj-halts-antarctic-whaling, last accessed 19 June 2014; Mohammad Rubaiyat Rahman, 'Battle for Whales in The Hague: Analysis of Judgment in *Australia v. Japan*', http://papers.ssrn.com/sol3/papers.cfm?abstract_id=2418817, last accessed 19 June 2014; Sir Geoffrey Palmer, 'A Victory for Whales: Sir Geoffrey Palmer QC Explains Aspects of the ICJ Decision', *New Zealand Law Journal* (2014), 124–8, http://papers.ssrn.com/sol3/ papers.cfm?abstract_id=2477544, last accessed 9 March 2015. See also Michael Johnson for an insightful analysis of judgments, in 'Whaling in the Antarctic – The ICJ Decision and its Consequences for Special Permit Whaling', *AYBIL* 32 (2015), 87–96. On the procedural aspects of New Zealand intervention, see Penelope Ridings, 'The Intervention Procedure in Whaling in the Antarctic: A Threat to Bilateralism?', *AYBIL* 32 (2015), 97–111.

[57] See, for example, William Aron, William Burke and Milton Freeman, 'Scientists versus Whaling: Science, Advocacy, and Errors of Judgment', *Bioscience* 12 (2002), 1137–40. As a reaction to the open letter submitted in 2002 by twenty-one scientists to the Government of Japan questioning its scientific whaling, these authors defended the scientific whaling of Japan and countered assertions, such as one stating that Japan did not meet minimum criteria for credible science, and that it refused to release information for independent review. The authors also cited numerous reports of the Scientific Committee of the IWC that JARPA made a very important contribution to the understanding of certain biological parameters, 1138. The authors said that: 'Sadly, the letter contains numerous errors of science and law and thus reflects poorly on the capability of the instigating organization and the care taken by the scientists endorsing this letter', 1138.

declaration, which excludes from the ICJ's jurisdiction any dispute concerning or relating to the delimitation of maritime zones, including the
territorial sea, the exclusive economic zone and the continental shelf, or
arising out of, concerning or relating to the exploitation of any disputed area
of, or adjacent to, any such maritime zone, pending its delimitation. The
jurisdictional dispute by Japan concerned the fact that part of the whaling
activities envisaged in JARPA II took place in maritime areas claimed by
Australia in what it asserts to be its Australian Antarctic Territory or in
an adjacent area (established before the 1959 Antarctic Treaty System,
which remains silent on such claims). However, while Japan had disputed
Australia's maritime claims relating to the Australian Antarctic Territory, it
did not submit a counter-claim to sovereign rights in those areas.

Australia argued that Japan had breached certain obligations under the
ICRW. It did not raise the argument that JARPA II was unlawful on the
basis that the whaling activities in the JARPA II programme had taken
place in the maritime areas over which Australia asserted sovereign rights
or in adjacent areas. Therefore, the nature and extent of Australia's claimed
maritime zones were immaterial to the dispute, which was focused on the
compatibility of Japan's activities with its obligations under the ICRW.[58]
The ICJ rejected Japan's jurisdictional argument and admitted the case for
adjudication on the basis of two Optional Clause declarations. Australia
very strongly advocated the 'evolution' of the 'object and purpose' of the
ICRW from the 'orderly regulating of the whaling industry' into, in fact, a
treaty with a preservationist, or at least strongly conservationist, 'object and
purpose' in relation to whale stocks. As a ground for such an 'evolution',
Australia indicated several recommendations of the IWC and amendments
to the Schedule. The Court, however, stated that amendments to the
Schedule and recommendations by the IWC 'may put an emphasis on
one or the other objective pursued by the Convention, but cannot alter its
object and purpose' (para. 56 of the Judgment). On the other hand, in
para. 45 of the Judgment, the Court said that '[t]he Commission has

---

[58] *Whaling in the Antarctic*, above n. 56, paras. 30–41; Donald Rothwell, 'The Whaling Case:
International Law Perspectives', *Law Council Review* 10 (April–July 2014), who says that:
'From an Australian perspective the decision by the ICJ in the *Whaling* case was a
vindication of a politically and legally risky strategy to challenge the international legal
validity of JARPA II. The decision of the court has set a precedent for the interpretation
of Article VIII of the ICRW which will become a reference point for all future conduct of
special permit whaling, especially in the Southern Ocean.' www.lawcouncil.asn.au/law
council/images/LawCouncilReview/Issue%2010%20Web.pdf, last accessed 25 February
2015, last accessed 25 February 2015.

amended the Schedule many times. The functions conferred on the Commission have made the Convention an evolving instrument.' The ICJ thus explained that the ICRW has evolved by way of amendments to its Schedule by a three-fourths majority of votes cast, according to Article III(2) of the ICRW, which, save for when a State resorts to the opting-out procedure, become binding on all States. It is the view of the present author that this is not sufficient in and of itself to lead to the conclusion that the ICRW is an 'evolving instrument'. As it is open to States to 'opt out' of any amendments to the Schedule to the ICRW that they find disagreeable, for such States, therefore, the ICRW remains relatively static and would only evolve to the extent that they have consented or otherwise actively (or imputably) acquiesced, and cannot be reviewed on its own but only in connection with other similar treaty regimes.[59]

In sum, the Court did not dwell in depth on the subject of the evolutionary interpretation of treaties, an area which attracted a vast body of literature. In particular, this is relevant in relation to the jurisprudence of the European Court of Human Rights (ECtHR) which, albeit extraneous to the present case, has, nevertheless, implications for the broader normative framework of international law.

Furthermore, Australia and Japan contended that it is conservation and sustainable exploitation, respectively, 'the object and purpose' of the ICRW, in the light of which the provision should be interpreted. According to Australia, Article VIII(1) should be interpreted restrictively given that the taking of whales is only permitted as an exception to the overall tenor of the ICRW. Such a restrictive reading of Article VIII would thus give effect to the ICRW's objective with regard to whale conservation. Japan argued that the power to regulate scientific whaling (that is to say, issue permits) should be assessed in the context of the freedom to engage in whaling ordinarily enjoyed by States under customary international law.[60]

The ICJ observed, on the basis of the Preamble and the relevant provisions of the ICRW, that neither a restrictive nor an expansive

---

[59] On 'evolutionary' and systemic outlook (systemic integration) points of the ICRW, also see Judge Cançado Trindade's Separate Opinion, paras. 25–40, www.icj-cij.org/docket/files/148/18146.pdf, last accessed 12 January 2015. On systemic integration in relation to the Judgment, see as well, Lilian del Castillo, 'Some Comments on the *Whaling in the Antarctic* Judgment', in Lilian del Castillo (ed.), *Law of the Sea, from Grotius to the International Tribunal for the Law of the Sea: Liber Amicorum Judge Hugo Caminos* (Leiden: Brill–Nijhoff, 2015), pp. 175–91, 182–90.

[60] *Whaling in the Antarctic*, above n. 56, para. 57.

interpretation of Article VIII would be justified. The ICJ noted that while programmes for purposes of scientific research should clearly be aimed at promoting scientific knowledge, they may also have aims other than either conservation or sustainable exploitation of whale stocks, as also reflected in the Guidelines issued by the IWC for the review of scientific permit proposals by the IWC Scientific Committee. For instance, at present, the Guidelines list three broad categories of objectives that, besides programmes aimed at 'improv[ing] the conservation and management of whale stocks, also envisage programmes which have as an objective the improvement of conservation and management of other living marine resources or the ecosystem of which the whale stocks are an integral part' and those focused on 'test[ing] hypotheses not directly related to the management of living marine resources'.[61]

The ICJ analysed the competence of States to grant whaling permits for scientific purposes. According to the ICJ, 'Article VIII gives discretion to a State party to the ICRW to reject the request for a special permit or to specify the conditions under which a permit will be granted' but 'whether the killing, taking and treating of whales pursuant to a requested special permit is for purposes of scientific research cannot depend simply on that State's perception'.[62] The ICJ analysed the legal requirements for the granting of a special permit authorising the killing, taking and treating of whales. First, the Court assessed whether the programme under which these activities occurred involved scientific research. Second, the Court considered whether the killing, taking and treating of whales was for purposes of scientific research. In considering this, the Court took into account whether, in the use of lethal methods, the programme's design and implementation are reasonable in relation to achieving its stated objectives. Notably, the ICJ observed that the standard in addressing the above is an objective one.[63] However, as Judge Owada noted in his Dissenting Opinion, 'design and implementation' is a new element of a standard of review, relied upon by Australia. Judge Owada was of the view that the Judgment does not explain why it is 'legitimate or appropriate' for the ICJ to expand the scope of the review by examining substantive aspects of JARPA II.[64]

---

[61] Ibid., para. 58.   [62] Ibid., para. 61.   [63] Ibid., para. 67.
[64] Judge Hisashi Owada, Dissenting Opinion, para. 32, www.icj-cij.org/docket/files/148/ 18138.pdf, last accessed 23 December 2014.

The idea of the application of the standard of review is considered to be novel in the practice of the ICJ.[65] According to Foster, it evokes the jurisprudence of the WTO in relation to Article 5(1) of the WTO Agreement on Sanitary and Phytosanitary Measures (SPS Agreement) in the *Canada–Continued Suspension of Obligations in the EC–Hormones Dispute, US–Continued Suspension of Obligations in the EC–Hormones Dispute* and *Australia: Measures Affecting the Importation of Apples from New Zealand* disputes before the WTO's Dispute Settlement Body.[66] Foster is of the view that the use of this technique by the ICJ offered practical benefits to the Court. It enabled the Court to decide the case through 'the medium of an objective process based on an expectation that an Article VIII research programme's design and implementation will be reasonable in relation to achieving stated objectives'.[67] Foster makes a very interesting point on the reversal of the burden of proof in this case, as in the classical use of the standard of review, the burden of proof rests with the Applicant (in the *Whaling* case it would have been Australia; but in fact it rested with Japan). As Foster explains, 'the Court's application of a standard of review in the *Whaling* case seems to have been connected with a relatively informal and malleable approach to the burden of proof'.[68]

It is unclear whether such an approach to the standard of review will be applied in other cases before the ICJ. However, the present author notes that in paragraph 69 of the Judgment, the ICJ made a very significant pronouncement which could indicate that its findings are of direct significance in this particular case but do not set general standards for the future:

> in applying the above standard of review, [the Court] is not called upon to resolve matters of scientific or whaling policy. The Court is aware that members of the international community hold divergent views about the appropriate policy towards whales and whaling, but it is not for the Court to settle these differences. The Court's task is only to ascertain whether the special permits granted in relation to JARPA II fall within the scope of Article VIII, paragraph 1, of the ICRW.[69]

---

[65] On this, see in-depth analysis in Caroline E. Foster, 'Motivations and Methodologies. Was Japan's Whaling Programme for Purposes of Scientific Research?', chapter to be published in Fitzmaurice and Tamada, above n. 56 (on file with the author of this study).

[66] Report of the WTO's Dispute Settlement Body, *Canada – Continued Suspension of Obligations in the EC–Hormones Dispute* (WT/DS320), and *US – Continued Suspension of Obligations in the EC–Hormones Dispute* (WT/DS321), paragraph 590, adopted on 14 November 1998. Report of the Appellate Body, *Australia – Measures Affecting the Importation of Apples from New Zealand* (WT/DS367), adopted on 17 December 2010. See Foster, above n. 65.

[67] Foster, above n. 65.   [68] Ibid.   [69] *Whaling in the Antarctic*, above n. 56, para. 69.

The ICJ noted the lack of transparency of the reasons for selecting particular sample sizes for individual research items (in particular in selection of Antarctic minke whales).[70] The Court came to the conclusion that while Article VIII of the ICRW exempts the granting of special permits for scientific whaling, this does not mean that scientific whaling is outside the scope of the ICRW; therefore whatever margin of appreciation in relation to scientific whaling ICRW State Parties and IWC Member States might enjoy (as pleaded by Japan), it is neither autonomous nor unlimited, and, therefore, must be subject to some objective – that is to say, universal to ICRW State Parties – standard.[71] The ICJ was of the view that JARPA II could properly be characterised as scientific research, based on its objectives; and it did not denounce lethal methods altogether. However, the ICJ found that important aspects of JARPA II's design and implementation were not reasonable in relation to its research objectives; and it called into question several issues relating to this Programme. Most importantly, the Court emphasised Japan's lack of willingness to cooperate with the IWC in the use of non-lethal scientific methods that had become available over the intervening period. The ICJ interpreted Article VIII of the ICRW and found that Japan had not sufficiently substantiated the scale of lethal sampling. The ICJ therefore ordered that Japan revoke any pending authorisation, permit or licence to kill, take or treat whales in relation to JARPA II, and refrain from granting any further permits under Article VIII(1) of the ICRW in pursuance of its Programme. Japan stated that it would abide by the Judgment but added that it 'regrets and is deeply disappointed by the decision'. Although, technically, the ICJ's decision does not impact on future scientific whaling by Japan, the ICJ noted that Japan will rely on the ICJ's findings 'as it evaluates the possibility of granting any future permits under Article VIII, paragraph 1, of the Convention'.[72]

As to the definition of the term 'scientific research' (which the ICRW lacks), the ICJ cited the views of one of the scientific experts of Australia, Mr Mangel, who maintained that scientific research (in the context of the ICRW) has four essential characteristics: defined and achievable objectives (be they questions or hypotheses) that aim to contribute to knowledge important to the conservation and management of stocks; 'appropriate methods', including the use of lethal methods only where the objectives of the research cannot be achieved by any other means;

---

[70] Ibid., para. 188.   [71] Ibid., para. 62.   [72] Ibid., para. 246.

peer review; and the avoidance of adverse effects on stock.[73] Japan had not offered an alternative definition.

As to the meaning of the term 'for purposes of' in Article VIII(1), Australia discussed two elements of a programme that impacted on the distinction between the grant of a special permit that authorises whaling 'for purposes of' scientific research, and whaling activities that do not fit within Article VIII, and thus, in Australia's view, violate paragraphs 7(b), 10(d) and 10(e) of the Schedule.[74] Australia considered that the quantity of whale meat generated by a programme for which a permit has been granted, and the sale of that meat, raises doubts about whether the killing, taking and treating of whales has actually been for purposes of scientific research.[75]

The ICJ was not persuaded by the definition of the Australian expert but did not deem it necessary to offer any general definition of scientific research;[76] rather, the ICJ analysed the meaning of the phrase 'for [the] purpose of', as a segment of the 'for purposes of scientific research' term, which appears to be the crucial part of the ICJ's reasoning but may prove to be rather difficult to interpret. Judge Hue noted that the division between 'scientific research' and 'in purpose of' in Article VIII(1) dictated the standard of review as articulated by the ICJ.[77]

According to Judge Bennouna, the failure of the ICJ to provide a definition of scientific research:

> might be regarded as something of a paradox. In effect, the Court seeks to determine the purpose of a given activity without having first clarified what this activity consists of. This is a perilous exercise. All the more so since what it turns out to consist in is a discussion of whether the design and implementation of a programme 'are reasonable in relation to its stated scientific objectives'.[78]

---

[73] Ibid., para. 74.   [74] Ibid., para. 90.   [75] Ibid., para. 91.   [76] Ibid., para. 86.

[77] Judge Hanquin Hue, Separate Opinion, para. 16. According to Judge Hue, the phrase for 'purpose of' cannot stand alone without the modifier 'scientific research'. www.icj-cij.org/docket/files/148/18152.pdf, last accessed 15 May 2015.

[78] Judge Mohamed Bennouna, Dissenting Opinion. www.icj-cij.org/docket/files/148/18144.pdf, last accessed 23 December 2014. A very interesting comment relating to the interpretation of Article VIII was made by Brighton, that the Court, by refusing to engage in the discussion whether JARPA II was for the purpose of commercial whaling, avoided a finding that Japan had acted in bad faith, Claire Brighton, 'Unraveling Reasonableness: A Question of Treaty Interpretation', *AYBIL* 32 (2015), 125–134, 134. On the issue of the burden of proof and good faith in the *Whaling* Case, see Julian Wyatt, 'Should we Presume that Japan Acted in Good Faith? Reflections on Judge Abraham's Burden of Proof Based Analysis', *AYBIL* 32 (2015), 146–167.

The ICJ expressed some concern about the rising sample sizes between Japan's first whaling programme JARPA and JARPA II. It also noted a certain lack of transparency in how its sample sizes were determined. The Court stated that JARPA II involved activities that in broad terms could be characterised as scientific research, but that 'the evidence does not establish that the design and implementation of the Programme are reasonable in relation to achieving its stated objectives'. The ICJ concluded that JARPA II is not 'for purposes of scientific research' pursuant to Article VIII(1) of the ICRW, and that Japan violated three relevant provisions (paragraphs 7(b), 10(d) and (e)) of the Schedule.

The ICJ did not find it necessary to pronounce on the scientific merit or importance of the scientific objectives in order to evaluate the purpose of the killing of whales under the JARPA II programme. The Court also declined to assess whether 'the design and implementation of the Programme are the best possible means of achieving its stated objectives'.[79] In order to analyse whether the use of lethal methods was for purposes of scientific research, the ICJ considered the reasonableness of the programme's design and implementation in relation to its stated scientific objectives.[80] However, crucially, the ICJ noted that Article VIII is an

---

[79] *Whaling in the Antarctic*, above n. 56, para. 88.

[80] Ibid., para. 88. It may be said that this test of reasonableness at least implicitly indicated some of the parameters of what constitutes 'reasonable' scientific research for the purpose of the ICRW. Any State intending to issue a permit under Article VIII must show that its programme only uses the necessary amount of lethal sampling to achieve its scientific objectives, both in a temporal and in a spatial rationale and methodology for creating a sampling size; that it uses the samplings from lethal research; and that lethal research permits are part of related research projects. Anastasia Telesetsky, Donald K. Anton and Timo Koivurova, 'ICJ's Decision in *Australia/Japan*: Giving up the Spear or Refining the Scientific Design?' ODIL 45 (2014), 328–40, 334. It may be noted that the Court has not mentioned the precautionary approach (principle) in this case. However, this question was raised by Judge ad hoc Hilary Charlesworth in her Separate Opinion, who said as follows: 'The precautionary approach to environmental regulation also reinforces this analysis of the conditions in which lethal research methods may be undertaken. The approach was formulated in Principle 15 of the Rio Declaration on Environment and Development in 1992 as "[w]here there are threats of serious or irreversible damage, lack of full scientific certainty shall not be used as a reason for postponing cost-effective measures to prevent environmental degradation". The precautionary approach entails the avoidance of activities that may threaten the environment even in the face of scientific uncertainty about the direct or indirect effects of such activities. It gives priority to the prevention of harm to the environment in its broadest sense, including biological diversity, resource conservation and management and human health. The essence of the precautionary approach has informed the development of international environmental law and is recognized implicitly or explicitly in instruments dealing with a wide range of

integral part of the Convention. It therefore has to be interpreted in light of the object and purpose of the Convention and taking into account other provisions of the Convention, including the Schedule. However, since Article VIII(1) specifies that 'the killing, taking, and treating of whales in accordance with the provisions of this Article shall be exempt from the operation of this Convention', whaling conducted under a special permit which meets the conditions of Article VIII is not subject to the obligations under the Schedule concerning the Moratorium on the catching of whales for commercial purposes, the prohibition of commercial whaling in the Southern Ocean Sanctuary and the Moratorium relating to factory ships. The ICJ held that the two elements of the phrase 'for the purposes of scientific research' were cumulative, the result of which was that even if a whaling programme involved scientific research, 'the killing, taking and treating of whales pursuant to such programme did not fall within Article VIII unless these actions are for purposes of scientific research'.[81]

Japan stated that the sale of meat as a means to fund research is permitted by Article VIII(2) and is common in fisheries research.[82] The ICJ was of the view that 'the fact that a programme involves the sale of whale meat and the use of proceeds to fund research is not sufficient, taken alone, to cause a special permit to fall outside Article VIII'. However, other elements would have to be examined, such as the scale of a programme's use of lethal sampling, which might suggest that the whaling is for purposes other than scientific research, and the granting of permits to use lethal sampling on a greater scale than is otherwise reasonable in relation to achieving the programme's stated objectives.[83]

---

subject-matter, from the regulation of the oceans and international watercourses to the conservation and management of fish stocks, the conservation of endangered species and biosafety', para. 6. www.icj-cij.org/docket/files/148/18158.pdf, last accessed 24 December 2014.

[81] *Whaling in the Antarctic*, above n. 56, para. 71. The decision of the Court not to define what scientific research is and to interpret separately the phrases 'scientific research' and 'purpose of' was puzzling at best. It is suggested that such a differentiation can lead to the conclusion that a project can involve 'scientific research' but not be for the 'purpose of scientific research'. The reasoning of the Court was found to be not fully satisfactory, since the Court was requested to interpret these words of Article VIII in light of their ordinary meaning and context. The Court, it is argued, could have defined scientific research in a *de minimis* manner 'as the testing of questions and hypotheses to further knowledge while avoiding adverse effects on the whale populations'. Telesetsky, Anton and Koivurova, above n. 80, 333.

[82] *Whaling in the Antarctic*, above n. 56, para. 92.   [83] Ibid., para. 94.

In Australia's view, the pursuit of policy goals, such as providing employment or maintaining a whaling infrastructure, could not reasonably justify the granting of permits on the basis of scientific research, as it would indicate that the killing of whales is actually taking place for the fulfilment of other policy outcomes.[84]

Japan contended that it would be within the rights of a State Party to conduct a programme of scientific research that is aimed at inquiry as to the possible resumption of commercial whaling on a sustainable basis on the part of that State Party.[85] In respect of this, the ICJ considered that whether motivations go beyond scientific research *per se* does not preclude the conclusion that a programme is for purposes of scientific research within the meaning of Article VIII. However, such motivation cannot justify the granting of a special permit for a programme that uses lethal sampling on a larger scale than is reasonable in relation to achieving the programme's research objectives. Crucially, the Court stated that the predetermined research objectives alone ought to be sufficient to justify the programme as designed and implemented.[86]

Further, the ICJ investigated whether, based on the evidence, the design and implementation of JARPA II were reasonable in relation to achieving its stated objectives.[87] Australia's main argument was that JARPA II was conceived in order to continue commercial whaling under the guise of scientific research.[88] Japan rejected Australia's characterisation of the factors that led to the establishment of JARPA. According to Japan, JARPA came about following Japan's acceptance of the Moratorium on commercial whaling, due to inadequate data on whale stocks to manage commercial whaling properly.[89] Australia pleaded that the goal of estimating natural mortality was 'practically unachievable' and the 'irrelevance' of the JARPA programme to estimating natural mortality was confirmed in 1994 when the IWC agreed to replace the NMP with another revised management tool, namely the RMP (discussed earlier in the present chapter), which did not rely on the type of information that JARPA obtained by lethal sampling.[90] Australia and Japan disagreed as to the usefulness of the RMP, which both Parties appraised as 'a conservative and precautionary management tool'.[91] The RMP, as discussed earlier, does not appear to yield the most credible results in terms of accuracy. In the view of the author of this study, it is perhaps a missed opportunity by the ICJ to have not analysed the RMP more extensively.

---

[84] Ibid., para. 95. [85] Ibid., para. 96. [86] Ibid., para. 97. [87] Ibid., para. 98.
[88] Ibid., para. 101. [89] Ibid., para. 102. [90] Ibid., para. 106. [91] Ibid., para. 107.

The Parties disagreed, however, on whether data collected by JARPA and JARPA II contributed to the RMP.[92]

The ICJ found that lethal methods appeared central to the design of JARPA II. The Parties disagreed as to the reasons for the use of such methods.[93] Japan stated that it had not used lethal methods more than it deemed necessary to meet research objectives and that lethal methods were 'indispensable' in JARPA II because the programme's first two objectives require data that can only be obtained from internal organs and stomach contents. Japan argued that non-lethal methods were not practical for minke whales.[94] Australia, relying on its experts' opinion, argued that Japan had 'an unbending commitment to lethal take', that 'JARPA II is premised on the killing of whales'[95] and that lethal methods should only be used when they are 'essential to the stated objectives of a programme'.[96] The ICJ noted that the Parties agreed that non-lethal methods are not a feasible means to examine internal organs and stomach contents, and that the evidence showed that, at least for some of the data sought by JARPA II researchers, non-lethal methods are not a workable solution.[97] The Court came to the conclusion that there was no evidence that Japan had examined whether it would be feasible to combine a smaller lethal take (in particular, of minke whales) and an increase in non-lethal sampling as a means to achieve JARPA II's research objectives. The absence of any evidence pointing to the consideration as to the feasibility of non-lethal methods was not explained.[98] Given the expanded use of lethal methods in JARPA II, the Court could not reconcile Japan's obligation to give due regard to IWC Resolutions and Guidelines with its statement that JARPA II uses lethal methods only to the extent necessary to meet its scientific objectives.[99]

In a comparison of sample sizes of JARPA II with those of JARPA, the ICJ also relied on expert opinion. The Court noted that Japan had stated that 'the research items and methods' of JARPA II were in principle the same as those used for JARPA. Australia noted that in practice Japan collected the same data under JARPA II, and Japan argued that broadly both programmes had as their purpose 'to further proper and effective management of whale stocks and their conservation and sustainable use'.[100] According to the ICJ, 'these similarities cast doubt on Japan's argument that the JARPA II objectives relating to ecosystem monitoring

---

[92] Ibid., para. 107.   [93] Ibid., para. 128.   [94] Ibid., para. 129.   [95] Ibid., para. 130.
[96] Ibid., para. 131.   [97] Ibid., para. 133.   [98] Ibid., para. 141.   [99] Ibid., para. 144.
[100] Ibid., para. 152.

and multi-species competition are distinguishing features of the latter programme that call for a significant increase in the minke whale sample size and the lethal sampling of two additional species'.[101] The ICJ concluded, therefore, that Japan's less than persuasive explanation for the decision to proceed with the JARPA II sample sizes prior to the final review of JARPA lent support to the view that those sample sizes and the launch date for JARPA II were not driven strictly by scientific considerations. This also appeared to support Australia's theory that Japan's priority was to effectively maintain its whaling operations without any disruption.[102]

The expert evidence was also decisive in the determination of sample sizes. In that respect the ICJ adopted a rather narrow approach. It did not seek to pass judgment on the scientific merits of the JARPA II objectives and on whether the activities of JARPA II could broadly be characterised as 'scientific research'. With regard to the setting of sample sizes, the Court was also not in a position to conclude whether a particular value for a given variable had scientific advantages over another. The ICJ sought only to evaluate whether the evidence supported a conclusion that the sample sizes were reasonable in relation to achieving JARPA II's stated objectives.[103] The Court stated that, taken together, the evidence relating to the minke, fin and humpback whale sample sizes provided scant reason and justification for the underlying decisions that generated the overall sample size. Therefore, the ICJ expressed its concerns about whether the design of JARPA II was reasonable in relation to achieving its stated objectives.[104]

Regarding sample sizes in relation to actual take, the ICJ observed that Japan's continued reliance on the first two JARPA II objectives to justify the target sample sizes, despite the discrepancy between the actual take and those targets, coupled with its statement that JARPA II can obtain meaningful scientific results based on the far more limited actual take, cast further doubt on the characterisation of JARPA II as a programme for purposes of scientific research. This evidence suggests that the target sample sizes are larger than are reasonable for achieving the purported objectives of JARPA II. The fact that the actual take of fin and humpback whales is largely, if not entirely, a function of political and logistical considerations further weakens the purported relationship between JARPA II's scientific research objectives and the specific sample size

---

[101] Ibid., para. 153.   [102] Ibid., para. 156.   [103] Ibid., para. 172.
[104] Ibid., para. 198.

targets for each species – in particular, the decision to engage in the lethal sampling of minke whales on a relatively large scale.[105]

The ICJ reiterated its view that JARPA II appeared to involve activities that could broadly be characterised as part of scientific research, but that the evidence was insufficient to establish that the programme's design and implementation were reasonable in relation to achieving its stated objectives. The Court concluded that the special permits granted by Japan for the killing, taking and treating of whales in connection with JARPA II had not been 'for purposes of scientific research' (pursuant to Article VIII(1) of the ICRW).[106] The Court was of the view that Japan had met the requirements of paragraph 30 concerning its JARPA II programme.[107]

The ICJ discovered that the special permits granted by Japan in connection with JARPA II did not fall within the provisions of Article VIII(1) of the ICRW; that Japan, by granting special permits to kill, take and treat fin, humpback and Antarctic minke whales in pursuance of JARPA II, had not acted in conformity with its obligations under paragraph 10(e) of the Schedule to the ICRW; that Japan had not acted in conformity with its obligations under paragraph 10(d) of the Schedule to the ICRW in relation to the killing, taking and treating of fin whales in pursuance of JARPA II; and that Japan had not acted in conformity with its obligations under paragraph 7(b) of the Schedule to the ICRW in relation to the killing, taking and treating of fin whales in the Southern Ocean Sanctuary in pursuance of JARPA II. The ICJ held, as stated earlier, that Japan should revoke any extant authorisation, permit or licence granted in relation to JARPA II, and refrain from granting any further permits in pursuance of that programme. The Court added that Japan was expected to take into account 'the reasoning and conclusions contained in this judgment as it evaluates the possibility of granting any future permits under Article VIII , paragraph 1, of the Convention'. This, as it was described, 'obscure' paragraph may lead to different interpretations, one of them being that any scientific programme regarding whaling by Japan will be illegal. It was also argued that such a statement was beyond the jurisdiction of the Court, which extended only to JARPA II.[108] According to de la Mare, Gales and Mangel, 'Although

---

[105] Ibid., para. 212.   [106] Ibid., para. 227.   [107] Ibid., para. 242.
[108] Ibid., para. 247; Dai Tamada, 'On the Way to Definitive Settlement of Dispute: Lessons from the *Whaling Case*', *Australian Yearbook of International Law* 32 (2015), 113–23, 118.

not explicitly noted by the ICJ, the Judgment highlights weaknesses of the review process within the IWC. Logical and scientific inconsistencies in JARPA II were pointed out in the IWC scientific committee's mandatory review of the original proposal.'[109] The same authors argue that in the case of scientific research permits, the Parties to the ICRW must state very clearly and in a detailed manner objectives and methods, and sample sizes must be capable of quantitative evaluation using normal scientific procedures. Long-term proposed research should specify intermediate objectives so the research can be adjusted or abandoned if they are not achieved.[110]

A particular aspect of this case is the extensive reliance of the ICJ on evidence submitted by expert witnesses. In the *Pulp Mills* case the ICJ had stated that,

> Regarding those experts who appeared before it as counsel at the hearings, the Court would have found it more useful had they been presented by the Parties as expert witnesses under Articles 57 and 64 of the Rules of Court, instead of being included as counsel in their respective delegations. The Court indeed considers that those persons who provide evidence before the Court based on their scientific or technical knowledge and on their personal experience should testify before the Court as experts, witnesses or in some cases in both capacities, rather than counsel, so that they may be submitted to questioning by the other party as well as by the Court.[111]

In the *Pulp Mills* case the use of experts resulted in heated separate judicial Opinions, which related to the way in which the ICJ had arrived at its findings. Both parties to the dispute had placed 'before the Court a vast amount of factual and scientific material'.[112] Some of these reports were prepared by experts, who, nevertheless, appeared before the ICJ as counsel for one of the parties to the dispute, which had meant that such experts could not be cross-examined by the other party or be questioned

---

[109] William de la Mare, Nick Gales and Marc Mangel, 'Applying Scientific Principles in International Law on Whaling', *Science and Law* 345 (2014), 1125–6, 1126, www.scien cemag.org/content/345/6201/1125.figures-only, last accessed 17 April 2015.

[110] Ibid., 1126.

[111] *Case Concerning Pulp Mills on the River Uruguay (Argentina v. Uruguay)*, ICJ Reports 2010, 15, para. 167. See Panos Merkouris, '*Case Concerning Pulp Mills on the River Uruguay (Argentina v. Uruguay)*: Of Environmental Impact Assessments and "Phantom Experts"', www.haguejusticeportal.net/index.php?id=11878, last accessed 14 May 2014.

[112] *Case Concerning Pulp Mills on the River Uruguay (Argentina v. Uruguay)*, above n. 111, para. 205.

by the ICJ, a fact which the Court considered important enough to mention in the body of the Judgment.[113]

Judges Al-Khasawneh and Simma felt that the Court might have benefited from the procedure provided for in Article 50 of the ICJ Statute, which provides that 'the Court may, at any time, entrust an individual, body, bureau, commission or other organisation that it may select, with the task of carrying out an enquiry or giving an expert opinion'.[114] Reliance upon Article 50 would have put to rest the concerns expressed regarding the practice of ICJ judges being advised by so-called 'phantom experts'.[115] These Judges were of the view that an application of Article 50, especially in highly complex cases, would put a stop to such a practice and would, thus, better serve the need for transparency, openness and procedural fairness.[116]

In the *Whaling in the Antarctic* case, the Parties made extensive use of experts who were subject to examination and cross-examination. Experts also were robustly examined from the Bench. Each expert submitted written testimony before giving oral evidence. However, as Peat argues, the non-appointment of experts by the Court in the *Whaling in the Antarctic* case was a missed opportunity. By doing so the ICJ could have obviated the need to imply an extra-textual standard of review which aimed at avoiding adjudication on the scientific merits of the programme and it would have enabled the Court to give effect to the ordinary meaning of the distinction between 'scientific research' and 'for the purpose of scientific research'.[117]

---

[113] See also Merkouris, above n. 111.

[114] Statute of the International Court of Justice, 26 June 1945, 2187 UNTS 90. See also Article 67 of the Rules of Court: '1. If the Court considers it necessary to arrange for an enquiry or an expert opinion, it shall, after hearing the parties, issue an order to this effect, defining the subject of the enquiry or expert opinion, stating the number and mode of appointment of the persons to hold the enquiry or of the experts, and laying down the procedure to be followed. Where appropriate, the Court shall require persons appointed to carry out an enquiry, or to give an expert opinion, to make a solemn declaration. 2. Every report or record of an enquiry and every expert opinion shall be communicated to the parties, which shall be given the opportunity of commenting upon it.'

[115] *Pulp Mills* case, above n. 111. Joint Dissenting Opinion of Judges Al-Khasawneh and Simma, para. 12, www.icj-cij.org/docket/index.php?p1=3&p2=3&case=135&p3=4, last accessed 15 May 2014; Merkouris, above n. 111.

[116] Joint Dissenting Opinion of Judges Al-Khasawneh and Simma, above n. 115, para. 14; see also Merkouris, above n. 111.

[117] Daniel Peat, 'The Use of Court-Appointed Experts by the International Court of Justice', BYIL 84 (2013), 271–303, 287–8.

A party can appoint experts/witnesses in accordance with its declared list of intended experts/witnesses (Articles 57, 62 and 65 of the ICJ Rules).[118] Australia called two experts during the public hearings: Professor Marc Mangel[119] and Nick Gales.[120] Japan called one expert, Professor Emeritus Lars Walløe.[121] The ICJ relied on expert evidence in this case in an exceptionally extensive manner when examining relevant elements of the programme's design and implementation: (1) use and scale of lethal research; (2) methods used to select sample sizes; (3) comparisons of target sample sizes and actual take; (4) programme timeframe; (5) scientific output of the programme; and (6) degree to which the programme coordinated its activities.[122]

This case demonstrates that the role of science in cases concerning environmental matters is as important as that of law, perhaps even more so. Steinar Andresen argues that the lack of scientific agreement on the status of whale stocks hampered progress for a long time within the Whaling Commission.[123] The same author also stresses that at times

---

[118] Article 57: 'Without prejudice to the provisions of the Rules concerning the production of documents, each party shall communicate to the Registrar, in sufficient time before the opening of the oral proceedings, information regarding any evidence which it intends to produce or which it intends to request the Court to obtain. This communication shall contain a list of the surnames, first names, nationalities, descriptions and places of residence of the witnesses and experts whom the party intends to call, with indications in general terms of the point or points to which their evidence will be directed. A copy of the communication shall also be furnished for transmission to the other party.' Article 62: '1. The Court may at any time call upon the parties to produce such evidence or to give such explanations as the Court may consider to be necessary for the elucidation of any aspect of the matters in issue, or may itself seek other information for this purpose. 2. The Court may, if necessary, arrange for the attendance of a witness or expert to give evidence in the proceedings.' Article 65: 'Witnesses and experts shall be examined by the agents, counsel or advocates of the parties under the control of the President. Questions may be put to them by the President and by the judges. Before testifying, witnesses shall remain out of court.'

[119] Distinguished Research Professor of Mathematical Biology and Director of the Center for Stock Assessment Research, University of California, Santa Cruz.

[120] Chief Scientist for Australia's Antarctic Programme.

[121] Professor Emeritus, University of Oslo; marine mammal adviser to the Government of Norway.

[122] De la Mare, Gales and Mangel, above n. 109, 1126. In particular, expert evidence was relied on in relation to what constitutes scientific research (paras. 73–86); in interpreting the phrase 'for purposes of' (paras. 87–97); and in assessing the JARPA II programme within the context of Article VIII of the Convention (paras. 98–227).

[123] Steinar Andresen, 'The Role of Scientific Expertise in Multilateral Environmental Agreements: Influence and Effectiveness', in Monika Ambrus, Karin Arts, Ellen Hey and Helena Raulus (eds.), The Role of 'Experts' in International and European

THE *WHALING IN THE ANTARCTIC* CASE

science is engaged in a 'value dispute', an example of which was the Norwegian catch of North Atlantic minke whales which, according to the IWC Scientific Committee, did not represent a threat to the population of minke whales. However, this finding was disregarded by the majority of the IWC, which still opposes the Norwegian catch, notwithstanding its endorsement by the IWC Scientific Committee. Such a situation, according to Andresen, is caused by a deep conflict over values. At times the regulatory body goes beyond the recommendations of the scientific advisory body, an example being the imposition of the Moratorium on whaling, which, according to Andresen, was taken against the backdrop of the anti-whaling movement headed by both the USA and Greenpeace.[124] It is quite obvious, as the history of the IWC demonstrates, that matters of whaling are very political and therefore the influence of 'pure' science is diminished. It may be expected that the *Whaling* case will set the standard regarding the use of experts in the adjudication of disputes that turn on scientific facts, the importance of which was first noted in the *Pulp Mills* case.

It was not in the remit of the ICJ to have discussed commercial whaling and also indigenous whaling. It made only some general observations so as to link scientific whaling to the whole nexus of rights and obligations of States under the ICRW, and clarified the issue of the margin of appreciation regarding the issuance of special permits. The ICJ also admitted the possibility of future commercial whaling on the part of Japan, which it felt the ICRW does not prohibit *per se*. In the meantime, Japanese, as well as Icelandic, scientific whaling in the north-western Pacific is to continue, and the recent ICJ case has no implications for that. The ICJ decision does not resolve questions relating to cultural diversity (discussed in Chapter 4). Most importantly, the ICJ decision has not settled fully and finally the question which the present author considers to be a crucial matter in relation to whaling, namely, what may ultimately be the 'object and purpose' of the ICRW. The total ban on commercial whaling, as at present – due to perceptions by some States, changes in socio-economic conditions, as well as the ecological approach – is not reconcilable with the

Decision-Making Processes. Advisors, Decision Makers or Irrelevant Actors? (Cambridge University Press, 2014), p. 115. The lack of consensus (or 'fragile consensus') within the IWC on the allocation of species is also noted by Jeffrey J. Smith, 'Evolving Conservation? The International Court's Decision in the *Australia/Japan* Case', ODIL 45 (2014), 301–27, 304.

[124] Andresen, above n. 123, pp. 118 and 119.

original purpose of sustainable whaling.[125] This issue is of particular importance in light of the Judgment's para. 56, which stated that 'amendments to the Schedule and recommendations by the IWC may put an emphasis on one or the other objective pursued by the Convention, but cannot alter its object and purpose', a statement that, of course in itself, may be subject to many divergent interpretations.

The question as to whether the ICJ is an appropriate forum to discuss scientific questions concerning whaling also arose. Both Judges Owada and Abraham suggested that the ICJ lacked the required expertise to do so.[126] There is also the issue of the application of the standard of 'objective reasonableness'.[127] What was the role of the ICJ in applying such a standard in this case: engaging in *de novo* review or leaving this to the discretion afforded to States issuing permits which is subject to review by the Scientific Committee and the IWC?[128] As has been correctly observed, the ICJ's decision revealed the weaknesses of the review process within

---

[125] See Judge Hisashi Owada, Dissenting Opinion, above n. 65, paras. 9–12. See also on this subject Judge Cançado Trindade, Separate Opinion, above n. 59.

[126] Judge Hisashi Owada said: 'On the question of what constitutes activities "for purposes of scientific research", it must first be said in all frankness that this Court, as a court of law, is not professionally qualified to give a scientifically meaningful answer, and should not try to pretend that it can, even though there may be certain elements in the concept that the Court may legitimately and usefully offer as salient from the viewpoint of legal analysis': para. 24. Judge Ronny Abraham was of the view that: 'Mais ce n'est pas le rôle de la Cour de dire si JARPA II a été conçu de la meilleure manière (c'est le rôle du comité scientifique de procéder à une évaluation sur cette question), mais seulement de décider s'il s'agit bien d'un programme poursuivant des fins scientifiques' (which is to say that Judge Abraham was of the view that: 'But it is not the role of the Court to say whether JARPA II was designed in the best way (this is the role of the Scientific Committee to conduct an assessment on this issue), but only to decide whether it is indeed a continuing programme for scientific purposes)', Judge Ronny Abraham, Dissenting Opinion, para. 38 (available in French only; English translation by the present author), www.icj-cij.org/docket/files/148/18141.pdf, last accessed 15 May 2014.

[127] Oral Proceedings, V. Lowe (CR 2013/22, p. 60, paras. 20–1).

[128] See Owada, Dissenting Opinion, paras. 29–49, above n. 64. See also the Dissenting Opinion of Judge Abdulqawi A. Yusuf on this point, who is of the view that the Court applied a standard of reasonableness in relation to the design and implementation of JARPA II that was not grounded in the practice and the law of the Court, para. 15. He is also critical of the reliance by the Court on the standard of review, which, according to him, is extraneous to the ICRW and not based on the applicable law (para. 12). Judge Yusuf also doubts whether a programme is for purposes of scientific research can be determined on the basis of the reasonableness of the scale of the use of lethal sampling: '[t]hus, the fact that the sample size of minke whales taken under JARPA II is much larger than that of JARPA makes no difference unless it is established first that both programmes are for purposes of scientific research', para. 31, www.icj-cij.org/docket/files/148/18148.pdf, last accessed 25 January 2015.

the IWC and its Scientific Committee, where science mixed with polit-ics,[129] not an uncommon phenomenon in intergovernmental fora where political considerations habitually determine outcomes. The view has been expressed that by relying on the test of reasonableness, 'the ICJ provided a clear, well-constructed Judgment focused on the logic, rather than details, of science', which could serve as a useful model in other disputes contain-ing complex technical issues. The ICJ's approach constitutes a model for dividing scientific issues from non-scientific questions in disputes involv-ing science, society and law.[130] It is also argued that by introducing the test of reasonableness in the design and implementation of scientific research, the Court has curbed the discretion of States under Article VIII of the ICRW. While States can still decide on the objectives of their research projects, they may find themselves limited as to how they can achieve those objectives based on this test.[131]

However, it may also be said that the ICJ decision has not been entirely injurious to Australian–Japanese relations given that Australia and Japan have in the meantime concluded the Japan–Australia Economic Partner-ship Agreement which will enter into force in 2015 to share military technology,[132] a rekindling of the bilateral relationship under Prime Ministers Tony Abbott and Shinzo Abe which was facilitated by the fact that Australia had not claimed that Japan was breaching any obligations owed to Australia per se.[133]

3.5.1   *Conclusions on the* Whaling in the Antarctic *case*

From the above review of the functioning of the IWC, and the develop-ments and events which have led up to the present era of evident conflict among its Members, it becomes clear that the ICRW, and the functioning of the IWC itself, is weighed down by many challenges and inherent weaknesses. This makes interstate cooperation on whaling regulation problematic, given its highly divisive nature and the fact that there is a high degree of disparity between the interests of the States involved. It may be said that the *Whaling in the Antarctic* Judgment has not

---

[129] De la Mare, Gales and Mangel, above n. 109, 1126.   [130] Ibid., 1126.

[131] Telesetsky, Anton and Koivurova, above n. 80, 355.

[132] More on this Bilateral Agreement is available at the following Australian governmental website: www.dfat.gov.au/fta/jaepa/, last accessed 20 December 2014.

[133] Shirley V. Scott and Lucia Oriana, 'International Convention for the Regulation of Whaling/International Court of Justice', *International Journal of Marine and Coastal Law* 29 (2014), 547–57.

immediately led to the amelioration of the atmosphere in the IWC, judging by proceedings at the 2014 meeting of the IWC. It was to be hoped that the ICJ Judgment would have contributed to arriving at a long-term policy relating to scientific whaling. The fact is, however, that the broad agreement that had at times been achieved within the IWC is far from certain nowadays. The Moratorium reached on commercial whaling – a success of the group of States that desire the definitive ban on whaling – is being denounced by those who oppose it as effectively being at odds with the object and purpose of the ICRW. It is extremely doubtful whether, in the absence of unanimity, any solution to the current deadlock could be found within the confines of the IWC, which was set up under an agreement between a relatively small number of more or less like-minded States with a common objective, principally, of imposing on themselves some proper system of regulation of their respective whaling industries in order to safeguard the longevity of their whaling industries by ensuring that whale stocks were not threatened with extinction.

It is apparent from a multiplicity of factors outlined above that the 'agenda' of the now numerous stakeholders has widened far beyond that. The IWC now has to attempt to operate as a forum within which irreconcilable conflicts of interest are resolved. The aspirations of the whaling nations, as they stand at present, simply cannot be met without some level, however contained, of resumption of commercial whaling. On the other hand, the aspirations of the preservationists, now a majority within the IWC, cannot be entirely fulfilled unless the possibility of any resumption of commercial whaling is abandoned. Therefore the most important and daunting question is whether the ICRW is still a relevant international instrument or whether it will have to be revised (or even abandoned as an obsolete treaty) given that it is falling short of meeting the current set of needs of the parties to it.

The aspirations of those groups that oppose whaling would extend to having even aboriginal and scientific whaling – currently exempted from the Moratorium – eventually phased out, as evidenced by the very strong protestations of civil society regarding the raising of aboriginal quotas for Greenland's Inuit. However, as matters stand at present, these aspirations are probably unlikely to be achieved in the near future. The Court observed that '[t]he preamble of the ICRW indicates that the Convention pursues the purpose of ensuring the conservation of all species of whales while allowing for their sustainable exploitation' (para. 56 of the Judgment), thus indicating that the

Convention was intended to reconcile the conservation of whales with their exploitation. As was noted, the Court in its Judgment made a very strong statement that the object and purpose of the ICRW cannot be changed through decisions of the IWC, but that only the focus can be different in so far as it concerns its object and purpose ('amendments to the Schedule and recommendations by the IWC may put an emphasis on one or the other objective pursued by the Convention, but cannot alter its object and purpose', para. 56 of the Judgment). In light of this statement, the suggestion to change the object and purpose of the Convention so as to eliminate all types of whaling can only be speculative at best. As the situation stands at present, there is no immediate possibility of the resumption of commercial whaling. Although such whaling was outside the remit of the Court's decision, the question may be asked whether the extended Moratorium is just a change of emphasis on the object and purpose of the Convention, or conversely the ICRW's object and purpose has already been changed by prohibiting commercial whaling through the amendment to the Schedule by the IWC.

It has even been suggested that, considering the current state of affairs at the IWC, the possibility of the withdrawal of the major whaling nations is real.[134] As was observed earlier in the present chapter, the ICJ Judgment has contributed only to a certain degree to the solving of these intractable problems within the IWC that are far more complex than just scientific whaling;[135] as the current deadlock would seem to be incapable of being overcome, within the ambit of the existing legal framework of whaling regulation, it may, indeed, be necessary to create something entirely new. One of the issues to which this case could potentially have contributed, though this was not elaborated in the Judgment, is the desirability of States acting on the basis of public concern (collective interest), which Australia claimed to be doing and for which it was credited.[136] According to

---

[134] Lisa Kobayashi, 'Lifting the International Whaling Commission's Moratorium on Commercial Whaling as the Most Effective Global Regulation of Whaling', *Environs* 29 (2006), 177–219, 205.

[135] See the same view as expressed by Palmer, above n. 56, 125: 'The decision tips the advantage to the conservation side in the Commission yet leaves unresolved the fundamental issue at the Commission as to whether commercial whaling will ever resume for those species for which it can be shown to be sustainable.'

[136] Malgosia Fitzmaurice, 'The International Court of Justice and International Environmental Law', in Christian Tams and James Sloan (eds.), *The Development of*

James Crawford, Australia invoked Japan's responsibility *erga omnes partes* under the ICRW.[137] During the proceedings, Australia claimed to act exclusively in defence of a general legal interest.[138] This case is yet another example of the question of the *locus standi* of States seeking to enforce public interests through ICJ litigation on the basis of the notions of obligations owed *erga omnes* and *erga omnes partes*.[139] The ICJ's jurisprudence in this matter is so varied that it does not allow one to draw more general conclusions;[140] however, as Tams opines, perhaps the *Whaling* case could be seen as a logical follow-up to the 2011 Judgment in the *Belgium* v. *Senegal* case. In that case, too, the Court had surprised commentators by going out of its

International Law by the International Court of Justice (Cambridge University Press, 2013), pp. 353–74: '[b]ecause of the general and longstanding public interest in the protection of marine mammals, this case is likely to define the public perception of the Court as a protector of environmental concerns', p. 377.

[137] James Crawford, 'Responsibilities for Breaches of Communitarian Norms: An Appraisal of Article 48 of the ILC Articles on Responsibility of States for Wrongful Acts', in Ulrich Fastenrath et al. (eds.), *From Bilateralism to Community Interest. Essays in Honour of Bruno Simma* (Oxford University Press, 2011), p. 236; James Crawford, *State Responsibility: The General Part*, chapter 11, 'Breaches of Communitarian Norms' (Cambridge University Press, 2013), pp. 362–94, 373.

[138] 'Australia does not claim to be an injured State because of the fact that some of the JARPA II take is from waters over which Australia claims sovereign rights and jurisdiction ... Every party has the same interest in ensuring compliance by every other party with its obligations under the 1946 Convention. Australia is seeking to uphold its collective interest, an interest it shares with all other parties.' Pleadings, CR 2013/18, p. 28, para. 19 (Burmester). As Tams observed, that was an unusual strategy as in other cases Australia had a dual approach, i.e. it emphasised the right to vindicate general interests but also stressed the Claimant State's special position, such as in the *Nuclear Tests* cases, where Australia and New Zealand emphasised both the special impact of nuclear testing on their territory and the interest of the international community in the banning of such tests. See *Nuclear Tests (Australia v. France)*, ICJ Pleadings, vol. I, pp. 14 and 43; *Nuclear Tests (New Zealand v. France)*, ICJ Pleadings, vol. I, pp. 8 and 49; Malgosia Fitzmaurice, above n. 136, pp. 358–9, commenting on this statement of Tams. See on this subject in detail, Christian Tams, *Enforcing Obligations* Erga Omnes *in International Law* (Cambridge University Press, 2005 (rev. edn 2010)), pp. 180 et seq.

[139] Christian Tams, above n. 138, chapter 4.

[140] On the one hand, we have *South West Africa*, Second Phase, Judgment, *ICJ Reports 1966*, p. 6 (rejection of standing to enforce interests of the international community) and *East Timor (Portugal v. Australia)*, Judgment, *ICJ Reports 1995*, p. 90 (jurisdictional limitations which prohibit public interest litigation), and on the other, *Barcelona Traction, Light and Power Company, Limited*, Judgment, *ICJ Reports 1970*, p. 3 (the *erga omnes* doctrine first mentioned) and *Questions relating to the Obligation to Prosecute or Extradite (Belgium v. Senegal)*, Judgment, *ICJ Reports 2012*, p. 422 (in which the ICJ recognised the standing of all treaty parties to enforce obligations *erga omnes partes*).

way to accept the applicant's standing to enforce a multilateral treaty protecting collective interests.[141]

In relation to *Whaling in the Antarctic*, there were views expressed that the current ecosystem approach and the notion of common heritage of humankind may be considered by States as matters that give rise to obligations *erga omnes* and *erga omnes partes*, and thus result in redress pursuant to Article 48 of the International Law Commission (ILC) Articles on State Responsibility (ASR).[142] As Urs persuasively argues, this case illustrates that multilateral agreements such as the ICRW are not a simple sum of bilateral relationships. Their multilateral effect is reflected by the interest of Australia and New Zealand in mutual compliance irrespective of their ability to make claims to specific injury arising out of Japan's violation.[143]

---

[141] Christian Tams, 'Roads Not Taken, Opportunities Missed: Procedural and Jurisdictional Questions Sidestepped in the Whaling Judgment', in Fitzmaurice and Tamada, above n. 56 (on file with the present author).

[142] Simone Borg, 'The Influence of International Case Law on Aspects of International Law Relating to Conservation of Living Marine Resources beyond National Jurisdiction', *Yearbook of International Environmental Law* 23 (2012), 44–79, 67–71. See also Giorgio Gaja, who also expressed the view that the protection of natural resources can be within the realm of interests of the international community and that the community interest can also be expressed through the imposition of certain restrictions on their exploitation. There is no doubt that the common heritage of mankind belongs to the category of concepts which engage general interest and that Article 48 of the Articles on State Responsibility is to be relied on in case of breaches of obligations involving community interests. Giorgio Gaja, 'The Protection of General Interests in the International Community', *General Course of Public International Law*, RCADI 364 (2011), 171–80. Shotaro Hamamoto was also of the view that multilateral environmental treaties are a source of collective interests, therefore arguing that Japan (even before the Judgment in the *Belgium* v. *Senegal* case) would have been in a difficult position to claim inadmissibility of the claim by Australia on the basis of lack of legal interest. According to Professor Hamamoto, the non-admissibility plea on the part of Japan, after *Belgium* v. *Senegal*, in the case against Australia, would be 'virtually hopeless', p. 6. 'Procedural Questions in the Whaling Judgment: Admissibility, Intervention and the Use of Experts', Japanese Society of International Law (19–21 September 2014), The Honourable Shigeru Oda Commemorative Lectures, 'ICJ Judgment on Whaling in the Antarctic: Its Significance and Implications', www.jsil.jp/annual_documents/2014/2014manuscript_hamamoto.pdf, last accessed 22 December 2014. See a very interesting comment of Kolb in relation to the exercise of the Court's discretionary powers in relation to the protection of common goods (whaling), Robert Kolb, 'Short Reflections on the ICJ's Whaling Case and the Review by International Courts and Tribunals of "Discretionary Powers"', *AYBIL* 32 (2015), 135–146.

[143] Priya Urs, 'Guest Post: Are States Injured by Whaling in the Antarctic?' *Opinio Iuris*, http://opiniojuris.org/2014/08/14/guest-post-states-injured-whaling-antarctic/, last accessed 24 December 2014. See also James Crawford, who argues that multilateral

Therefore, 'as a result, irrespective of whether the ICRW was intended to prohibit commercial whaling as a conservationist effort, or simply to regulate states' access to a common resource, this emphasis by the Court reaffirms this trajectory in the development of international law'. It may be noted that the Seabed Disputes Chamber of the International Tribunal for the Law of the Sea (ITLOS) has referred to Article 48 of the ASR as stating that obligations to preserve the environment of the high seas and in the Area may be *erga omnes*, owed to the international community as a whole, or *erga omnes partes*, owed 'to a group of States [providing] that the obligation is established for the protection of a collective interest of the group'.[144]

A different view from that adopted by the Court in the *Whaling* case on the question of standing (Article 48 of the ASR) has been expressed, namely that, though the Court's view might be justified in the case of Conventions such as the Genocide Convention or the Convention against Torture, it has no *raison d'être* in the case of the ICRW, even taking into account the allegedly 'special' character of whales.[145] This view raises a host of important legal questions (analysis of which exceeds the framework of this chapter). Lastly, this case has perhaps heralded a new era of the Court regarding science, which 'is a

---

'law-making' treaties have become the dominant source of obligations among States in the contemporary world. 'Chance, Order, Change: The Course of International Law', RCADI 365 (2013), 9–390.

[144] Paragraph 180 of the 2010 *Advisory Opinion on Responsibilities and Obligations of States Sponsoring Persons and Entities with Respect to Activities in the Area*, Seabed Disputes Chamber of the International Tribunal for the Law of the Sea (ITLOS Case No. 17), www.itlos.org/fileadmin/itlos/documents/cases/case_no_17/adv_op_010211.pdf, last accessed 18 January 2015. On this Opinion, see Donald K. Anton, Robert A. Makgill and Cymie R. Payne, 'Advisory Opinion on Responsibility and Liability for International Seabed Mining (ITLOS Case No. 17): International Environmental Law in the Seabed Disputes Chamber', http://ssrn.com/AuthorID=371838, last accessed 18 January 2015; http://ssrn.com/abstract=1793216, last accessed 14 May 2014; Ilias Plakokefalos, 'Seabed Disputes Chamber of the International Tribunal for the Law of the Sea, *Responsibilities and Obligations of States Sponsoring Persons and Entities with Respect to Activities in the Area* (Advisory Opinion)', *Journal of Environmental Law* 24 (2012), 1–11. At the time of this Advisory Opinion, there were views expressed that the ICJ should follow this example. Tim Stephens, 'Law of the Sea Symposium – Comment' http://opiniojuris.org/2013/05/27/law-of-thesea-symposium/, last accessed 15 May 2014, and Andre Nollkaemper, 'International Adjudication of Global Public Goods: The Intersection of Substance and Procedure', SHARES Research Paper 9/2012, 2.

[145] Hironobu Sakai, 'After the Whaling Case: Its Lessons from a Japanese Perspective', chapter to be published in Fitzmaurice and Tamada, above n. 56 (on file with the present author), pp. 10–11.

cornerstone of studies on biodiversity'.[146] There is no doubt that with the increasing number of environmental cases before the Court, science will become a significant element of the Court's adjudication of cases.

3.6   Post-judgment developments

3.6.1   Japanese position after the Judgment

It is considered that the Judgment of the ICJ was shocking for Japan, including the official institutions and bodies such as the Ministry of Foreign Affairs, the Fisheries Agency (which did not expect such strong language from the Court), politicians and whalers. It may be said that the Judgment was 'truly a bolt from the blue', according to senior members of the Japan Whaling Association and the Japanese Institute of Cetacean Research (ICR), the operational wings of Japanese scientific whaling.[147]

The unanimous resolution adopted, on 16 April 2014, by the Agriculture and Fisheries Committee of the House of Representatives of the Japanese Diet stated, inter alia, that the whaling Judgment will have a serious adverse effect on Japan's whale research, its whale meat market and its traditional culture of eating whale meat; and it urged the government to continue the whale research, to exercise diplomatic means not to be sued again, to budgetise for the work to redraft JARPA II, and to continue a strong whaling policy, including the possible option of withdrawing from the ICRW.[148] Of great importance for Japan was paragraph 246 of the Judgment.[149] It was understood, on the one hand, 'as a warning not to continue research whaling in the North West Pacific, and, on the other hand, as an invitation to resume research whaling in the

---

[146] Alexander Gillespie, 'Science, Value and People: The Three Factors that Will Define the Next Generation of International Conservation Agreements', *Transnational Environmental Law* 1 (2012), 169–82, 170.

[147] Akiho Shibata, Presentation during the workshop on the resumption of Japanese scientific whaling, organised by Queen Mary University of London on 13 March 2015 (on file with the author).

[148] Ibid.

[149] 'The Court sees no need to order the additional remedy requested by Australia, which would require Japan to refrain from authorizing or implementing any special permit whaling which is not for purposes of scientific research within the meaning of Article VIII. That obligation already applies to all States parties. It is to be expected that Japan will take account of the reasoning and conclusions contained in this Judgment as it evaluates the possibility of granting any future permits under Article VIII, paragraph 1, of the Convention.'

Antarctic'.[150] According to the Foreign Ministry, the warning element of this paragraph was included in the phrase 'any future permits', i.e. as containing the implicit message that Japan should reconsider not only whaling in the Antarctic, but also the programme in the North West Pacific (scheduled to commence on 22 April 2015). The Foreign Ministry interpreted paragraph 246 in a more extensive manner than the wording of this paragraph. It presumed that the Judgment has the legal potential, although not yet determinative, to recognise the *locus standi* of all Parties to the ICRW to bring a case before the ICJ of alleged non-compliance by other Parties. It also noted the possibility of a request for interpretation of the Judgment being lodged by Australia and/or New Zealand, in the event Japan were to decide soon after the Judgment to continue research whaling in the North West Pacific in April 2014.[151]

On 18 April 2014, the Minister of Agriculture, Forestry and Fisheries of Japan, Mr Joshimasa Hayashi, issued a policy statement concerning the future of whaling in the light of the ICJ Judgment and its effect on Japan's basic policy on whaling. He said that the Judgment confirms that one of the purposes of the ICRW is sustainable exploitation of whale resources. In light of this, Japan has confirmed its policy of the resumption of commercial whaling by conducting research whaling.[152] The statement provides the following programme in relation to whaling during the fiscal year 2014: (1) the cancellation of the Second Japanese Whale Research Programme in the Antarctic (JARPA II) in accordance with the ICJ Judgment; (2) limitation of research objectives and reduction in the scale of the research activities of the Second Japanese Whale Research Programme in the North West Pacific (JARPN II); (3) for research programmes in the fiscal year 2014/15, Japan would take various necessary measures in the light of the Judgment (such as studies of feasibility or practicability of non-lethal methods such as DNA biopsy samplings in the North West Pacific).[153] For the fiscal year 2015, Japan set out the following targets: Japan intends to conduct in-depth review of the design of whale research programmes in the Antarctic and in the North West Pacific, with the aim of submitting new research programmes to the Scientific Committee of the IWC by autumn 2015, which will take into account the criteria mentioned in the Judgment. Japan's

[150] Shibata, above n. 147, at 5.   [151] Ibid., 5.
[152] www.jfa.maff.go.jp/e/pdf/danwa.pdf, last accessed 20 March 2015. See also the chapter by Joji Morishita, 'IWC and the ICJ's Judgment', to be published in Fitzmaurice and Tamada, above n. 56 (on file with the present author).
[153] Ibid.

design of the new programme will follow an internationally open and highly transparent process with the participation of renowned scientists from Japan and abroad, and through other processes including discussions at the IWC Scientific Committee's workshop and coordination with other institutions conducting relevant studies.[154] On 9 June 2014, the Prime Minister of Japan, Mr Shinzo Abe, said to the parliamentary commission: 'I want to aim at the resumption of commercial whaling by conduction of whaling research in order to obtain scientific data indispensable for the management of whale resources.'[155] Mr Hayashi initiated a 'whale week', inviting people to dine on whale meat in his ministry. He said that this '"whale week" campaign was part of efforts to let Japanese people know that whaling and eating whale meat are part of their culture'.[156]

3.6.2 The post-Judgment meeting of the IWC (Portorož, Slovenia)

The post-Judgment meeting of the IWC in Slovenia was very interesting from the point of view of the many references by the members of the Commission to the Judgment.[157] All three States submitted statements concerning the Judgment. Australia's understanding of the Court's Judgment, *inter alia*, was that it concluded that JARPA II was not a programme for the purposes of scientific research pursuant to Article VIII. Australia welcomed the decision of the Court that Japan 'shall revoke any extant authorization, permit or licence to kill, take or treat whales in relation to JARPA II, and refrain from granting any further permits under Article VIII, paragraph 1, of the Convention, in pursuance of that programme'. Australia urged the IWC to ensure that it 'considers the guidance from the Court and incorporates its learned judgment into the practices of the Commission'.[158]

According to Japan, the Court decided that, on the one hand, the permits should be revoked, but, on the other hand, the objective of the ICRW includes 'to provide for the proper conservation of whale stocks and thus make possible the orderly development of the whaling industry';

---

[154] Ibid.
[155] 'Japanese Prime Minister Shinzo Abe to work towards commercial whaling hunt despite ICJ ruling', *ABC News*, www.abc.net.au/news/2014-06-10/japanese-pm-to-push-for-return-to-commercial-whaling/5511110, last accessed 23 March 2014.
[156] Ibid.
[157] 65th meeting of the IWC in Slovenia, http://iwc.int/iwcs-65th-meeting-closes-with-progress—and-prais, last accessed 23 December 2014.
[158] IWC65/OS/Australia.

and that '[a]mendments to the Schedule and recommendations by the IWC may put an emphasis on one or the other objective pursued by the Convention, but cannot alter its object and purpose'. The Judgment also stated that '[i]t is to be expected that Japan will take account of the reasoning and conclusions contained in this Judgment as it evaluates the possibility of granting any future permits under Article VIII, paragraph 1, of the Convention' and although '[t]he Court finds that the use of lethal sampling *per se* is not unreasonable in relation to the research objectives of JARPA II', the Court found nevertheless that 'the special permits granted by Japan in connection with JARPA II do not fall within the provisions of Article VIII, paragraph 1, of the International Convention for the Regulation of Whaling'. In light of the Judgment, Japan therefore announced its course of actions on 18 April 2014 through the Statement by the Minister of Agriculture, Forestry and Fisheries that Japan would submit a new research plan based upon international law and scientific evidence to the Scientific Committee of the International Whaling Commission (IWC), which would be based on the criteria mentioned in the Judgment. (See on this Section 3.6.1.)[159]

New Zealand submitted a Draft Resolution to the IWC for 'Whaling under Special Permit'. The gist of the proposed Resolution was reliance on the ICJ Judgment in the functioning of the IWC. In this document New Zealand relied on the findings of the Court concerning lethal methods, design of a programme and the test of reasonableness.[160] Japan

---

[159] IWC56/OS/Japan.

[160] The document stated that the IWC: '1. Instructs the Scientific Committee, in its review of new and existing special permit research programmes, to provide advice to the Commission on: (a) whether the design and implementation of the programme, including sample sizes, are reasonable in relation to achieving the programme's stated research objectives; (b) whether the elements of the research that rely on lethally obtained data are likely to lead to improvements in the conservation and management of whales; (c) whether the objectives of the research could be achieved by non-lethal means or whether there are reasonably equivalent objectives that could be achieved non-lethally; (d) whether the scale of lethal sampling is reasonable in relation to the programme's stated research objectives, and non-lethal alternatives are not feasible to either replace or reduce the scale of lethal sampling proposed; and (e) such other matters as the Scientific Committee considers relevant to the programme, having regard to the decision of the International Court of Justice, including the methodology used to select sample sizes, a comparison of the target sample sizes and the actual take, the timeframe associated with a programme, the programme's scientific output; and the degree to which a programme coordinates its activities with related research projects. 2. Instructs the Scientific Committee to consider and revise how it reviews special permit research programmes, including in relation to the Annex P: Process for the Review of Special Permit Proposals

has not supported the proposed Resolution on the grounds that it suggested that special permit research programmes should be subject to approval by the IWC, which goes against Article VIII of the ICRW and beyond the ICJ Judgment. In contrast, some Latin American anti-whaling nations criticised the proposal as legitimising a special permit research programme. No consensus was achieved and the proposed Resolution was adopted by 35 votes in support, 20 votes against and 5 abstentions. As is the case for all Resolutions adopted by the IWC, this Resolution is legally non-binding. The Resolution requires all members of the IWC to put future scientific whaling programmes to the IWC's Scientific Committee for guidance. Japan, however, said that they would not be following the Resolution because they interpreted the ICJ's Judgment differently (as meaning that scientific research was not subject to the approval of the IWC) and would proceed with the new round of research whaling in the Southern Ocean that they had already declared. According to New Zealand, it is essential to ensure that the reasoning and conclusions contained in the ICJ's Judgment are fully taken into account in any future consideration by the IWC of special permit programmes.[161]

The effect of the Resolution on the IWC's future policy regarding special permits and the new whaling research programme (Section 3.6.3) is still to be determined. This Resolution, being, like all Resolutions of the IWC, of a non-binding character, Japan is free not to follow it. It is to be expected that opposition from anti-whaling countries may be even stronger than in the past because of the ICJ Judgment, which in turn might lead to more contentious confrontations at the IWC. However, it has to be observed that Japan expressed its commitment to follow the ICJ Judgment, terminated JARPA II and pledged to follow the Judgment in the preparation of new research. Therefore, '[i]f there is sufficient

and Research Results from Existing and Completed Permits, in light of the matters set out in paragraph 1 above, for consideration by the Commission. 3. Requests that no further special permits for the take of whales are issued under existing research pro-grammes or any new programme of whale research until: (a) the Scientific Committee has reviewed the research programme to enable it to provide advice to the Commission in accordance with the instructions above; and (b) the Commission has considered the report of the Scientific Committee and assessed whether the proponent of the special permit programme has acted in accordance with the review process described above; and (c) the Commission has, in accordance with Article VI, made such recommendations on the merits or otherwise of the special permit programme as it sees fit.' IWC/65/14 Rev1 Agenda item 15.

[161] IWC/65/OS New Zealand.

willingness among the IWC members to take advantage of the ICJ Judgment for promoting positive dialogue, rather than confrontation, the IWC65 [meeting] could be marked as a turning point in the whaling dispute'.[162]

3.6.3   New Scientific Research Programme in the Antarctic Ocean

On 18 November 2014, Japan announced its plans to take 333 minke whales in the Antarctic. It submitted a draft of the New Scientific Research Programme in the Antarctic Ocean (NEWREP-A) to the Chairman of the IWC Scientific Committee and the IWC Secretariat. The new programme is proposed to last for the duration of twelve years and it established 'intermediary targets' with a review by the IWC Scientific Committee after six years. The programme also provides for collaboration with the Commission for the Conservation of Antarctic Marine Living Resources (CCAMLR) and several Japanese research institutes (such as those on polar issues and fisheries).[163] Japan's Institute of Cetacean Research endorsed a lethal hunt and stated that '[a]fter giving serious scientific consideration, it has been concluded that age data at the annual scale can be obtained only through lethal sampling methods, and thus lethal methods need to be employed under this program'.[164] Japan's Commissioner, Joji Morishita, said at the IWC's 2014 meeting: 'we will be submitting a new research plan in [the] Antarctic Ocean so that we can start from 2015'; '[a]ll these activities, as we have been arguing [, are] perfectly in line with international law, a scientific basis, as well as ICJ judgement language'.[165]

It has been said that the fundamental logic of structuring the programme has undergone a significant re-orientation, based on the ICJ Judgment, as exemplified by:[166] (1) the main objective being the improvement of the application of the Revised Management Procedure to Antarctic minke whales; (2) identifying very strictly the scientific data that is absolutely necessary to achieve the main objective and that

---

[162] Morishita, above n. 152.

[163] For the full document, see 'Proposed Research Plan for New Scientific Whale Research Program in the Antarctic Ocean (NEWREP-A)', the Government of Japan, www.jfa. maff.go.jp/j/whale/pdf/newrep–a.pdf, last accessed 26 December 2014. See also 'Japan to expand its Antarctic whaling area', Sydney Morning Herald, The Environment, www. smh.com.au/environment/whale-watch/japan-to-expand-its-antarctic-whaling-area-2014 1118-11pa1l.html, last accessed 23 March 2015.

[164] Sydney Morning Herald, above n. 163.   [165] Ibid.   [166] Shibata, above n. 147, 14.

cannot be obtained by non-lethal methods, which, in the NEWREP-A case, came to be identified as the Age at Sexual Maturity (ASM); (3) the sample size of lethal take would be based on the most reliable and accurate parameter to obtain the required result, rather than a wide range of potential sample sizes, which, in the NEWREP-A case, came to be 333 Antarctic minke whales annually in order to detect ASM 50 per cent with annual increase of 0.1 per year older or younger difference; (4) as a consequence, the sample size is determined by the most reliable, and thus most scientifically reasonable, parameter.[167] The Expert Review Panel on JARPA II convened in February 2014, one month before the ICJ Judgment, actually made a recommendation to considerably increase the efforts and resources allocated to the ecosystem-modelling aspect of JARPA II.[168] Japan's resumed scientific whaling was met with criticism in Australia and New Zealand. It may be said that there is a certain degree of scepticism concerning the change in scientific whaling by Japan. Clapham, with experience in the IWC Scientific Committee, suggested that the Judgment of the ICJ should be treated as no more than a temporary setback in this type of whaling by Japan, admittedly with some 'superficial' changes to bring it line with the ICJ ruling.[169]

Concluding remarks

Lawyers frequently do not feel comfortable with science. However, as the *Whaling* case indicated, science and law are at times two sides of one coin; and in order to reach a legal decision it is indispensable to analyse the scientific evidence. Not all lawyers share this view, as was demonstrated by the opinions of certain Judges, doubting whether the Court had sufficient expertise to deal with matters of science. Be that as it may, whaling issues cannot be discussed without science and, in the *Whaling* case, the experts were all scientists and their evidence played a fundamental role in the Court's Judgment. The functioning of the IWC is based on science and one of the main issues that has been repeatedly raised in connection with the work of the IWC is the

---

[167] Ibid., 14.

[168] Ibid., 14 (Report of the Expert Workshop to review JARPA II, SC/65b/Rep02 (2014), p. 39, Section 10.2.1).

[169] Philip Clapham, 'Japan's Whaling Following the International Court of Justice Ruling: Brave New World or Business as Usual?', *Marine Policy* 51 (2014), 238–41, 238.

purported lack of a sound scientific basis for decision-making. Generally speaking, the role of science in environmental law is very complex.[170] Overall, we witness a trend in the valorisation of science and, more particularly, science-based policy-making, in various instances of interstate cooperation, be they in treaty-based international or supranational organisations, the WTO or transnational policy networks. The argument goes that practice at the level of international cooperation seems to find science attractive for its objectivity, freedom from bias and independence from the theories within which the resultant data is rationalised.[171]

Peel explains that international environmental law is perhaps the area of international law in which reliance on science is most pronounced, given that it aims at the prevention of environmental pollution and at the protection of nature.[172] Peel's analysis of risk theory and the application of technical, expert processes to international law clearly indicates that they are far from clear, especially viewed from the perspective of cultural theory.[173] Furthermore, there are two competing regulatory paradigms that are dominant in international debates and disputes over health and environmental risks: sound practice and the precautionary principle, which are based on regulatory principles found in United States law and in European Union law. As Peel explains, the US notion of sound science fosters the need for a high standard of scientific proof in order to enact regulations addressing risk. Conversely, the precautionary principle admits the possibility for regulation to be based on pre-emptive protective measures where, for instance, there is good cause to legislate but insufficient unequivocal evidence per se. Under the precautionary principle, protective measures addressing potentially severe health or environmental risks should not be postponed if there is no scientific certainty.[174] What these two approaches share is scientific evidence for risk assessment as the point of departure. However, the significance of the available evidence is evaluated differently under these two distinct approaches 'in light of differing sensitivities to uncertainties and differing levels of emphasis placed on social and economic matters'.[175]

---

[170] See generally on this subject: Jacqueline Peel, *Science and Risk Regulation in International Law* (Cambridge University Press, 2010); Caroline E. Foster, *Science and the Precautionary Principle in International Courts and Tribunals. Expert Evidence, Burden of Proof and Finality* (Cambridge University Press, 2011).
[171] Peel, above n. 170, p. 65.   [172] Ibid., p. 68.   [173] Ibid., p. 105.   [174] Ibid., p. 168.
[175] Ibid., p. 169.

The dilemma of scientific proof and evidence is palpable in proceedings before international courts and tribunals, including cases which concern environmental protection, not only in the *Whaling in the Antarctic* case. Another, earlier, example is the 1999 *Southern Bluefin Tuna* case.[176] The main issue in that case was the implementation of the 1993 Convention on the Conservation of Southern Bluefin Tuna, concerning a possible experimental fishing programme for bluefin tuna. Lacking such a programme, Japan had adopted a unilateral 'pilot programme' of experimental fishing, without the prior agreement of New Zealand and Australia. The 'pilot programme' took an additional 1,464 tonnes of fish, in excess of Japan's total allowable catch (TAC) allocation of 6,065 tonnes. In 1999, Japan stated its plans to start a full experimental fishing programme with immediate effect. The *Southern Bluefin Tuna* case illustrates the questions of interpretation of scientific data and the approaches to scientific research which may yield different results concerning one particular species. Foster explains that a key issue, in interpreting catch data for the purposes of virtual population analysis, has been how to estimate the fish which were present in areas that had been fished previously but not in a particular year. A focus of the Japanese scientific evaluation had been to estimate the ratio of the mean density of fish in unfished areas to that in fished areas. Depending on the approaches adopted to measuring fish density, the results were completely different.[177] Foster notes that many cases before international courts and tribunals indicate that the judges have a challenging job in evaluating conflicting scientific evidence presented by the parties.[178]

The work of the IWC entails complex issues of scientific data and, in general, the application of science in the context of a mutual lack of cooperation and confidence. No doubt science is closely linked with politics in the IWC. The problematic relationships between members of

---

[176] *Southern Bluefin Tuna (Australia v. Japan; New Zealand v. Japan)*, (2000) 119 ILR 508.
[177] Foster, above n. 170. A very important case on the use of experts (albeit not concerning living resources) was *Case Concerning Pulp Mills on the River Uruguay*, above n. 111, see Joint Dissenting Opinion of Judges Al-Khasawneh and Simma, www.icj-cij.org/docket/files/135/15879.pdf, last accessed 24 December 2014.
[178] Foster, above n. 170, p. 84. In the *Pulp Mills* case (above n. 111), Judges Al-Khasawneh and Simma observed that experts 'would be drawn into questions of legal interpretation through their involvement in the application of legal terms'. However, it is up to the adjudicative agency, in discharging its judicial function, to 'interpret legal terms, to pronounce on questions of law, to perform the legal categorisation of factual issues, and to carry out assessments relating to the burden of proof', para. 12, Joint Dissenting Opinion of Judges Al-Khasawneh and Simma, above n. 177.

the IWC do not leave much hope for solving the impasse in which this body has been for a very long time. It cannot be said, as emphasised earlier in this chapter, that the Judgment in the *Whaling* case solved all contentious problems pertaining to the functioning of the IWC; but, at least in relation to scientific whaling, it gave some guidance for the future. However, it is considered that the important aspect of the ICJ Judgment is that it was the first time that an independent body, not the IWC, made an assessment of scientific whaling by Japan. The ruling is a condemnation of an 'intractably mired process used by the IWC Scientific Committee', while reviewing and discussing scientific programmes, which never ended in an agreement 'on either endorsement or condemnation of a scientific whaling programme'.[179]

The post-Judgment developments both in Japan and in the IWC are not very straightforward and are quite confusing. The 18 April 2014 statement of the Minister of Agriculture, Forestry and Fisheries of Japan that 'Japan has confirmed its policy of the resumption of commercial whaling, by conducting research whaling' (which was reaffirmed by the Prime Minister), clearly indicates that Japan has not abandoned its aspirations for the resumption of commercial whaling, even if they are limited in scope and confined to one whale species, expecting that at some point in the future the Moratorium on commercial whaling will be lifted. Such expectations are strongly supported by cultural arguments. It can be presumed that the resumption of commercial whaling will not be supported by other State Members of the IWC, among them not only the two litigants in the ICJ case, but also a very strong Latin American group. Such a situation will lead to further tensions and mutual distrust.

---

[179] Clapham, above n. 169, 239. According to Clapham, discussions and reports by the SC, with the full presence of Japan, included evasive formulations: 'Some members felt . . . In contrast others disagreed.'

4

Cultural diversity

Introduction

Whaling raises questions beyond merely that of the law, given that it is so inextricably linked to, among other things, the concept of cultural diversity – a concept that is of great importance to other disciplines, including that of social anthropology. The present chapter is devoted mainly to those legal issues that are often argued from the standpoint of cultural diversity. To this end, the chapter will give some degree of consideration to the chief anthropological questions that arise. The concept of cultural diversity (or cultural identity) within the context of grounds to justify whaling is most frequently analysed and discussed in relation to indigenous whaling, given that this is a category of whaling that is outside the scope of the current IWC Moratorium on commercial whaling. (On cultural diversity in relation to indigenous peoples, see Chapter 7.) However, there is also another pertinent aspect of whaling that is often neglected, relating to Japanese, Norwegian, Icelandic and Faroese whaling, which States claim that their engagement in whaling, and their consumption of whale products, is an expression of their national identities. Therefore, when juxtaposed to the practices of other nations, their whaling customs are considered as an expression of their cultural diversity. There will be no definite answers given, as cultural diversity is a complex and divisive issue, not least due to its highly discursive and indeterminate nature. There is also a further related contentious issue that compounds the complexity of the issues relating to whaling, namely, that of animal rights, that is often juxtaposed against rights to cultural diversity in the whaling debate, and which will be discussed in Chapter 5. This chapter therefore will be devoted to the often neglected issue of cultural diversity relating to non-indigenous people in relation to whaling.

4.1 General outline

This section deals with general issues of cultural diversity, such as its meaning, what its elements are, and the context in which it is applied. The section is, however, more of an overview of pertinent questions than an in-depth analysis of the concept, which indeed has already been widely researched and written about.[1] In this context, it would be outside the scope of the present chapter to dwell in detail on the controversies that relate to the tensions between universal standards and particular assertions of culture.[2]

It was in the Universal Declaration of Human Rights (UDHR)[3] (Article 27(1)) that the right 'freely to participate in the cultural life of the community' was first asserted. However, this right has been the subject of a wide variety of interpretations.[4] It has been claimed that the meaning of this right, in a somewhat elitist reading, related to high culture (the 'high arts' and *belles lettres*), and that, according to this reading, the role of the State was to safeguard the masterpieces of art rather than the specific way of life or the traditions of communities, or such matters as religion and languages that are fundamental to the expression of minority identity.[5] Again, in the 1966 International

---

[1] See numerous publications of Will Kymlicka on multiculturalism that also deal with cultural diversity: such as *Multicultural Odysseys: Navigating the New International Politics of Diversity* (Oxford University Press, 2007); *Politics in the Vernacular: Nationalism, Multiculturalism and Citizenship* (Oxford University Press, 2001); *Multicultural Citizenship: A Liberal Theory of Minority Rights* (Oxford University Press, 1995). See also Alexandra Xanthaki, 'Multiculturalism and International Law: Discussing Universal Standards', *Human Rights Quarterly* 32 (2010), 21–48; S. James Anaya, 'International Human Rights and Indigenous Peoples: The Move Toward the Multicultural State', *Arizona Journal of International & Comparative Law* 21 (2004), 9–34; Alejandro Fuentes, 'Cultural Diversity and Indigenous Peoples' Land Claims. Argumentative Dynamics and Jurisprudential Approach in the Americas', PhD dissertation, http://rwi.lu.se/wp-content/uploads/2012/08/Alejandro-Fuentes-doctoral-thesis.pdf, last accessed 20 December 2014.

[2] See, for example, Hilary Charlesworth, 'Human Rights and the UNESCO Memory of the World Programme', in Michele Langfield, William Logan and Máiréd Craith (eds.), *Cultural Diversity, Heritage and Human Rights* (New York: Routledge, 2010), p. 25. See also 1993 Vienna Declaration and Programme of Action Adopted by the World Conference on Human Rights in Vienna on 25 June 1993, www.ohchr.org/EN/ProfessionalInterest/Pages/Vienna.aspx, last accessed 24 December 2014.

[3] Universal Declaration of Human Rights (UDHR) General Assembly Resolution 217(III), 10 December 1948, www.un-documents.net/a3r217a.htm, last accessed 24 December 2014.

[4] Athanasios Yupsanis, 'The Meaning of "Culture" in Article 15(1)(a) of the ICESCR – Positive Aspects of the CESCR's General Comment No. 21 for the Safeguarding of Minority Cultures', GYIL 55 (2012), 345–83, 350.

[5] Ibid., 350.

Covenant on Economic, Social and Cultural Rights (ICESCR),[6] a similar, yet distinct right was asserted, namely: the right of everyone 'to take part in cultural life' (Article 15(1)(a)).[7]

To define culture is not without its complexities; let alone to define it in relation to cultural diversity. As was noted in 1952, there were sixty-four definitions of culture employed by anthropologists.[8] The starting point is the definition adopted by the United Nations Educational, Scientific and Cultural Organization (UNESCO), a body which has made fundamental pronouncements concerning cultural diversity, has sponsored declarations and conventions in this regard, and has adopted a different approach in its definition of culture to that above-referred. The UNESCO definition rejected the 'elitist' notion of culture and, aided by social anthropology,[9] arrived at the following definition of cultural diversity, namely, as being 'the whole complex of distinctive spiritual, material, intellectual and emotional features that characterize a society or social group. It includes not only the arts and letters, but also modes of life, the fundamental rights of the human being, value systems, traditions and beliefs.'[10]

This definition also includes ways of social organisation, for instance how individuals live together. The Declaration, in particular its elements of culture, such as 'way of life', 'modes of life' and 'ways of living together', has to be read together with Article 1(1) of the 1996 Declaration of Principles of International Cultural Cooperation, which states that 'each culture has a dignity and value which must be respected'. Such phrasing of the definition of culture is of fundamental importance for minority cultures, as it presumes the obligation of a State to provide necessary conditions for their protection and preservation.[11] Fuentes explains that, under this definition, culture has at least two different aspects, covering, on the one hand, the individual and, on the other, the societal (that is to say, those aspects that pertain to social groups). From an individual point of view, culture, amongst other things, is a

---

[6] International Covenant on Economic, Social and Cultural Rights (ICESCR), 16 December 1966, 993 UNTS 3.

[7] On this, see Yupsanis, above n. 4.   [8] Ibid., 349.   [9] Ibid., 351.

[10] UNESCO, Mexico City Declaration on Cultural Policies, adopted at the World Conference on Cultural Policies, Mexico, 6 August 1982, http://portal.unesco.org/culture/en/files/12762/11295421661mexico_en.pdf/mexico_en.pdf, last accessed 24 December 2014; 1996 Declaration of Principles of International Cultural Cooperation, http://portal.unesco.org/en/ev.php-URL_ID=13147&URL_DO=DO_TOPIC&URL_SECTION=201.html, last accessed 18 January 2015.

[11] Yupsanis, above n. 4, 352.

source of meaning about life, and equips a human being with the necessary tools to reflect upon herself or himself and to take rational decisions. From a societal point of view, culture provides a shared/common meaningful framework, which allows human beings to construct their commonness and togetherness, and to build common supportive societal structures which are necessary for the organisation of human society.[12]

The anthropological definition of culture was further endorsed by General Comment 21 of the ICESCR,[13] according to which cultural rights are essential for the 'maintenance of human dignity and positive social interaction between individuals and communities in a diverse and multicultural world' (first paragraph). General Comment 21 (thirteenth paragraph) adheres to a broad notion of culture, and includes in this definition the following:

> The Committee considers that culture, for the purpose of implementing article 15(1)(a), encompasses, *inter alia*, ways of life, language, oral and written literature, music and song, non-verbal communication, religion or belief systems, rites and ceremonies, sport and games, methods of production or technology, natural and man-made environments, food, clothing and shelter and the arts, customs and traditions through which individuals, groups of individuals and communities express their humanity and the meaning they give to their existence, and build their world view representing their encounter with the external forces affecting their lives.

An important feature of the definition of culture adopted by the ICESCR is its dynamic character. Following the anthropological approach to culture, determining what practices are encompassed by the notion of culture within the context of the ICESCR is not a task frozen in time, but is, rather, a dynamic process that is not aimed at setting or promoting any one type or set of values over others, as somehow being fit for all individuals in homogenous societies. The ICESCR also stressed that social phenomena such as migration, globalisation, integration and assimilation have brought individuals together at a time when they also strive to maintain their distinct identities.[14] Yupsanis notes that the

---

[12] Fuentes, above n. 1, 17. See also Kymlicka, *Multicultural Citizenship*, above n. 1, p. 76.

[13] Committee on Economic, Social and Cultural Rights, General Comment No. 21, Right of everyone to take part in cultural life (art. 15, para. 1(a)), UN Doc. E/C.12/GC/21 (2009), www1.umn.edu/humanrts/gencomm/escgencom21.html, last accessed 24 December 2014.

[14] Yupsanis, above n. 4, 356.

ICESCR's approach to the notion of culture effectively departs from the essentialist approach in which culture is seen as a set of hermetically 'closed compartments and isolated manifestations'.[15] According to Yupsanis, '[t]his evolutionary and dynamic understanding of culture seems to be the most important contribution of social anthropology to international law's conceptions of cultural life, inherently rejecting essentialist views of cultural purity'.[16] Such an approach supports the idea that multiculturalism helps to integrate and strengthen society as a whole, rather than to fragment it.[17]

The Human Rights Committee (HRC) of the International Covenant on Civil and Political Rights (ICCPR),[18] similarly to UNESCO, departed from a narrow elitist understanding of culture and adopted a broad reading that includes in its meaning traditional activities such as fishing and hunting. There are several cases in which the HRC has applied a wider reading of the notion of culture.

Furthermore, there are several UNESCO-related international law instruments dealing with culture. Mention must also be made of the 1989 UNESCO Recommendation on Safeguarding of Traditional Culture and Folklore, which contains the recommendation that

> Member States bring this Recommendation to the attention of the authorities, departments or bodies responsible for matters relating to the safeguarding of folklore and to the attention of the various organizations or institutions concerned with folklore, and encourage their contacts with appropriate international organizations dealing with the safeguarding of the folklore of sub-national groups.[19]

In 2005, UNESCO sponsored a Convention on the Protection and Promotion of the Diversity of Cultural Expressions.[20] This Convention

---

[15] Ibid., 356.   [16] Ibid., 356.   [17] Ibid., 356.

[18] Article 27, General Comment No. 23, adopted on 6 April 1994, Human Rights Committee (Fiftieth session, 1994), Compilation of General Comments and General Recommendations Adopted by Human Rights Treaty Bodies, UN Doc. HRI/GEN/1/Rev.1 at 38 (1994), www1.umn.edu/humanrts/gencomm/hrcom23.htm, last accessed 24 December 2014; see also Xanthaki, above n. 1, at 27. *Bernard Ominayak, Chief of the Lubicon Lake Band* v. *Canada*, Communication No. 167/1984, CCPR/C/38/D/167/1984. www1.umn.edu/humanrts/undocs/session45/167-1984.htm, last accessed 24 December 2014.

[19] 1989 UNESCO Recommendation on Safeguarding of Traditional Culture and Folklore, http://portal.unesco.org/en/ev.php-URL_ID=31038&URL_DO=DO_TOPIC&URL_SEC TION=201.html, last accessed 26 December 2014.

[20] 2005 UNESCO Convention on the Protection and Promotion of the Diversity of Cultural Expressions, 2440 UNTS 311.

plainly adheres to the anthropological (that is to say, to the wider) definition of culture. Article 1 of the Convention supports, amongst other things: the protection and promotion of the diversity of cultural expressions; efforts to foster inter-culturality in order to develop cultural interaction in the spirit of building bridges among peoples; and the recognition of the distinctive nature of cultural activities, goods and services as vehicles of identity, values and meaning.

> The objectives of the Convention are to be achieved in conformity with the Charter of the United Nations, the principles of international law and universally recognized human rights instruments, and the Parties reaffirm their sovereign right to formulate and implement their cultural policies and to adopt measures to protect and promote the diversity of cultural expressions and to strengthen international cooperation to achieve the purposes of this Convention.
>
> (Article 5)

As in the other relevant UNESCO instruments concerning cultural diversity, dignity plays a fundamental role in recognising cultures of minorities and indigenous peoples (Article 2(3)). There are also other instruments sponsored by UNESCO that, generally, deal with culture, but that also relate to particular groups such as indigenous peoples. Mention must be made of the 1972 UNESCO Convention Concerning the Protection of the World Cultural and Natural Heritage under which tangible items of indigenous cultural and natural heritage may be listed (with their free, prior and informed consent).[21] Furthermore, there is the 2003 UNESCO Convention for the Safeguarding of the Intangible Cultural Heritage, in which States determine what will be added to the so-called Representative List of the Intangible Cultural Heritage of Humanity. This Convention appears to be of particular importance for indigenous peoples, although it has been subjected to certain criticism relating to its weak implementation scheme.[22]

---

[21] 1972 UNESCO Convention Concerning the Protection of the World Cultural and Natural Heritage, 1037 UNTS 151. See also UN Expert Mechanism on the Rights of Indigenous Peoples; Frederico Lenzerini, 'Cultural Rights and Cultural Heritage', 2012 ILA Final Report of the Group on Indigenous Rights, 1–31, at p. 23, www.ila-hq. org/download, last accessed 24 December 2014.

[22] 2003 UNESCO Convention for the Safeguarding of the Intangible Cultural Heritage, 2368 UNTS 3; Siegfried Wiessner, 'Culture and Rights of Indigenous Peoples', in Ana Filipa Vrdoljak (ed.), *The Cultural Dimension of Human Rights. Collected Courses of the Academy of European Law* (Oxford University Press, 2013), p. 134.

As mentioned earlier, the ICESCR's right to culture includes the right to participation.[23] There are several other human rights instruments which also recognise the right to culture, including the International Convention on the Elimination of All Forms of Racial Discrimination (CERD), Article 5(e)(vi);[24] the Convention on the Rights of the Child (CRC), Article 31;[25] and the ICCPR, Article 27.[26] Will Kymlicka has observed that multiculturalism is never 'risk free, but where these fortunate circumstances exist, it becomes *la belle risque* – a modest but manageable risk worth taking in the pursuit of fairer and a more inclusive society'.[27] Kymlicka has noted that in some societies (perhaps less so in Western democracies), there has been to a certain degree a retreat from multiculturalism directed at certain groups, and that there has been a 'reassertion of the most assimilative and exclusionary policies'.[28] This observation may have implications for non-indigenous whaling justified on cultural diversity grounds.

Whaling as a practice linked to, or defended on the basis of, cultural diversity is highly controversial even in the, arguably, clearer case of whaling on the part of indigenous peoples. An even more complex and emotional problem arises in relation to whaling in Norway, Iceland and Japan, as well as the less well-known hunting of pilot whales by the Faroe Islands, where it can also be argued that it constitutes an exercise of the right to cultural diversity. As one author noted, 'cultural relativism surfaces here'.[29] The anti-whaling lobby disseminates the idea that the call for the abolition of whaling reflects 'a new, global

---

[23] Xanthaki, above n. 1, 26.

[24] 1966 International Convention on the Elimination of All Forms of Racial Discrimination (CERD), 660 UNTS 195, 'The right to equal participation in cultural activities'.

[25] 1989 Convention on the Rights of the Child (CRC), 1577 UNTS 3, 44, '1. States Parties recognize the right of the child to rest and leisure, to engage in play and recreational activities appropriate to the age of the child and to participate freely in cultural life and the arts. 2. States Parties shall respect and promote the right of the child to participate fully in cultural and artistic life and shall encourage the provision of appropriate and equal opportunities for cultural, artistic, recreational and leisure activities.'

[26] 1966 International Covenant on Civil and Political Rights (ICCPR), 999 UNTS 171, 'In those States in which ethnic, religious or linguistic minorities exist, persons belonging to such minorities shall not be denied the right, in community with the other members of their group, to enjoy their own culture, to profess and practise their own religion, or to use their own language', http://treaties.un.org/doc/Publication/UNTS/Volume%20999/volume-999-I-14668-English.pdf, last accessed 20 December 2014.

[27] Kymlicka, *Multicultural Odysseys*, above n. 1, p. 21.   [28] Ibid., p. 52.

[29] Peter Stoett, 'Of Whales and People: Normative Theory, Symbolism and the IWC', *Journal of International Wildlife Law and Policy* 8 (2005), 151–75, 167.

consciousness'[30] and, further, that '[t]he Japanese, Norwegians, and Icelanders are the vociferous leaders of a small minority of nation-States'. However, does this, in itself, mean that they are wrong to insist on the practice? 'In the environmental policy world, there are no angels.'[31]

4.2   Cultural diversity and non-indigenous whaling

This section deals with non-native whaling from a cultural diversity standpoint. It includes an analysis of Japanese, Norwegian and Icelandic whaling, and of the Faroe Islands' hunting of pilot whales. The issue of mainstream whaling – that is to say, whaling that is neither indigenous nor conducted in relation to scientific research – has been a thorny and contentious one that has resulted in the overall ban of commercial whaling within the IWC, to which at present there is no solution, considering the intransigent positions of both camps of IWC Member States. It will be of interest, however, to present also arguments that support the right to cultural diversity of non-indigenous peoples, an issue which is frequently neglected and which gives rise to rather negative reactions.

In 1995, ninety-five States adopted the Kyoto Declaration and Plan of Action during the International Conference on the Sustainable Contribution of Fisheries to Food Security (hosted by Japan, with technical assistance from the Food and Agriculture Organization (FAO)). The sixth paragraph of the Declaration calls for an 'increase in the respect and understanding of social, economic and cultural differences among States and regions in the use of living resources, especially cultural diversity in dietary habits, consistent with management objectives'.[32]

4.2.1   Japan

Japan's reaction to the imposition of the IWC Moratorium and its scientific whaling was analysed earlier. This section deals with Japanese coastal whaling supported on the part of Japan on the basis of its connection to cultural diversity.[33] This chapter will deal primarily with

[30] Ibid., 167.   [31] Ibid., 167.

[32] 1995 Kyoto Declaration and Plan of Action on Sustainable Contribution of Fisheries and Food Security, www.fao.org/docrep/006/ac442e/AC442e3.htm, last accessed 24 December 2014.

[33] See, on this subject, Keiko Hirata, 'Why Japan Supports Whaling', *Journal of International Wildlife Law and Policy* 8 (2005), 129–49, 129; David R. Keller and Dan Goodman, 'Straights of Strife: Japanese Whaling, Cultural Relativism, and International

Japanese Small Coastal Whaling (JSCW), which has been the subject matter of many of the IWC's Resolutions, in which concern was expressed about the commercial aspects of this community-based whaling. Japan strongly opposes the prohibition of whaling in general, including coastal whaling. Japan makes its views known at successive IWC meetings. Masayuki Komatsu, the Alternative Commissioner of Japan to the IWC and an official at the Japanese Fisheries Agency, has criticised the United States government on the basis that it promotes the rights of the indigenous peoples (Inuit) of Alaska to whaling, while, at the same time, opposing the Japanese hunt for minke whales under the coastal whaling scheme. Commissioner Komatsu stated at the 2002 IWC meeting: 'Japan is tired of asking year after year for 50 minke whales from an abundant stock for our traditional coastal whalers only to have the United States vote against it; yet we have always supported the Alaskans' taking of almost 280 bowhead whales.'[34] The same situation arose at the 2003 meeting.

As Hirata observes: 'the schism between Japan and the anti-whaling camp at the IWC has widened substantially over the years'.[35] Japanese JSCW whaling has been significantly downscaled since the imposition of the Moratorium. There are only eight small firms engaged in coastal whaling, hunting for species that are, according to Japan, outside the jurisdiction of the IWC, namely, Baird's beaked whale and pilot whale. Coastal whaling is a small operation; before the Moratorium on whaling there were only nine whaling boats in operation. Since the Moratorium,

Politics', in Peggy Connolly, Becky Cox-White, David R. Keller and Martin G. Leever (eds.), *Ethics in Action: A Case-Based Approach* (Malden, Mass.: Wiley-Blackwell, 2009); Arne Kalland and Brian Moeran, *Japanese Whaling, End of an Area* (New York: Routledge) 1993 (reprinted); Brian Moeran, 'The Cultural Construction of Value. "Subsistence", "Commercial" and Other Terms in the Debate about Whaling', *MAST (Maritime Anthropological Studies)* 5 (1992), 1–16; see, in depth on Japan and whaling, Judith Wouters, 'Japan and the IWC: Investigating Japan's Whaling Policy Objectives', Master's Dissertation, University of Leuven, 2008–9, www.scriptiebank.be/sites/default/files/e4c466ef30d18f4c25bfeaeb883f2058.pdf, in particular pp. 103–19, where the author critically evaluated all arguments by Japanese scholars and politicians regarding cultural identity and whaling. Last accessed 14 January 2015.

[34] Cited in Hirata, above n. 33, 137. Note, however, that in 2007, at the Conference for the Normalization of the International Whaling Commission, Working Group 3 on Cultural Diversity recommended that Japan's small-type coastal whalers should be permitted to catch minke whales. Conference on Normalizing the IWC – Tokyo, 13–15 February 2007, IWC/M08/INFO 2, www.jfa.maff.go.jp/j/whale/w_document/pdf/iwc_houkoku.pdf, last accessed 11 July 2015.

[35] Hirata, above n. 33, 138.

only five whaling boats have been operational. The various enterprises have paired up and shared vessels in order to avoid collapse. These enterprises are bound by annual quotas issued by the Japanese government, and their whaling activities are monitored by the government. Hirata is of the view that this small-scale coastal whaling has not attracted the anti-whaling lobby's attention despite the controversy surrounding the extent of the IWC's jurisdiction over small and medium cetaceans and over waters within the coastal State's jurisdiction. However, coastal whaling has often been discussed in the IWC's forum due to the claim of Japan that whaling connected to cultural diversity is comparable to indigenous whaling, and therefore Japan's request for quotas to be set for minke whales for coastal whaling is legitimate. Japan argued that its small fishing villages depend on whaling for subsistence and survival, to the same extent as may the Inuit peoples.[36] Therefore, the Japanese IWC Commissioner argued that expanding whaling opportunities for these villages would help diminish their suffering.[37] Small-scale whaling has also received the support of Western scholars, especially when it 'secures historically-based practices of socially-defined human groups that value whaling activities on a multidimensional basis'.[38] In that respect, coastal whaling has also attracted significant international attention. People living in such coastal villages claim that they should be allowed large quotas to hunt for Baird's beaked whales in order to continue their ancestors' tradition.

The Japanese are of the view that the ban of whaling and consequently on eating whale meat is a form of cultural imperialism on the part of the West due to a lack of understanding of Japanese customs and culture. From Japan's point of view, there is no real inherent difference between the dietary habits of different human cultures – be it the eating of whale meat or the eating of sardines or beef.[39] The Japanese have used also the 'cultural rights' discourse in relation to their right to eat whale meat. Hirata explains that Japanese views on whaling are based on three underlying perspectives: the belief that the Japanese have been eating whale meat for thousands of years and that

[36] The following villages depend on whaling: Abashiri, Ayukawa, Wadaura, Taiji, Ukushima and Arikawa. See Kalland and Moeran, above n. 33, 18–42.
[37] Keller and Goodman, above n. 33, p. 393.
[38] Oran R. Young, 'Subsistence, Sustainability, and the Sea Mammals: Reconstructing the International Whaling Regime', Ocean & Coastal Management 23 (1994), 117–27, 122.
[39] Keller and Goodman, above n. 33, p. 393.

they have a distinct and unique whale-eating culture ('*gyoshoku bunka*') that is not shared with every nation; that it is more appropriate to approach the consumption of whale meat, while undoubtedly relating to a mammal, as being more akin to the consumption of fish – that it should not, thus, be loaded with the sensibilities that may be attached to the consumption of large sea mammals; and that Western objections are essentially cultural imperialist interference in Japanese cultural identity and diversity.[40]

Hirata explains, however, that whale meat eating, while it existed previously, had not been commonplace in Japan until after the Second World War, due to the necessity to feed the population. This assertion, however, is not supported by the work of other authors, such as Kalland and Moeran. These authors describe a long-standing cultural tradition of the whale distribution in villages, based on the ritual of reciprocity that continues to be practised when the first whale of the hunting season has been caught.[41] The long-standing tradition of Japanese whale meat eating has also been confirmed by other scholars, such as Iino and Goodman, who assert that the Japanese have been eating it for over 2,000 years, and that large cetaceans have been hunted for over 400 years.[42] Kalland and Moeran also mention that, for centuries, all parts of the whale – blubber, skin and cartilage – have been used. Each and every whale-hunting village developed its own whale-eating tradition and practices. According to these authors, food has great symbolic value in Japan, and 'cuisine is one of the strongest markers of social identity in Japan' where there are numerous examples of such 'food identity'.[43] For example, the coastal towns of Abashiri and Ayukawa specialise in minke meat, Wada in Baird's beaked whales and Taiji in pilot whales and dolphins.[44]

The downscaling of small-scale Japanese whaling has also adversely affected local tourism.[45] Whale meat was consumed in these villages in connection with the most important religious events, and whales also

---

[40] Hirata, above n. 33, 141–4.   [41] Kalland and Moeran, above n. 33, p. 143.

[42] Yasuo Iino and Dan Goodman, 'Japan's Position in the International Whaling Commission', in William C. G. Burns and Alexander Gillespie (eds.), *The Future of Cetaceans in a Changing World* (Ardsley, NY: Transnational Publishers, 2003), p. 7.

[43] Kalland and Moeran, above n. 33, p. 147.

[44] Milton M. R. Freeman, 'Culture-Based Conflict in the International Whaling Commission: The Case of Japanese Small-Type Whaling', in Burns and Gillespie, above n. 42, p. 50.

[45] Ibid., p. 53.

have considerable cultural (including religious) symbolism. For instance, there are members of those communities who believe that whaling is connected to their sensibilities about how to be on good terms with the Shinto deities, their ancestors' souls and the souls of deceased whales in order to make a safe and financially successful journey.[46] Since whales have for centuries provided a source of food and employment, they are equated with prosperity and security, particularly in coastal whaling towns. Several cultural events, including ceremonies (both religious and secular), take place, such as 'kujira kuyo' and 'kujira matsuri'.[47] Some ceremonies are aimed at ensuring a peaceful repose for the souls of whales hunted by villagers in the past, and these customs may be seen as integral to the communities that practise them, given that these practices have not stopped after whaling ceased in those areas. Women pray at shrines for whalers' safety, for a good catch and so on, and Shinto priests officiate at purification ceremonies on whaling boats. There are also important Buddhist ceremonies for the souls of hunted whales and for the souls of whalers (seeking forgiveness for taking the lives of whales and for the impact on their karma for having taken the lives of whales).

Unlike other nations, the Japanese utilise all parts of the whale (including fat, soft tissue and cartilaginous parts). According to some accounts, the Japanese have been using cetaceans for 6,000 years and the cooking of whale meat features in the first cookery book in Japan, the *Ryori Mono-gator*, which appeared in 1643.[48] The basic philosophy concerning the eating of whale meat in Japan is 'Geiniku Choumikata': that is to say, making good use of the whale's meat – the efficient consequent use of a life destroyed.[49] In earlier times, whaling was conducted by hand-held harpoons (the 'tsukitori-ho' method). In the seventeenth century many other methods were developed, such as nets and the use of boats (the 'amitori' method). Such diversified methods of capture require skilled manpower. The shore-based factories manufactured various products (including food and whale-based insecticide for rice fields). In addition, artisans were employed to maintain boats. In that respect, there was a

---

[46] See Milton Freeman et al., *Inuit, Whaling, and Sustainability (Contemporary Native American Communities)* (Lanham Md.: Altamira Press, 1998), pp. 149, 150. See also on that Iino and Goodman, above n. 42, p. 7.

[47] Freeman, above n. 44, p. 48.

[48] Jun Akamine, 'Intangible Food Heritage: Dynamics of Whale Foodways in the Age of Whale Meat Rarity', in *Senri Ethnological Studies, No. 84, Anthropological Studies of Whaling* (Osaka: National Museum of Ethnology, 2013), p. 214.

[49] Ibid., p. 223.

whole raft of individuals, whalers, artisans, manufacturers and so on who were involved in, and depended on, the local whaling industry that dominated the local economy, thus giving rise, in the Middle Ages, to the use of the term 'whaling towns' to denote those coastal communities.[50] After the Japanese whaling grounds were discovered, Japanese small-type whaling continued and most of the meat obtained that way was consumed locally.

A significant aspect of small-type whaling in Japan is its social dimension. Minke boat crews constitute a recognised social unit and they continue to socialise outside the whaling season. The whaling season lasts only six months; however, the boat owner continues to pay the crew a partial wage during the non-whaling season, in order to support crew social solidarity throughout the year.[51] The strong cultural aspect of whaling cannot be underestimated. In whaling towns, there is a symbolic link between whale meat consumption and longevity, good health and vitality. This places whale meat firmly in local food and ceremonial culture. There is also a gift ceremony linked to giving whale meat. In 1987, about 1,500 bottles of sake were distributed in Ayukawa during the minke whale First Catch ('hatsuryo') ceremonies in anticipation of a return gift of whale meat.[52]

Some of the whale meat is exchanged for money that is also assessed as culturally appropriate behaviour, not primarily aimed at economic gain. This, however, may lead to adverse perceptions of small-type Japanese whaling as somehow being essentially a commercial endeavour and therefore banned under the terms of the Moratorium.[53] Against this, it was explained by one of Wada's residents: '[t]hrough the meat gift-giving custom, we have a complex social networking arrangement. This area has a system that depends on forty whales at the moment, but if the quota disappears, so does our social system.'[54]

Furthermore, the Japanese have a long tradition of equating whales with fish. For instance, at the level of semantics, the Japanese script symbol used to denote the notion 'whale' contains a component that denotes the notion 'fish'. As to the issue of cultural imperialism referred to earlier, the Japanese public is resentful of any Western interference in its cultural practices regarding the hunting and eating of whales as long as this is done in a sustainable manner. Japan regards this as 'Japan bashing' and considers it particularly hypocritical given the slaughter of

---

[50] Freeman, above n. 44, p. 41.   [51] Ibid., p. 43.   [52] Ibid., p. 44.   [53] Ibid., p. 47.
[54] Cited in ibid., p. 48.

cattle and other mammals such as kangaroos in parts of the Western world. Some Japanese view the attitude of Westerners towards their whaling as an expression of racism, and that 'white Europeans do not tolerate the culturally unique cuisines of non-white people'.[55] The grievance concerning Western imperialism strengthens the attitude of the Japanese to resist Western approaches to their whaling customs. However, Hirata aptly observes that these views fail to take into account the fact that Norwegians and Icelanders are also criticised for hunting and eating whales.

Iino and Goodman explain the reasons why the Japanese are so adamant about the right to whaling, notwithstanding that whaling does not contribute significantly to national GDP and that whale meat no longer constitutes a significant part of the diet of most Japanese. The answer given is very succinct: they say that it is a 'matter of principles'.[56] The most fundamental of these principles are that marine resources should be managed in accordance with scientific principles; that the Parties to the ICRW should fulfil their obligations in good faith; and that respect for cultural diversity is an important aspect of international cooperation. In the view of Japan, by ignoring these principles, the majority of the Parties to the ICRW have imperilled the world community's ability to manage its resources in a responsible manner, and the IWC should return to its functions as defined by the ICRW.[57] Japan argues that there is a racialist undercurrent to Western attitudes towards, and opposition to, Japan's whaling that amounts to cultural imperialism through the imposition of Western cultural values on Japanese society.[58]

One of the unresolved legal issues is the nature of Japanese small-type whaling. Freeman regards Japan's coastal whaling as a combination of indigenous and commercial whaling.[59] It may be considered that the concept of indigenous whaling has been applied in a selective and inconsistent manner in the IWC, and that its relationship to commercial whaling has not been very clearly defined. Indeed, the IWC has never consistently dealt with the question of money transactions in subsistence whaling. It was accepted in the case of Greenland and Russia that their indigenous peoples may buy and sell meat, on condition that it be used

[55] Freeman, above n. 44, p. 42.   [56] Iino and Goodman, above n. 42, p. 8.
[57] Ibid., p. 9.
[58] M. Komatsu and S. Misaki, *Whales and the Japanese: How We Have Come to Live in Harmony with the Bounty of the Sea* (Tokyo: Institute of Cetacean Research, 2003), p. 32.
[59] Freeman, above n. 44, p. 53.

locally, which term, according to Freeman, has not been defined precisely in the IWC. Freeman further argues that aboriginal whaling is exempted from the Moratorium due to the dependence of these culturally defined peoples on whales and whale products 'for cultural, religious, ceremonial, nutritional, and economic reasons'.[60] The view may be expressed that the small-type whalers of Japan share the same characteristics with the indigenous peoples of Greenland and Russia. However, Freeman notes that the dependency on whales and whale products is subject to a different interpretation by the IWC. He argues that the 'dependence' on whaling by communities in Japan cannot be easily linked with 'dependence' of indigenous peoples in Russia, whose lifestyles are significantly at variance with those of communities enjoying a comfortable living in Japan. However, Freeman states that small-type whaling communities share common cultural traditions with aboriginal peoples who engage in whaling, such as an effective and unbroken connection with the past, Buddhist and Shinto religious traditions linked to whaling, whaling-related festivals, payment in whale meat by the whaling crews, and whaling techniques.[61] The use of cash for payment of wages, fees and taxes had existed in feudal times, as did whaling festivals. Moreover, the avoidance of paying fees and taxes as a means to maximise profit on the part of whalers would be in conflict with Confucian obligations that exist in Japan, aimed at maintaining and preserving matters such as family enterprise (*seigyou*) and traditions, 'a powerful cultural imperative, implying a high degree of moral obligation'.[62]

As observed above, in general the Japanese argue that they have a spiritual link with animals they use for food and say a special prayer before the meal expressing gratitude for these animals ('*itadakimasu*').[63] It may be said that, in light of the above, the IWC practice of focusing exclusively on any commercial aspect of small-type whaling (and concerning whaling in general) in Japan fails to take into account the bigger picture, as it misses the cultural and religious dimensions of small-type Japanese whaling.[64]

---

[60] Ibid., p. 54.   [61] Ibid., p. 55.

[62] Ibid., pp. 55–6 and 61, citing Theodore C. Bestor, 'Socio-Economic Implications of Zero Catch Limit on Distribution Channels and Related Activities in Hokkaido and Myiagi Prefectures, Japan', IWC/41/SE1 (1989), 77. It must be noted, however, that due to the lack of whale meat at the markets in Japan, as an effect of the Moratorium, part of the sales of minke and beaked whales moved from the local market to a wider distribution.

[63] Komatsu and Misaki, above n. 58, pp. 154, 155.   [64] Freeman et al., above n. 46, p. 574.

4.2.2   Iceland

This section deals with the less well-known issue of cultural diversity and whaling in Iceland.[65] The approach to whales from the point of view of environmentalists and Icelandic fishers (whalers) is very different. Whales are a symbol of nature for many environmentalists, whilst Icelandic fishers have far less romantic views of these marine mammals. As Einarsson explains, the Icelandic small-scale fishermen view animals and nature in a utilitarian and anthropocentric manner. There is no doubt that when the interests of whales and fishermen conflict, 'it is evident in the fishermen's anthropocentric view that the animals have to be sacrificed'.[66] Iceland's attitude towards opposing environmentalists propagating the elimination of whaling, and the ban on whaling, evolved, no doubt, from commercial considerations and a resistance to capitulate to pressure from outside actors such as other IWC States. Iceland opposes the IWC Moratorium, which it regards as constituting a limitation on its sovereignty, including how it determines its own fisheries policy (which, from Iceland's standpoint, includes whaling).[67] The anti-whaling lobby argues that the whaling industry is unfit to act as custodian of the world's whales given that it is motivated by another objective: namely, the pursuit of profit. On the other hand, whalers categorise environmentalists as driven by emotions, irrational, sentimental and naive about the necessity of hunting animals for food.[68]

The whole attitude towards whales in Iceland seems to be entirely different from that in non-whaling Western States where, symbolism and totemic significance of whales aside, the issue of whaling is not part of the usual politics or of public debate. For Icelanders, on the other hand, whales constitute an integral part of life with implications for their sense of national identity.[69] Fishers in Iceland see whales as predators, and there are numerous stories of whales sinking boats. In that respect,

[65] This section is based on Niels Einarsson, *Culture, Conflict and Crises in the Icelandic Fisheries*, Uppsala Studies in Cultural Anthropology No. 48 (Uppsala Universitet, 2011).
[66] Ibid., p. 55.
[67] Anne Brydon, 'In the Eye of the Guest: Icelandic Nationalist Discourse and the Whaling Issue', http://digitool.library.mcgill.ca/view/action/singleViewer.do?dvs=1374935032269~27&loca le=en_GB&show_metadata=false&VIEWER_URL=/view/action/singleViewer.do?&DELI VERY_RULE_ID=6&adjacency=N&application=DIGITOOL-3&frameId=1&usePid1= true&usePid2=true 237, 342, 372, last accessed 20 December 2014.
[68] Ibid., 370.
[69] Niels Einarsson, 'A Sea of Images: Fishers, Whalers, and Environmentalists', in *Culture*, above n. 65, p. 81.

whales are animals that compete with, and deprive, fishers of herring and other fish.[70] They are thought to consume millions of tonnes of fish, while fishers have to face increasing quotas that limit their catch. Icelandic fishers claim that, since the imposition of the Moratorium on whaling, there is a large (and growing) number of whales that endangers their livelihood, and that, therefore, they should be justified in treating whales as pests. Einarsson has observed that: '[n]ot only are fishers forbidden to hunt whales, but they also must accept that whales may literally be eating away their basis for subsistence'.[71] Therefore, fishers' notion of whales is formed by what is thought of their role in the ecosystem and how they influence fish stocks and consequently the livelihood of fishers.[72] Animals are seen as competitors for scarce resources.

Einarsson also notes that the attitudes of fishers towards whales are based on their everyday engagement with nature. He explains that when animals and humans compete for food, particularly when utilitarian and anthropocentric views of the ecosystem dominate, animals are often treated as pests.[73] Einarsson challenges the perception of whalers as brutes who are 'less than human'.[74] To this effect, he poses a question:

> But what alternatives are there for people like Icelandic fishers apart from a utilitarian, human-centered view of nature? Isn't species-ism and the exclusion of some animals from the moral community almost a necessary prerequisite for fishing? To Icelandic fishers the arguments of Western conservationists who see themselves as 'standing in for' nature ... are not valid because they are not based on the practitioner's way of knowing the realities of fishing. It is totally alien to fishers' anthropocentric cultural model of the 'Great Chain of Being' when animals are given moral standing on a level with humans.[75]

The core, therefore, of the understanding of the attitudes of Icelandic fishers towards whales has to be based on an acceptance of divergent perceptions and images of cetaceans and their role in the livelihood of an Icelandic fisher. It is purely a practitioner's point of view, making their living through whaling.[76] Similarly to Japan, the image of a whale has had a historical meaning since the ninth and tenth centuries. The Icelandic word for windfall or godsend, 'hvalreki', literally means 'stranded whale'. The most interesting observation by Einarsson is that, generally, in Iceland there is no great local demand for whale meat – other than that for consumption in the tourist industry – but rather Icelanders claim

---

[70] Ibid., p. 82.   [71] Ibid., p. 84.   [72] Ibid., p. 84.   [73] Ibid., p. 91.   [74] Ibid., p. 91.
[75] Ibid., p. 91.   [76] Ibid., p. 97.

their right to harvest, which remains the core of Icelandic whaling policy. He also noted that recently the rhetoric has moved away from the right to hunt to the duty to do so in the name of non-discriminatory sustainable use of natural resources, without the exclusion of any animal species. Einarsson notes that '[t]his ethical dimension of duty is an interesting recent development, a new facet of existing discourse and an escalation of the stakes involved'.[77]

4.2.3   Norway

The history of Norwegian whaling is very long and complex, and has partially been covered in the discussion in earlier parts of the present publication. This section is principally devoted to contemporary issues of whaling in Norway and to questions that arise in connection with cultural considerations.[78] Norway continues with commercial whaling, having opted out of the Moratorium. Since the imposition of the Moratorium (1985–6) until 2013 it hunted around 20,000 whales.[79] In Norway, all non-legal discussion concerning whaling focuses on the question of cultural diversity and on the ethics of whaling.

It would be helpful to look at the question of whaling in this State against a general background of the concept of Norwegian organised environmentalism that 'consists of two interrelated anomalies'.[80] One anomaly is that this is a State-friendly society, which trusts State institutions, and where civil society has a close working relationship with governmental bodies. The other anomaly (and this is a very important factor in relation to whaling in Norway) is the local community perspective in which animal rights fail to enter the definition of environmentalism. This particular feature appears to distinguish environmentalism in Norway from that in other States. Therefore, it may be said that 'these interrelated anomalies make the case of Norway unique within international environmentalism'.[81]

---

[77] Ibid., p. 98.
[78] Information from EFTEC, 'Norwegian Use of Whales: Past, Present and Future Trends', Final Report for the Society for the Protection of Animals (WSPA), 2011, www.wspa.org.au/Images/Whaling_Full_report_tcm30-21294.pdf, last assessed 25 December 2014.
[79] See International Whaling Commission, http://iwc.int/table_objection, last accessed 25 December 2014.
[80] Gunnar Grendstad, Per Selle, Kristin Strømsnes and Øystein Bortne, *Unique Environmentalism. A Comparative Perspective* (New York: Springer, 2006), p. 9.
[81] Ibid., p. 9.

Local communities have a very practical view of nature, as designed to serve human beings, similarly to Iceland. The support of local-community based whaling (and seal hunting) is based on an organic way of life, in which the local community is closely connected to nature through its utilisation of resources. Therefore, the support and general opinion in Norway relating to whaling and sealing 'should be understood as protection of Norwegian local communities as well as rational harvest of nature'.[82]

Norwegian whaling has acquired a symbolic value of independence and self-determination. Local governments have a very strong position in these matters and the central government cannot overrule them easily. The Norwegian economy does not depend on whaling. However, to a certain degree whaling still plays an important role in the local economy of small communities; it also has a cultural significance for them.[83] Greenpeace was not successful in Norway, as its policy towards animal rights was alien to Norwegians, who doubted that animals' interests should be accorded a privileged position.[84] There are also historical and political elements to it, such as nation-building and the democratisation process in the late nineteenth century. It is linked with the development of Norwegian statehood, with significant support given to local communities. This perspective is a part of Norwegian political culture as a defining element of Norwegian environmentalism.[85] From local communities' perspective, in which there is a merger between nature and culture, animals' rights are excluded from environmentalism. The Norwegian environmentalism means that people can support environmental concerns, but at the same time they do not object to whaling and sealing. According to Grendstad et al., the exclusion of animal rights from Norwegian environmentalism defines its unique character. However, there is no doubt that the approach to animal rights in Norway excludes harming them and includes minimising pain and suffering. Inflicting pain is punished by law.[86]

However, in the event of conflict between animal rights and welfare and local communities' interests, the latter will prevail. According to Grendstad et al., there is a great difference between small-scale harvesting, beneficial to small communities, and large-scale industrial harvesting, which does not promote the interests of these small communities. Finally, it may be said that hunting has a long tradition in Norway and is considered a legitimate activity. Therefore in this 'pragmatic and

---

[82] Ibid., p. 25.   [83] Ibid., pp. 25, 103.   [84] Ibid., p. 103.   [85] Ibid., pp. 103–4.
[86] Ibid., p. 110.

instrumental culture, it becomes irrational not to take advantage of resources that are readily available at almost no cost'.[87] For some Norwegians whaling is a part of culture, a symbol of their distinctive national character. It is more than food; this is a part of their way of life.[88]

Norway represents a very interesting phenomenon in relation the environment: on the one hand, it is well known for its love of nature; but on the other hand, it approaches natural resources in a utilitarian way: 'Norwegians love their mountains at home but use the sea as a resource.'[89] There is a dualism in the attitude towards nature, which has kept Norway prosperous. Natural resources of the sea are to be 'revered and harvested'.[90] Whaling in Norway is not connected with the need for food but rather is 'imbued' in its culture (in particular in the northern villages, which have been engaged in whaling for centuries) and is a symbol of Norway's distinctive national character.[91] Whale hunting is seen as no different from hunting other animals such as deer. Thus, it would be a simplification to label everybody in Norway 'an environmentalist', especially in rural areas where environmentalists are seen as city types, telling rural people how to live.[92] The aggressive anti-whaling campaign, as conducted by Sea Shepherd, antagonised Norwegians and contributed to the rise of patriotic feelings.[93]

Rothenberg is correct in saying that as environmental concerns have become increasingly multicultural, there is a challenge as to how to find a way to pursue cultural diversity, and to reconcile it with a globally accepted governance of nature, in particular when it is not confined to one State. He is of the view that Norway's argument would be stronger if whaling was justified within the framework of global environmental problems, instead of relying on a tired reply of the lack of understanding of Norway's long-standing whaling tradition.[94] Anthropological studies indicate that whalers in Norway treat whaling as a 'profession' and are puzzled by their image as 'brutes', as they are well informed and ecologically aware. Whalers and their families are proud of whaling, as in the local context it represents honourable men's work.[95] They approach

---

[87] Ibid., p. 111.

[88] David Rothenberg, 'Love of Nature vs. Love of Respect. Non-Violence in Practice in Norway', in Andrew Light and Eric Katz (eds.), *Environmental Pragmatism* (London: Routledge, 1996), p. 259.

[89] Ibid., p. 259.   [90] Ibid., p. 259.   [91] Ibid., p. 258.   [92] Ibid., p. 253.

[93] Ibid., p. 261.   [94] Ibid., p. 259.

[95] Harald Beyer Broch, 'North Norwegian Whalers' Conceptualization of Current Whale Management Conflicts', in Milton M. R. Freeman and Urs P. Kreuter (eds.), *Elephants*

whaling purely as a means of getting food, they would not want to inflict unnecessary pain, and they respect animals. However, the animal rights ideology is completely alien to them, considering human suffering in the world. They insist that whales, being animals, are different from people and that all animals are placed on Earth for the benefit of people.[96] 'Obviously, animal rights' activists and people living by any occupation involving the killing of animals, will never agree on those issues.'[97]

However, this argument of a long cultural tradition is the most frequently submitted one at the forum of the IWC by both Japan and Norway. Both these States argue that they are being denied pursuit of their tradition of whaling, unlike indigenous peoples, because they use modern methods. Such a position, according to Norwegians, is intolerable. Their ambassador to the IWC stated as follows: 'Norway no longer accepts what she perceives as cultural imperialism imposed by the majority of the members of the International Whaling Commission on the local communities of the nations and peoples who want to exercise their sovereign cultural right to be different.'[98]

4.2.4 Faroe Islands

In comparison to the countries discussed above, Faroese hunting of pilot whales is known and analysed to a lesser degree. It is purely coastal hunting (so-called 'grind', which is the hunting of pilot whales, which migrate) and is arguably outside the jurisdiction of the IWC.

The arguments put forward on the part of the government in favour of whaling involve a mixture of historical, cultural and environmental considerations.[99] The Faroese have killed pilot whales for at least 1,200 years and claim that they are not in danger of extinction as stated by the North Atlantic Marine Mammal Commission (NAMMCO) and by the American Cetacean Society (ACS). The International Union for

---

and Whales. Resources for Whom? (Basle: Gordon and Breach Science Publishers, 1994), 203–17, 209.
[96] Ibid., 212.   [97] Ibid., 213.
[98] IWC (2006) Chairman's Report of the Forty-Fourth Annual Meeting (IWC, Cambridge), cited in Alexander Gillespie, International Environmental Law, Politics, and Ethics (2nd edn, Oxford University Press, 2014), p. 89.
[99] Elin Brimheim, http://elinbrimheimheinesen.blogspot.co.uk/2012/05/10-arguments-against-pilot-whaling-and.html, last accessed 24 December 2014.

Conservation of Nature (IUCN) also is of the view that the pilot whale hunt is 'probably sustainable'.[100] In the Faroe Islands, pilot whales have been an important source of food for the inhabitants since the islands were first colonised. The whales are taken in an organised drive hunt, or *grind*. The hunt is opportunistic; when whales are sighted, local fishing vessels cooperate to drive the whales onto designated beaches. Once ashore, they are killed by severing the neck arteries and veins using a specialised knife. The catch is then evaluated by designated officials who measure and mark the whales. The catch is divided into shares following specified rules and distributed free of charge to hunt participants and all adult residents in the district.[101]

Regulation of the Faroese pilot whale hunt is based on old Norse laws and deals with all aspects of the hunt, including driving procedures, beaching, killing methods, valuation, distribution and beach clean-up.[102] There are no quotas, but certain beaches or entire whaling districts can be closed when harvests are considered sufficient. The hunt is supervised by elected '*grindforemen*', who are under the supervision of the '*sýslumaður*', or district sheriff. The *sýslumaður* also oversees the valuation and division of the catch, and is responsible for keeping records of the harvest. In recent years, the pilot whale catch in the Faroes has ranged between 228 and 2,909. From 1709 to 1999, a total of 246,434 pilot whales were caught in 1,766 pods. There has been an average of 6.1 *grinds* per year in that period, and *grind* size has ranged from 1 to 1,200 whales, with a mean of 139.5 whales per *grind*.[103]

In defence of Faroese pilot whale hunting it has been stated:

---

[100] Brimheim, *Why we should let Faroe islanders hunt whales*, ibid. It may be said, however, that there are not very detailed records relating to pilot whales' abundance. An indication of long-term historical trends in the abundance of pilot whales around the Faroe Islands can be gained from an analysis of catch data (records go back to 1584). There is little current information on the abundance of pilot whales in the North-west Atlantic. Pilot whales were subject to an intensive drive fishery in Newfoundland from 1947 to 1972, and this fishery, it is believed, reduced the stock to very low levels. Abundance at the onset of the fishery was likely to have been about 60,000 animals. An aerial survey in eastern Newfoundland and Labrador waters was conducted and estimated 13,167 whales (95% C.I. 6,731 to 19,602). The population has likely not yet recovered to its pre-exploitation size. It appears that pilot whales are also abundant in the offshore waters of the north-eastern USA.

[101] NAMMCO, Status of Marine Mammals in the North Atlantic, the Long-Finned Pilot Whale, www.nammco.no/Nammco/Mainpage/MarineMammals/long-finned_pilot_whale. html, last accessed 24 December 2014.

[102] Ibid.   [103] Ibid.

They have never set out to look for pilot whales: they kill them only when a school is discovered close to shore, and only if one of a small number of designated beaches is near enough to use as a landing ground. According to NAMMCO, pilot whales number more than 750,000, and each year the slaughter is estimated to take less than 0.1 per cent of the population. Records have been kept since 1584 – which makes this the longest recorded tradition of any human–animal interaction. Experts think the practice has been going on for more than 1,200 years. The '*grindadráp*' (whale hunt) is not merely something from the Faroese past. It is a reminder of their relationship to the sea, and the meat is still a favourite delicacy.[104]

Widespread criticism concerning the cruelty of killing was rebutted by an argument that, at present, whales are not being stabbed and hacked to death with spears and hooks but that spears are not permitted and hooks are rounded to enable a quick kill.[105] The new method of killing, inserting a type of knife into the blowhole, still does not ensure a quick death.[106] Arguments are put forward that all killing is cruel, including also killing of other animals.[107] It is argued that whale meat is a very important foodstuff for the Faroese, and claims that it does not belong to

---

[104] Tim Ecott, 'Why We Should Let Faroe Islanders Hunt Whales', *Spectator*, 1 February 2014. The same author makes the following arguments: 'Wouldn't it be better if high-profile marine campaigns left the Faroese alone and focused on the more immediate and pressing threats to ocean ecosystems? Only this week a factory was discovered in Pu Qi in China that is processing more than 600 whale sharks a year. The world's largest fish, a harmless plankton feeder, is known to be dwindling fast across the tropics. In the Mediterranean, a combination of vested interests (some criminal) and lax European Union laws have resulted in the decimation of tuna populations. In the St Lawrence River in Canada, a small population of beluga whales is being poisoned by PCBs. Around 100 million sharks of all species are being caught worldwide to feed the Asian market for sharkfin soup. In many areas, 90 per cent of large carnivorous sharks have been removed from the ecosystem. In India and Sri Lanka, there is a burgeoning fishery for giant manta ray gills to make "blood purifiers" for the Chinese medicine trade. Parrotfish and conch are being overfished in the Caribbean, allowing algae to lay waste to the coral reefs. The list could go on and on and on. Endangered fish species are commonly found on most British restaurant tables and, due to overfishing, our once superabundant cod populations continue to show little sign of recovery. These are the marine issues that I worry about. There is one ocean on our planet, not six or seven or more according to labels on a chart. All that sea is connected to form a giant system that we have neglected and continue to plunder. Let's not victimize one tiny human population who are carrying on a tradition that will in all probability die out naturally in time. For now, let them eat whales.'

[105] Ibid.   [106] Gillespie, above n. 98, p. 92.

[107] Ibid. See also 'Whaling in Faroe Islands – in Brief', Prime's Minister's Office, January 2012, www.whaling.fo/Files/Filer/whaling/IN%20BRIEF%20JAN%202012.pdf, last accessed 24 December 2014.

the twenty-first century are dismissed as continental sensibilities and prejudices, and an encroachment on the culture of the Faroese and on their right to decide on their own way of living. Similarly to in other whaling nations, it is also asserted that the dominant approaches of the Western world (namely, the anti-whaling sentiment) to nature are sentimental and ethnocentric and overlook the fact that the livestock industry across the Western world is also 'insensitive' to the fate of animals.[108] In the *grind* there is, as described above, an element of its being a part of nature:

> In concrete terms, the danger to participants of thrashing tails, often mentioned in accounts of the kill, is still present. In this respect it retains the characteristic of the precarious exploitation of untamed environment of pre-modern times, as opposed to controlled and industrialized exploitation of nature characteristic to modern Western societies today ... The whales must be killed like land mammals, but to do so, the men must partially enter the whales' own environment ... *grind* by definition is 'based on an instantaneous relation between man and a prey'.[109]

Sanderson views the lack of understanding and the international pressure to conform as a result of the ambiguity of the *grind* as a form of subsistence hunt for food, independent of industrial development, conducted, however, with a large degree of organisation within a modern Western society. Western societies, according to this author, cannot accommodate congruence between the 'social' and the 'wild'.[110] In a highly romanticised assessment of the *grind*, Sanderson says that pilot whale hunting represents 'a meeting and merging of the boundaries between land and sea, between the social and the wild, between culture and nature'.[111]

The majority of these arguments are disputed by environmentalists, including the claim that pilot whales are not endangered and that Faroese hunting is sustainable. Thus, at the meeting of ASCOBANS in 2012, it was decided that, given the lack of relevant data, Faroese hunting could not be considered sustainable within the context of the meaning of the definition of sustainability in ASCOBANS. This was a decision based on

---

[108] Ibid.
[109] Kate Sanderson, '*Grind* – Ambiguity and Pressure to Conform – Faroese Whaling and the Anti-Whaling Protest', in Milton M. R. Freeman and Urs P. Kreuter (eds.), *Elephants and Whales. Resources for Whom?* (Basle: Gordon and Breach Science Publishers, 1994), pp. 187–210, 195.
[110] Ibid., p. 195.   [111] Ibid., p. 199.

application of the precautionary principle.[112] The method of killing of the entire pods was also disputed. On the other hand, NAMMCO experts are of the view that:

> Pilot whales are likely one of the most abundant *odontocetes* in the North Atlantic. The harvesting of pilot whales that continues today in the Faroe Islands has proven sustainable over a period of more than 300 years, and in 1997, NAMMCO concluded that the drive hunt was sustainable ... The population off Newfoundland is likely recovering after a period of excessive harvesting. In some other areas, bycatch of pilot whales in fisheries continues, but apparently at relatively low and decreasing levels.[113]

Concluding remarks

In the view of the present author, there are strong arguments on both sides of the cultural whaling dilemma. An unbiased and balanced approach is to be recommended, though it has to be said that emotions relating to whaling prevent any rational discussion. Non-aboriginal whaling described in this chapter fulfils in many aspects the elements of a multitude of definitions of culture, which were presented above, and in particular there is a very strong feature of societal interaction. The opinions, however, concerning this type of whaling, are not informed by definitions but rather by strong feelings coupled with scarce and variable scientific data.

Ethics and cultural diversity are linked by strong emotions; but such emotions are rarely accompanied by an in-depth knowledge about the subject matter.[114] In the view of the present author, there will never be agreement concerning cultural diversity regarding whaling. There are a multitude of arguments based on philosophy, political considerations and also bioethics, and none of them gives any solution to the problem of whaling as being permissible within cultural diversity and of whether

---

[112] 19th ASCOBANS Advisory Committee Meeting, Galway, Ireland, 20–22 March 2012, AC/19/Doc.5-01 (S), Document: 5-01, Pilot Whale Hunt in the Faroe Islands.

[113] NAMMCO, Status of Marine Mammals in the North Atlantic, the Long-Finned Pilot Whale, www.nammco.no/webcronize/images/nammco/635.pdf, last accessed 30 March 2015.

[114] Ibid.; Ole Torrissen et al., 'Food for Thought: Good Ethics or Political and Cultural Censoring in Science?', *ICES Journal of Marine Science* 69 (2012), 3–5, http://icesjms. oxfordjournals.org/content/early/2012/03/06/icesjms.fss016.full.pdf+html, last accessed 10 July 2015.

whaling is an ethical activity. It is incontestable that '[i]t is a matter of fact, supported by several surveys, that attitudes towards whaling differ among people, and this is clear, furthermore, that dominant attitudes, pro or con, co-vary with whether the nation is engaged in whaling or not. The 'cultural gulf' is increasing between whaling and non-whaling nations.'[115] With perhaps a certain degree of simplification, it was stated that attitudes towards whaling as an expression of cultural identity vary depending on whether the nation is engaged in whaling or not. The majority of people in Norway and Japan are pro-whaling, whilst in States such as the UK and Germany there is a strong anti-whaling culture.[116]

Several arguments have been put forward concerning the ethics of whale hunting. Bioethicists consider the hunting of endangered animals to be unethical. However, ethical arguments alone are not persuasive when they are at odds with science. As a consequence of the Moratorium, several species have recovered.[117] Torrissen et al. are of the view that

> the conclusion must be that there is no generally accepted argument against whaling as such. Most ethicists would concede that if whaling threatens the survival of a species, then it is unethical to continue to harvest that species. However, whether survival is threatened is obviously dependent on the species in question, and if a certain whale species such as the minke whale [is] shown to have recovered to a level that allows risk-averse sustainable harvesting, then the argument from threats to survival fails.[118]

It is the present author's understanding that, despite views to the contrary, Japanese coastal whaling shares similarities to indigenous whaling given that it is limited to small communities that have historically engaged in this activity and for whom whaling has particular cultural significance. As mentioned earlier in the chapter, in Japan there are beliefs in whaling communities that attach spiritual meaning to the whale. The whaling of Norway, Iceland and the Faroe Islands appears to be based on strong beliefs that it is part of the cultural rights of these nations, given their history of whaling. There is no doubt they share a similar utilitarian approach to whaling: whales are part of nature but also a natural resource of the sea, to be consumed, no different from fish.

The cultural aspect of whaling in these whaling countries is also based on a perceived national 'duty' to engage in whaling as a means of resisting the dominant Western/continental cultural trends and sensibilities. There are

[115] Ibid., 2.   [116] Ibid., 2.   [117] Ibid., 2.   [118] Ibid., 2.

further arguments submitted in support of whaling that concern State sovereignty over natural resources, including the conviction that sustainable whaling (for minke whales, which are believed no longer to be endangered) is outside the remit of international regulation and therefore a matter of national purview. The general view in these countries is that dominant Western sensibilities concerning whaling appear unjustifiable and hypocritical, given that they seem to focus selectively on whales while other mammal killings are not met with such systematised opposition by other anti-whaling States. Western anti-whaling States are also accused of sentimentalism (mawkishness) and anthropomorphism by projecting human values onto whales, often not taking into account the fact that whales are regarded as any other animal by the people of whaling nations. In fact, some whaling nations' public consciousness regards whales to be more akin to fish, while in other cases, Iceland being the notable example, they are considered pests that compete with the fishing industry due to the large volume of fish that they consume. Therefore, it may be said that the attitude to whales in Iceland is even antagonistic to a certain degree.

Kalland's views are worth describing as they paint in a vivid way the cultural rift between whaling and non-whaling nations. He analyses the 'myth' of a whale, which is perceived as a pure creature, somewhat 'between and betwixt' a fish and a mammal. According to Kalland, pro-whaling nations talk about a 'whale' in the singular, lumping together all whale species, of which there are about seventy. Thus an image has been created of a 'super whale' drawing on all existing species: the whale is the largest animal on earth (the blue whale); it has the largest brain on earth (the sperm whale); it sings nicely (the humpback whale); it has nurseries (some dolphins); it is friendly (the grey whale); it is endangered (the blue whale), etc. 'Such a creature does not exist.'[119] The whale has acquired totemic features, being portrayed as a beautiful, gentle and loyal creature, whilst whalers are brutal, greedy, butchers, savages, evil, etc. As Kalland says, whalers make excellent enemies as very few nations are engaged in whaling; therefore, as he says, they are 'ideal scapegoats for environmental disasters and human cruelty to animals'.[120] Kalland further explains that it could have been possible for consumptive and

---

[119] Arne Kalland, 'Whose Whale Is That? Diverting the Commodity Path', in Milton M. R. Freeman and Urs Kreuter (eds.), *Elephants and Whales. Resources for Whom?* (Basle: Gordon and Breach Science Publishers, 1994), pp. 159–86, 178–9.

[120] Ibid., pp. 164–5.

non-consumptive uses of whales to coexist. However, the cultural framework which has turned a whale into a super whale, and a super whale
into a commodity, has 'decommoditised' whale meat and oil and created
a picture of an evil whaler. As a result, a 'super whale' cannot coexist with
whaling practices. Moreover, urban dwellers impose their totems on
others and this, according to Kalland, has led to totemisation of whales
and cultural imperialism, which has caused the whaling issue to arrive at
a stalemate.[121]

As Stoett has observed, in the case of whaling 'cultural relativism
surfaces'.[122] He aptly noted that:

> The anti-whaling lobby often has pushed forward a powerful idea that
> efforts to abolish whaling are reflective of a new, global consciousness.
> Clearly enough, the Japanese, the Norwegians, and Icelanders are the
> vociferous leaders of a small minority of nation-states. But does this, in
> itself, make them wrong? In the environmental policy world, there are no
> angels. Surely the most consistent and powerful proponent of the anti-
> commercial whaling stance, the United States, the world's biggest polluter
> in several areas, the Mecca of the wasteful consumption-oriented culture
> itself, is subject to rather harsh criticism regarding its own environmental
> policies.[123]

Stoett also asks an important question about the possibility of the
'integration' of Japanese into mainstream Western culture regarding
whaling: 'Shouldn't modern Alaskan or coastal aboriginals be similarly
integrated, so that they, too, overcome their insensitive urge to kill
advanced mammals and seals?'[124] Stoett notes that there is no doubt
that science has a fundamental role to play in the sense of legitimising
global governance decisions and directions, and has a key function to
fulfil in wildlife governance. Science, however, is inexorably linked to
ethics, and, as Stoett explains, 'what is good, what is right, what is
justified is intrinsic to all scientific enterprise'.[125] As was perceptively
stated, 'culture has become a powerful weapon on the global political
battlefield. Cultural arguments have become politically "correct, and real"
and "pure" culture is perceived to be good.'[126] This attribute of 'purity' is
lacking from the notion of non-indigenous whaling.

There is no straightforward solution to these issues, which are highly
politicised and involve exchanges that are rife with accusations of hyp-
ocrisy. As we have seen, a persistent ethical issue that appears in debates

---

[121] Ibid., p. 179.   [122] Stoett, above n. 29, p. 167.   [123] Ibid., p. 167.
[124] Ibid., p. 168.   [125] Ibid., p. 169.   [126] Kalland, above n. 119, p. 183.

about whaling is the method of hunting, and the pain and suffering caused to whales, which is part and parcel of a greater problem of 'animal harm'.[127] While the harming or killing of animals by indigenous peoples is accepted (at least to some extent)[128] by the society, non-indigenous harm to animals (or cruelty), such as the killing of seals in Canada, and the shooting and trapping of birds (despite EU legislation) in the Mediterranean, is more complex, and evokes more negative reactions but still is culturally condoned. As Nurse phrased it: '[t]o many Mediterranean men, hunting is a way of life rather than a sport or recreation'.[129] Nurse noted that, to hunters, legislation protecting birds is a stumbling block in the enjoyment of their culture.[130] He stated perceptively that

> [w]here cultural acceptance of animal harm is strong and legal and regulatory regimes are weak and/or poorly implemented, animal harm will continue both as a means of resistance and as a means of reassessing cultural identity which may integrate animal harm and masculinities into cultural practices that result in animal deaths. The reality of animal killing that is socially construed to be acceptable within a country or a region such as the Mediterranean is that it has meaning to the people who carry out the killing but also to the society which endorses that killing.[131]

Gillespie makes some very apt observations on cultural pluralism and nature in general, which apply very much to the context of the whaling debate and which the present author fully supports. In a situation where a species is on the verge of extinction and there is a choice between, on the one hand, killing it off completely due to cultural needs and, on the other hand, allowing it to survive and recover in the future, then the choice of the second option will be beneficial for the future of the culture itself, if the species is allowed to flourish. He strongly opines that 'to kill off a species now in the name of cultural tradition is to kill off the culture'.[132] Therefore, survival of species should trump cultural considerations. The States which consider whaling and eating whale meat as part of their culture may, however, rebut this argument by claiming that hunting of species of whales that are not endangered could be culturally defensible and not abhorrent. Such a view is partly based on the concept

---

[127] Angus Nurse, *Animal Harm. Perspectives on Why People Harm and Kill Animals* (Farnham: Ashgate, 2013), see in particular chapter 6, 'Animal Harm, Culture and Self-Expression', pp. 137–68.

[128] See, on the controversial Makah hunt, Chapter 5 of this publication.

[129] Nurse, above n. 127, p. 148.   [130] Ibid., p. 148.   [131] Ibid., p. 151.

[132] Alexander Gillespie, 'The Ethical Question in the Whaling Debate', *Georgetown Int'l Env'l Law Review* 9 (1997), 375.

of sustainable use (i.e. use that does not lead to long-term decline) of non-endangered species of whales, in the manner of the utilisation of any other marine resource (as, in the view of some of these States, the whale is not a unique mammal but rather akin to fish). It can be said that such an approach at present has been abandoned by the majority of the State Members of the IWC. It may also be said that there is no clear understanding of the definition and content of sustainable use, whether it is consumptive or non-consumptive.

Cultural relativism should not be an excuse for any actions which culture may wish to condone: '[t]hus culture should not be seen as a panacea for environmental destruction, nor for that matter, environmental protection'.[133] In the view of the present author, the question of animal welfare is beyond the debate on cultural diversity and cruelty to animals and should not be justified on such a ground or treated as an expression of cultural identity of groups of people. Rather, it relates to the question of ethics about how undue suffering should be prohibited irrespective of cultural sensitivities (which will be discussed in Chapter 5). However, the author of this study admits that at times it is very difficult to isolate the question of animal suffering from it being a part of tradition and the expression of cultural diversity.

There is no clear solution to the problem of the protection of animals and cultural relativism. It cannot be denied that, as Gillespie observes, in this very sensitive and difficult sphere of the expression of culture,[134] frequently decisions that are made have a strong political background, as many States decide in an arbitrary way which cultural practices they will support and which they will not, notwithstanding many definitions of culture. As was seen from the above discussion, such a view is shared by many lawyers, scientists and philosophers.

---

[133] Ibid., 375.   [134] Gillespie, above n. 98, p. 89.

5

Environmental ethics, animal rights and the law

Introduction

This chapter, which is closely related to the previous one, examines the complex issue of animal rights, particularly in connection with whaling. It has been established in the previous chapter that certain States claim the right to cultural diversity, which includes taking whales. The question may be posed how this claim can be reconciled with the rights of animals (including whales). The animal rights theory, which is diversified, is part and parcel of ethics and philosophy. There are several very different schools of thought regarding the rights of animals. We can ask the following question: can whaling be banned on the basis of the animal rights approach, or does the theory of cultural diversity of nations, which identifies itself with the hunting of whales, override concerns for the rights of animals? There is not one simple answer to this very complex problem; and this chapter does not purport to give one. It analyses the issue of the rights of animals and their importance in relation to whaling. Cultural diversity and the rights of animals command a very individual approach, as they concern sensitive questions of which each and every person has a very different understanding.

5.1 Animal rights: outline of general issues

This section concerns the position of animals in overall nature from the standpoint of ethics and philosophy. For, as was stated by Coyle and Morrow, '[e]nvironmental law without a sense of philosophy and history is a pale and bloodless creature'.[1]

The discussion in the field of philosophy regarding the relationship between humans and nature, be it the natural habitat or other animals, is

---

[1] Sean Coyle and Karin Morrow, *The Philosophical Foundations of Environmental Law, Property Rights and Nature* (Oxford: Hart Publishing, 2004), p. 215.

as old as philosophical inquiry itself.[2] This relationship has puzzled all manner of thinkers, including lawyers, philosophers and anthropologists. Lévi-Strauss noted that animals are good to think with, not just good to eat.[3] There are different approaches to assessing what the value of nature might be, including doing this on a utilitarian basis, thus finding that it has essentially an instrumental value, or on a more discursive basis with a view to finding some inherent or intrinsic value.[4] The first of these approaches is based on the material purpose; it serves the use to which it may be put. Inherent value, on the other hand, is premised upon the value that each entity possesses of itself, not as an object of utility. It can also be labelled as nature's amenity value; though it could sensibly be argued that it falls within its instrumental value, given that it has an amenity value from the standpoint of human society. Intrinsic value has at times been referred to as a moral value.[5] For example, the Convention on Biological Diversity (CBD), in its Preamble, expressly acknowledges the intrinsic value of biological diversity. As Bowman observes, 'the precise wording, in which intrinsic value is not merely itemized as one in a catalogue of motivations, but set apart from the list of anthropocentric justifications which follow, seems to give particular emphasis to this moral dimension'.[6]

As Peterson explains, apart from different anthropological and philosophical approaches to animal rights, there is a host of unresolved issues, such as consideration of whether rights are bestowed upon all animal species or only those with some closer connection to human cultures such as domesticated animals, or others historically used for food and transport, and in general whether there is a division between wild and

[2] See Catherine Redgwell, 'Life, the Universe and Everything: A Critique of Anthropocentric Rights', in Alan Boyle and Michael Anderson (eds.), *Human Approaches to Environmental Protection* (Oxford University Press, 1996), pp. 1–89; Dale Jamieson, *Ethics and the Environment. An Introduction* (Cambridge University Press, 2008); Peter Singer, *Animal Liberation* (New York: Harper Perennial, 2001); Roderick Frazier Nash, *The Rights of Nature. A History of Environmental Ethics* (Madison, Wis.: Wisconsin University Press, 1989); Aubrey Manning and James Serpell, *Animals and Human Society* (Abingdon: Routledge, 1994); Michael P. T. Leahy, *Against Liberation. Putting Animals in Perspective* (Abingdon: Routledge, 1993); Sue Donaldson and Will Kymlicka, *Zoopolis: A Political Theory of Animal Rights* (Oxford University Press, 2011).

[3] Claude Lévi-Strauss, *The Savage Mind* (Chicago University Press, 1968).

[4] Michael Bowman, 'The Philosophical Foundations of International Wildlife', in Michael Bowman, Peter Davies and Catherine Redgwell, *Lyster's International Wildlife Law* (2nd edn, Cambridge University Press, 2010), p. 62.

[5] Ibid., pp. 62–3.   [6] Ibid., p. 67.

domestic animals. According to some views, there is a perceived conflict between the environment and animals. The solution to this conflict lies in the existence of two separate but equal regimes for wild nature and animals towards which historically and socially human society has certain responsibilities. Such a model is criticised for being based on a false assumption that existence in the wild and domestication are entirely separate, which can be both inaccurate and destructive. These divisions do not account for the fact that humans are also animals, and that they evolved biologically as a consequence of natural phenomena, and that they continue to evolve socially and biologically due to the interaction between nature and culture. Another theory is that of the so-called moral pluralism, which presupposes that many systems of value could sensibly coexist – the opposite of monism, which traces all value to one original source. Under this theory, different approaches are needed for different aspects of the non-human world. There is also the theory of pragmatism (rejecting such philosophical assumptions that appear to be based on more discursive idealist foundations). A pragmatic approach to preserving nature is not based on any perceived intrinsic value but on whatever value there is in preserving non-human goods, presumably from a human standpoint. The theories that find the approval of Peterson are based on the individual protection of animals and the integration between animals and humans; on the notion of a community which bridges the dividing line between domestic and wild animals. A further way to connect people with animals is through placing them within an all-encompassing idealist/metaphysical context, such as the Abrahamic religions which provide a theological context within which humans and other life forms are 'God's creations' and humans, as the most refined aspect of this creation, are responsible for the stewardship of nature and all it contains. However, as Peterson argues, most theories are aimed at reconciliation: the holistic, the individualistic and the religious share a common conviction that the anthropocentric value system is the basic issue.[7]

However, from the point of view of international law, as helpful as these inquiries are, matters are not so clearly taxonomised. Different instruments deal with different aspects of the ecosystem, including animals – be they endangered or abundant – and the natural habitat. For instance, several Conventions that protect animals are in force,

---

[7] Dale Peterson, *Moral Lives of Animals* (London: Bloomsbury Press, 2011), pp. 141–61.

including the 1992 CBD,[8] the 1971 Convention on Wetlands of International Importance especially as Waterfowl Habitat,[9] the 1979 Berne Convention on the Conservation of European Wildlife and Natural Habitats[10] and the 1973 Convention on International Trade in Endangered Species of Wild Fauna and Flora.[11] This generation of Conventions that protect animals differs fundamentally from the very early agreements aimed at the protection of certain species. For instance, treaties such as the 1900 Convention on the Preservation of Wild Animals, Birds and Fish in Africa[12] and the 1902 Convention to Protect Birds Useful for Agriculture 'no longer can be considered especially enlightened',[13] given that they were purely of an anthropocentric nature, whose main purpose was the protection of certain species of birds and animals useful for human beings rather than being aimed at the welfare of animals per se. These early treaties did not prohibit the killing of some animals that are now strictly protected, such as birds of prey. Bowman correctly observes that modern international agreements that deal with the protection of animals focus mainly on rare, threatened and endangered species, without, however, going as far as commanding that they be treated as individual living creatures deserving 'respect and consideration' in their own right. Moreover, Bowman reminds us that domestic animals generally seem to lack any international protection and suffer frequently from terrible cruelty inflicted upon them. Therefore, Bowman suggests that they ought to be the subject of international regulation.[14] The welfare of animals, on the one hand, and the protection of animal species, on the other, are separate matters. As Bowman notes, 'those who hunt or trap animals for sport or financial gain are sometimes keen conservationists, but are seldom moved by any consideration of animal welfare'.[15] Animal welfare and the prohibition of cruelty in dealing with animals are in the

---

[8] 1992 Convention on Biological Diversity, 1760 UNTS 79.
[9] 1971 Convention on Wetlands of International Importance especially as Waterfowl Habitat, 996 UNTS 245.
[10] 1979 Berne Convention on the Conservation of European Wildlife and Natural Habitats, 1284 UNTS 209.
[11] 1973 Convention on International Trade in Endangered Species of Wild Fauna and Flora, 993 UNTS 245.
[12] 1900 Convention on the Preservation of Wild Animals, Birds and Fish in Africa, 4 IPE 1607.
[13] 1902 Convention to Protect Birds Useful for Agriculture, 94 BFSP 715; see also Michael Bowman, 'The Protection of Animals under International Law', *Connecticut J. Int'l Law* 4 (1989), 487–90.
[14] Bowman, above n. 13, 488.   [15] Ibid.

present author's view a different matter from philosophical questions of animal rights. The humane treatment of animals is already legally enforceable in many States, as, for instance, is the humane treatment of animals during hunts in many States.[16] In some countries, such as Sri Lanka, the Constitution imposes an obligation on citizens and the State to 'value all forms of life', no doubt due to the Buddhist majority culture.

As mentioned earlier, the discourse relating to the relationship between animals and humans has been the subject of philosophical debate for centuries. One important philosopher who made pronouncements on this subject is Immanuel Kant.[17] He took the view that animals were 'man's instruments', 'needing protection only in so far as to assist humans in relating to each other'. According to Kant, the treatment of animals by humans reflected the social relations between humans. Another important philosopher, Descartes, took the view that 'brutes' (animals) lack the capacity to feel their own suffering or pain. Animals are machines which may resemble humans physically but which lack a soul; thus they cannot feel anything:[18] an astounding conclusion given that animals must surely have reacted in exactly the same way as they do today towards any harm or perceived threat. Jeremy Bentham supported the rights of animals and expressed the view that a fully grown animal is actually more rational than an infant, thus admitting a more anthropomorphic basis to his approach.[19]

There are numerous theories relating to the place of animals in our universe and the relationship between animals and humans. The direct anthropocentric approaches that characterised early environmental treaties were replaced by approaches that recognise an intrinsic value of the environment and the fauna and flora it contains.[20] Recent approaches place humans as an element of nature, acknowledging the interdependence between human beings and other animal species.[21] This approach underpins the 1982 World Charter for Nature.[22] Its Preamble states that '[m]ankind is a part of nature and life depends on the uninterrupted

---

[16] Ibid., p. 674.

[17] Immanuel Kant, *Lectures on Ethics*, ed. and trans. Peter Heath, ed. J. B. Schneewind (Cambridge University Press, 1997).

[18] René Descartes, *Discourse on Method and Meditation on First Philosophy*, trans. John Cottingham, Robert Stoothoff and Dugald Murdoch (Cambridge University Press, 1991).

[19] Jeremy Bentham, *The Principles of Morals and Legislation* (Amherst, NY: Prometheus Books, 1988), pp. 310–11.

[20] Redgwell, above n. 2, p. 73.   [21] Ibid., p. 73.

[22] World Charter for Nature, GA A/RES/37/7 (1982); 22 ILM (1983) 455.

functioning of natural systems which ensure the supply of energy and nutrients' and that '[e]very form of life is unique, warranting respect regardless of its worth to man, and, to accord other organisms such recognition, man must be guided by a moral code of action'. Such an approach to the environment can be termed 'weak anthropocentrism'.[23]

The animal rights debate, however, has undergone a significant change since the advent of recent modern international law and with publication of the book of Peter Singer, *Animal Liberation*.[24] In this book, Singer went as far as to compare the plight of animals and the value of their liberation with the similar aspects of the anti-racist, anti-homophobic and feminist causes. Human domination over animals was the last form of discrimination that remained unaddressed; and animals lacked the capacity and agency to defend their own 'interests'. Singer drew an analogy between racism and 'speciesism' (that is to say, discrimination against species that, according to this notion, is extreme given the human domination over other animal species) in the theory and practice of the area of experimentation. He writes that blatant speciesism results in painful experiments on other races, justified on the grounds of their usefulness and the contribution to the development of science. He reminds us that under Nazism, German doctors, some of them well known in their area, habitually experimented on Jews, Slavs and Roma given that they were perceived, and therefore treated, as inferior to 'the Aryan race' of which the Germanic peoples were considered to be the most 'pure'.[25] Therefore, Singer and other authors, proponents of animal rights, sought to make the case that humans and animals, given that they have a lot in common, such as sharing the capacity to suffer, ought to somehow be treated equally. Singer argued that humans should not reject animal interests on the basis that animals do not belong to the human species, as this is a blatantly speciesist/discriminatory attitude, exhibiting the approach that only those belonging to a certain species enjoy some superior moral status.[26] As pointed out above, Singer's own arguments against speciesism are based on philosophical questions relating to ethics.

---

[23] See, for example, Redgwell, above n. 2, p. 73.   [24] Singer, above n. 2.

[25] Ibid., p. 83.

[26] See also Peter Singer, 'Animal Liberation at 30', *New York Review of Books*, 15 May 2003. Singer's review essay analysed the following books: Roger Scruton, *Animals Rights and Wrongs* (London: Metro, 2000); Paola Cavallieri, *The Animal Question: Why Non-Human Animals Deserve Human Rights* (Oxford University Press, 1992); David De Grazia, *Taking Animal Rights Seriously* (Cambridge University Press, 1996); and Matthew Scully, *Dominion: The Power of Man, the Suffering of Animals, and the Call to Mercy*

More specifically, his views fall within the notion of 'bio-centrist' ethics ('bioethics'). Under the approach that he advocates, it is ethically indefensible to differentiate between the interests of members of our own species and those of animals. He nevertheless admits that there may be difficulties connected with this concept, as it 'requires us to estimate what the interests are in an endless variety of different circumstances'.[27] The same author ponders that dilemmas of the ethical approach based on the principle of equal consideration of interests 'can only be rough approximation',[28] if they can be resolved at all. Singer's approach to animals is 'utilitarian',[29] based on 'assessing acts by calculating value of their consequences',[30] a task that is very complex in relation not only to animals but also to humans.

It may be said that our treatment of animals may be due simply to ignorance or lack of full awareness of their conditions.[31] In broad brushstrokes, the arguments against speciesism take either a rights-based approach or are premised on the grounds of ethics. The rights-based approach is represented by Cavallieri. She submits several interesting – and controversial – arguments to substantiate the extension of the realm of human rights protection to animals. For example, she analyses and compares animals with the situation of slaves and their denial of human rights protection, even after they were freed. However, the most interesting is the theoretical basis of her study in which Cavallieri follows the concept of the 'basic right' of Ronald Dworkin.[32] She advocates the rights of animals based on the notion of the universal application of human rights over all human beings irrespective of whether they are within or outside a particular human rights regime, including 'non-paradigmatic' cases.[33] She argues that this framework of human rights protection should be extended even further to include animals within the paradigm of Dworkin's basic human right, which, according to Cavallieri, constitutes the fundamental political framework in a decent society. She argues as follows:

(New York: St Martin's Press, 2003), www.nybooks.com/articles/archives/2003/may/15/animal-liberation-at-30/, last accessed 26 January 2014.

[27] Singer, above n. 26.

[28] Singer's comments are in the review of the book of David De Grazia, above n. 26.

[29] For example, Redgwell, above n. 2, p. 76.   [30] Jamieson, above n. 2, p. 32.

[31] Ibid., pp. 115–16.

[32] Ronald Dworkin, *Taking Rights Seriously* (London: Duckworth, 1977), pp. 179–83.

[33] Cavallieri, above n. 26, pp. 76–9.

If, so far as women are concerned, this takes the form of law on equality
that may play an active role in fostering social transformation, in the case
of nonhumans what is in question is instead a legal change aimed at
removing the status of property which is the basic obstacle to the enjoyment of the denied rights. In this sense, the shift from the condition of
objects to that of subjects of legal rights does not appear as a point of
arrival but rather as the initial access to the circle of possible beneficiaries
of that 'egalitarian plateau' from which contemporary political philosophy
starts in order to determine any more specific individual right.[34]

Dworkin professed the idea of all having equal rights to concern and
respect deriving from equal dignity of all persons.[35] Dworkin's theory is
based on what he terms the intrinsic value of everyone's life, which he
treats as an objective concept.[36] Dworkin presents a list of so-called
baseline rights, the status of which is uncertain given that economic
rights are not globally recognised as universal human rights.[37] Brown
noted difficulties with this concept, due to the ambiguity of the notion of
the absolute minimum standard of human rights 'that is required to
display a good faith attempt to treat all human beings with equal
dignity'.[38] Cavallieri professes the idea that the 'egalitarian plateau'
(a concept introduced by Dworkin) sets the boundary for human beings
to remain within its boundaries. She is of the view that the boundaries of
the protection offered by the 'egalitarian plateau' should be extended
to include animals. However, as Singer observes, such a rights-based
approach as advocated by Cavallieri is not supposed to resolve every
conflict of interests and rights. He further explains that her notion of
rights as a part of the basic political framework of a decent society means
that certain rights are not necessarily absolute, and may be subject to
specific restrictions to these 'rights'.[39]

---

[34] Ibid., p. 142.
[35] '[W]e might say that individuals have a right to equal concern and respect in the design
and administration of the political institutions which govern them. This is a highly
abstract right.' Ibid., p. 180.
[36] Ibid., 198–9. On the critique of Dworkin's theory of egalitarianism, see also Alexander
Brown, *Ronald Dworkin's Theory of Equality. Domestic and Global Perspective* (Basingstoke: Palgrave Macmillan, 2009).
[37] Ronald Dworkin, *Is Democracy Possible Here? Principles for a New Political Debate*
(Princeton University Press, 2006). See also on this subject, John Rawls, *The Law of
Peoples* (Cambridge, Mass.: Harvard University Press, 1999), p. 37.
[38] Brown, above n. 36, p. 139.
[39] Singer, above n. 26. Singer gives as an example 'Typhoid Mary' (Mary Mallon), who was
compulsorily quarantined because she carried a lethal disease. He further adds that a
government may be entitled to restrict the movements of humans or animals who are a

Similar views based on the intrinsic value and supporting a rights-based approach were voiced by Regan, a strong supporter of the sanctity of life for all, including animals.[40] His views are premised on the assumption that everything that has inherent value has it equally. Gradation of value is unacceptable because it is 'perfectionist' and could potentially be enlisted to justify discrimination. Such a view, he says, is predicated upon the idea that some creatures embody preferred qualities, that is to say, certain 'perfections'. Therefore, such an approach could lead to sacrifices of creatures that are less than 'perfect', which is morally abhorrent.[41] According to Regan, such rights are not absolute. Under certain circumstances they can be compromised in cases of, for instance, self-defence by the innocent – 'prevention' cases. However, certain exceptions to the equal application of rights presented by Regan are controversial and may put in doubt the principle of equal inherent value.[42]

In the view of the present author, the most crucial distinction between theories which may be termed 'theories of animal welfare' and 'theories of animal rights' is based on the question of cruelty and suffering of pain. The line between these two theories is very fine, and, although many authors try to draw very fast and clear distinguishing lines, there is no clear-cut distinction apart perhaps from approaches to pain and suffering, as represented by animal welfare and Regan animal rights. Singer was of the view that animal suffering is acceptable if there is no other way to satisfy fundamental human needs. Regan criticises this view given that neither anti-cruelty laws nor animal welfare sufficiently protect animals. As Kalland explains, according to this view, hunting even when humanely conducted is incompatible with Regan's philosophy given that the death of the animal is inevitable. In that respect, laws aimed at minimising pain and suffering do not address any 'inherent' 'rights' animals might have to life. What is more, Kalland finds Singer's theory difficult to implement as there is not a precise definition of what are 'important human needs'.[43] We should also mention the school of

---

danger to the public, but nevertheless must show the concern and respect due to them as possessors of basic rights.

[40] Tom Regan, *The Case for Animal Rights* (Berkeley: University of California Press, 1983); see also Peter Singer and Tom Regan (eds.), *Animal Rights and Human Obligations* (Englewood Cliffs, NJ: Prentice Hall, 1976).

[41] Ibid., p. 243.   [42] Jamieson, above n. 2, p. 120.

[43] Arne Kalland, *Unveiling the Whale: Discourses on Whales and Whaling* (New York: Berghahn Books, 2009), p. 8.

thought, in similar vein to Bentham's argument, that animals should enjoy rights on the basis that they are at least as autonomous as human beings, without the full mental capacities to which human society, generally, affords human rights protection. According to this argument, therefore, animals should be granted only basic rights.[44]

There are also other scholars (Sunstein and Leslie) who adopt a somewhat more pragmatic attitude, which is perhaps not as far-fetched or radical as to accord animals full autonomy, in the sense of liberating them completely from human subjugation. They argue that sometimes wild animals can have more decent lives under human control than when completely free. This group of scholars would ban all practices that bring suffering to animals and amount to cruelty and neglect. These authors understand animal rights as legal protection against their harm; an idea that is so far the least controversial. Moreover, such rights should also involve a moral claim for such legal protection. These scholars argue that such an approach to animal rights should be met with general consent given that there is little doubt that animals have certain rights.[45]

Another approach to rights of animals is based on an integrated, all-encompassing notion of a general right of nature or the environment. In that sense, animals are a subset. Animals enjoy rights as a part of ecosystems and their rights derive therefrom. There are different schools of this ecological approach. The most far-reaching is represented by Arne Næss, who coined the term 'deep ecology', advocating a deeper, more 'spiritual' approach to nature.[46]

There is clearly no uniform and generally accepted approach to animal rights. Several approaches can be distinguished, including the rights-based; the utilitarian; the damage-limitation approach that Sunstein and Leslie seem to propose; and the ecological approach. All these

---

[44] Mary Anne Warren, 'The Rights of the Non-Human World', in Robert Elliot and Arran E. Gare (eds.), *Environmental Philosophy* (University Park: Penn. State University Press, 1983), p. 109.

[45] Cass R. Sunstein, 'The Rights of Animals: A Very Short Primer', The Law School, University of Chicago, John M. Olin Law and Economics Working Paper No. 157 (2D Series) Public Law and Legal Theory Working Paper No. 20, 2006, www.law.uchicago. edu/academics/publiclaw/uindex.html, last accessed 20 December 2014); Jeff Leslie and Cass R. Sunstein, 'Animals Rights Without Controversy', John M. Olin Law and Economics Working Paper No. 283 (2D Series), Public Law and Legal Theory Working Paper No. 120, 2006 www.law.uchicago.edu/academics/publiclaw/.index/html, last accessed 20 December 2014.

[46] Arne Næss, 'The Shallow and the Deep. Long Range Ecology Movement', *Inquiry* 16 (1973), 95–100.

approaches make interesting points and raise certain issues. For instance, if we adopt the rights-based approach, questions arise as to how far we can extend it and how many rights we can accord to animals. Let us argue that it is indisputable that we ought to protect animals from cruelty and neglect; but do they enjoy the full right to life and the full autonomy that arguably, at least at the level of legal principle, are afforded to human beings in functioning liberal democracies? These questions cannot be resolved by simply changing the degree of according rights to animals. As Redgwell observes, there is a 'strong-rights approach' and a 'weak-rights approach' to nature. The first of these approaches is characterised by elevating all of nature (animals, trees, and so on) to the same rights level as humans. The second of these approaches is a watered-down version of the strong-rights approach, 'where moral and legal considerability have been conflated in the loose use of "rights talk"'.[47]

The traditional views on animal rights, which Donaldson and Kymlicka term 'Animal Rights Theory' (ART), can be summarised as protection rights bestowed on all conscious or sentient beings, human and non-human animals alike.[48] Such views were the subject of critical observations such as those of Alexander Gillespie[49] and Donaldson and Kymlicka.[50] Gillespie is of the view that environmental ethics should move from the individual moral approaches to animals towards an integrated approach of seeking inherent value in complete communities or ecosystems, as opposed to individual animals.[51] The critique of the classical ART views by Donaldson and Kymlicka is based on the division between 'selfhood' and 'personhood'. There are many ART views expressed according to which these two notions are effectively equated, since animals are sentient selves and should be treated as persons.[52] According to some authors, personhood can only be found in human beings, and is contingent on other attributes (such as language). Donaldson and Kymlicka are of the view that it is almost impossible to draw a coherent and sharp distinction between these two concepts, and such a distinction is not even conceptually sustainable as it attempts to draw a single line in what is a continuous process, or 'series of continua in which individuals move at different stages of life'.[53]

---

[47] Redgwell, above n. 2, p. 83.   [48] Donaldson and Kymlicka, above n. 2, p. 24.
[49] Alexander Gillespie, 'The Ethical Question in the Whaling Debate', *Georgetown International Environmental Law Review* 9 (1997), 355–87, 384.
[50] Donaldson and Kymlicka, above n. 2, p. 223.   [51] Ibid., p. 384.   [52] Ibid., p. 26.
[53] Ibid., p. 26.

According to Donaldson and Kymlicka, the traditional approaches to animal rights have many implications that identify a range of negative rights, such as the right not be tortured, experimented on, owned, enslaved, imprisoned or killed. Extending such negative rights to animals therefore would result in the prohibition of animal keeping, animal testing and animal eating, and the collapse of the pet industry, a large part of the agriculture industry, and so on.[54] However, Donaldson and Kymlicka believe that such an ART approach is not sufficiently developed, and the conceptualisation of the relationships between animals and humans should go much further. They developed a citizenship (for domestic animals), sovereignty (for wild animals) and denizenship (for liminal animals) theory which is farther reaching than the traditional ART theory, and is based on the premise that a universal theory of animal rights has to be more specific and take into account more complex relationships between humans and non-human animals.[55] Their theories differ in relation to domesticated, wild and liminal animals. In relation to the issue of whaling, this theory could be of interest, as it would indicate that the entire cetacean species ought to be entirely sovereign; that is to say, not prejudiced in any way by the activity of humans.

In general, the traditional theory of animal rights is based on the principle of 'letting them be', with the minimum (or no) interference from humans, as expressed by, among others, Singer[56] and Francione.[57] Wild animals should enjoy sovereignty, similar to that enjoyed by States. Animal sovereignty is based on the premise that animals are not passive recipients of humans' benign or harmful actions but have the capacity to 'pursue their own good and shape their own communities'.[58] Such a concept should also have strictly delimited boundaries. Donaldson and Kymlicka explain that while recognising wild animal sovereign rights to a habitat, they are not referring to parks where humans retain sovereignty, exercising stewardship over animals and nature, but they mean relations between sovereign entities resting on a similar claim to authority. Humans in animal territory should not play the role of stewards and managers but that of guests/visitors to a foreign territory.[59]

---

[54] Ibid., p. 49.   [55] Donaldson and Kymlicka, pp. 50–69.
[56] Singer, above n. 2, p. 251.
[57] Gary Francione, *Animals as Persons: Essays on Abolition of Animal Exploitation* (New York: Columbia University Press, 2008), p. 13.
[58] Donaldson and Kymlicka, above n. 2, p. 170.   [59] Ibid., p. 170.

Since ethical issues relating to legally protecting the life and welfare of animals cannot be answered in an unequivocal non-contingent manner, and, given the absence of some universal theory that would satisfy all philosophers (and lawyers) dogged by this issue, it is the view of the present author that the most acceptable, least controversial and most practical approach is that which Sunstein and Leslie propose. It is not as far reaching as the strong-rights approach, and it sets out acceptable and workable postulates based on animal welfare. It does not aspire to establish new theories but offers a practical solution, the implementation of which would benefit animals. The welfare approach and conservation, although they may appear to be two sides of the same coin, have a different theoretical basis. Welfare is fundamentally concerned with ethical issues (reduction of animal suffering), while conservation is based on science and economic assumptions based on a foundation of anthropocentric concern. However, these two approaches may converge at times.[60]

5.2 Rights of whales

The analysis below is devoted to arguments regarding whales and whaling from the standpoints of ethics and animal rights. The seminal work on this subject remains D'Amato and Chopra's essay.[61] They claim that whales are species with intelligence even higher than that of humans and that they are 'the most specialized of all mammals'. 'They are intelligent, they have their own community, and they can suffer.'[62] However, as these authors claim, whales have no means of self-defence, although those who have been attacked by whales may well refute this. D'Amato and Chopra submit moral arguments against the killing of whales in general. They rely on our duty to future generations due to the intrinsic value of whales, without calculating their utility to human beings. They are of the view that it is almost impossible to draw sharp and clear lines between moral and legal rights, as there is a considerable overlap between them.[63] D'Amato and Chopra rely on the term 'entitlements'

---

[60] Stuart R. Harrop, 'From Cartel to Conservation and on to Compassion: Animal Welfare and the International Whaling Commission', *Journal of International Wildlife Law and Policy* 6 (2003), 79–104, 79–80.

[61] Anthony D'Amato and Sudhir K. Chopra, 'Whales: Their Emerging Right to Life', AJIL 85 (1991), 21–62; see also Hope M. Babcock, 'Putting a Price on Whales to Save Them: What Do Morals Have to Do with It?' *Environmental Law* 43 (2013), 1–33.

[62] D'Amato and Chopra, above n. 61, 21–2.   [63] Ibid., 53.

rather than 'rights' when talking about the rights of whales, by which, as jurists, they understand legally enforceable rights. They claim that entitlements may overlap with morality. Strictly speaking, however, if an interest is not legally enforceable, it is not a legal entitlement, despite whatever 'strong considerations' may favour it.[64]

D'Amato and Chopra rely on and modify the definition of entitlement by Calabresi and Melamed[65] and, in particular, draw upon two aspects of entitlement, as understood by them. One aspect appears when there are conflicting interests between (two or more) people or groups of people and then the State must decide which of the conflicting parties is entitled to prevail; the other aspect constitutes intervention by a State to enforce a decision.[66] D'Amato and Chopra transfer this argument to the field of international law and argue that a whale as a sentient being 'is in the process of being assigned an entitlement of life'. They further develop the argument that in any conflict between whale and whaler, the whaler lacks (or will lack in the foreseeable future) an entitlement to hunt and kill whales. The second element of entitlement is also present as, according to these authors, the international community has intensified its efforts to protect whales, at the national and international levels.[67] In that respect, the second element of their argument is essentially that some extraneous agent – in the case of whales, the international legal system/s – must step in and defend the survival interests of whales.

These authors examine possible 'counterclaims' which conflict directly with whatever entitlement whales have to the right to life. These are hunting for scientific research and aboriginal whaling, which are currently outside the scope of the IWC Moratorium. Japanese scholars submit several reasons (counterclaims) for the justification of scientific whaling, the most important being that taking samplings of whales proves which whale species are endangered. However, the authors of this article counter this argument by observing that in advance of sampling no one can be certain whether the particular species is endangered. D'Amato and Chopra state that, 'since Japanese whalers are concededly killing all these whales in a state of *a priori* uncertainty about whether the species are endangered, one result might be that the process of lethal "sampling" itself could reduce species of whales below the critical level

[64] Ibid., 55.
[65] Guido Calabresi and David Melamed, 'Property Rules, Liability Rules and Inalienability: One View of the Cathedral', *Harvard Law Review* 85 (1972), 1089–1128.
[66] D'Amato and Chopra, above n. 61, 53.   [67] Ibid., 53–4.

necessary for reproduction'.[68] The second fundamental argument discussed by these authors relates to the perceived cultural bias regarding Japanese whaling, already discussed in Chapter 4. However, these authors argue that the continued killing of whales on cultural grounds further solidifies 'a pervasive attitude among the population that the whale was meant for artistic and gustatory benefits of humans'.[69]

Arguments such as those of D'Amato and Chopra are not universally accepted by scholars. Whales take a special place in symbolism and have become almost totemic in the deference that we are told we must show towards these mammals. As Kalland points out, the concept of a 'super-whale' has developed, based on mythical characteristics (see on this Chapter 4).[70] Kalland is also of the view that it is dangerous to single out one species of animals as more ecologically important than others, as all animals play a role in ecosystems. Such an approach is akin to the theory based on viewing animals from an environmental perspective. Environmentalists have an integrated approach to animals, and their value is understood in terms of how they contribute to the healthy functioning of ecosystems. The proponents of this theory frequently mock the attention granted to so-called 'charismatic megafauna' (lions, whales, orang-utans) when less attractive but more useful ecological entities are ignored or devaluated.[71] Similarly to Kalland, some Japanese anthropologists express the view that European and North American culture might see whales as special beings through the depictions in Western media that may have created a new species, a 'media whale'.[72] It is interesting to note the arguments put forward by Judges Mohamed Bennouna and Abdulqawi A. Yusuf in dissent in the ICJ *Whaling in the Antarctic* case, which noted that the issue of whaling is emotionally charged, featuring in history, literature culture and mythology, and that whales have an iconic status.[73]

---

[68] Ibid., 55.   [69] Ibid., 57.   [70] Kalland, above n. 43, p. 28.

[71] Anna L. Peterson, *Being Animal. Beasts and Boundaries in Nature Ethics* (New York: Columbia University Press, 2013), p. 30.

[72] Views of Japanese scholars such as Motohori Lawashima, Karsuki Morita and Kayo Ohamagari have been summarised by James M. Savelle and Nobuhiro Kishigami, 'Anthropological Research on Whaling: Prehistoric, Historic and Current Contexts', in Nobuhiro Kishigami, Hisashi Hamaguchi and James M. Savelle (eds.), *Senri Ethnological Studies, No. 84, Anthropological Studies of Whaling* (Osaka: National Museum of Ethnology, 2013), pp. 1–51.

[73] Judge Mohamed Bennouna, Dissenting Opinion, *ICJ Reports 2014*, www.icj-cij.org/docket/files/148/18144.pdf, last accessed 24 December 2014; Dissenting Opinion of Judge

The argument by D'Amato and Chopra that whales should be singled out as deserving total protection was supported by Mence, who suggested a practical solution that the right to life of whales should be incorporated into the text of the ICRW, with the Scientific Committee advising which species qualify as 'borderline persons'. With respect to such species (e.g. blue, sperm, fin, humpback, right and killer whales, as well as bottlenose dolphins), the Moratorium should be replaced by a permanent ban on whaling.[74]

5.3   Conclusions on animal rights

The question of the application of the various theories of animal rights to whales, in the view of the present author, cannot provide a satisfactory basis for practical regulation of whaling. All general animal rights theories, of which there are many, offer very conflicting views, whether they are those of Singer, Regan or Donaldson/Kymlicka. The arguments of sovereignty accorded to wild animals are incapable of practical implementation at present, in the real world, even if one were to agree with them in theory.

Therefore, if we are to apply any theory to whales within the ambit of the ICRW, as things stand at present, it would not be a total ban on whaling, but an animal welfare approach, to limit their suffering. The application of welfare theory is not without problems itself. States which are advocates of humane killing of whales are accused of being hypocritical, as they do not extend the same policy under their jurisdictions in relation to all animals, both domesticated and wild, which frequently are killed in a cruel way and die violently and over a long period of time.[75] Gillespie suggested that the idea of killing whales humanely should be supported by States that practice consistently humane killing of all animals. Whales must be killed humanely but so must other animals.[76] One such step was the banning of cold harpoons; but not enough has been done in relation either to primary or to secondary killing.[77]

The subject of humane killing of whales has been on the agenda of the IWC since 1960, when the main criterion was the speed of the killing, i.e.

Abdulqawi A. Yusuf, *ICJ Reports 2014*, para. 2, www.icj-cij.org/docket/files/148/18148. pdf, last accessed 24 December 2014.

[74] David Mence, 'The Cetacean Right to Life', *International Journal in Context* 11 (2015), 17–39, at 33–4.

[75] Gillespie, above n. 49, 363.   [76] Ibid., 366.   [77] Harrop, above n. 60, 92.

aiming for instant death. In 1980, the Workshop on Whale Killing Methods defined humane killing as '[c]ausing its death without pain, stress or distress perceptible to the animal. This is an ideal. Any humane killing technique aims first to render an animal insensitive to pain as swiftly as it is technically possible.'[78] Therefore the definition of humane killing within the Workshop on Whale Killing Methods in the 1990s focused on finding a way of inflicting the least possible pain and the quickest possible death. Gillespie notes that there is no uniformity between the members of the IWC as to what is a 'humane' method of killing. Certain States (such as Japan, France, Norway, Denmark and Antigua and Barbuda) argued that what is considered as 'humane' is a subjective judgement, and reflects a cultural and traditional background. Due to continuing differences, the offensive term 'humane' was removed from the titles of the Working Group on Welfare Consideration of Whale Killing Methods and the related Workshop on Whale Killing Methods. Gillespie argues that 'the broad contention is that "humane" consider-ations are ultimately subjective, and as such, have no place in inter-national forums such as the IWC, ... is mistaken'.[79] It may be noted as well that Japan argued that considerations of humane methods of whale killing are outside the jurisdiction of the IWC in general, and in particu-lar in relation to small cetaceans, in relation to which there is no agreement as to the IWC's jurisdiction.[80] There was also some improve-ment in the killing methods in the Faroe Islands.[81]

Despite the lack of a uniform approach to the issue of the term 'humane', Gillespie is of the overall view that the IWC 'has succeeded admirably in reducing infliction of pain on hunted species, as well as their time of death'.[82] At its sixty-fifth Annual Meeting in 2014, the IWC agreed to reflect on the full scope of the IWC's considerations of welfare within the Terms of Reference of the Whale Killing Methods and Welfare Issues Group and to initiate a programme of work to address some of the key human activities with the potential to adversely affect cetacean welfare.[83]

In sum, the dilemma raised in the Introduction about the interrelation-ship between the right to cultural diversity and animal rights will remain unresolved for many reasons, including the lack of any single convincing or widely accepted animal rights theory and the disagreement on what exactly

---

[78] Cited by Gillespie in 'Humane Killing: A Recognition of Universal Common Sense in International Law', *Journal of International Wildlife Law and Policy* 6 (2003), 1–29, 2.
[79] Ibid., 3.   [80] Ibid., 22.   [81] Ibid., 23–4.   [82] Ibid., 21.
[83] International Whaling Commission, https://iwc.int/welfare, last accessed 23 March 2015.

is comprised in the right to cultural diversity. Thus, the way forward should be moving away from an animal rights discourse towards the almost universally accepted theories of animal welfare, which, even considering such differences as there are (such as the meaning of the word 'humane'), would seem to be capable of resolution. Even so, there remain areas of conflict between the animal welfare approach and the right to cultural diversity (which, for instance, may be used to support the retention of less humane killing methods). In the view of the present author, notwithstanding the strength of claims of the right to cultural diversity, these have to be trumped by claims of animal welfare. In this respect it is notable that this is one area in which the IWC has succeeded in sufficiently resolving disagreement among its members to achieve a considerable, and in many ways surprising, level of success. Such considerations should be present when there is an increase in interest in animal rights, termed 'the animal turn'.[84]

5.4   Intergenerational equity in relation to whaling

The next question which pertains, in the view of the present author, to the issue of the position of animals within the general structure of the relationship between humans and animals is the theory of intergenerational equity, as it concerns the preservation of nature. The initial views concerning this theory were critical of its allegedly anthropocentric character and questioned whether the rights of animals were taken into account in preservation of the environment for future generations. Edith Brown Weiss, the author of this theory, denied such allegations and expressly confirmed that animals are also beneficiaries in her theory.[85]

5.4.1   The concept of intergenerational equity

The 1946 ICRW was indeed pioneering in acknowledging in its Preamble, 'the interest of the nations of the world in safeguarding for future generations the great natural resources represented by the whale stocks'. Intergenerational equity directly links generations to environmental issues. As was explained by Brown Weiss, who introduced and elaborated this concept, the use of our natural resources raises at least three kinds of

---

[84] Katie Sykes, 'The Appeal to Science and the Formation of Global Animal Law', SSRN: *EJIL* (forthcoming, 2015), available at http://SSRN.com/abstract=2632812, last accessed 14 August 2015.

[85] Edith Brown Weiss, *In Fairness to Future Generations: International Law, Common Patrimony, and Intergenerational Equity* (Ardsley, NY: Transnational Publishers, 1989).

equity problems between generations: depletion of resources for future generations; degradation in the quality of resources; and discriminatory access to use and benefit from resources received from past generations.[86] There is a multitude of ways in which depletion of natural resources may occur: present generations may deplete a more expensive natural resource, thus making it unavailable (or available only at a higher price) for future generations; natural resources may also be exploited by present generations that are ignorant of their potential economic importance to subsequent generations. In some cases the present generation may exhaust certain natural resources by destruction of areas of high biological diversity. Depletion may reduce the diversity of resources available for adapting to climate change; for instance, the destruction of forests can result in an increase of global greenhouse emissions.[87] Degradation of the quality of the environment also poses questions of equity. The quality of the natural environment (globally and locally) has been degraded, particularly in the last fifty years. Pollution – which degrades many areas of the environment, such as oceans, air, fresh water, soil and land – affects the uses that future generations can make of the environment and the cost of doing so.

The question of preserving the environment for future generations was raised as early as 1893 in the *Pacific Fur Seal Arbitration*.[88] This arbitration concerned a dispute between the United Kingdom and the United States in which the United States suggested the necessity of adopting measures to protect fur seals on the high seas, that is to say, in maritime areas over which extended the freedom of the high seas, including the freedom of fishing. The United States presented complex arguments to counter the right of the freedom of the high seas and pleaded that, amongst other things, 'no possessor of property, whether an individual man, or a nation, has an absolute title to it. His title is coupled with a trust for the benefit of mankind', and that '[t]he title is further limited. The things themselves are not given him, but only the usufruct or increase. He is but the custodian of the stock, or principal thing, holding it in trust for the present and future generations of man.'[89]

---

[86] Edith Brown Weiss, 'Implementing Intergenerational Equity', in Malgosia Fitzmaurice, David Ong and Panos Merkouris (eds.), *Research Handbook on International Environmental Law* (Cheltenham: Edward Elgar Publishing, 2011), p. 100.

[87] Ibid., p. 101.

[88] *Pacific Fur Seals (Great Britain* v. *United States)*, Moore's International Arbitration, 755 (1893). Brown Weiss, above n. 86, p. 101.

[89] Also relevant is the following: 'The earth was designed as the permanent abode of man through ceaseless generations. Each generation, as it appears upon the scene, is entitled only to use the fair inheritance. It is against the law of nature that any waste should be

Every generation would certainly at least have an interest in using the environment and natural resources. However, how could this interest be elevated to a legal right and, moreover, a right the defence of which rests on an earlier generation given that it cannot be defended by the actual rights-holders (namely, subsequent generations)? The main problem is finding a balance between the needs of present generations and the interests of future generations, taking into account such factors as poverty, which may prevent certain communities from equitable sharing of their legacy.[90]

The notion of intergenerational equity is formed on the basis of two relationships: that between generations at different temporal points and that between organised human society and the environment/ecosystem. Accordingly, each generation could sensibly be regarded as the steward of the ecosystem and all its natural resources, and as being morally responsible for the fair and sustainable management of it in order to pass it on to the next generation in the state that each generation has found it.

The human species is thus responsible for man-made degradation of the ecosystem. The notion of equality is at the core of the legal framework connecting generations, in their care and use of the natural system. The concept of intergenerational equity is based on the idea of a partnership between generations themselves and between natural systems and generations. The present generation holds the natural environment in trust for future generations as its beneficiary with the right to use it. Each generation has an obligation to pass on to future generations the natural environment in a state no worse than that in which it was received from past generations.[91]

Brown Weiss identified three aspects of the notion of intergenerational equity: namely, the conservation of diversity of natural and cultural resources (or conservation of options); the conservation of environmental quality (or conservation of quality); and the equitable or non-discriminatory access to the earth and its resources (or conservation of access). The first principle means that each and every generation has an

---

committed to the disadvantage of the succeeding tenants. The title of each generation may be described in a term familiar to English lawyers as limited to an estate for life; or it may with equal propriety be said to be coupled with a trust to transmit the inheritance to those who succeed in at least as good a condition as it was found, reasonable use only excepted. That one generation may not only consume or destroy the annual increase of the products of the earth, but the stock also, thus leaving an inadequate provision for the multitude of successors which it brings into life, is a notion so repugnant to reason as scarcely to need formal refutation.'

[90] *Fur Seal Arbitration*, above n. 87, 102.   [91] Brown Weiss, above n. 85, p. 102.

obligation to conserve the natural and cultural diversity of resources so as not to restrict the options available to future generations to meet their own needs and satisfy their own values. Conservation of quality means that every generation must maintain the quality of the natural environment so it can be passed on to future generations in no worse condition than that inherited from past generations. Equitable access means that each generation has a non-discriminatory right to access and benefit from the natural environment.[92]

These principles should meet three criteria. First, they should encourage equality among generations by introducing a balance in the use of natural resources; that is to say, using natural resources in a manner that is not exclusionary to future generations, on the one hand, and does not impose undue burdens on the present generation, on the other hand. Second, the present generation should not interfere with or predict the values of future generations, but rather it should allow flexibility to future generations in how they pursue their own goals and aims. Third, these principles should be reasonably clear as to be applicable in different social and legal systems.[93]

The rights of future generations as well as the notion of keeping our planet in trust for future generations are not new ideas. Many MEAs and soft-law documents drafted over a substantial period of time mention in their preambles the invocation to future generations.[94] This might all

---

[92] Ibid., p. 103.   [93] Ibid.

[94] See, for instance, International Convention for the Regulation of Whaling: 'The Governments ... Recognizing the interest of nations of the world in safeguarding for future generations the great natural resources represented by whale stocks ...'; the 1979 Bonn Convention on the Conservation of Migratory Species of Wild Animals (19 ILM (1979) 15: 'The Contracting Parties ... Aware that each generation of man holds the resources of the earth for future generations and has an obligation to ensure that this legacy is conserved and, where utilised, is used wisely ...'; Convention on International Trade in Endangered Species of Wild Fauna and Flora, 12 ILM (1973) 1085: 'Recognizing that wild fauna and flora in their many beautiful and varied forms are an irreplaceable part of natural systems of the earth which must be protected for this and generations to come...'; the 1979 Convention on Migratory Species of Wild Animals, 19 ILM (1980) 15: 'Recognizing that wild flora and fauna constitute a natural heritage of aesthetic, scientific, cultural, recreational, economic and intrinsic value that needs to be preserved and handed on to future generations ...'; Principle 2 of the Stockholm Declaration on Human Environment (11 ILM (1972) 1416): 'The natural resources of the earth, including the air, water, land, flora and fauna and especially representative samples of natural ecosystems, must be safeguarded for the benefit of present and future generations through careful planning or management, as appropriate'; Principle 3 of the 1992 Rio Declaration on Environment and Development, 31 ILM (1992) 874: 'The right to development must be fulfilled so as to equitably meet developmental and environmental needs of present and future generations.'

constitute useful evidence in any judicial exercise to establish whether this notion has crystallised into a general principle of law that is supported by developments in conventions or custom.

The question of intergenerational equity has also been the subject of national and international case law. One such case in national courts concerning the application of this principle is the 1993 *Minors Oposa* claim heard in the Supreme Court of the Philippines.[95] It must be mentioned, however, that national courts have not always been willing to apply this concept. In courts in Pakistan it has been invoked but has never been applied. In Bangladesh, in the 1997 case *M. Farooque* v. *Bangladesh and Others*,[96] the petitioners submitted that they were representatives not only of their own generation but of generations to come, relying on the *Minors Oposa* claim. However, the Court rejected this argument, stating that in the Philippines minors had *locus standi*, since the Constitution of the Philippines grants the fundamental right to a clean environment, a right which does not exist in Bangladesh.

The concept of intergenerational equity has also been applied in international case law. The ICJ, and several of its Judges in separate or dissenting opinions, has referred to this concept. Judge Weeramantry was a great supporter of this concept, the *Nuclear Tests II* case being a case in point.[97] The ICJ also dealt with this issue in the *Nuclear Weapons* Advisory Opinion.[98] There are some other examples of this concept being argued before the ICJ. For instance, in the *Gabčíkovo–Nagymaros Project*, the ICJ referred to future generations in the following terms:

---

[95] *Minors Oposa* v. *Secretary of the Department of Environment and Natural Resources*, Supreme Court of the Philippines, 30 July 1993, 33 ILM (1994) 173.

[96] 9 DLR (AD) (1997) 1.

[97] *Request for an Examination of the Situation in Accordance with paragraph 63 of the Court's Judgment of 20 December 1974 in the Nuclear Tests (New Zealand v. France) Case*, Order of 22 September 1995 (Dissenting Opinion of Judge Weeramantry), *ICJ Reports 1995*, p. 317.

[98] 'The use of nuclear weapons could constitute a catastrophe for the environment. The Court also recognizes that the environment is not an abstraction but represents the living space, the quality of life and the very health of human beings, including generations unborn. The existence of the general obligation of States to ensure that activities within their jurisdiction and control respect the environment of other States or of areas beyond national control is now part of the corpus of customary international law relating to the environment' (para. 29); '... the use of nuclear weapons would be a serious danger to future generations. Ionizing radiation has the potential to damage the future environment, food and marine ecosystem, and to cause genetic defects and illness in future generations' (para. 36). *Legality of the Threat or Use of Nuclear Weapons, Advisory Opinion, ICJ Reports 1996*, p. 226.

Owing to new scientific insights and to a growing awareness of the risks for mankind – for present and future generations – of pursuit of such interventions at an unconsidered and unabated pace, new norms and standards have been developed, set forth in a greater number of instruments during the last two decades.[99]

Notably, the national Constitutions of several States contain invocations to future generations. Some authors are of the view that this is an affirmation of the concept of intergenerational equity as one that amounts to a general principle of law.[100] Three types of clauses relating to intergenerational justice may be distinguished: general clauses;[101] ecological generational justice;[102] and financial generational justice.[103]

---

[99] *Case Concerning the Gabčíkovo–Nagymaros Project (Hungary v. Slovakia), ICJ Reports 1997*, para. 140.

[100] Joerg Chet Tremmel, 'Establishing Intergenerational Justice in National Constitutions', in Joerg Chet Tremmel (ed.), *Handbook of Intergenerational Justice* (Cheltenham: Edward Elgar Publishing, 2006); see also the very critical analysis of this concept by Vaughan Lowe, 'Sustainable Development and Unsustainable Argument', in Alan Boyle and David Freestone (eds.), *International Law and Sustainable Development* (Oxford University Press, 1999), 19–38; and Alan Boyle in the same book, 'Codification of International Environmental Law and the International Law Commission: Injurious Consequences Revisited', pp. 61–87.

[101] Tremmel, above n. 100, p. 191. There are several Constitutions with such clauses: e.g. Poland, Preamble to the Constitution: 'Recalling best traditions of the First and Second Republic, obliged to bequeath to future generations all that is valuable from over a thousand years' heritage'; Switzerland, Preamble to the Federal Constitution: 'In the name of God Almighty! Whereas, we are mindful of our responsibility towards creation; . . . are conscious of our common achievements and our responsibility towards future generations'; Estonia, Preamble to the Constitution: 'Unwavering in our faith and with unwavering will to safeguard and develop a state . . . which shall serve to protect internal and external peace and provide security for present and future generations, the Estonian people . . . adopted the following Constitution.

[102] Numerous clauses, such as Argentina, Constitution, Article 41, clause 1: 'All inhabitants are entitled to the right to a healthy and balanced environment fit for human development in order that productive activities shall meet present needs without endangering those of future generations; and shall have the duty to preserve it. As a first priority environmental damage shall bring about obligations to repair according to law'; Poland, Constitution, Article 74, clause 1: 'Public authorities shall pursue policies ensuring ecological security of current and future generations'; South Africa, Constitution, Article 24: 'Everyone has the right (a) to an environment that is not harmful to their health or well-being; and (b) to have the environment protected, for the benefit of present and future generations, through reasonable legislative and other measures that prevent pollution and ecological degradation, promote conservation, and secure ecologically sustainable development and use of natural resources while promoting justifiable economic and social development.'

[103] Estonia, Constitution, Article 116: 'proposed amendments to the national budget or to its draft, which require a decrease in income, and increase in expenditures, as prescribed

One of the most revolutionary proposals of Brown Weiss was her suggestion for the establishment of an 'Ombudsman' to represent the interests of future generations and thus to overcome the inherent temporal limitations on future generations asserting their rights in person. This idea appeared, however, to be rather far-fetched, if not indeed unworkable, at the time. However, certain States did set up special bodies whose function was to represent such interests to varying degrees or with regard to particular areas of policy. In 1993, the French government established a 'Council for the Rights of Future Generations', tasked with considering issues related to nuclear power. This body, however, lapsed when France resumed nuclear testing in the Pacific.[104] Israel is another example, where its Parliament, the Knesset, established a 'Commission for Future Generations' (now defunct) tasked with assessing draft bills that were of particular relevance for future generations within the area of the environment, natural resources, development, health, the economy, planning and construction, education, quality of life, technology and all matters which were determined by the Knesset Constitution, Law and Justice Committee as having particularly important consequences for future generations. In practice this body dealt with protecting children.[105] In 2007, the Hungarian Parliament enacted legislation establishing an 'Ombudsman for Future Generations', vested with broad powers, including advising the Parliament on the impact of certain legislation on future generations and intervening to enjoin activities that could have a detrimental impact on them. In 1980, the United Nations General Assembly adopted a Resolution proclaiming 'the historical responsibility of States for the preservation of nature for present and future

---

in draft national budget, must be accompanied by the necessary financial calculations, prepared by the initiators, which indicate the sources of income to cover the proposed expenditures'; Article 216, clause 5 of the Constitution: 'it shall be neither permissible to contract loans nor provide guarantees and financial sureties which would engender a national public debt exceeding three-fifths of the value of the annual gross domestic product. The method for calculating the value of the annual gross domestic product and national public debt shall be specified by statute'; Germany, Article 109, clause 2 of the Basic Law: 'The Federation and the Länder shall perform jointly the obligations of the Federal Republic of Germany resulting from legal acts of the European Community for the maintenance of budgetary discipline pursuant to Article 104 of the Treaty Establishing the European Community and shall, within this framework, give due regard to the requirements of overall economic equilibrium'; and Article 115(1): 'The borrowing of funds and the assumption of surety obligations guarantees, or other commitments that may lead to expenditures in future fiscal years, shall require authorization by a federal law specifying or permitting computation of the amounts involved.'
[104] Brown Weiss, above n. 86, p. 110.   [105] Ibid., p. 110.

generations'.[106] It called upon States, 'in the interests of present and future generations', to take 'measures ... necessary for preserving nature'.[107]

The above examples can be taken as indicating that there is a certain degree of concern from States regarding future generations. Conversely, it could also be argued that these examples do not amount to much, particularly given that, in the case of some States, these mechanisms no longer exist (e.g. France and Israel) or have been scaled down (Hungary) or were aimed at other outcomes (as may be the case with Israel's mechanism which, when it was operational, did no more than protect the rights of existing children and of a generation of children 'born tomorrow', not extending as far ahead as to include all successive future generations).[108]

The concept of intergenerational equity seems to feature particularly prominently in international environmental law. One could argue that it is, in fact, a leading concept in this field. However, its normative content remains imprecise and its practical application ambiguous. It is unclear whether it has acquired the status of a principle of law, and, if so, whether its normative content has crystallised; or whether it remains an abstract notion encountered in the discourse of a range of social science and humanities disciplines. Attempts to invoke it before national courts have largely been unsuccessful; and before international courts and tribunals, intergenerational equity has not acquired great prominence.

5.4.2   Intergenerational equity and the ICRW

This section will deal with intergenerational equity in relation to whaling, within the context of the ICRW. Particularly relevant in this respect is the analysis of conservation methods adopted by the IWC and the review of three types of whaling – commercial, scientific and indigenous – in connection with the preservation of whale stocks for future generations.

The ordinary meaning of the Preamble suggests that under the ICRW regime the sustainable use of whales had clearly been envisioned. An example is the expression in the Preamble,

> [r]ecognizing that in the course of achieving these objectives, whaling operations should be confined to those species best able to sustain

---

[106] Historical Responsibility of States for the Preservation of Nature for Present and Future Generations, 30 October 1980, A/RES/35/8, para. 1.
[107] Ibid., para. 3.
[108] S. Shoham and N. Lamay, 'Commission for Future Generations', in Tremmel, above n. 100, pp. 244–98.

exploitation in order to give an interval for recovery to certain species of whales now depleted in numbers.

Therefore, it is the view of the present author that a complete ban of commercial whaling activities would not be necessary to fulfil the demands for intergenerational equity given that these could still be met with some degree of commercial whaling taking place, so long as whaling stocks are not threatened with extinction so as to harm the interests of successive generations of humankind. Without doubt the overexploitation of whale stocks is very detrimental for future generations. It may be noted, however, that in the *Whaling in the Antarctic* case, it was suggested by Australia that the objectives of the ICRW have changed and any exploitation of whales, even sustainable, was no longer permissible. However, as was explained in Chapter 3, the Court did not accept this argument.

It is not absolutely clear whether the IWC promotes the principle of intergenerational equity. On the one hand, it may be argued that the IWC does not fully foster intergenerational equity, especially considering the exempted category of scientific whaling and expanding quotas allocated for aboriginal whaling. On the other hand, the IWC Moratorium on commercial whaling and the creation of whale sanctuaries can be said to promote intergenerational equity considerations indirectly. The introduction of the Moratorium, without doubt, bolstered the maintenance of whaling stocks for future generations. On the other hand, sustainable use of resources is an aspect of the notion of intergenerational equity. In light of this, it can be argued that a total ban on sustainable commercial whaling is contrary to the principle of equality between generations, as it unfairly disadvantages the present generation in favour of future generations.

It may be noted, however, that the lack of a coherent policy and cooperation between the IWC Member States is also one of the factors interfering with attempts to introduce long-lasting conservation methods of preserving whale stocks for future generations which would be capable of accommodating the interests of all State Parties to the ICRW. In this context, mention must be made of the 'Future of the IWC' process, which was established in 2007. Its main aim, to have regard for future generations, i.e. to improve the conservation of whales, unfortunately failed due to the lack of consensus.[109]

---

[109]   International Whaling Commission, http://iwc.int/future, last accessed 20 October 2014. See on this Joji Morishita, 'The Truth about the Commercial Whaling Moratorium', *Senri Ethnological Studies, No. 84, Anthropological Studies on Whaling* (Osaka: National Museum of Ethnology, 2013), pp. 337–83.

The Judgment in the *Whaling in the Antarctic* case did not deal expressly with the concept of intergenerational equity. However, Judge Cançado Trindade, in his Separate Opinion, mentioned that '[i]ntergenerational equity comes again to the fore in the present case of *Whaling in the Antarctic*' (referring to the ICRW Preamble on preserving whale stocks for future generations). He also stressed this concept's temporal dimension.[110] In addition, he analysed other environmental conventions from the point of view of the rights of future generations. Scientific whaling per se should expand our knowledge of whales, thus having the potential to contribute to the preservation of whale stocks for future generations. However, as evidenced by the *Whaling* case, unreasonable taking of whales by means of excessive lethal methods could be counter to the interests of future generations.

By virtue of Article V(1)(c) of the ICRW, the IWC can designate certain marine areas as sanctuaries for whales where whaling is entirely prohibited. Sanctuaries are designed to provide whales with a refuge from whaling, allowing species to recover from the kind of serious over-exploitation that occurred throughout the twentieth century. According to the Australian government, their aim is to benefit long-term whale conservation by, *inter alia*, facilitating the recovery of seriously depleted great whale populations by, for instance, protecting important areas such as feeding or breeding grounds and migratory routes, and developing non-lethal economic uses of cetacean species (such as ecotourism and whale watching).[111]

There are two international sanctuaries: the Indian Ocean Sanctuary (IOS) and the Southern Ocean Sanctuary (SOS). The first international whale sanctuary was established in 1938 in the Antarctic, and had only been intended to maintain unexploited stock levels for potential future whaling. It became open to whaling in 1955.[112] The IOS prohibits whaling throughout the Indian Ocean extending north from fifty-five degrees south. It will be reviewed every ten years.[113] The SOS was established in 1994 to protect whales from commercial whaling. It prohibits commercial whaling in former Antarctic whaling grounds,

---

[110] Separate Opinion of Judge Cançado Trindade, *Whaling in the Antarctic*, www.icj-cij.org/docket/files/148/18146.pdf, last accessed 24 March 2015, para. 43.

[111] www.environment.gov.au/coasts/species/cetaceans/international/iwc.html, last accessed 20 November 2014.

[112] www.environment.gov.au/coasts/publications/pubs/iwc-factsheet-sanctuaries.pdf, last accessed 20 November 2014.

[113] Ibid.

south of forty degrees south. This sanctuary will be reviewed every ten years.[114] It may be added that Japan lodged an objection to the SOS, which means that when commercial whaling is resumed, Japan will not be bound by it. The main point of the dispute is that any amendment to the Schedule, on the basis of which the sanctuary may be established, can only be effected on the basis of scientific findings, which Japan argues were lacking, a claim which has been refuted by Australia and New Zealand.[115] Other proposals for sanctuaries – such as those by Brazil, Argentina and South Africa, who first proposed the establishment of a 'South Atlantic Whale Sanctuary' in 2001, and by Australia and New Zealand in 2000 – have so far failed to gain support in the IWC.[116]

What is more, there are also national whale sanctuaries, such as the Australian Whale Sanctuary, which has been established to protect all whales and dolphins found in Australian waters. Under the Environment Protection and Biodiversity Conservation Act 1999 (the EPBC Act) all cetaceans (whales, dolphins and porpoises) are protected in Australian waters. The Australian Whale Sanctuary includes all Commonwealth waters from the three nautical mile State waters limit out to the boundary of Australia's EEZ (that is to say, out to 200 nautical miles, and beyond in some places). Within the Sanctuary it is an offence to kill, injure or interfere with a cetacean. Severe penalties apply to anyone convicted of such offences. The Australian Whale Sanctuary comprises the Common-wealth (that is to say, the Australian 'Commonwealth'/federal territorial) marine area, beyond the coastal waters of each Australian constituent State and the Northern Territory. It includes all of Australia's EEZ.[117]

Such national sanctuaries are outside the jurisdiction of the IWC. The position of whale sanctuaries vis-à-vis the rights of future generations can be compared to that of the effect of the Moratorium on those rights. That is to say, simply in terms of the theory of intergenerational equity, they are required only to the extent that they are essential to maintaining the balance, in terms of whale stocks and their possible exploitation, between

---

[114] Ibid.

[115] Annual Report, Whaling Commission, 2001. International Whaling Commission, https://iwc.int/annual-reports-iwc, last accessed 24 March 2015.

[116] See on this the in-depth Report of the International Panel of Independent Legal Experts On: 'Special Permit ("Scientific") Whaling Under International Law', Paris, 12 May 2006, www.ifaw.org/sites/default/files/international-panel-scientific-whaling.pdf, last accessed 24 December 2014.

[117] www.environment.gov.au/coasts/species/cetaceans/conservation/sanctuary.html, last accessed 20 November 2014.

present and future generations. In relation to both the Moratorium and sanctuaries, it needs to be understood that the theory of intergenerational equity can require no more than that the present generation pass on to future generations whale stocks with the potential for exploitation in no worse state than that enjoyed by the present generation. Those who are looking for more than this are not so much doing it for the benefit of future generations as in the interests of changing the usage of whale stocks by the present generation as an end in itself.

Concluding remarks

As was explained in the Introduction, Chapter 4 and the present chapter should in fact be read together, as they analyse the interrelationship between the right to cultural diversity and animal rights. These considerations are one of the most complex issues relating to whaling. The problem of this troubled relationship has become even more controversial when animal rights have been treated as an extension of human rights, which is a logical result of treating animals as persons.[118] Based on this approach, animals would be granted certain inviolable rights. This in turn would lead to questions of the universality of animal rights, and to exceptions/limitations to animal rights that may be granted on the basis of the right to cultural diversity (analysed in Chapter 4). One aspect of this relationship is the question of animal welfare, which is an area of many divergent views. Certain practices in the name of the right to cultural diversity, for instance ritual sacrifices of animals, could be condemned or tolerated, depending on personal views, whilst wanton cruelty would be unequivocally condemned.[119] There is a host of uncomfortable questions regarding the right to cultural diversity in order to justify such cruelty as bull fighting in Spain or bear baiting in Turkey.[120] However, what is necessary at the interstate normative level is consistency and coherence; this does not mean that culturally sensitive exemptions ought not to be granted, rather it means that they ought to be granted evenhandedly and not denied to a State when they have been granted to other States. Admittedly, considering the emotional and frequently irrational attitudes to the right to cultural diversity, it is perhaps a naive, if not impossible, suggestion to fulfil. For instance, why

---

[118] Donaldson and Kymlicka, above n. 2, p. 44.
[119] Paula Casal, 'Is Multiculturalism Bad for Animals?' *Journal of Political Philosophy* 11 (2003), 1–22.
[120] Donaldson and Kymlicka, above n. 2, p. 45.

should comparable (to whaling) pain and suffering of animals for the production of food products and clothes, and for animal testing in the industries of non-whaling nations, be tolerated, while whaling nations are admonished by international organisations such as the IWC? Unlike indigenous whaling, other whaling promoted within the context of cultural diversity (Norwegian, Icelandic, Japanese and Faroese) has a much less sympathetic reception from the animal welfare/animal rights theorists. Bio-ethicists are of the view that 'the most powerful rejoinder to critics of whaling nations like Japan and Norway is to point to cultural bias: singling out whales among larger animals for special ethical considerations and protection is not based on scientific criteria but on cultural prejudice alone'.[121]

As was evident from the general overview of animal rights approaches and theories, there are several schools, and the choice of any approach is a personal one. The author of this study favours a pragmatic approach in relation to animal rights and cultural diversity, not so much based on philosophical theories as on animal welfare. In coming to assess the situation as it currently stands, it seems to the present author that the only achievable standard appears to be within the realm of animal welfare (reduction of suffering and pain). The animal rights approach is not widely accepted (or followed), as it is less compromising than the animal welfare approach. The noble theory of Donaldson and Kymlicka (animals as citizens and animal sovereignty) cannot be realistically implemented when one has regard to what may be the dominant sensibilities in our societies. The UK, Germany and New Zealand have perhaps tenuously argued that the IWC has a moral responsibility to admit these considerations into debates that take place within it. It is argued that the Schedule to the ICRW, by referring to the methods of whaling and the types of apparatus and appliances to be used, supports the view that the IWC may reasonably develop the mandate to discuss matters such as whale welfare.[122] Whale welfare has remained on the agenda of the IWC since 1981. A Working Group has been established on this issue, and several workshops have been held on this topic.[123] There are more very encouraging developments in the area of the welfare

---

[121]   Ole Torrissen et al., 'Food for Thought: Good Ethics or Political and Cultural Censoring in Science?', *ICES Journal of Marine Science* 69 (2012), 3–5, http://icesjms.oxford journals.org/content/early/2012/03/06/icesjms.fss016.full.pdf+html, last accessed 10 July 2015, 3.

[122]   Michael Bowman, 'Wildlife and Welfare', in Bowman, Davies and Redgwell, above n. 4, p. 684.

[123]   Ibid., p. 684.

of whales adopted at the IWC sixty-fifth Meeting in 2014. These include the new Action Plan, which comprises reports from Contracting Governments on the methods used to kill whales and the effectiveness of those methods, as well as, *inter alia,* the very serious animal welfare concerns that arise through large whales becoming entangled in fishing gear or other marine debris.[124]

Due to the need for whale welfare, the present author is of the view that even where indigenous/aboriginal whaling is justified on grounds relating to cultural diversity, it should be subject to welfare requirements (this question will be examined in detail in Chapter 7). These complex questions are unlikely to be solved by falling back on the usual arguments; all parties to the debate must reassess their seemingly intransigent positions. However, it may be observed that, as the law stands at present, States do have an obligation to observe standards of welfare towards animals. Therefore, it was suggested that animal welfare could be accorded some measure of legal significance in the form of a meta-principle, i.e. one relevant to 'the interpretation and amplification of norms established by other means'.[125] For instance, references to nature conservation treaties in the regulation of capture of animals may be accepted as giving permission for scrutiny on the grounds of welfare considerations. There are, however, serious shortcomings relating to such an approach, one being the vague and very diverse content of the obligation of animal welfare (internationally and nationally), and another being that the interpretation of treaties in the light of animal welfare might be expressly excluded by a treaty provision. Therefore, there is no doubt that the best way forward is to include express provisions to this effect.[126]

Finally, the author of the present study posed a question, namely, whether the considerations of future generations in relation to whaling are evident in the practice of the IWC and the States. There appears not to be a straightforward reply to this question, as explained above in relation to the establishment of sanctuaries and the imposition of the Moratorium.

[124] International Whaling Commission, http://iwc.int/welfare, last accessed 18 January 2015. It may be noted that the NAMMCO is also concerned with humane killing methods, 'NAMMCO Expert Group Meeting on Assessment of Whale Killing Data', 2010, www.nammco.no/webcronize/images/Nammco/948.pdf, last accessed 17 April 2015.
[125] Bowman, above n. 122, p. 681.   [126] Ibid., pp. 681–2.

The IWC and its interaction with other organisations and conventions

Introduction

As we have seen in earlier parts of the present publication, the legal regime relating to the international regulation of whaling had been a relatively simple collection of general international rules that permitted whaling overall but which had introduced certain restrictions in order to allow diminishing whale stocks to recover. That relative simplicity gave way to a more contentious and complex regulatory system, culminating in the Moratorium (that is to say, a total ban) on commercial whaling, though with certain exceptions that have generated much controversy. Over recent decades, significant developments have taken place in international policy-making, in that we have witnessed, among other things, the growing influence of environmental concerns, including concerns over animal welfare (explored in the previous chapter).

Presently, the ICRW remains the starting point of any legal discussion concerning whaling by States that are parties to that instrument. That said, as discussed in previous parts of the present publication, there is a whole raft of international legal agreements (alongside the acts of important interstate bodies such as the Human Rights Committee) that have implications for whaling, in that they touch upon specific aspects of whaling, including the rights of indigenous peoples and the protection of endangered species. In that respect, understanding the interplay between the ICRW regime and other international instruments is fundamental to addressing the legalities of whaling at the interstate level. The present chapter deals with this without going into too much detail about the content, jurisdictional scope and functions of other instruments. Rather, this chapter focuses on the relationships themselves. It does not purport to analyse all the relationships with all possible treaty regimes and organisations; its purpose is to illustrate questions of cooperation and coexistence between the IWC and other regimes and possible issues of fragmentation. The importance of the collaboration of the IWC with other international bodies and conventions (discussed in the following paragraphs) was explicitly acknowledged by the IWC in its Resolution adopting the 'Berlin Initiative'.[1] This chapter analyses the relationship between the ICRW and the following treaties: the Agreement on Cooperation in Research, Conservation and Management of Marine Mammals in the North Atlantic; the Agreement on the Conservation of Small Cetaceans of the Baltic, North East Atlantic, Irish and North Seas (ASCOBANS); the Agreement on the Conservation of Cetaceans of the Black Sea, Mediterranean Sea and Contiguous Atlantic Area (ACCOBAMS); the Convention on the Conservation of Antarctic Marine Living Resources (CCAMLR); the 1979 Convention on the Conservation of European Wildlife and Natural Habitats (the 'Bern Convention'); the 1982 United Nations Law of the Sea Convention (UNCLOS); the Convention on Biological Diversity (CBD); and the Convention on International Trade in Endangered Species of Wild Fauna and Flora (CITES).

The relationship between the ICRW and the European Union (EU) will also be examined. The exponential growth of international multilateral environmental agreements (MEAs) has generated some concerns about potential conflicts and overlaps in their interactions.[2]

The first part of this chapter analyses the scope for cooperation and potential conflict between the ICRW (including the IWC) and the other international bodies and regimes from an operational standpoint, whilst the second part deals with the issue of normative conflict.

The development of international law has led to the emergence – and to a robust evolution – of norms typically associated with international environmental law. The protection of the environment has been the subject of numerous MEAs and has also resulted in the emergence of certain norms in international custom, such as the prohibition of transboundary pollution. States therefore are obliged (on the basis of both MEAs and international custom) to protect the environment, particularly regarding those aspects of their behaviour that have transboundary environmental implications. One such area of environmental protection is that of biological diversity, which is covered by various international

---

[1] 'The Berlin Initiative on the Strengthening the Conservation Agenda of the International Whaling Commission', Annex C, Resolution 2003-1, Adopted during the fifty-fifth Annual Meeting, Annual Report of the International Whaling Commission, 2003.

[2] Alexander Gillespie, *Whaling Diplomacy: Defining Issues in International Environmental Law* (Cheltenham: Edward Elgar Publishing, 2005), pp. 318–26.

agreements, including various MEAs: the CBD;[3] CITES;[4] and the 1979 Convention on the Conservation of Migratory Species of Wild Animals (CMS).

6.1   The role of the IWC and other organisations in the regulation of whaling: general introduction

There are several issues that arise in connection with the relationship between various organisations in respect of whaling and areas of competition between their respective functions.[5] Some general and most fundamental questions of competence of the IWC and other international organisations remain unresolved. As Gillespie observes, the initial intention behind setting up the IWC was that it would serve as the sole body charged with whaling-related issues. That said, the IWC was not designed as an exclusive club of whaling nations; rather, as discussed earlier, it was set up to act in the interest of all nations to safeguard whale stocks for the longevity of the whaling industry and for future generations.[6] In the history of the IWC there have been certain conflicts with other competing bodies.[7]

There are several legal questions which relate indirectly to the position of the IWC (and its competence) in relation to other relevant treaties and organisations. Of particular relevance to the relationship of the IWC with other bodies is the interpretation accorded to Article 65 of UNCLOS.[8] Some authors, such as Gillespie, interpret this provision as according to the IWC the status of 'central and uppermost international authority for cetaceans'. However, there are different interpretations which focus on the word 'organisations' (in its plural form) in Article 65 as clearly indicating that there may be other whaling organisations, equally competent to decide on whaling matters, and that the IWC lacks the exclusive role in this area. Such a restrictive interpretation of Article 65, denying the central role of the IWC, is also supported by Canada. A narrow interpretation of UNCLOS Article 65 has implications for the character of relationships between the IWC and any other organisations that may have competences in relation to whaling.

---

[3] Convention on Biological Diversity, 1760 UNTS 79.
[4] Convention on International Trade in Endangered Species of Wild Fauna and Flora, 993 UNTS 243.
[5] Gillespie, above n. 2, pp. 318–21.   [6] Ibid., p. 323.   [7] Ibid., p. 328.   [8] Ibid., p. 31.

6.2 The IWC and the North Atlantic Marine Mammal Commission

6.2.1 Brief introduction to the North Atlantic Marine Mammal Commission

NAMMCO was set up on the basis of the Agreement on Cooperation in Research, Conservation and Management of Marine Mammals in the North Atlantic.[9] NAMMCO developed from the North Atlantic Committee for Coordination of Marine Mammals Research (NAC).[10] NAMMCO was set up in order to focus on modern approaches to the study of the marine ecosystem as a whole, and to understand better the role of marine mammals in this system, through regional cooperation. NAMMCO and its Member States strive to strengthen and further develop effective conservation and management measures for marine mammals in a holistic manner.[11]

The main reason for the establishment of NAMMCO was dissatisfaction with the functioning of the IWC and, arguably, the lack of any rational management of whales by the IWC. There were, however, other reasons. NAMMCO's jurisdiction covers all types of cetaceans and extends over pinnipeds, marine ecosystems, multi-species interaction and management issues. The IWC, as it stands at present, is not the most efficient forum for dealing with small cetaceans as its jurisdiction in this area is contested. NAMMCO members were also in need of a forum that could provide objective (in their view) information about marine mammals;[12] consequently, they established an investigative and management body capable of addressing the needs of coastal communities and indigenous peoples.[13]

---

[9] Agreement on Cooperation in Research, Conservation and Management of Marine Mammals in the North Atlantic, signed in Nuuk, Greenland, on 9 April 1992 and entered into force ninety days later on 8 July 1992: www.nammco.no/webcronize/images/Nammco/659.pdf, last accessed 17 April 2015. See also David D. Caron, 'The International Whaling Commission and the North Atlantic Marine Mammal Commission: The Institutional Risks of Coercion for Consensual Structures', AJIL 89 (1995), 154–74.

[10] Grete Hovelsrud-Broda, 'NAMMCO – Regional Cooperation, Sustainable Use, Sustainable Communities', in William Burns and Alexander Gillespie (eds.), *The Future of Cetaceans in a Changing World* (Ardsley, NY: Transnational Publishers, 2003), p. 144; Brettny Hardy, 'A Regional Approach to Whaling: How the North Atlantic Marine Mammal Commission is Shifting the Tides for Whale Management', *Duke Journal of Comparative and International Law* 17 (2006), 169–98.

[11] NAMMCO, www.nammco.no/Nammco/Mainpage/, last accessed 18 April 2015.

[12] Hovelsrud-Broda, above n. 10, pp. 145–6.   [13] Ibid., p. 146.

The Parties to the Agreement are Norway, Iceland, Greenland and the Faroe Islands. The main focus of the Agreement is to study the marine ecosystem as a whole, and to achieve a better understanding of the role of marine mammals in this system.[14] NAMMCO is structured as follows. The Council is the NAMMCO decision-making body. It meets annually in order to review advice it requested from the NAMMCO Scientific Committee, to coordinate recommendations for further scientific research and to review hunting methods for marine mammals in areas under the jurisdiction of its Members. The Management Committee puts forward proposals for conservation and management and recommendations for scientific research with respect to stocks of marine mammals. At present, there are two Management Committees. The Scientific Committee provides scientific advice in response to requests from the Council.[15] The Committee on Hunting Methods provides advice on hunting methods. NAMMCO developed and implemented a 'Joint Control Scheme for the Hunting of Marine Mammals', which includes international observation of sealing and whaling activities in the NAMMCO Member States, and which is monitored by the Committee on Inspection and Observation. It may be noted that NAMMCO Members have not pooled sovereign powers and surrendered to NAMMCO; rather, NAMMCO exists to achieve a degree of coordination in their regional efforts, and its powers are merely advisory. In that regard, NAMMCO does not set whaling quotas, despite certain suggestions to this effect, but does advise NAMMCO members on such matters. In general, it is considered that NAMMCO does not have binding regulatory powers over its members.

6.2.2 The relationship between the IWC and NAMMCO

The NAMMCO Agreement contains a general clause (Article 9) stating that, '[t]his Agreement is without prejudice to obligations of the Parties under other international agreements'. Provisions purporting deference to other agreements are not uncommon. However, such provisions can be insufficient when formulated in general terms, without reference to specific agreements, or without any allusion to how normative conflicts are to be resolved. According to Caron, NAMMCO poses a

---

[14] www.nammco.no/, last accessed 3 November 2014.   [15] Ibid.

challenge to the IWC, although 'strictly speaking, the organization does not conflict with the IWC'.[16] From a legal point of view, both Norway and Iceland opted out of the Moratorium; therefore their commercial whaling is legal. Caron accepts that, but observes that NAMMCO and the action of both these States challenge the legitimacy of the IWC.[17] Caron was right in stating that Inuit peoples, in relation to aboriginal whaling, viewed NAMMCO as a useful addition, or even an alternative, to the IWC.

Whilst NAMMCO has limited and relatively clear-cut functions, nevertheless its relationship with the IWC has a potential for conflict and could be quite challenging, given that – unlike the IWC – its membership does not include any non-whaling nations, whose interests and views are therefore not represented. NAMMCO is a regional organisation; in contrast the IWC has a broader and more pluralistic representation, and their respective remits are disparate. The IWC obligations may conflict with those of NAMMCO for Iceland and Norway, who are members of both organisations (as well as indirectly for Denmark through Greenland's and the Faroe Islands' membership on NAMMCO). Should NAMMCO offer an alternative management scheme, States such as Norway and Iceland (or any other State sharing the membership of both organisations) 'will need to walk a fine line to reconcile their obligations'.[18] The legal position of Greenland and the Faroe Islands is also complicated. They are not members of the IWC in their own capacity, given that they are Danish dependencies. Consequently, they are bound by IWC decisions through Denmark,

---

[16] Caron, above n. 9, 165. Henriksen is of the view that the relationship between the IWC and NAMMCO can be challenging, although in theory, since they share the same objective, there should be no conflicts. The IWC Moratorium on commercial whaling is applicable to the North Atlantic. The Faroe Islands is permitting hunting for the pilot whale, a small cetacean that is not regulated through the IWC. NAMMCO may not adopt decisions permitting commercial whaling without prejudicing the obligations of its member states. Tore Henriksen, 'North Atlantic Marine Mammal Commission (NAMMCO)' (to be published in *The Encyclopaedia of Multilateral Environmental Agreements* (Cheltenham: Edward Elgar Publishing, 2016) (on file with the author).

[17] Caron, above n. 9, 165.

[18] Howard S. Schiffman, 'The Competence of Pro-Consumptive International Organisations to Regulate Cetacean Resources', in Burns and Gillespie, above n. 10, p. 185. It is also argued that the IWC can use NAMMCO to great effect. For example, it could provide data to the IWC on species for which the IWC is lacking such data. It could also assist the IWC to monitor aboriginal whaling in a more efficient manner. Hardy, above n. 10, 194–8.

which requests every year quotas of whales (minke whales, fin whales, bowhead whales and humpback whales) on behalf of Greenland's Inuit peoples. Both the IWC and NAMMCO adopt non-binding Resolutions relating to what could be termed management of whale stocks in relation to environmental issues (such as pollution, habitat and hunting methods).

One of the grounds for possible conflict and contention with the IWC is NAMMCO competence over small cetaceans (such as narwhal and beluga whales). The point at issue is that several IWC Resolutions relate to the management of such whales, and certain IWC members, such as the United Kingdom, accept IWC competence over such whales. However, several other IWC members deny that the IWC has such competence. Conversely, if States accept that the IWC possesses such competence, to the exclusion of other international actors, then the position of Norway and Iceland, which are parties to both the ICRW and NAMMCO, may theoretically result in a conflict, in particular because NAMMCO recommends (but does not allocate) total quotas not only for stocks of large whales but also for narwhal and beluga.[19] Quotas for narwhal and beluga whales are set unilaterally by Greenland, which is a NAMMCO member in its own capacity. Therefore, from the point of view of setting quotas for whaling, there should be no conflict as the IWC (at least at present) does not set any quotas for narwhal and beluga.

NAMMCO develops policy recommendations and appears to have the remit to carry out scientific research in connection with all whale species in the North Atlantic, be they great, small or medium-sized. It may be observed, however, that NAMMCO does not have the power to make binding recommendations. Norway and Iceland continue to whale commercially due not to their membership of NAMMCO but because they have opted out of the IWC Moratorium. We have to be mindful, again, about the limited powers of NAMMCO (it does not set quotas), so if some conflict arose, it would be regarding whale stock management in general rather than in relation to a specific allocation. Therefore, in practice there is little, if any, possibility of conflicting jurisdictions. In theory, it cannot be denied, however, that parallel governance of NAMMCO and the IWC may lead to possible

---

[19] See, for instance, NAMMCO Annual Report of the Management Committee for Cetaceans, 3–4 September 2008, Greenland, p. 12.

jurisdictional overlaps and conflicts between them, at least for the States that are members of both organisations. Notwithstanding such a possibility, the view held by the majority of experts is that the IWC's general functional character and its holistic approach to the management of whale stocks leave no doubt whatsoever that the IWC still remains the central organisation in charge of whaling and a forum for cooperation.[20]

6.3   The IWC and the 1979 Convention on the Conservation of Migratory Species of Wild Animals

The CMS may have overlapping jurisdiction with the ICRW.[21] The CMS operates as an umbrella convention which contemplates subsequent agreements that may be within the context of Article IV(3) (styled as 'AGREEMENTS') or within the context of Article IV(4) (styled as 'agreements'). These subsequent agreements may be reached between State Parties that are Range States of migratory species listed in CMS Appendix II, 'where these should benefit the species and should give priority to those species with unfavourable conservation statuses' (that is to say, those species whose survival faces some degree of threat). Such agreements may cover 'any population or any geographically separate part of the population of any species or lower taxon of wild animals, members of which periodically cross one or more national jurisdiction boundaries'.

The CMS includes two Appendices: Appendix I, which covers 'endangered migratory species', and Appendix II, which covers migratory species with unfavourable conservation statuses and 'those which have conservation status which would significantly benefit from international cooperation that could be achieved by international agreement'.

---

[20] Schiffman, above n. 18, p. 185. The same view is expressed by Hardy, who says forcefully, 'Despite the fact that NAMMCO has not become an alternative to the IWC, NAMMCO can still provide lessons on how the IWC could operate', above n. 10, 171. NAMMCO is no rival to the IWC, for the following reasons, *inter alia*: 'it does not manage large cetaceans alone; it has a mission to develop research on ecosystem interactions between marine mammals and the ocean environment before developing management schemes; it has not developed a binding regulatory scheme for consumption of large whales that would include quotas or other management tools; most importantly the IWC, as a global organisation, has benefits to offer which NAMMCO as a small-scale regional one cannot' (Hardy, above n. 10, 189–90).

[21] Gillespie, above n. 2, p. 332.

In 2000, a Memorandum of Understanding was concluded between the Conference of the Parties (COP) of the CMS and the IWC.[22] The Memorandum's objective is to establish a framework of information sharing and consultation between the IWC and the CMS, supplemented in 2001 by the objective to pursue mutually supportive action in relation to small cetaceans. The relationship of the CMS with other international treaties is regulated by Article XII, which states that 'nothing in this Convention shall prejudice the codification and development of the Law of the Sea by the United Nations Conference on the Law of the Sea' and '[t]he Provisions of this Convention shall in no way affect the rights and obligations of any Party deriving from any existing Treaty, Convention or Agreement'. As Gillespie notes, the importance of the first paragraph of this Article relates to Article 65 of UNCLOS, which concerns the management of cetaceans. All else being equal, the second paragraph expresses some deference to earlier Conventions, such as the ICRW.[23] This approach had already been adopted by some Conventions concluded under the auspices of the CMS, such as ACCOBAMS. The non-conflicting relationship between the CMS and the IWC is illustrated by examples of the CMS listing of great whales, which is in line with IWC decisions.[24] In relation to small cetaceans, the determination of the scope of the jurisdiction of both instruments was debated in 1988 and 1994 at the Meetings of the CMS COP. It was decided that in the common areas of interest for both Conventions (such as small cetaceans), the CMS should focus on the migratory aspects of species, whilst the IWC (Scientific Committee) should deal with their habitat and population.[25] At present, due to the lack of certainty with regard to the IWC's jurisdiction over small cetaceans, the CMS appears to fill this void and to have become the leading Convention in this area, and this has not been contested by the IWC.[26]

---

[22] Ibid., p. 332. The Memorandum of Understanding between the CMS and the IWC was negotiated at Adelaide in 2000 (fifty-second IWC Meeting (with reservations of Japan, Norway and the Dominican Republic)).

[23] Gillespie, above n. 2, p. 333.

[24] Gillespie gives examples such as the upgrading of several species of whales (fin, sei and sperm) to Annex I of the CMS, in addition to the already listed humpback, right and bowhead whales according to the IWC's listing. The CMS also added to Annex II Antarctic minke whale after the initial refusal to do so, as it was decided that the IWC would give better protection to this species. See Gillespie, above n. 2, p. 333.

[25] CMS Proceedings of the Second Meeting of the Conference of the Parties (1988), 35–6; CMS Proceedings of the Fourth Meeting (1994), 52, cited in Gillespie, above n. 2, p. 333.

[26] IWC, 41st Report (1991); see also, 'Linkages with Other Conventions', CMS Bulletin, No. 5 (1996), p. 6.

6.4 The IWC and the Agreement on the Conservation of Small Cetaceans of the Baltic, North East Atlantic, Irish and North Seas

ASCOBANS[27] and ACCOBAMS (see Section 6.5) are 'agreements' within the context of Article IV(4) (rather than 'AGREEMENTS' under Article IV(3) of the CMS), which means that they are stand-alone agreements, albeit closely connected to the CMS.[28] AGREEMENTS under Article IV(3) are limited to species listed in Appendix II. During the negotiations of ASCOBANS, not all small cetaceans of the Baltic and North Seas were listed under Appendix II of the CMS.[29]

ASCOBANS is a regional regime. Its territorial scope encompasses maritime zones under the jurisdiction of the parties to the Agreement. ASCOBANS applies to 'all small cetaceans found within the area of the agreement' (Article 1.1). Small cetaceans are defined as 'any species, subspecies or population of toothed whales Odontoceti except the sperm whale' (Article 1.2(a)). The sperm whale is the only member of the order of Odontoceti that is not considered a small cetacean. This definition does not include the minke whale as it belongs to the order of Mysticeti (baleen whales). As Churchill noted, the imprecise definition of small cetaceans is explained by uncertainty at the time of the negotiation of ASCOBANS as to what species of small cetaceans were found in the North and Baltic Seas.[30]

ASCOBANS is open and applicable to any Range State, which is defined as a State 'that exercises jurisdiction over any part of the range of a species covered by this agreement, or a State whose flag vessels, outside national jurisdictional limits but within the area of the agreement, are engaged in operations adversely affecting small cetaceans' (Article 1.2(f)). As Churchill aptly observes, the second category of States seems purely theoretical given that all parts of the geographical extent of

---

[27] ASCOBANS was concluded in 1991 as the Agreement on the Conservation of Small Cetaceans of the Baltic and North Seas (ASCOBANS) under the auspices of the Convention on Migratory Species (CMS or Bonn Convention) and entered into force in 1994. In February 2008, an extension of the agreement area came into force, which changed the name to 'Agreement on the Conservation of Small Cetaceans of the Baltic, North East Atlantic, Irish and North Seas'. Lithuania, Belgium and the United Kingdom have yet to ratify the amendment. See www.ascobans.org/the_agreement.html, last accessed 3 November 2014. Robin Churchill, 'The Agreement on the Conservation of Small Cetaceans of the Baltic and North Seas', in Burns and Gillespie, above n. 10, pp. 283–313.

[28] Ibid., p. 287.　　[29] Ibid., p. 289.　　[30] Ibid., p. 289.

ASCOBANS are located in the national jurisdiction of its Contracting Parties.[31] There are currently ten Parties to ASCOBANS.[32]

The basic purpose of ASCOBANS is to promote close cooperation 'in order to achieve and maintain a favourable conservation status for small cetaceans' in the Baltic and North Seas and, after the amendment of Article 2.1, also the Irish Sea. The conservation aims are set out in the Conservation and Management Plan, which appears as an Annex to ASCOBANS, and which requires parties, among other things, to endeavour to establish the prohibition under national law of the intentional taking and killing of small cetaceans, and the obligation to release immediately any animals caught alive and in good health; to reduce pollution harmful to small cetaceans; to modify fishing gear and practices to reduce bycatches; to prevent significant disturbances (such as those caused by seismic testing and whale-watching) to small cetaceans; to carry out population surveys and research into the causes of their decline; and to report bycatches and stranding. The Plan is couched in rather vague and hortatory language.[33] In 1997, at the Second Meeting, the ASCOBANS Parties defined more specific conservation objectives. The Working Group stated that it was necessary to have specific population levels so the effectiveness of conservation measures could be evaluated. It was recommended that certain interim measures should aim at restoring population levels at 80 per cent of carrying capacity (that is to say, at a level that represents 80 per cent of the level that a given ecosystem could sustain).[34] The Parties also adopted other resolutions concerning more specific issues, such as bycatches and pollution. Article 8.2 of ASCOBANS provides that 'the provisions of this agreement shall in no way

[31] Ibid., p. 290.
[32] Belgium, Denmark, Finland, France, Germany, Lithuania, the Netherlands, Poland, Sweden and the United Kingdom. Non-party Range States are: Estonia, Ireland, Latvia, Norway, Portugal and Spain. The Agreement Area is defined as follows: '... the marine environment of the Baltic and North Seas and contiguous area of the North East Atlantic, as delimited by the shores of the Gulfs of Bothnia and Finland; to the south-east by latitude 36°N, where this line of latitude meets the line joining the lighthouses of Cape St Vincent (Portugal) and Casablanca (Morocco); to the south-west by latitude 36°N and longitude 15°W; to the north-west by longitude 15° and a line drawn through the following points: latitude 59°N/longitude 15°W, latitude 60°N/longitude 05°W, latitude 61°N/longitude 4W; latitude 62°N/longitude 3°W; to the north by latitude 62°N; and including the Kattegat and the Sound and Belt passages.'
[33] Churchill, above n. 27, p. 296.
[34] Report of ASCOBANS, Report of the Fourth Meeting of the Advisory Committee (1977), 43, cited in Churchill, above n. 27, p. 295.

affect the rights and obligations of a Party deriving from any other existing treaty, convention, or agreement'. Churchill's assessment of ASCOBANS is very cautious. He is of the view that the Conservation and Management Plan was not really ever fully implemented by the Parties (in such areas as bycatches and pollution prevention); therefore, the overall effect of ASCOBANS on its parties and their behaviour appears to have been rather limited.[35]

The ICRW is a much broader treaty regime whose task is to regulate whaling; ASCOBANS is a regional treaty. As the subject of the regulation under the ASCOBANS regime, namely, small cetaceans, gives rise to concerns about potential conflict with the IWC, it becomes necessary to delineate the precise scope of the jurisdiction of the IWC with regard to small cetaceans. As was noted several times, the IWC has continuously attempted to regulate small cetaceans. Interestingly, however, during deliberations on Draft Resolution 9 in Working Group II of ASCOBANS, the representative of the IWC observed that 'the IWC is the global body responsible for the conservation and management of large whales'.[36]

With respect to the powers of the IWC over the management of whales and the concurring jurisdiction under the ASCOBANS regime, the interpretation of Article 65 of UNCLOS is also of some relevance, as in the instance of NAMMCO. However, it is quite clear that ASCOBANS is a regional agreement, thus not usurping in any way the power to decide on small cetaceans' management at a broader and more multilateral level. Relevant to ASCOBANS is the jurisdictional matter of the territorial scope of the IWC's governance: for instance, whether it is empowered to regulate whaling in marine zones within the jurisdiction of State Parties to the ICRW. Conflict may arise if certain Resolutions of the IWC regarding the management of small cetaceans conflict with those adopted by the ASCOBANS Meeting of the Parties (MOP). However, this is an unlikely scenario, given that the IWC has expressly acknowledged ASCOBANS as one of the Conventions which may affect whale management and that, at present, it does not really exercise jurisdiction over this type of whales.[37]

---

[35] Ibid., p. 311.
[36] Daniel Owen, 'The Interaction between the ASCOBANS MOP and the IWC, NAMMCO and EC', Doc. AC15/Doc.30(O), www.ascobans.org/sites/default/files/document/AC15_30_InstitutionalInteractions_1.pdf, last accessed 19 April 2015, 18.
[37] The 'Berlin Initiative' Resolution, Preamble, 4th recital.

Owen points in his Report to several examples of already existing cooperation between the IWC and the ASCOBANS MOP.[38] As this author observes, several Resolutions adopted by the ASCOBANS MOP indicate a collaborative relationship between these two regimes, such as in relation to bycatches and chemical pollution. As to bycatches, the ASCOBANS MOP Resolutions support bycatch thresholds set by the IWC Scientific Committee, and rely on the advice on bycatch thresholds provided by the IWC/ASCOBANS Working Group on Harbour Porpoises.[39] Regarding chemical pollution, ASCOBANS MOP Resolutions note several of the IWC initiatives, such as the IWC intersessional meeting on the effects of chemical pollution on cetaceans[40] and the IWC Pollution 2000+ Programme. The IWC appears to support the role of ASCOBANS in these initiatives.[41] The active role of the IWC in the work of the ASCOBANS MOP, in which the IWC has observer status, was confirmed by the IWC Secretariat's paper, which states that IWC observers are allowed to play an active role in the meetings of both ASCOBANS and the Advisory Committee. Moreover, the advice provided by the IWC Scientific Committee to ASCOBANS appears to be quite appreciated.[42] The IWC Secretariat's paper emphasised that there is very effective cooperation between ASCOBANS and ACCOBAMS and the IWC, and that the ASCOBANS MOP and the Advisory Committee nominate observers to participate in meetings of the IWC and the IWC Scientific Committee.[43] The IWC has also collaborated with the ASCOBANS on the SCANS I and SCANS II projects regarding small cetaceans in the European part of the Atlantic Ocean and in the Baltic Sea.[44]

Finally, it may be added that there are proposals concerning the amendment of ASCOBANS to widen its jurisdictional scope to cover all cetaceans.[45] Having analysed provisions of ASCOBANS and the ICRW, Irini Papanicolopulu and Tullio Scovazzi concluded that the

---

[38] Owen, above n. 36, 24-7.

[39] ASCOBANS MOP 2 - Resolution on incidental take of small cetaceans (7th recital and paragraphs 5 and 7); MOP 3 - Resolution No. 3; Owen, above n. 36, 25.

[40] ASCOBANS MOP 1 - Resolution on the Implementation of the conservation and management plan (Action I); Owen, above n. 36, 25.

[41] ASCOBANS MOP 3 - Resolution No. 8 (paragraphs 6 and 13); MOP 3 - Resolution No. 7 (6th recital); MOP 4 - Resolution No. 8 (paragraph 3); Owen, above n. 36, 25.

[42] Owen, above n. 36, 25-6.   [43] Ibid., 26.   [44] Ibid., 26.

[45] On this, see the document prepared for the fifteenth meeting of the Advisory Committee of ASCOBANS, Irini Papanicolopulu and Tullio Scovazzi, 'The Implications of the Extending of the Scope of ASCOBANS to All Cetaceans. Legal Aspects', 2008, www.ascobans.org/pdf/ac15/ac15-29.pdf, last accessed 28 December 2014.

interpretation of Article 8.2 of ASCOBANS clearly indicates that any treaty concluded before the adoption of ASCOBANS should generally prevail over it, as is the case of the ICRW. Since the ICRW does not contain any clauses concerning its relationship to other treaties, it follows that, all other things being equal, for States which are Parties to both ASCOBANS and the ICRW, the ICRW ought generally to prevail.[46] ASCOBANS neither prohibits whaling nor actively permits it. The effect of the Moratorium would be for the parties to ASCOBANS that are also parties to the ICRW (and that have not previously opted out of the Moratorium) to be under the obligation to refrain from any commercial whaling of any kind of cetacean,[47] notwithstanding the silence of ASCO-BANS in this respect. Thus, no substantive contradictions appear to arise in practice between the IWC and ASCOBANS.

6.5   The IWC and the Agreement on the Conservation of Cetaceans of the Black Sea, Mediterranean Sea and Contiguous Atlantic Area

ACCOBAMS is also an agreement within the context of Article IV(4) of the CMS. Article I(1)(a) of ACCOBAMS defines its territorial scope:

> [t]he geographic scope of this Agreement, hereinafter referred to as the 'Agreement area', is constituted by all the maritime waters of the Black Sea and the Mediterranean and their gulfs and seas, and the internal waters connected to or interconnecting these maritime waters, and of the Atlantic area contiguous to the Mediterranean Sea west of the Straits of Gibraltar.[48]

---

[46] Ibid., 5.   [47] Ibid., 5.

[48] 1996 Agreement on the Conservation of Cetaceans of the Black Sea, Mediterranean Sea and Contiguous Atlantic Area (ACCOBAMS), www.accobams.org/index.php?option= com_content&view=category&layout=blog&id=68&Itemid=1, last accessed 18 January 2015. ACCOBAMS further specifies that 'the Black Sea is bounded to the southwest by the line joining Capes Kelaga and Dalyan (Turkey); the Mediterranean Sea is bounded to the east by the southern limits of the Straits of the Dardanelles between the lighthouses of Mehmetcik and Kumkale (Turkey) and to the west by the meridian passing through Cape Spartel lighthouse, at the entrance to the Strait of Gibraltar; and the contiguous Atlantic area west of the Strait of Gibraltar is bounded to the east by the meridian passing through Cape Spartel lighthouse and to the west by the line joining the lighthouses of Cape St Vicente (Portugal) and Casablanca (Morocco)'. There is a pending amendment to ACCOBAMS aimed at extending the jurisdiction of the Agreement to include the EEZ of Portugal. The Parties are: Albania, Bulgaria, Croatia, France, Georgia, Greece, Italy, Lebanon, Libya, Malta, Monaco, Montenegro, Morocco, Portugal, Slovenia, Syria, Tunisia and Ukraine.

There is a difference regarding cetaceans covered by ASCOBANS and those covered by ACCOBAMS. ASCOBANS covers only small cetaceans, whilst ACCOBAMS covers all cetaceans: great and small. Article I(2) of ACCOBAMS states: '[t]his Agreement applies to all cetaceans that have a range which lies entirely or partly within the Agreement area or that accidentally or occasionally frequent the Agreement area, an indicative list of which is contained in Annex 1 to this Agreement'.

The main objective of ACCOBAMS is set out in its Article II:

> 1. Parties shall take co-ordinated measures to achieve and maintain a favourable conservation status for cetaceans. To this end, Parties shall prohibit and take all necessary measures to eliminate, where this is not already done, any deliberate taking of cetaceans and shall co-operate to create and maintain a network of specially protected areas to conserve cetaceans.
> 2. Any Party may grant an exception to the prohibition set out in the preceding paragraph only in emergency situations as provided for in Annex 2, paragraph 6, or, after having obtained the advice of the Scientific Committee, for the purpose of non-lethal *in situ* research aimed at maintaining a favourable conservation status for cetaceans . . .

The scope of jurisdiction of ACCOBAMS covers all cetaceans in the area of the Agreement. Therefore there is real potential for conflict between ACCOBAMS and the ICRW. The Preamble of ACCOBAMS expressly recognises the precedence of the ICRW over it, as it recognises '[t]he importance of other global and regional instruments of relevance to the conservation of cetaceans, signed by many Parties, such as the International Convention for the Regulation of Whaling'. According to Owen, an analysis of cooperation between the IWC and ACCOBAMS, based on their reports, indicates a practice of close cooperation on the level of workshops, assessments, research and monitoring. According to the paper presented by the IWC on its cooperation with other organisations, the most effective cooperation was with ASCOBANS and ACCOBAMS.[49] For example, a paper issued by the IWC Secretariat in 2003 on cooperation between ACCOBAMS and the IMO Scientific Committee mentions at least two topics of mutual interest for both in relation to large cetaceans: ship strikes and fin-whale conservation. That paper concludes with a statement that there are a number of areas of common interest in which cooperation is very valuable.[50] The scope of the ICRW and ACCOBAMS could be an area of conflict, as the ICRW also relates to the commercial

---

[49] Owen, above n. 36, 24.   [50] Ibid., 24.

taking of cetaceans whereas ACCOBAMS is a conservation instrument only, which completely bans any taking of whales within the ACCOBAMS territorial jurisdiction. Possible conflicts around this issue would arise when the Moratorium on commercial whaling has been lifted, if any State Parties which were parties to both agreements decide to recommence any commercial whaling in areas also covered by ACCOBAMS. This conflict should be resolved in accordance with the relevant rules of the law of treaties.

6.6   The IWC and the Convention on International Trade in Endangered Species of Wild Fauna and Flora

CITES is a very complex, global convention, a full description of which would exceed the scope of the present publication. In brief, at its inception, CITES was elaborated as an essentially trade-related instrument, rather than one primarily aimed at the conservation of species, as may be the case for the Convention on Biological Diversity. Article 2 of CITES lists 'fundamental principles' of achieving the objectives of the Convention. CITES consists of the framework Convention and three Appendices listing species to which different levels of trade restrictions apply. For instance, Annex I is the strictest, given that it prohibits all trade in species listed therein, as such trade is detrimental to their survival.

CITES contains a provision (namely, Article XIV) relating to 'the Effect [of] International Conventions', where it states that with regard to trade in marine species listed in Appendix II, the signatories to CITES are to be 'relieved of the obligations imposed on [them] under the provisions of the present Convention ... [if their actions are] in accordance with the provisions of such other treaty, convention or international agreement'. Article XV of CITES deals with amendments to its Appendices I and II. When amendments to these Appendices are made, the CITES Secretariat is under a duty to 'consult other Parties and interested bodies on the amendment'. With regard to marine species, it is necessary for the CITES Secretariat to 'consult intergovernmental bodies having a function in relation to those species especially with a view to obtaining scientific data these bodies may be able to provide and to ensuring coordination with the conservation measures enforced by such bodies'. In that respect, CITES contemplates the need for cooperation with other regimes with overlapping subject matters and/or mandates, thus including the IWC.

As Gillespie has noted, the need for cooperation between CITES and other international bodies has been very much on the agenda of CITES. In 2000 a Resolution was adopted in which the Parties to CITES expressly recognised the IWC as having primary legal competence for the management and conservation of whales in which, *inter alia*, it recalls that 'great whales have not generally recovered from the depletion brought about by commercial exploitation'. The Resolution noted that the IWC has taken 'increasingly vigorous action to provide for the effective conservation and management of whales which are of interest to all nations of the world' and, most importantly, recognised the need for CITES and the IWC to cooperate and exchange information on international trade in whale products and affirmed that any illegal international trade in Appendix I whale specimens undermines the effectiveness of both the IWC and CITES. The Resolution also encouraged other Parties to CITES which are not Parties to the ICRW to accede to it.[51]

In 2002, Mexico proposed a Resolution on cooperation between CITES and the IWC.[52] As Gillespie explains, the possible overlap between CITES and the ICRW/IWC with regard to cetaceans was noted early on by the IWC. The IWC offered to act as a scientific adviser to CITES, and also adopted a Resolution which affirmed the IWC's perceived precedence in whaling matters, and which referred to the perceived 'supportive' role of CITES.[53] With regard to that IWC Resolution, CITES responded with three Resolutions in which it acknowledged the leading role of the IWC regarding the regulation of cetaceans. In a very important Resolution (Resolution 2.9, Trade in Certain Species and Stocks of Whales Protected by the International Whaling Commission

---

[51] Ibid., 337. CITES COP Resolution 11.4 adopted at Gigiri, Kenya, 2000. CITES has 180 Parties.

[52] Gillespie, above n. 2, p. 335. For a general commentary on the relationship between CITES and the IWC, see an excellent monograph by Ed Couzens, *Whales and Elephants in International Conservation Law and Politics: A Comparative Study* (Abingdon: Routledge, 2014), pp. 55–71, 155–66. On similar problems with competing jurisdictions in fisheries management, see Margaret Young, *Trading Fish, Saving Fish: The Interactions between Regimes in International Law* (Cambridge University Press, 2011), pp. 134–88; and also Erick Franckx, 'The Protection of Biodiversity and Fisheries Management: Issues Raised by Relationship between CITES and LOSC', in David Freestone, Richard Barnes and David Ong (eds.), *The Law of the Sea: Progress and Prospects* (Oxford University Press, 2006), p. 210.

[53] Appendix D: 'Resolution to the CITES', Special Meeting, Tokyo 1978, IWC 30th Report (1980), 2, cited in Gillespie, above n. 2, p. 335.

from Commercial Whaling),[54] CITES perceived itself as a supporting institution, accorded the IWC a leading role, and emphasised the need for international cooperation, especially due to the IWC's inability to effectively control alone the trade in meat and other whale products. The Resolution called on the CITES Parties 'not to issue any import or export permit or certificate for introduction from the sea, under this Convention for primarily commercial purposes for any specimen of species or stock protected from commercial whaling by the International Convention for the Regulating of Whaling'. According to Gillespie, that Resolution did not differentiate between species listed in the CITES Appendices I and II, and thus this equation negated the distinction between these Appendices, and, were it to have effect within CITES, would surely have to amount to an amendment to CITES; an event which would therefore trigger the necessity for the CITES rules on subsequent amendments to be satisfied.

Gillespie also observes that Resolutions such as that mentioned above clearly demonstrate the deference of CITES towards the IWC's decisions in these matters.[55] The Resolution was reflected by changes to the CITES Appendices. In 1975, the species of whales – blue, humpback, grey, right and bowhead – were listed in Appendix I. At the meeting in Costa Rica, the whole order of whales (two families and seventy-eight species) was listed in Appendix II for trade purposes (the exceptions of Appendix II were already listed in Appendix I). Certain State Parties to CITES attempted to list all whale species in Appendix I. In 1983, Bryde's, beaked, pygmy and minke whales (with the exception of the West Greenland stock) were added to Appendix I.[56] It may be noted that the Faroe Islands are excluded from the scope of CITES. All listing in CITES and the trade regulation consequently do not affect this territory. Greenland is included.

Gillespie notes an interesting statement by CITES to the effect that '[t]here is no positive evidence that any putative population of Minke whales is endangered in terms of the literal interpretation of the criteria . . . for the CITES'.[57] CITES' action was dictated by the fact that no scientific evidence to suggest they were not endangered was available and that the IWC listed them as a protected stock. As Gillespie explains, in 1985 (the year of the implementation of the Moratorium on commercial whaling) a last attempt was made to add all whale species to Appendix I and a 'slow-down' on cetacean issues commenced. The 'slow-down' has shown that

---

[54] Gillespie, above n. 2, p. 336.   [55] Ibid., p. 337.   [56] Ibid., p. 337.   [57] Ibid., p. 338.

CITES has done all it could in order to ascertain the primacy of the IWC at its forum, as the 'IWC has become the primary battle-ground for these issues'.[58]

In the period 1985–94, the focus of CITES shifted towards trade of other species, most notably towards the African elephant. CITES also adopted several important Resolutions which review the procedure for having species listed in the CITES Appendices (the 'Berne Criteria'). The most significant Resolution was the 1994 Resolution 9.24,[59] which called for new, more stringent criteria of listing than those included in the 'fundamental principles of [CITES]', which nevertheless retained their importance.[60] That Resolution established six Annexes by which the listing and relocation of species between Appendices should be assessed. There are several new, additional elements of the assessment procedure which were included in that Resolution, the most important being that regarding the Annex on 'conservation and management', according to which proponents of conservation and management should be consulted as to the legal status, species management and control measures pertaining to species.[61] Gillespie observed that there is some discrepancy between the objectives of that Resolution, given that it states: '[r]ecalling that international trade in all wild fauna and flora under the purview of the Convention' while also stating: '[n]oting the competence of certain inter-governmental organizations in relation to the management of marine species'. Here, CITES attempts to assert some right to oversee all questions of international trade relating to wild fauna and flora, while it also tries to acknowledge the competence of other organisations which may have an interest in species within the scope of CITES.[62] Annex 6 and its section on Conservation and Management further detailed the methods of reconciliation of these two objectives. It recommended that, in respect of species under the jurisdiction of other international organisations, it is necessary to consult and take their views into account before making amendments to the CITES Appendices, and to provide details of the instruments relating to the management of these species.

By 1994, the question of whales reappeared on the agenda of CITES when the issue of trade in illegal whale meat arose, as well as attempts made to de-list certain species of cetaceans from Appendix I, which

[58] Ibid., p. 338.
[59] Adopted at COP 15, www.cites.org/eng/res/all/09/E09-24R15.pdf, last accessed 29 December 2014.
[60] Gillespie, above n. 2, p. 338.   [61] Ibid., p. 339.   [62] Ibid., p. 339.

prohibits all trade in products derived from species listed therein.[63] The attempts to de-list certain cetaceans aimed at depriving the IWC of the leading role in listing of cetaceans. Those efforts, led by Japan and Norway, were unsuccessful. During discussions it was noted that the IWC was essentially a dysfunctional organisation, and that there were other organisations, such as NAMMCO, the World Trade Organization (WTO), and CITES, which appeared better suited than the IWC.[64] A further factor that exacerbated the lack of support for the IWC was its inability to adopt the Revised Management Scheme, a fact that was a stumbling block in the effective management of whales. That was observed in a letter of concern from the CITES Secretariat to the IWC, to which the IWC responded to reassure CITES of the 'real progress' in negotiations for the adoption of the RMS.[65]

There are several other Resolutions (in addition to those mentioned above) on the subject of the relationship between the IWC and CITES, by which CITES 'recognizes the IWC's primary competence for the management of whales, [and] notes the risk of illegal trade', and also acknowledges the 'important role' of CITES in 'supporting the IWC decisions',[66] and by which CITES recommends 'that the Parties agree not to issue any import or export permit, or certificate for introduction from the sea, under this Convention for primarily commercial purposes for any specimen of a species or stock protected from commercial whaling by the International Convention for the Regulation of Whaling'.

The IWC has responded with eight Resolutions expressing its gratitude to CITES for its cooperation, and calling for improved mechanisms to prevent illegal trade. The relationship between the IWC and CITES has further been consolidated in 2009 Resolution Conf. 11.4 (Rev. CoP12), on 'Conservation of Cetaceans, Trade in Cetacean Specimens and the Relationship with the International Whaling Commission', which recognises IWC primary competence for the management of whales.[67] The gist of that Resolution is the encouragement of cooperation between CITES and the IWC.[68]

---

[63] Ibid., p. 339.   [64] Ibid., p. 340.   [65] Ibid., pp. 340–1.

[66] CITES, www.ssn.org/Meetings/cop/cop14/Factsheets/Cetaceans_EN.pdf, last accessed 28 December 2014. The 1996 Resolution on Cooperation between the IWC and CITES; the IWC's 1998 Resolution.

[67] Resolution Conf. 11.4 (Rev. CoP12), www.cites.org/eng/res/11/11-04.php, last accessed 29 December 2014.

[68] Conference of the Parties (of CITES), '... WELCOMES the work of the IWC in this respect and URGES CITES Parties to explore the issue of illegal trade in whale meat and

Finally, in 2013, the CITES Conference of Parties (COP) 16 adopted the document on 'Cooperation with Organizations and Multilateral Environmental Agreements', making the following statement with regard to the IWC:

> [i]n accordance with Resolution Conf. 11.4 (Rev. CoP12) on Conservation of cetaceans, trade in cetacean specimens and the relationship with the International Whaling Commission, the Secretariats of CITES and IWC have advised each other about meetings of mutual interest, revised the schedule of species and stocks protected from commercial whaling by the International Convention for the Regulation of Whaling, and otherwise exchanged information of mutual interest.[69]

Various MEAs have clauses similar to that of CITES Article XV, which seek to reconcile provisions existing in different agreements. Gillespie noted that the formulation of this Article raises questions, such as what international organisations CITES must consult, and how one ensures coordination with that body.[70] In case of whaling, the answers to both questions are straightforward; as was explained earlier in this chapter, there is good cause for other organisations to regard the ICRW and IWC as, respectively, the regime and institution that have primary authority over whaling matters, as evidenced by a long-standing practice, described in this section.

It is interesting to note that both Norway and Japan at the CITES COP 10 on the one hand valued the links with the IWC and, on the other hand, criticised the failure of the IWC to complete the RMS, and opined that this would eventually frustrate the scientific basis for CITES decision-making.[71] However, some other Parties, such as St Lucia, at meetings of CITES have expressed concern regarding the relationship between CITES and the IWC, as well as the possible need for a new Whaling Convention which would take account of sustainable utilisation.

---

the geographic origin of meat apparently illegally traded and to cooperate with the CITES Secretariat in the collection of information on this subject; ENCOURAGES the IWC to keep CITES Parties fully informed through the CITES Secretariat and the Standing Committee between meetings of the Conference of the Parties on all related developments regarding the illegal trade in whale products; INVITES all countries concerned to cooperate to prevent illegal trade in whale meat, and to report to the CITES Secretariat on any development regarding this issue; and DIRECTS the Secretariat to share with the IWC any information it collects regarding illegal trade in whale meat . . .'.

[69] Cooperation with Organizations and Multilateral Environmental Agreements, www.cites.org/en.pdf g/cop/16/doc/E-CoP16-13.pdf, last accessed 29 December 2014, para. 55.
[70] Gillespie, above n. 2, p. 344.   [71] Couzens, above n. 52, p. 61.

CITES has witnessed many arguments by Japan on the change of listing of whales that were argued very strongly during the 2007 COP. Japan listed in a document fourteen points setting out the reasons for the downlisting of certain whale species and the proposals for more modern managing of whale stocks.[72] The debate over the status of whales within the remit of CITES can be briefly summarised as involving Japan and some of the CITES States seeking to undermine the authority of the IWC as the leading body in the management of whale stocks and noting the lack of scientific data. Other CITES States, led by Australia, view the IWC as the competent institution in whaling matters.[73]

Gillespie noted that the group of those States which have not accepted the leading authority of the IWC in whaling matters is effectively 'charging the CITES to adjudicate' and that such de facto adjudication 'may be made by the CITES deciding to take actions which are not in accordance with the wishes of the IWC'.[74] Furthermore, Gillespie ana-lysed the problems which may arise with this. CITES has no mandate to adjudicate de facto upon the decisions of the IWC, and in doing so, CITES would contravene international law and its own provisions (Article XV). Acting in any such manner, CITES would also pave the way and set precedent for 'any international organization to challenge the authority of any other international organization which deals with an overlapping subject simply by asking its members to evaluate the per-formance of the other body, and then voting to decide whether it will, or will not, usurp its role either by direct or indirect means'.[75] Therefore, Gillespie concludes that such forum shopping could overall undermine the rule of international law.[76] However, it is open to State Parties to CITES to make unilateral statements to the effect that they do not wish to be bound by the provisions of the Convention relating to trade in a particular species listed in the Appendices. That is to say, it is open to them to make reservations so long as any such reservation is in accord-ance with Articles XV, XVI and XXIII of the Convention. Relevant to the making of reservations is also Resolution Conf. 4.25 (Rev. CoP14).[77]

[72] Ibid., p. 164.
[73] Peter Sand, 'Japan's "Research Whaling" in the Antarctic Southern Ocean and in the North Pacific Ocean in the Face of the Endangered Species Convention (CITES)', RECIEL 17 (2008), 56–71, 60–1. See the view that the IWC and the CITES represent two somewhat parallel autonomous regimes that complement and supplement one another.
[74] Gillespie, above n. 2, p. 344. [75] Ibid., p. 345. [76] Ibid., p. 345.
[77] www.cites.org/eng/res/04/04-25R14.php, last accessed 29 December 2014.

Japan, Iceland and Norway have appended reservations with regard to certain types of whale.[78] It may be said that these States are not the only ones to lodge reservations in relation to whaling.[79]

Couzens is of the view that in the intervening years the whole pro-whaling debate has shifted the focus away from the IWC and towards CITES, with anti-whaling States trying to promote the IWC given that the Moratorium is within the context of the latter. However, as he explains, in general the discourse relating to the best method of utilising animals has changed, with the different terminology and with the new understanding of the complexity of the ecosystem in question.[80]

6.7   The IWC and the 1980 Convention on the Conservation of Antarctic Marine Living Resources

The objective of the CCAMLR[81] is the conservation of Antarctic marine living resources, which are defined as: 'the populations of fin fish, molluscs, crustaceans and all other species of living organisms, including birds, found south of the Antarctic Convergence' (Article I(2)). Article II(3) sets out principles of conservation:

[78] Japan has lodged reservations with regard to the common (Northern) minke whale (except for the Appendix II population of West Greenland), the Antarctic minke whale, the sei whale (except the population in the North Pacific (taking them for scientific research), and between the Equator and the Arctic), the Bryde's whale, the fin whale, the Irrawaddy dolphin and Baird's beaked whale: Appendix I. Iceland has lodged reservations concerning the common (Northern) minke whale, the sei whale (unrestricted), the blue whale, the fin whale, the humpback whale, the sperm whale and the northern bottlenose whale. It also lodged reservations over various Appendix II cetaceans, the West Greenland population of the humpback whale, seven species of dolphin, the killer whale and one species of porpoise. Norway has reservations concerning the common (Northern) minke whale (except for the Appendix II population of West Greenland), the Antarctic minke whale, the sei whale (except the populations of the North Pacific and between the Equator and the Antarctic) and the sperm whale (except for the populations in the North Pacific and between the Equator and the Antarctic), the fin whale (only concerning the populations in the North Atlantic off Iceland and Newfoundland and its southerly region near America) and the sperm whale. Couzens, above n. 52, pp. 165–6.

[79] For example, Palau has made a reservation concerning the common (Northern) minke whale (except for the Appendix II population of West Greenland) and the sperm whale. St Vincent and the Grenadines have lodged a reservation in relation to the humpback whale: Couzens, above n. 52, p. 166.

[80] Couzens, above n. 52, p. 166.

[81] 1980 Convention on the Conservation of Antarctic Marine Living Resources (CCAMLR), 1329 UNTS 48, part of the Antarctic Treaty System. CCAMLR has twenty-six Parties.

(a) prevention of decrease in the size of any harvested population to levels below those which ensure its stable recruitment ...;

(b) maintenance of the ecological relationships between harvested, dependent and related populations of Antarctic marine living resources and the restoration of depleted populations to the levels defined in sub-paragraph (a) ...; and

(c) prevention of changes or minimisation of the risk of changes in the marine ecosystem which are not potentially reversible over two or three decades, taking into account the state of available knowledge of the direct and indirect impact of harvesting ...

Article VII establishes the Commission for the Conservation of Antarctic Marine Living Resources, whose function is to give effect to the objectives and principles set out in Article II.

With regard to the relationship between the ICRW and the 1980 CCAMLR, the most important provisions of the latter are Articles VI and XXIII(3). Article VI states that: '[n]othing in this Convention shall derogate from the rights and obligations of Contracting Parties under the International Convention for the Regulation of Whaling'. Article XXIII(3) provides as follows: 'The Commission's Scientific Committee shall seek to develop cooperative working relationships, as appropriate, with inter-governmental organizations and non-governmental organizations which could contribute to their work, including ... the International Whaling Commission.'[82] The marine resources managed by the CCAMLR specific-ally exclude whales and seals, as pre-eminence is given to the pre-existing ICRW and to the Antarctic Seals Convention (ASC).[83] In practice, the IWC and the CCAMLR Commission and the Scientific Committee have established good cooperation in areas of mutual interest. The IWC has adopted Resolutions noting the first research collaboration of the IWC and CCAMLR under the joint SOWER 2000 and POLLUTION+ 2000 research programmes, and calling for greater collaboration with the CCAMLR.[84]

---

[82] Article IX(5) states that: '[t]he Commission shall take full account of any relevant measures or regulations established or recommended by ... existing fisheries Commissions responsible for species which may enter the area to which this Convention applies, in order that there shall be no inconsistency between the rights and obligations of a Contracting Party under such regulations or measures and conservation measures which may be adopted by the Commission'.

[83] A. Fabra and V. Gascón, 'The Convention on the Conservation of Antarctic Marine Living Resources (CCAMLR) and the Ecosystem Approach', *International Journal of Marine and Coastal Law* 23 (2008), 567–98, 574.

[84] Gillespie, above n. 2, p. 331. See also the Resolution on Cooperation between the IWC and the CCAMLR at the IWC's thirty-first Meeting, Report (Argentina and Chile

6.8   The IWC and trade restrictions

Trade restrictions are among the tools that may be utilised by the IWC to regulate the conservation of whales. Whilst there is no express provision in relation to trade restrictions in the ICRW, the IWC habitually issues Resolutions enjoining trade restrictions in relation to both whale products and whaling equipment, as indirect means of enhancing conservation. In the absence of express authorisation under the Whaling Convention, such as exists with respect to limitations imposed on whaling, the legal effect of such Resolutions is unclear and challenged.

A considerable problem with which the IWC struggles is pirate whaling, to which a partial solution has been found in trade restrictions, both in whale products and in whaling equipment.[85] In 2001, in the Resolution on Commercial Whaling, the IWC urged Norway not to issue export permits for whale products. As Gillespie observes, this was especially emphasised due to the linkages with CITES and its listing of some proposed species for export.[86] There are also several IWC Resolutions dealing with the restriction on the sale of whaling vessels and equipment.[87] As Gillespie explains, the IWC had always intended to be the leading organisation in the overseeing of all trade in whaling products

---

reserved their position on this resolution and reiterated it in 1982). Resolution IWC 2000 and 2003-1.

[85] Nicole Millar, 'Polar Pirates: Friend or Foe? Should the Definition of Piracy Be Altered to Exclude the Activities of Sea Shepherd in the Southern Ocean?', dissertation, University of Otago, October 2013, www.otago.ac.nz/law/research/journals/otago065270.pdf, last accessed 28 December 2014. Unilateral trade restrictions have been used by the United States and the United Kingdom. For instance, the United States unilaterally threatened to apply trade restrictions under the Pelly Amendment (discussed in earlier chapters of the present publication) and the Packwood-Magnuson Amendment against Japan in order to stop Japan from upholding reservations relating to the imposition of the Moratorium.

[86] IWC Resolution on Commercial Whaling, IWC/ 53/26, Rev. Agenda Item 9.2; Gillespie, n. 2 above, p. 326.

[87] IWC 24th Report (1977), 22; IWC 28th Report (1976), 31.33. 1979 Resolution, Appendix 9: Importation of Whale Products from Non-Member Countries, IWC 30th Report (1980), 38; 1980 Resolution, Appendix 6: Resolution Aimed at Discouraging Whaling Operation Outside the IWC Regulation, IWC 31st Report (1981), 30. Appendix F: Resolution on the Transfer of Whaling Equipment etc., Special Meeting, IWC 28th Report (1980), 30, specifically urged that all Member States of the IWC should take all practical measures to prevent the transfer of factory ships, whale catchers or gear, apparatus or appliances which are used in whaling operations and also to discourage the provision by their citizens of expertise and assistance necessary to conduct such whaling operations.

and equipment. The IWC has issued several Resolutions on the importation of whale products from non-IWC States.[88]

After the establishment of CITES, the trade aspects of illegal whale
meat and whaling equipment were dealt with by both the IWC and
CITES. Further attempts to import illegal whale meat resulted in an
IWC Resolution which also refers to the obligations of the ICRW State
Parties and IWC members under CITES.[89] At the Fort Lauderdale
meeting, a CITES Resolution was passed which, among other things,
stressed the importance of cooperation and exchange of information
between the IWC and CITES.[90] In 1995 and 1996, the IWC noted the
CITES Resolution favourably, and also passed another Resolution which
referred to complex questions of tracing the source of illegal trade in
whale meat and products, especially in light of the fact that a level of legal
trade of whale meat was taking place, and in light of existing dated
stockpiles.[91] However, the involvement of the IWC in the monitoring
and prohibition of the sale of illegal whale meat is not without controversy, as Japan suggested that the IWC lacked the necessary competence
concerning the trade in whale products in relation to domestic markets.[92]
Japan offered cooperation concerning the sale of whale meat but this led
to challenges from other States as to the quality of information that Japan
would submit. The suggestion of peer review of the samples analysed
in market surveys was objected to by Norway and Japan.[93] In 1998, both
States reiterated their willingness to supply information voluntarily;
however, they expressed their misgivings as to whether the IWC was
the appropriate forum for domestic trade matters, and suggested that

[88] For instance, Appendix E: Resolution on the Importation of Whale Products from Non-
IWC Member Countries, Special Meeting, Tokyo, 1978, IWC 30th Report (1980), 8. This
Resolution called upon IWC Members to 'prevent import of any whale or product thereof
taken by a whale catcher or processed, at a land station or factory ship which is registered
with, partially or wholly owned by, or under the jurisdiction of any State not a party to
this Convention'.

[89] In 1994, larger quantities of whale meat were discovered en route to Japan. This resulted
in the IWC's Resolution on International Trade in Whale Meat and Products (Appendix
7, IWC 45th Report, pp. 45–6). This Resolution referred to the obligation under the
ICRW and CITES 'relating to international trade in whale products'. CITES, for its part,
also addressed this problem, such as in Resolution 9.2 at the Fort Lauderdale meeting.
This Resolution referred to the discovery of the illegal trade in whale meat. This
Resolution also observed that there was no adequate monitoring system in existence.

[90] Resolution 9.12 CITES.

[91] Resolution on Improving Mechanisms to Prevent Illegal Trade in Whale Trade, Appendix 7, at p. 45.

[92] IWC 47th Report (1997), p. 21.   [93] IWC Report (1948), p. 24.

CITES and/or the WTO would be more appropriate.[94] That was a reason for which both Norway and Japan did not support the Resolution on the Cooperation between the IWC and CITES in 1998, presenting the view that the IWC was encroaching on the competence of other organisations.[95]

It must also be noted that Denmark frequently abstained from IWC Resolutions relating to the cooperation between the IWC and CITES (such as the Resolutions of the IWC in 1999 and 2001 which recalled that 'all species of whales in the Schedule be listed in Appendix I of the CITES' and requested that 'the Government of Norway refrain from issuing export permits for whale products'). As Altherr and Lonsdale argue, 'by taking these positions, Denmark essentially expressed opposition to the moratorium, the CITES trade ban, and the EU legislation with respect to whales'.[96] In 2007, Denmark also abstained from the Resolution which stressed the importance of the Moratorium and confirmed that the revocation of the CITES trade ban could weaken the Moratorium, thus calling on the parties not to support the downlisting of whale species from Appendix I of CITES. However, in June 2007, despite Greenland's support for Japan's proposal for the CITES Appendix I list (listing of all cetaceans) to be reviewed, Denmark did not break the EU's consensus, and voted against this proposal.[97] In parallel, CITES continued dealing with issues of illegal trade. One of its initiatives was the decision of the CITES COP to call on the Parties to make an inventory of the frozen whale meat and products possessed in commercial quantities; and to collect DNA samples from stockpiles for identification purposes.[98] The competence of CITES on matters of trade in illegal whale meat and other whale products was not challenged by Japan, which suggested continuous updates on this subject matter.[99] Theoretically, the WTO could be a proper forum for dealing with issues of restrictions on whale-related products, as indeed has been suggested by Japan and

[94] IWC, fiftieth Meeting, 1998 (1999), p. 9.   [95] Ibid., at p. 52.

[96] Sandra Altherr and Jennifer Lonsdale, 'Breaking Ranks: Denmark Goes Alone on Whaling Policy', www.hsi.org/assets/pdfs/breaking_ranks_may_2012.pdf, last accessed 28 December 2014.

[97] Ibid., p. 16.

[98] E.g. Decision 10.40, regarding cooperation in monitoring illegal trade in whale parts and derivatives.

[99] Japanese Proposal to transfer Southern Hemisphere Minke from Appendix I to Appendix II, Prop. 11.16:6.

Norway, as a means of passing restrictive attitudes of the IWC. However, to date, these issues have not been raised in the forum of the WTO.[100]

6.9 The IWC and the 1979 Convention on the Conservation of European Wildlife and Natural Habitats

The 1979 Convention on the Conservation of European Wildlife and Natural Habitats (the 'Bern Convention')[101] was adopted within the context of the Council of Europe (CoE). All State Parties to the Bern Convention must take action to: promote national policies for the conservation of wild flora and fauna and their natural habitats (including migratory species (Article 1)); have regard to the conservation of wild flora and fauna in their planning and development policies, and in their measures against pollution; promote education and disseminate general information on the need to conserve species of wild flora and fauna and their habitats; encourage and coordinate research related to the purposes of the Convention and also cooperate to enhance the effectiveness of these measures through: coordination of efforts to protect migratory species; and the exchange of information and the sharing of experience and expertise.[102] Appropriate legislative and administrative measures must be adopted to conserve the wild fauna species listed in Appendix II of the Bern Convention. The following are prohibited in relation to species listed in this Appendix: all forms of deliberate capture and keeping and deliberate killing; the deliberate damage to or destruction of breeding or nesting sites; the deliberate disturbance of wild fauna, particularly during the period of breeding, rearing and hibernation; the possession of and internal trade in these animals, alive or dead, including stuffed animals and any part or derivative thereof. Appendix III of the Bern Convention applies to 'all species not mentioned in its Appendix II'.[103]

---

[100] See, in depth, on similar possibilities in relation to fish, Young, above n. 52.

[101] 1284 UNTS 209, http://conventions.coe.int/Treaty/Commun/QueVoulezVous.asp?NT= 104&CM=8&DF=&CL=ENG, last accessed 31 January 2015.

[102] www.coe.int/t/dg4/cultureheritage/nature/bern/default_en.as, last accessed 28 December 2014.

[103] The Convention has four Appendices: Appendix I (strictly prohibited: flora); Appendix II (strictly prohibited: fauna); Appendix III (protected fauna – all species not mentioned in Appendix II); Appendix IV (prohibited means of capture; killing; or other forms of exploitation). There are 168 Parties.

The Parties have sought primarily to implement the objectives of the Bern Convention concerning habitat protection through the ongoing development of a coordinated series of protected areas, known as the Emerald Network. These obligations are now primarily discharged by EU Member States through adherence to the EU's General Directive 92/43 EEC (Habitats Directive). The primary enforcement mechanism of the Bern Convention is its innovative system of case files, whereby the Bern Convention's institutions respond to complaints alleging a failure to meet the requisite conservation standards.[104] Cetaceans are listed in Appendix II (List of strictly protected species) and in Appendix III (List of protected species) to the Bern Convention. About thirty species are listed in Appendix II and all others in Appendix III. The Faroe Islands and Greenland are not included in the scope of the Bern Convention. As long as the Moratorium on whaling is in place, there is very little scope for conflict between the listings of the Bern Convention and the management of whales under the ICRW. However, in the event that the Moratorium were to be lifted, there would arise the possibility of a conflict related to whales listed in Appendix II, which prohibits deliberate killing and capture of all species listed therein. It may be noted that the Bern Convention allowed States to make reservations in relation to listings. Therefore, in cases of States which made such a reservation in relation to whales included in the reservation, there would be no conflict. For example, Iceland at the time of ratifying the Bern Convention appended a reservation excluding six species of whales, including minke whales.

6.10   The IWC and the European Union

Under EU law, cetaceans (whales, dolphins and porpoises) are protected by General Directive 92/43 EEC (Habitats Directive)[105] and by Council Regulation No. 338/97 that implements CITES.[106] The

---

[104] http://us.whales.org/en/issues/in-depth/bern-convention-1979, last accessed 24 December 2014.

[105] Council Directive 92/43/EEC of 21 May 1992 on the conservation of natural habitats and of wild fauna and flora, Official Journal (OJ) L 206, 22/07/1992 P. 0007–0050, EUR-lex, http://eur-lex.europa.eu/LexUriServ/LexUriServ.do?uri=CELEX:31992L0043:EN:html, last accessed 28 December 2014.

[106] Council Regulation (EC) No. 338/97 of 9 December 1996 on the protection of species of wild fauna and flora by regulating trade therein, OJ L 61, 3.3.1997, P. 1–69, EUR-lex, http://eur-lex.europa.eu/smartapi/cgi/sga_doc?smartapi!celexapi!prod!CELEXnumdoc&lg=en&

Directive is the means by which the EU meets its obligations under the Bern Convention. In 2008, for the first time, the EU adopted a common position for the IWC Annual Meeting relating to proposals for amendments to the ICRW and its Schedule.[107] Prior to the sixtieth Annual Meeting of the IWC, and in relation to the 2008 EU common position regarding the IWC, the Danish Commissioner to the IWC informed the other EU Member States that Denmark would invoke 'Declaration 25', an annex to the Maastricht Treaty, with regard to EU Member States' overseas countries and territories, in order to exempt such territories from the effects of the common position.[108] At the IWC meeting, Denmark explained its stand in relation to the EU's common position and its intention to conform to it. However, Denmark made clear that the common position does not extend over Denmark's overseas territories, namely, Greenland and the Faroe Islands, where it conflicts with their interests. It therefore informed the meeting that when Denmark made an intervention in the IWC, it would be to pursue the interests of its overseas territories, particularly those of Greenland.[109] In March 2009, EU Member States agreed on a common position with regard to their dealings at the IWC Annual Meetings from 2009 to 2011.[110] Denmark did not refer to Declaration 25. This may be because Declaration 25 was an Annex to the Maastricht Treaty, which remained in force until 2009 but was superseded by the Lisbon Treaty.[111] There is no agreement as to the legal position of Declaration 25 regarding territories of Denmark and whaling. One legal analysis finds that Declaration 25 is no longer valid and that Denmark is now under an obligation to

---

numdoc=31997R0338&model=guichett, last accessed 28 December 2014. It may be noted that not all Member States of the EU are parties to the ICRW (the Czech Republic, Cyprus, Latvia, Malta and Greece are not parties). Two autonomous overseas territories of Denmark – the Faroe Islands and Greenland – are excluded from the scope of the EU. Greenland has a population of 56,000 and the Faroe Islands a population of 49,000. Mainland Denmark has a population of 5.5 million.

[107] Council Decision 9818/08.

[108] www.eurotreaties.com/maastrichtfinalact.pdf, last accessed 28 December 2014. See also Altherr and Lonsdale, above n. 96.

[109] Annual Report of the IWC 2008, 2, cited in Altherr and Lonsdale, above n. 96, pp. 9–10.

[110] EU Council Decision 7146/09 of 3 March 2009, cited in Altherr and Lonsdale, above n. 96, p. 10.

[111] V. Miller (2011): Declaration 25 of the Treaty on European Union: Danish Territories and Whaling. Standard Note SN 5980, dated 24 May 2011, provided to the Members of Parliament, cited in: Altherr and Lonsdale, above n. 96, p. 11.

comply with the EU Common Position for the IWC, regarding its overseas territories, and with EU environmental law.[112]

Other legal analyses support the view that Denmark may only take a different position to that of the other EU IWC members with respect to IWC decisions.[113] In autumn 2011, EU IWC members negotiated a new EU Council Decision for the common EU position to be taken at the subsequent three IWC meetings.[114] Denmark submitted a written statement opposing the EU Council Decision and stating that the common EU position was unbalanced in relation to the mandate of the IWC and 'therefore unable to contribute sufficiently to the endeavours to secure sustainable conservation and management of whales through a well-functioning IWC. Consequently Denmark cannot vote in favour of the proposal.' This stand was justified by Denmark with reference to its overseas territories (without explicitly invoking Declaration 25 in relation to the Maastricht Treaty). Denmark further argued that the EU position is for a large part 'incompatible with the interests of the Faroese and Greenland and it will be impossible to find solutions where these interests can coincide with the EU position'.[115]

6.11   The IWC and the 1982 United Nations Convention on the Law of the Sea

This part of the chapter deals with general aspects of the relationship between the IWC and UNCLOS.[116] UNCLOS contains several provisions

---

[112] ClientEarth (2010): 'The Proposed Reform of the International Whaling Convention and EU Voting Rules', www.clientearth.org/reports/100520-marine-protection-eu-voting-and-iwc-f.pdf, last accessed 28 December 2014.

[113] Ludwig Krämer (2010), 'Negotiating and Voting on Whale Protection within the IWC. Analysis for the International Fund for Animal Welfare', http://opinion-former-resources.politics.co.uk/microsites2/364355/graphics/ifawlegalpaperiwc.pdf, last accessed 28 December 2014.

[114] Proposal for a Council Decision establishing the position to be adopted on behalf of the European Union at the next five meetings of the International Whaling Commission including the related inter-sessional meetings with regard to proposals for amendments to the International Convention on the Regulation of Whaling and its Schedule, /* COM/2011/0495 final – 2011/0221 (NLE), http://eur-lex.europa.eu/legal-content/EN/TXT/?uri=CELEX:52011PC0495, last accessed 28 December 2014, 167.

[115] EU Council, 12 December 2011, Inter-institutional file 2011/0221 NLE, cited in Altherr and Lonsdale, above n. 96, p. 10.

[116] United Nations Convention on the Law of the Sea (UNCLOS), 1833 UNTS 3; Agreement Relating to the Implementation of Part XI of the Convention of 10 December 1982, 1836 UNTS 41.

that deal with marine resources (namely, Articles 56 and 57 concerning the Specific Legal Regime of the Exclusive Economic Zone (EEZ) and the Rights, Jurisdiction and Duties of the Coastal State in the EEZ; Articles 61 and 62 concerning the Conservation of Living Resources; Article 64 concerning Highly Migratory Species; and Articles 65 and 120 concerning Marine Mammals).

It may be said that several UNCLOS provisions concerning marine resources aim at both the conservation and the utilisation of such resources (the balancing of which is a complex matter), which, according to some views, UNCLOS broadly achieves.[117] The UNCLOS provisions also promote the duty of State Parties and UNCLOS-related bodies to cooperate with other international regimes and organisations.

The legal regime of UNCLOS and the conservation of living marine resources has been widely analysed and will not be the subject of the present chapter, which analyses the most pertinent aspects of UNCLOS that concern whaling. The most important aspect of UNCLOS for the management of living natural resources, such as whales, is that concerning the EEZ, in which, according to UNCLOS, States have jurisdiction over natural resources. UNCLOS Article 61 provides that '[t]he coastal State shall determine the allowable catch of the living resources in its exclusive economic zone' and that it shall also 'ensure through proper conservation and management measures that the maintenance of the living resources is not endangered by over-exploitation'. Article 61 also imposes a duty on coastal States to cooperate 'as appropriate' with competent international organisations, 'whether sub-regional, regional or global'. This provision acknowledges the important role of scientific evidence. The objective of Article 62 is the promotion by the coastal State of 'optimum utilization of the living resources in the exclusive economic zone without prejudice to article 61'. Schiffman argues that the legality of a State's actions in relation to the exploitation of its own natural resources may be presumed, unless there is conflict with treaty obligations or there is clear evidence of interference with the rights of other States in exploiting their own maritime resources.[118]

Article 64, concerning migratory species, is a provision the objectives of which are both utilisation and conservation.[119] The most important Article in relation to marine mammals is Article 65, stating that

---

[117] Schiffman, above n. 18, p. 171.   [118] Ibid., p. 172.

[119] Article 64: '1. The coastal State and other States whose nationals fish in the region for the highly migratory species listed in Annex I shall cooperate directly or through

Nothing in this Part restricts the right of a coastal State or the competence of an international organization, as appropriate, to prohibit, limit or regulate the exploitation of marine mammals more strictly than provided for in this Part. States shall cooperate with a view to the conservation of marine mammals and in the case of cetaceans shall in particular work through the appropriate international organizations for their conservation, management and study.

Article 65 should be read together with Article 120 of UNCLOS, which states that 'Article 65 also applies to the conservation and management of marine mammals in the high seas.' Article 120 ought to be analysed in conjunction with Article 87(2), which imposes the duty of 'due regard' to the interests of other States in the exercise of the freedom to fish in the high seas, and which must be consistent with 'their treaty obligations' (Article 116(a)). As was noted in Chapter 2, it may be presumed that by the reference to an 'international organization' in Article 65 is meant the IWC, despite some views to the contrary. Schiffman is of view that the formulation of Article 65 indicates that, in case of marine mammals, conservation objectives are paramount, as it permits coastal States the introduction of stricter standards for marine mammals than for other marine species[120] and therefore confirms the special conservation status accorded under UNCLOS to marine mammals. It may be inferred from the formulation of Article 120, which transposes to the high seas the application of Article 65, that it permits therein the same 'stricter' approach to conservation and the management of marine mammals.[121] The special 'stricter' provisions of Article 65 with regard to the protection of marine mammals are, for instance, exemplified within the context of the IWC by the Moratorium on commercial whaling. Such an approach, however, appears to be somewhat contradicted by steadily rising quotas of humpback whales allocated for indigenous peoples by the IWC. Saying that, it has to be noted that Article 65 is only permissive, rather than mandatory, with respect to stricter regimes relating to cetaceans. Therefore the formulation of Article 65, despite its appearance of according to

---

appropriate international organizations with a view to ensuring conservation and promoting the objective of optimum utilization of such species throughout the region, both within and beyond the exclusive economic zone . . .'.
[120] Schiffman, above n. 18, p. 171.
[121] Nele Matz-Lück and Johannes Fuchs, 'Marine Living Resources', in Donald R. Rothwell, Alex G. Oude Elferink, Karen N. Scott and Tim Stephens (eds.), *The Oxford Handbook on the Law of the Sea* (Oxford University Press, 2015), p. 508; Schiffman, above n. 18, p. 171.

marine mammals special conservation status, is characterised by a lack of a precise definition of what is a 'stricter' approach to the conservation of marine mammals. Thus the whole concept is vague and loosely defined, giving rise in practice to many possible interpretations.

6.12   The IWC and the Convention on Biological Diversity

The CBD[122] has three main objectives:

(1) The conservation of biological diversity;
(2) The sustainable use of the components of biological diversity;
(3) The fair and equitable sharing of the benefits arising out of the utilisation of genetic resources.

The CBD sets general approaches to conservation (*in situ*; *ex situ*) and regulates, at least in broad terms, access and sharing of indigenous knowledge and the position of developing States. General provisions of the CBD were supplemented by the Cartagena Protocol on Biosafety[123] and the Nagoya Protocol on Access and Benefit-sharing,[124] which are independent treaties. The CBD, as such, has evolved through many Strategic Plans, such as the Strategic Plan for Biodiversity 2011–20, including Aichi Biodiversity Targets.[125]

In light of the 'dysfunctional character' of the IWC and the perhaps inadequacy of the ICRW, there are views which promote the CBD as a replacement or a supplement for the ICRW, given that the CBD has introduced broader environmental and biological perspectives regarding conservation of marine species, but lacking, however, a more precise

---

[122] Convention on Biological Diversity, 5 June 1992, 1760 UNTS 143. See on this Convention: Catherine Redgwell, 'The Biodiversity Convention and Biosafety Protocol', in Michael Bowman, Peter Davies and Catherine Redgwell, *Lyster's International Wildlife Law* (2nd edn, Cambridge University Press, 2010), pp. 587–649.

[123] 2000 Cartagena Protocol on Biosafety, 2226 UNTS 208.

[124] 2010 Nagoya Protocol on Access and Benefit-sharing, www.cbd.int/abs/, last accessed 20 January 2015.

[125] 'This plan provides an overarching framework on biodiversity, not only for the biodiversity-related conventions, but for the entire United Nations system and all other partners engaged in biodiversity management and policy development. Parties agreed to translate this overarching international framework into revised and updated national biodiversity strategies and action plans within two years. Additionally, in decision X/10, the Conference of the Parties decided that the fifth national reports, due by 31 March 2014, should focus on the implementation of the 2011–2020 Strategic Plan and progress achieved towards the Aichi Biodiversity Targets.' www.cbd.int/sp/default.shtml, last accessed 20 January 2015.

approach to the conservation of marine ecosystems.[126] There are authors
who refer to particular provisions of the CBD as applicable to whaling,
such as: Article 3 (avoidance of environmental harm); Article 5 (cooperation); and Article 14 (assessment of environmental projects posing
significant risks for biodiversity).[127] It was also suggested that the CBD
may play a significant role in the increased role of marine sanctuaries, as,
'properly used, sanctuaries have the potential to provide the best scientific data for us to understand – and to protect – biodiversity'.[128] However, according to Couzens, the establishment of sanctuaries has become
a highly politicised matter within the IWC.[129] One might also argue that
the CBD is essentially a framework treaty with general pronouncements
and therefore normatively weaker than a purposive legal instrument.
A framework treaty with imprecise pronouncements would lead only to
more interpretative disputes and thus fewer concrete results, and, thus,
its effectiveness would most likely be low. The new strategic plans, still
having very much a framework character, are not offering much in the
way of detailed management of, for example, whaling stocks. Therefore,
in the view of the present author, the usefulness of the CBD in relation to
whaling and the ICRW is limited to general guidance in matters of
contemporary approaches to conservation (such as the use of the precautionary approach, as professed by the CBD).

6.13   The United Nations Environment Programme

The United Nations Environment Programme (UNEP)[130] relates to the
general protection of marine mammals with no specific provision for the
narwhal. The Global Plan of Action for the Conservation, Management and
Utilisation of Marine Mammals (MMAP) was developed between 1978 and
1983 jointly by UNEP and the United Nations Food and Agriculture
Organization (FAO), in collaboration with other intergovernmental and

---

[126] On this, see Patricia Birnie, 'The Framework for Cooperation', in William C. G. Burns
and Alexander Gillespie (eds.), *The Future of Cetaceans in a Changing World* (Ardsley,
NY: Transnational Publishers, 2003), p. 103.

[127] Sand, above n. 73, 60.   [128] Couzens, above n. 52, p. 201.   [129] Ibid.

[130] UNEP, 'Overview of UNEP's Marine Mammal Action Plan', www.unep.org/regional
seas/Marinemammals/downloads/m_m_action_plan.doc, last accessed 31 December
2014. See also Boris M. Culik, 'Review of Small Cetaceans. Distribution, Behaviour,
Migration and Threats', Marine Mammal Action Plan/Regional Seas Reports and Studies no. 17, UNEP/CMS Regional Seas, www.unep.org/regionalseas/publications/reports/
RSRS/pdfs/rsrs177.pdf, last accessed 1 January 2015.

non-governmental bodies concerned with marine mammal issues, in response to growing international concerns about the status, and the need for conservation, of marine mammal populations worldwide. The MMAP was subsequently adopted by UNEP's Governing Council in 1984, and endorsed by the governing bodies of leading international organisations dealing with issues relevant to marine mammals, such as the FAO, the IWC and the International Union for the Conservation of Nature (IUCN). The MMAP was also endorsed by the UN General Assembly and UNEP was designated as its Secretariat.

The MMAP's fundamental objective is to promote the implementation of a multilateral policy for conservation, management and utilisation of marine mammals. This policy should be widely acceptable to governments and the public. The MMAP is built along five lines, namely, policy formulation, regulatory and protective measures, improvement of scientific knowledge, improvement of law and its application, and enhancement of public awareness. Species covered by the MMAP include all marine species of mammals (cetaceans, pinnipeds and sirenians), as well as riverine species of dolphins, seals and otters. At present, the MMAP is incorporated in particular regional Seas Programmes.

6.14   The question of fragmentation of international law relating to the protection of whales

As we have seen in the present publication, there is a whole raft of international instruments of legal effect that relate to different aspects of whaling. Thus, at the current level of development of international law, and in particular international environmental law, the question of coordination of treaties can appear very complex.

Some have direct implications for the regulation of whaling (as is the case of the ICRW), whilst others have as their direct or incidental subject matter the conservation of whale species. For instance, while UNCLOS cannot be sensibly held to be about 'whales' *per se*, its provisions do have implications for the management of whale stocks, given that these are part of the living natural resources over which UNCLOS extends. Given the multiplicity therefore of treaties that have implications for whaling, however direct or marginal, it is no surprise that perceptions of fragmentation arise. While the views on fragmentation may differ,[131] what is undisputed is the fact

---

[131] See the International Law Commission Report of the Study Group, Fragmentation of International Law: Difficulties Arising from the Diversification and Expansion of

that the multiplicity of treaties may give rise to an exponential number of perceived conflicts between norms found in different instruments. As Prost reminds us, the issues surrounding perceptions of fragmentation are not limited to general international law; rather, each and every separate area of international law, each special regime, has started debating the issue of its own fragmentation from the corpus of international law.[132] Prost identifies several stages in the debate surrounding fragmentation. The first one was focused on two issues, according to Prost: the functional 'autonomization' of special regimes and the multiplication of international courts and tribunals. As to the issue of special regimes, Prost explains, international lawyers are divided into two groups. The first group is of the view that a special regime which is characterised by a comprehensive system of secondary norms (its own sources and its own system of State responsibility) becomes a self-contained and self-sufficient system, which does not rely on norms of general international law in its approach to its own substantive norms, including their interpretation and implementation.[133] The second group is of the view that it would be problematic to find at present any regimes that are characterised by a total independence from international law (which is the majority view), 'whether it is characterized as "general"; "traditional"; or "fundamental", or not'.[134] Therefore, the notion of a self-contained regime, in its purest form, would be appropriate for a subsystem of public international law, distinct in all aspects, which would not fall back on any general rules of customary law or treaty law.[135]

The International Law Commission's (ILC's) Study Group on Fragmentation accorded to general international law some subsidiary role in all legal regimes, even the most articulated and developed.[136] As was observed by the Study Group, there is no uniform definition or notion of a self-contained regime.[137] In the narrowest sense, this term is used in

---

International Law (A/CN.4/L.682) (13 April 2006) for the most authoritative observations of issues surrounding normative conflict relating to, among many other things, competing regimes and so on. See also the symposium on fragmentation, *Michigan Journal of International Law* 25 (2003–4), 845–1349.

[132] Mario Prost, *The Concept of Unity in Public International Law* (Oxford: Hart Publishing, 2014), p. 9.

[133] Ibid., pp. 10–11.

[134] Nele Matz-Lück, 'Norm Interpretation Across International Regimes', in Margaret Young (ed.), *Regime Interaction in International Law. Facing Fragmentation* (Cambridge University Press, 2012), p. 206.

[135] Ibid., pp. 206–7.   [136] Report of the ILC Study Group, above n. 131.

[137] On self-contained regimes, see Bruno Simma and Dirk Pulkowski, 'Of Planets and the Universe: Self Contained Regimes in International Law', EJIL 16 (2006), 483–529.

relation to the special set of secondary rules under the regime of State responsibility, which have primacy over general rules concerning the consequences of a violation. In a broader meaning, this term is used to denote interrelated wholes of primary or secondary rules, or so-called 'systems' or 'subsystems', that regulate some particular areas somewhat differently to general law, also in the sense of the modification or exclusion from the realm of general international law of certain norms such as, for example, the rules of interpretation.[138]

Similarly divisive has proved to be the issue of the diversity of international courts and tribunals, as the view has varied from perceiving their multitude as a threat to the unity of international law, almost to anarchy; to a less apocalyptic view, which approached the problem as largely theoretical and a largely positive development allowing a broader entrenchment of legality, standardisation and the rule of law in disparate fields of interstate policy and regulation.[139] The ILC Study Group has adopted a position, on the one hand, that views the diversity of international courts and tribunals as a positive phenomenon that responds to new technical and functional requirements in discrete areas. On the other hand, it acknowledged that conflicts may arise, which defeat the unity of international law.[140] Prost noted that recent studies regarding fragmentation are not focused on basic considerations regarding the phenomenon of fragmentation, such as whether or not it is desirable; but rather concern the identification of solutions to managing the variety, or to 'ordering the pluralism' through finding relevant principles and techniques in order to bring coherent order to this variety.[141] Technical solutions in ordering the chaos of multi-legal orders may, as indicated

---

[138] Report of the ILC Study Group, above n. 131, paras. 128 and 133.

[139] On the techniques of dealing with regime and rule conflict in adjudication under international law, see James Crawford and Penelope Nevill, 'Relations between International Courts and Tribunals: The "Regime Problem"' in Young, above n. 134, pp. 235–60.

[140] Prost, above n. 132, p. 10.

[141] The classical publication on this subject matter is: Campbell McLachlan, 'The Principle of Systemic Integration and Article 31(3)(c) of the Vienna Convention', ICLQ 54 (2005), 279–320; Campbell McLachlan, 'The Evolution of Treaty Obligations in International Law', in Georg Nolte (ed.), *Treaties and Subsequent Practice* (Oxford University Press, 2014), pp. 69–79; Philippe Sands, 'Treaty, Custom and Cross-fertilization of International Law', *Yale Human Rights and Development Journal* 1 (1998), 85–121; Panos Merkouris, 'Debating the *Ouroboros* of International Law: The Drafting History of Article 31(3)(c)', ICLR 9 (2007), 1–31; Matz-Lück, above n. 134, pp. 201–34; Dirk Pulkowski, *The International Law and Politics of International Conflict* (Oxford University Press, 2014), in particular, pp. 272–98;

by the ILC Study Group report, be found in the interpretative tools in which the most prominent role is accorded to Article 31(3)(c) ('systemic integration') of the 1969 Vienna Convention on the Law of Treaties (VCLT)[142] (and to its mirror norms as they are thought to exist in custom with regard to disputes involving a State not party to the VCLT – as the VCLT is generally held to reflect customary norms) and such principles of normative interpretation including *lex specialis derogat legi generali* and *lex posterior derogat legi priori*.

It may be noted that the principle of normative interpretation contained in Article 31(3)(c) VCLT was rarely relied upon, and was almost dormant, until the statement of the ICJ in the *Oil Platforms* case, and the work of the ILC Study Group on Fragmentation which acknowledged it. We now observe the continued interest in this principle, the role of which has gone from marginal to very significant in the interpretation of treaties;[143] although this has not been a development that has been universally heralded as positive.[144] International courts and tribunals at

---

Gabriel Orellana Zabalza, *The Principle of Systemic Integration: Towards a Coherent International Legal Order* (Münster: LIT, 2012); Hans van Gellecum, 'Environmental Law in the Context of Article 31(3)(c) of the Vienna Convention on the Law of Treaties: Reconciling Treaty Interpretation and Progressive Environmental Norms: The *Pulp Mills* Case and Beyond', Social Science Research Network, http://papers.ssrn.com/sol3/papers.cfm?abstract_id=1989468, last accessed 29 December 2014; Prost, above n. 132, p. 11; Panos Merkouris, *Article 31(3)(c) VCLT on the Principle of Systemic Integration: Normative Studies in Plato's Cave* (Boston and Leiden: Nijhoff/Brill, 2015).

[142] 1969 Vienna Convention on the Law of Treaties (VCLT), 1155 UNTS 331.

[143] See, for example, some of the latest publications on the EJIL Talk! blog: Kushtrim Istrefi, '*RMT* v. *The UK*: Expanding Article 11 of the ECHR Through Systemic Integration', www.ejiltalk.org/r-m-t-v-the-uk-expanding-article-11-of-the-echr-through-systemic-integration/, last accessed 19 March 2015; and Panos Merkouris, 'Keep Calm and Call (no, not batman but . . .) Articles 31–32 VCLT: A Comment on Istrefi's Recent Post on *RMT* v. *UK*', www.ejiltalk.org/keep-calm-and-call-no-not-batman-but-articles-31-32-vclt-a-comment-on-istrefis-recent-post-on-r-m-t-v-the-uk/, last accessed 5 August 2014.

[144] *Oil Platforms (Islamic Republic of Iran v. United States of America)*, Judgment, *ICJ Reports 2003*, p. 161. See the controversial view expressed by Judge Buergenthal, who took a very restrictive approach to Article 31(3)(c). According to his view, the Court's jurisdiction is limited only to the matters which the parties agreed to submit to it and this impacts on the applicable law in interpreting the treaty before it. Such a limitation will not allow the ICJ to rely on all other sources of international law, notwithstanding the source, including the UN Charter. Judge Buergenthal, Separate Opinion, paras. 22–4, www.icj-cij.org/docket/files/90/9729.pdf, last accessed 5 August 2014. Judge Higgins was quite sceptical as to the use (or rather misuse) of Article 31(3)(c) and she was of the view that the Court should have relied on the ordinary meaning of the terms of Article XX(1)(d), an approach that was commended in this case. Judge Higgins, Separate Opinion, www.icj-cij.org/docket/files/90/9721.pdf, p. 49, last accessed 5 August 2014.

times have different understandings of Article 31(3)(c) VCLT, as was the case in the WTO *EC–Biotech* case. The adjudicative panel had (albeit not expressly) disagreed with the notion of 'relevant rules'. The *Biotech* panel addressed the question of whether provisions in the Cartagena Protocol were relevant rules within the context of Article 31(3)(c), and whether all parties to the Cartagena Protocol must simultaneously be WTO members. The adjudicative panel ruled that this was necessary, and was criticised for it. The fundamental question was whether Article 31(3)(c) requires the full participation in both treaties; or whether the relationships between States may be analysed on an individual basis.[145] This line of reasoning appears to be still prevalent in the WTO, as in the 2011 *European Communities – Measures Affecting Trade in Large Civil Aircraft* case, in which the WTO Appellate Body stated that '[o]ne must exercise caution in drawing from an international agreement to which not all WTO members are party'.[146]

At present, it may be said that Article 31(3)(c) has gained some more weight in the interpretation of treaties. In the *Whaling in the Antarctic* case,[147] the concept of systemic integration was relied upon, to some extent, by all Parties to the dispute. It cannot be said, however, that it played a significant role in their pleadings (the ICJ in its Judgment did not address this issue).[148] In principle, it would appear that for the protection of whales, it would be beneficial to interpret the ICRW in the broader context of the other treaties, such as the CBD and CITES, as well as the general principles underlying international environmental law, such as the precautionary principle.[149] Such an

---

[145] *European Communities – Measures Affecting the Approval and Marketing of Biotech Products*, Report of the Panel, WT/DS291/R, adopted 21 November 2006, para. 7.68; Pulkowski, above n. 141, pp. 290–1.

[146] *European Communities – Measures Affecting Trade in Large Civil Aircraft*, WT/DS316/AB/R, adopted 18 May 2011, para. 843.

[147] *Whaling in the Antarctic*, www.icj-cij.org/docket/files/148/18136.pdf, last accessed 28 December 2014.

[148] On all issues raised regarding the law of treaties in this case, see Malgosia Fitzmaurice, 'The Whaling Convention and Thorny Issues of Interpretation', in Malgosia Fitzmaurice and Dai Tamada (eds.), *Whaling in the Antarctic: The Judgment and its Implications* (Brill–Nijhoff, forthcoming, 2016). On file with the author.

[149] Judge ad hoc Hilary Charlesworth analysed the possible role of this principle for whaling, especially when there is a lack of scientific certainty. She said: 'Both Parties to this dispute endorsed the precautionary approach at a theoretical level, although they disagreed about its application to the facts. In my view, the precautionary approach requires that non-lethal methods of research be used wherever possible. In relation to Article VIII, which contemplates the killing of the subject of research by the research

approach, it seems, would also provide a technical solution in a rather complex patchwork of norms that exist in different instruments concerning whales and whaling. There was never any hint during the *Whaling* case indicating that there is fragmentation of norms regarding issues of whaling. However, as was exemplified by the Judgment, the impact of the principle of systemic integration to the final outcome was insignificant.

The proper understanding of the workings of this provision as well as its connection with evolutionary interpretation and subsequent practice remain unresolved. The *Whaling in the Antarctic* case exemplified the argument that there is no one uniform understanding of the legal nature of the principle of systemic integration, one of the contentious issues being whether it also includes a temporal element. Judge Cançado Trindade[150] supported the view that systemic integration is somewhat akin to, if not coterminous with, the evolutionary interpretation of treaties, and relied on the *Namibia* Advisory Opinion, which is an important case in relation to the dynamic interpretation of treaties. He also cited many cases of the European Court of Human Rights (ECtHR), in which there has been an evolutionary approach to the interpretation of the European Convention on Human Rights (ECHR), as examples of systemic integration, which he equates with evolutionary interpretation. This approach tallies with the one adopted by the ILC Study Group on Fragmentation, which noted that Article 31(3)(c) VCLT has two interlinked aspects: a mechanism to connect and harmonise different legal regimes; and the temporal element which gives a ground for the evolutionary interpretation of treaties, thus avoiding conflict between treaties. As Arato observes, 'the two aspects of VCLT 31(3)(c) are connected and codependent'. In fact, Arato explicitly analyses 'evolutive interpretation' of the ECHR by the ECtHR as based on Article 31(3)(c), therefore treating these two institutions as coterminous.[151] The invocation of Article 31(3)(c) in the *Whaling* case

---

activity, an implication of the precautionary approach is that lethal methods must be shown to be indispensable to the purposes of scientific research on whales' (para. 10).

[150] www.icj-cij.org/docket/files/148/18146.pdf, para. 27, last accessed 28 December 2014. See also Torp Helmersen, who holds the view that evolutive interpretation and systemic integration are distinct concepts, 'Evolutive Treaty Interpretation: Legality, Semantics and Distinctions', *European Journal of Legal Studies* 6 (2013), 127–48, 146–8.

[151] Julian Arato, 'Constitutional Transformation in the ECtHR: Strasbourg's Expansive Recourse to International Rules of International Law', *Brook. J. Int'l L.* 37 (2012), 349–88, 355.

was not in relation to remedying any perceived fragmentation, but rather in relation to strengthening the argument of the development over time of the object and purpose of the ICRW, in line with other environmental conventions, and thus exemplifying through comparisons with other international instruments its alleged evolutionary development, as was pleaded by Australia. The reliance on the principle of systemic integration to overcome fragmentation between various treaty regimes is perhaps premature, as this method is still evolving and there are many different perceptions and ways of implementation of this principle. There are doubts whether it results in any greater coherence or effectiveness. There is, thus, a need for significant research to be done in order to reach persuasive conclusions in respect of the role of systemic integration relating to the fragmentation.[152]

The fragmentation in the field of whaling regulation is to some extent remedied as a result of a certain degree of coherence due to the presence of communications and norms (such as Memoranda of Understanding; provisions such as Article VI of the CCAMLR; and Resolutions adopted by ASCOBANS) between the relevant international organisations, which acknowledge the ICRW regime as responsible for the conservation and management of large whales at the multilateral level. Nevertheless, there are still some tensions between competing organisations, such as the IWC and NAMMCO.

The remaining question is whether the regime of whaling under the IWC can be characterised as a 'self-contained' regime in the wider notion of a subsystem. The present author is of the view that such characterisation of the IWC would not be correct. Undoubtedly, whaling is a discrete area of international law, but the IWC is not the only organisation which sets the rules for whaling, nor is the set of rules that results from the law-making activity of the IWC a subsystem of international law which does not fall back on general international law. There are neither special principles of 'international whaling law' nor a different set of rules for the interpretation of the ICRW (as was evidenced by the *Whaling in the Antarctic* case in which the Court applied the rule of interpretation as established by the VCLT to the ICRW). Therefore, from the point of view of fragmentation of international law, a suggestion that whaling under the IWC is a self-contained regime is not justified.

---

[152] Matz-Lück, above n. 134, p. 234.

6.15   Conflicts between treaty norms and the 1969 Vienna Convention on the Law of Treaties

Much has been written on the conflict of treaties.[153] This part of the chapter focuses mainly on possible conflict of environmental treaties and the ICRW. There is a commonly shared view that the VCLT does not solve in a satisfactory manner the issue of the conflict of treaties.[154] In general, only the primacy of the United Nations Charter (UN Charter) as an international treaty is uncontested (confirmed by Article 30(1) VCLT). Article 103 of the UN Charter expressly states that any conflict between a provision in some international treaty and any UN Charter provision must be resolved in a way that prioritises the latter.

However, while techniques adopted in Article 30 VCLT are workable where parties to an earlier and a later treaty are the same, there are problems with determining the subject matter of treaties where there is some overlap.[155] As Klabbers correctly observes, matters become more complex when the parties to the treaty are not identical, a situation provided for in Article 30(4) VCLT.[156] The ILC, while drafting the conflict clause, relied on three maxims concerning the solution of conflicts between treaties: *lex posterior, lex priori* and *lex specialis*.

According to Article 59 VCLT, if two conflicting treaties deal with the same subject matter and are concluded by identical parties, following the *lex posterior* rule the later treaty prevails. The *lex posterior* rule cannot solve all types of treaty conflict and its opposite, the *lex priori* rule, is sometimes applied by courts, adding to uncertainty surrounding the conflict of treaties.[157] *Lex specialis derogat legi generali* is not part of Article 30 VCLT due to its substantive orientation (the substance of the treaty). The application of

---

[153] Seyed Ali Sadat-Akhavi, *Methods of Resolving Conflict between Treaties* (Leiden: Brill Academic Publishers, 2003); K. N. Dahl, 'The Application of Successive Treaties Dealing with the Same Subject-matter', *Indian Journal of International Affairs* 1 (1974), 17, 279–318; J. B. Mus, 'Conflicts between Treaties in International Law', NILR 45 (1998), 208–32; Joost Pauwelyn, *Conflict of Norms in Public International Law: How WTO Law Relates to Other Rules of International Law* (Cambridge University Press, 2003); Ahmad Ali Ghouri, 'Determining Hierarchy Between Conflicting Treaties: Are Vertical Rules in the Horizontal System?' *Asian Journal of International Law* 2 (2012), 235–66; Christopher J. Borgen, 'Resolving Treaty Conflicts', *Geo. Wash. Int'l L. Rev.* 37 (2005), 573–648; Jan Klabbers, 'Beyond the Vienna Convention: Conflicting Treaty Provisions', in Enzo Cannizzaro (ed.), *The Law of Treaties Beyond the Vienna Convention* (Oxford University Press, 2011), p. 192; Surabhi Ranganathan, *Strategically Created Treaty Conflicts and the Politics of International Law* (Cambridge University Press, 2015).
[154] See e.g. Klabbers, above n. 153, p. 194.   [155] Ghouri, above n. 153.
[156] Klabbers, above n. 153, pp. 194–5.   [157] Ghouri, above n. 153, 18.

this maxim is not without problems, such as those relating to deciding which treaty ought to be considered the more specific and which the more general: a complex task in most of the situations that involve treaties with overlapping – but not coextensive – thematic content.[158]

As a result of the seemingly inconclusive formulation of Article 30 VCLT, several treaties include clauses setting out the principles concerning their relationship to other international legal agreements, particularly with regard to their temporal features. Such provisions are called 'conflict clauses'.

The Report of the ILC Study Group on Fragmentation of International Law distinguishes various categories of such clauses.[159] There are clauses:

(1) prohibiting the conclusion of incompatible subsequent agreements (this clause is an express nullification of the *lex posterior* rule) (for instance, Article 8 of the NATO Treaty);[160]

(2) permitting subsequent 'compatible' treaties, thus an affirmation of the *lex posterior* rule (Article 311(3) UNCLOS);[161]

(3) providing in the subsequent treaty that it 'shall not affect' the earlier Treaty, thus a limitation to the *lex posterior* rule (Article 30 of the Geneva Convention on the High Seas);[162]

(4) providing in the subsequent treaty that, among the parties, it overrides an earlier treaty (which is in fact a modification *inter se* of the treaty);

(5) abrogating expressly in the subsequent treaty the earlier treaty (Article 311 UNCLOS, according to which, between parties to it and to the 1958 Law of the Sea conventions, the former shall prevail);

---

[158] Klabbers, above n. 153, p. 200. On this maxim, see in depth the Report of the ILC Study Group on 'Fragmentation of International Law', above n. 131, pp. 56–122.

[159] Report of the ILC Study Group, above n. 131, p. 135.

[160] 'Each Party declares that none of the international engagements now in force between it and any other of the parties or any third States is in conflict with the provisions of this treaty, and undertakes not to enter any international engagement in conflict with this Treaty.'

[161] 'Two or more States Parties may conclude agreements modifying or suspending the operation of provisions of this Convention, applicable solely to the relations between them, provided that such agreements do not relate to a provision derogation from which is incompatible with the effective execution of the object and purpose of this Convention, and provided further that such agreements shall not affect the application of the basic principles embodied herein, and that the provisions of such agreements do not affect the enjoyment by other States Parties of their rights or the performance of their obligations under this Convention.'

[162] 'The provisions of this Convention shall not affect conventions or other international agreements already in force, as between States parties to them.'

(6) maintaining expressly in the subsequent treaties earlier compatible treaties (Article 311(2) UNCLOS);[163] and

(7) promising that future agreements will abrogate earlier treaties (Article 307 of the EU Treaty (Article 234 EC)) providing that the rights and obligations of members ensuing from treaties concluded before the membership are not affected. The members, however, commit to take action so as to abrogate those treaties.[164]

The issue of conflicts between obligations deriving from environmental treaties is equally puzzling and complex. It may be briefly noted that the relationship between treaties that belong to different regimes is an unresolved problem, such as relations between instruments constituting part of trade and environmental regimes, an attempt to accommodate which may result in 'obscure and ambiguous formulations', such as in the Protocol on Biosafety to the CBD to the effect that 'trade and environment agreements should be mutually supportive with a view to achieving sustainable development'.[165]

In that respect, the present author is of the view that subsequent communications (clarifications, declarations, statements and so on) that have been accepted by the relevant States could amount to useful evidence of how particular normative conflicts ought to be resolved. However, it is stated that such vague clauses are a method

---

[163] 'This convention shall not alter the rights and obligations of States parties which arise from other agreements compatible with this convention and which do not affect the enjoyment by other States parties of their rights or the performance of their obligations under this Convention.'

[164] Report of the ILC Study Group, above n. 131, p. 135.

[165] See, on this, Sadat-Akhavi, above n. 153, pp. 213–47; Sabrina Safrin, 'Treaties in Collision? The Biosafety Protocol and the World Trade Organization Agreements', AJIL 96 (2002), 606–28, 617. See e.g. Cartagena Protocol on Biosafety to the Biodiversity Convention and its relationship to the obligations of the parties under the WTO covered agreements. The Protocol includes provisions concerning its relationship with the trade instruments, but leaves many other important treaty relations unaddressed (such as its relationship to, for example, the International Plant Protection Convention, the Chemical Weapons Convention and the Biological Weapons Convention). The preamble to the Protocol includes the following formulations: 'Recognizing that trade and environment agreements should be mutually supportive with a view to achieving sustainable development; Emphasizing that this Protocol shall not be interpreted as implying a change in the rights and obligations of a Party under any existing international agreements; Understanding that the above recital is not intended to subordinate this Protocol to other international agreements.' Report of the ILC Study Group, above n. 131.

to emphasize the importance of harmonizing interpretation. This may work well between treaties that are part of the same regime and share a similar object and purpose or carry a parallel 'ethos' – e.g. between several environmental or trade instruments *inter se*. But it cannot be assumed *a priori* that a similar readiness exists as between parties to treaties across regimes, treaties that seek to achieve physically incompatible solutions, or are inspired by very different (perhaps opposite) objectives in situations experienced as zero-sum games. In such cases, at the end of the day, one treaty must be preferred over the other.[166]

As Matz explained, the legal interdependence of agreements is one of the reasons why international environmental law is subject 'to conflicts, contradictions and doubling of efforts'.[167] Matz distinguishes several possible areas of conflict between instruments, namely: in international instruments having different legal natures; in instruments with a different geographical scope; between agreements with different points of view or with different objectives; between original and modified agreements; and between treaties that in particular regulate, in principle, the same subject matter but which have different parties.[168]

There are very many possible variations of conflicts between environmental treaties: they can have similar approaches but differ with regard to their aims and political objectives; and they may not even be based on similar foundational approaches. It is very difficult to establish clear-cut differences between various types of conflict.[169] There are instances of international environmental agreements in which the ICRW is expressly mentioned as having priority in matters relating to whaling, such as in the CCAMLR (discussed earlier in this chapter). Article VI of the CCAMLR reads as follows: '[n]othing in this Convention shall derogate from the rights and obligations of Contracting Parties under the International Convention for the Regulation of Whaling . . .'. As highlighted by Wolfrum, such a clause establishes the priority of the ICRW but does not entirely displace the application of the CCAMLR to whales should it be possible for the CCAMLR to be applied in a manner compatible with the rights and obligations under the ICRW. In practice, the CCAMLR becomes operational when either the ICRW does not cover certain

---

[166] Report of the ILC Study Group, above n. 131, p. 141.
[167] Rüdiger Wolfrum and Nele Matz, *Conflicts in International Environmental Law* (Berlin: Springer, 2003), p. 4. On this subject, see also Malgosia Fitzmaurice and Olufemi Elias, *Contemporary Issues in the Law of Treaties* (Utrecht: Eleven International Publishing, 2005), pp. 314–48.
[168] Wolfrum and Matz, above n. 167, p. 6.   [169] Ibid., pp. 7, 12.

species or the IWC fails to reach agreement on an issue. Moreover, according to Article IX(5) of the CCAMLR, the Commission must take full account of any relevant measures or regulations established or recommended by existing fisheries commissions, which also includes the IWC.[170] Wolfrum also mentions Article XII(2) of the CMS, which states that its provisions do not affect the rights and obligations of State Parties under other international agreements. Wolfrum argues that, in practice, a State Party to the ICRW could object to the protection of humpback whales (which are protected under Appendix I of the CMS) and this would not necessarily be seen as a violation of the CMS.[171] Other relevant provisions also regulate the conflict between environmental agreements by way of 'conflict clauses', which have the common purpose of clarifying the relationship between the instruments of international law, including treaties, although their formulations can vary considerably[172] (Article 22 of the CBD).

Another example may be found in a provision of the 1991 Environmental Protocol to the Antarctic Treaty. According to the Final Act of the Eleventh Antarctic Treaty Special Consultative Meeting, nothing in the Protocol on Environmental Protection is to derogate from rights and obligations of Parties under the CCAMLR, the Convention for the Conservation of Antarctic Seals and the ICRW. As Wolfrum and Matz observe, the intention of the clause is to establish that the rights and obligations of State Parties stemming from these Conventions are not prejudiced. However, these clauses are not entirely clear.[173] Although there is no doubt that the right to hunt whales is not limited under the 1991 Environmental Protocol to the Antarctic Treaty, it is not entirely clear whether the Protocol also relates to activities going beyond those permitted by these Conventions (such as fishing out of season).[174] The question may thus arise whether such an activity would be a violation of the Protocol. The answer is that it would not be a violation, as fishing, notwithstanding its character (legal or illegal), is to be dealt with under the CCAMLR.[175]

Furthermore, under the saving clause of Article 22(1) of the CBD, Wolfrum and Matz comment that, though at first sight the clause provides for the priority of existing treaties, it contains a qualification that may reverse this result and make the application of these clauses

---

[170] Ibid., p. 60.   [171] Ibid., p. 61.
[172] Ibid., p. 122; Fitzmaurice and Elias, above n. 167, p. 332.   [173] Ibid., p. 334.
[174] Wolfrum and Matz, above n. 167, p. 123.   [175] Ibid., p. 124.

even 'more obscure'.[176] Article 22(1) provides, in fact, that only instruments which do not harm the environment will prevail over the CBD. Such a clause may pose serious interpretative problems, as there are no criteria indicating when the implementation of rights and obligations poses a serious threat to biological diversity. Therefore, according to Wolfrum and Matz, there are doubts whether such a clause will succeed in the prevention or solving of conflicts. Wolfrum and Matz also have reservations towards Article 22(2). As they note, this clause demonstrates the necessity of precisely formulating clauses that do not leave room for interpretation. Otherwise the objective of conflict clauses, to establish competences and prevent conflicts, cannot be met.[177]

As to the ICRW and UNCLOS, Article 311(2) of UNCLOS may be of importance to their interplay. It states as follows:

> 2. This Convention shall not alter the rights and obligations of States Parties which arise from other agreements compatible with this Convention and which do not affect the enjoyment by other States Parties of their rights or the performance of their obligations under this Convention.

In such a case, there are several questions that arise as to the compatibility of the ICRW with UNCLOS, such as whether, for instance, indigenous whaling is compatible with the UNCLOS provisions on the management of marine living resources and marine mammals.

Finally, recourse may be had to the provisions of the VCLT in order to solve the issue of conflicting environmental treaties. The question may first be posed as to whether Article 31 VCLT (on interpretation) can be applied to resolve such conflicts. The VCLT does not appear to be appropriate to deal with the task of harmonisation of MEAs,[178] given that there are some inherent problems, such as those relating to the difficulty in precisely ascertaining the common object and purpose of such treaties. There are some general objectives, such as sustainable development, in most MEAs. However, such objectives are too general, and frequently lack a sufficiently precise definition to allow interpretative techniques to resolve apparent conflicts. As Matz states, 'unless two treaties share an object and purpose element, Article 31 does not generally provide for better harmonization in the interpretation process of treaties'.[179] Equally, as is the case for general international law, Article 30 VCLT is not very helpful in relation to environmental law. Matz in

---

[176] Ibid., p. 123.   [177] Ibid.   [178] See, in depth, ibid., pp. 129–59.   [179] Ibid., p. 138.

particular highlights the difficulties in the interpretation of the phrase 'the same subject matter', which could be interpreted either broadly or restrictively.

The instructive example of the complex nature of the coexistence of various treaties and the inadequacy of Article 30 VCLT is the relationship between the ICRW and the NAMMCO Agreement. At first glance, it would appear that these two treaties deal with the same subject matter, that is to say, management of whales. Therefore, it would appear that Article 30(3) and (4) VCLT is perfectly suited to deal with normative conflicts between them. However, analysis of these two treaties evidences that the concept of 'the same subject matter' is a matter of a considerable complexity. Closer scrutiny reveals that the IWC regulates whaling in all its aspects (holistically), including allocation of quotas at a global level, and NAMMCO is a regional organisation with very limited functions, which only partially (in fact to a very limited degree) overlap with those of the IWC. It may also be noted that the limited membership of NAMMCO (out of four members, only two are also members of the IWC) restricts the scope of the subject matter of this organisation to matters of interest to these few members.

Concluding remarks

It may be said that in relation to whales' management, there is some degree of fragmentation. There is no doubt that the ICRW is the main international instrument to manage whales and whaling holistically. However, there is also a host of other MEAs which, at least to a limited degree, are concerned with whales. Most of them, by the way of formal provisions or subsequent practice, accept the leading role of the IWC. Therefore the scope of conflict is very limited. All these MEAs are of a conservation character, which tallies with the present policy of the IWC. However, if in the future the IWC allows the resumption of commercial whaling, there will be a clash of objectives between the IWC and these MEAs. Speculatively, there is potential for conflict between the trade restriction on whale products and whale-related equipment promoted by the IWC and the free-trade objectives of the World Trade Organization (WTO). This issue has never been raised within the forum of the WTO and it is unlikely to become the subject of a dispute.

The conflict between norms of various treaties is one of the legal issues still awaiting resolution. Neither the rules of the VCLT nor the provisions contained in treaties are sufficiently clear to provide a straightforward rule. Even conflict clauses do not appear to render always clear results and resolve disputes. Such an example is the oblique and ambiguous formulation of Article 22 of the CBD.

As noted by Matz: '[b]ecause the law of treaties cannot provide a forum for the coordination of the content of treaties, different approaches must be considered'.[180] It would appear that cooperation between various entities could be an answer but, as was stated above, this sometimes fails as well.

---

[180] Ibid., p. 159.

Indigenous whaling

Introduction

This chapter is devoted to indigenous whaling, which is one of the forms of whaling provided for by the ICRW. It is based on certain assumptions, including: that certain indigenous peoples possess a right to whaling as an aspect of their right to cultural diversity; and that such indigenous peoples, as holders/beneficiaries of such rights affirmed by international law, may be reasonably held to be under certain obligations vis-à-vis the upholding of the rule of law, including international law relating to environmental protection of the world's endangered biodiversity. Such assumptions bring to the fore whatever tensions might exist between different legal regimes relating to, on the one hand, cultural diversity and, on the other, environmental protection. There are several examples of aboriginal/indigenous whaling which illustrate this problem; the best known are the Makah peoples of the State of Washington, USA, and the Inuit peoples in Greenland.

The compatibility and harmonisation issues that arise in relation to aboriginal whaling, environmental protection and whale welfare are complex; and practice, thus far, clearly indicates the complications resulting from the reconciling of these occasionally conflicting policy objectives.

7.1 Cultural diversity and indigenous peoples

This section is not meant to present an in-depth analysis of the legal regime pertaining to indigenous peoples' cultural diversity, as it is the subject matter of many publications and its full analysis is beyond the scope of this chapter. A general introduction is of relevance, however, as some indigenous peoples consider whaling as an expression of their cultural identity.

Central to the rights of minorities and indigenous peoples is Article 27 of the International Covenant on Civil and Political Rights (ICCPR):[1]

> In those States in which ethnic, religious or linguistic minorities exist, persons belonging to such minorities shall not be denied the right, in community with the other members of their group, to enjoy their own culture, to profess and practise their own religion, or to use their own language.

The construct of this Article was subject to some criticism as being rather vague. General Comments 21 and 23 of the Human Rights Committee (HRC) were instrumental in clarification of this Article in relation to minority rights.[2]

The HRC's case law contributed to further understanding of the rights of indigenous peoples. There are several instruments and General Comments which relate directly to such rights. For example, in 2000 the United Nations Sub-Commission on the Promotion and Protection of Human Rights approved and revised the United Nations Draft Principles and Guidelines on the Protection of the Cultural Heritage of Indigenous Peoples,[3] which were based on the premise of a separate legal regime for the protection of indigenous heritage.[4] These Principles take a comprehensive approach to the definition of indigenous heritage which includes all artefacts, cultural expressions – such as works of art, music, dance and ceremonies – traditional knowledge, human remains and burial grounds. The 1989 International Labour Organization (ILO) Indigenous and Tribal Peoples Convention[5] has implications for the cultural rights of

---

[1] International Covenant on Civil and Political Rights, 999 UNTS 171, entered into force 23 March 1976; Athanasios Yupsanis, 'Article 27 of the ICCPR Revisited: The Right to Culture as a Normative Source for Minority/Indigenous Participatory Claims in the Case Law of the Human Rights Committee', *Hague Yearbook of International Law* 26 (2013), 359–410.

[2] General Comment 21, www1.umn.edu/humanrts/gencomm/hrcom21.htm, last accessed 21 April 2015; General Comment 23, www1.umn.edu/humanrts/gencomm/hrcom23.htm, last accessed 21 April 2015; Yupsanis, above n. 1, 361–4, 364–70.

[3] UN Economic and Social Council (ECOSOC), Commission on Human Rights, Human Rights of Indigenous Peoples: Report of the Seminar on Draft Principles and Guidelines for the Protection of the Heritage of Indigenous Peoples, UN Doc. E/CN.4/Sub2/2000.26, 19 June 2000, www.refworld.org/docid/3b00f28018.html, last accessed 25 December 2014.

[4] Siegfried Wiessner and Marie Battiste, 'The 2000 Revision of the United Nations Draft Principles and Guidelines on the Protection of the Heritage of Indigenous People', *St Thomas L. Rev.* 13 (2000), 383–90, 383; Wiessner, 'Culture and Rights of Indigenous Peoples', in Ana Filipa Vrdoljak (ed.), *The Cultural Dimension of Human Rights. Collected Courses of the Academy of European Law* (Oxford University Press, 2013), pp. 117–56, 135–8.

[5] 1989 ILO Convention No. 169 Concerning Indigenous and Tribal Peoples in Independent Countries, 1650 UNTS 383, Articles 1–19.

indigenous peoples, as it grants indigenous peoples control over their legal status and guarantees their right to ownership of land and possession of the total environment they occupy or use.[6]

General Comment 21 of the Committee on Economic, Social and Cultural Rights (CESCR) refers directly to the right to culture of indigenous peoples in paragraphs 36 and 37. Paragraph 36 is of particular importance, as it states that indigenous peoples enjoy collective rights

> to ensure respect for their right to maintain, control, protect and develop their cultural heritage, traditional knowledge and traditional cultural expressions, as well as the manifestations of their sciences, technologies and cultures, including human and genetic resources, seeds, medicines, knowledge of the properties of fauna and flora, oral traditions, literature, designs, sports and traditional games, and visual and performing arts. States parties should respect the principle of free, prior and informed consent of indigenous peoples in all matters covered by their specific rights.[7]

It should, however, be mentioned that the character of indigenous peoples' collective rights (including cultural rights) is somewhat controversial. The legal integrity of collective rights of indigenous peoples, as opposed to their individual rights, is not universally accepted. However, the 2007 United Nations Declaration on the Rights of Indigenous Peoples (UNDRIP) is unequivocal about this. In its Preamble, UNDRIP states that '[i]ndigenous people possess collective rights which are indispensable for their existence, well-being and integral development as peoples'.[8] Several views were expressed that such a collective right is vital for their self-realisation and survival as a societal group.[9] It may be said that

---

[6] Articles 1–19.   [7] General Comment 21, above n. 2.

[8] 2007 United Nations Declaration on the Rights of Indigenous Peoples, adopted 13 September 2007, by affirmative vote of 143 States, 4 against (the United States, Canada, Australia and New Zealand), 11 abstentions (Azerbaijan, Bangladesh, Bhutan, Burundi, Colombia, Georgia, Kenya, Nigeria, Russia, Samoa and Ukraine), www.un.org/esa/socdev/unpfii/documents/DRIPS_en.pdf, last accessed 23 November 2014.

[9] See e.g. '[The] shift away from positivist, state dominated dialogue toward a more inclusive framework that is much more responsive to the ideals enshrined in the Charter of the United Nations ... has created [for indigenous peoples] a space for them to move an agenda of promoting and encouraging respect for their human rights within this formal international organization, including the collective rights to their culture, their land, and self-government as an essential part of their individual self-realization.' International Law Association, The Hague Conference 2010, Rights of Indigenous Peoples, Professor Siegfried Wiessner, Chair; Dr Federico Lenzerini (Italy), Rapporteur, 3. See also Wiessner, 'Culture and Rights', above n. 4, p. 134.

indigenous peoples constitute a prototype of an organic group of human beings, who aspire to lead the same way of life and to spend their entire lives together. At present, such peoples frequently lead lives in self-defined broadly autonomous communities, sharing similar beliefs, and most importantly have an attachment to their land, on which they were the original dwellers. Therefore, a collective spiritual relationship to their land is what separates them from other surrounding groups, and, often, they are denominated as minorities within an overall outsider State.[10]

The right to culture based on dignity is also a cornerstone of the approach adopted in relation to indigenous peoples, as enshrined in Article 15(1) of UNDRIP,[11] which provides that: '[i]ndigenous peoples have the right to the dignity and diversity of their cultures, traditions, histories and aspirations which shall be appropriately reflected in education and public information.' The cultural rights of indigenous peoples have to be approached and understood in harmony with the fundamental rights underlying the Declaration, as part of the whole nexus of indigenous rights. Therefore, such rights have to be viewed together with the right of self-determination (Article 3)[12] and the right to autonomy or self-government in matters relating to their internal and local affairs and to financing their autonomous function.[13] It must be noted that indigenous peoples' right to culture is interlinked with their rights to land and natural resources (Articles 25 and 26). Their special relationship with land and nature distinguishes them from other types of social minority. Of importance are also the UNDRIP provisions that prohibit their forced assimilation (Article 8(1)), genocide (Article 7(2)) and their relocation and forced displacement (Article 10).[14]

---

[10] Wiessner, 'Culture and Rights', above n. 4, pp. 124–5.

[11] United Nations Declaration on the Rights of Indigenous Peoples, above n. 8. See also Article 11(1), below n. 16.

[12] Article 3: 'Indigenous peoples have the right to self-determination. By virtue of that right they freely determine their political status and freely pursue their economic, social and cultural development.'

[13] Article 4: 'Indigenous peoples, in exercising their right to self-determination, have the right to autonomy or self-government in matters relating to their internal and local affairs, as well as ways and means for financing their autonomous functions.' See also Article 46(1). See also other Articles which are of importance: participatory right in decision-making (Article 18); obligation of States to consult; and to obtain 'free, prior and informed' consent to legislative acts which may affect indigenous peoples (Articles 19, 32 (2)); rights to improve their social and economic conditions (Articles 17, 21, 22, 24); rights to development (Article 23); the right to international cooperation (Articles 26, 39, 41, 42); rights to redress and reparation (Articles 8(2), 28).

[14] Wiessner, 'Culture and Rights', above n. 4, p. 143.

The cultural rights of indigenous peoples are also set out in UNDRIP Articles 11–14.[15] Article 11 grants indigenous peoples the right to practise and revitalise their traditions and culture;[16] Article 12 concerns indigenous peoples' right to practise their spiritual and religious traditions;[17] Article 13 refers to indigenous peoples' intangible heritage;[18] and Article 14 concerns their right to establish and control their educational systems.[19]

CESCR General Comment 21 promotes free, prior and informed consent regarding culture. This is further strengthened by paragraph 36 of General Comment 21, which states that:

> States parties must . . . take measures to recognize and protect the rights of indigenous peoples to own, develop, control and use their communal lands, territories and resources, and, where they have been otherwise

[15] Ibid., p. 144.

[16] Article 11: '1. Indigenous peoples have the right to practise and revitalize their cultural traditions and customs. This includes the right to maintain, protect and develop the past, present and future manifestations of their cultures, such as archaeological and historical sites, artefacts, designs, ceremonies, technologies and visual and performing arts and literature. 2. States shall provide redress through effective mechanisms, which may include restitution, developed in conjunction with indigenous peoples, with respect to their cultural, intellectual, religious and spiritual property taken without their free, prior and informed consent or in violation of their laws, traditions and customs.'

[17] Article 12: '1. Indigenous peoples have the right to manifest, practise, develop and teach their spiritual and religious traditions, customs and ceremonies; the right to maintain, protect, and have access in privacy to their religious and cultural sites; the right to the use and control of ceremonial objects; and the right to the repatriation of their human remains. 2. States shall seek to enable the access and/or repatriation of ceremonial objects and human remains in their possession through fair, transparent and effective mechanisms developed in conjunction with indigenous peoples concerned.'

[18] Article 13: '1. Indigenous peoples have the right to revitalize, use, develop and transmit to future generations their histories, languages, oral traditions, philosophies, writing systems and literatures, and to designate and retain their own names for communities, places and persons. 2. States shall take effective measures to ensure that this right is protected and also to ensure that indigenous peoples can understand and be understood in political, legal and administrative proceedings, where necessary through the provision of interpretation or by other appropriate means.'

[19] Article 14: '1. Indigenous peoples have the right to establish and control their educational systems and institutions providing education in their own languages, in a manner appropriate to their cultural methods of teaching and learning. 2. Indigenous individuals, particularly children, have the right to all levels and forms of education of the State without discrimination. 3. States shall, in conjunction with indigenous peoples, take effective measures, in order for indigenous individuals, particularly children, including those living outside their communities, to have access, when possible, to an education in their own culture and provided in their own language.'

inhabited or used without their free and informed consent, take steps to return these lands and territories.[20]

This obligation is a clear link with the rights of indigenous peoples, where free, prior and informed consent is one of the fundamental rights

---

[20] General Comment 21 also states as follows: '1. Cultural rights are an integral part of human rights and, like other rights, are universal, indivisible and interdependent. The full promotion of and respect for cultural rights is essential for the maintenance of human dignity and positive social interaction between individuals and communities in a diverse and multicultural world. 2. The right of everyone to take part in cultural life is closely related to the other cultural rights contained in article 15: the right to enjoy the benefits of scientific progress and its applications (art. 15(1)(b)); the right of everyone to benefit from the protection of moral and material interests resulting from any scientific, literary or artistic production of which they are the author (art. 15(1)(c)); and the right to freedom indispensable for scientific research and creative activity (art. 15(3)). The right of everyone to take part in cultural life is also intrinsically linked to the right to education (arts. 13 and 14), through which individuals and communities pass on their values, religion, customs, language and other cultural references, and which helps to foster an atmosphere of mutual understanding and respect for cultural values. The right to take part in cultural life is also interdependent on other rights enshrined in the Covenant, including the right of all peoples to self-determination (art. 1) and the right to an adequate standard of living (art. 11). 3. The right of everyone to take part in cultural life is also recognized in Article 27, paragraph 1, of the Universal Declaration of Human Rights, which states that "everyone has the right freely to participate in the cultural life of the community..."', above n. 2. General Comment 23, *inter alia*, includes the following statements: '1. Article 27 of the Covenant provides that, in those States in which ethnic, religious or linguistic minorities exist, persons belonging to these minorities shall not be denied the right, in community with the other members of their group, to enjoy their own culture, to profess and practise their own religion, or to use their own language. The Committee observes that this article establishes and recognizes a right which is conferred on individuals belonging to minority groups and which is distinct from, and additional to, all the other rights which, as individuals in common with everyone else, they are already entitled to enjoy under the Covenant'; and para. 6.2, 'Although the rights protected under article 27 are individual rights, they depend in turn on the ability of the minority group to maintain its culture, language or religion. Accordingly, positive measures by States may also be necessary to protect the identity of a minority and the rights of its members to enjoy and develop their culture and language and to practise their religion, in community with the other members of the group. In this connection, it has to be observed that such positive measures must respect the provisions of articles 2.1 and 26 of the Covenant both as regards the treatment between different minorities and the treatment between the persons belonging to them and the remaining part of the population. However, as long as those measures are aimed at correcting conditions which prevent or impair the enjoyment of the rights guaranteed under article 27, they may constitute a legitimate differentiation under the Covenant, provided that they are based on reasonable and objective criteria', above n. 2. See also Amanda Barratt and Ashimizo Afadameh-Adeyemi, 'Indigenous Peoples and the Right to Culture: The Potential Significance for African Indigenous Communities of the Committee on Economic, Social and Cultural Rights: General Comment 21', *African Human Rights Journal* 11 (2011), 560–88.

accorded to them. In that respect, should the government of a State Party take measures that affect the cultural rights of indigenous peoples within their territory, it should do so with the free and informed consent of those groups likely to be affected by any such measure. This right is enshrined in Article 19 of UNDRIP. It states as follows:

> States shall consult and cooperate in good faith with the indigenous peoples concerned through their own representative institutions in order to obtain their free, prior and informed consent before adopting and implementing legislative or administrative measures that may affect them.

The right to free, prior and informed consent was also confirmed by the HRC in the case of *Àngela Poma Poma* v. *Peru*, which stated that in the case of the imposition of measures which would substantially compromise or interfere with the culturally and economically significant activities of the members of minority or indigenous communities, free, prior and informed consent is necessary.[21]

There are additional cases in which the HRC reaffirmed the right to culture of indigenous peoples, in the context of the application of the ICCPR. For example, in the *Kitok* v. *Sweden*[22] and *Ominayak* v. *Canada*[23] cases, the HRC interpreted the cultural guarantees under Article 27 of the ICCPR to extend to economic and social activities that the indigenous group relied upon.[24] It is, however, important to note that such a right of indigenous peoples to cultural diversity is neither unlimited nor absolute; rather, it is subject to a balancing act by the State authorities, as is the case of other human rights, such as the right to privacy. Therefore, as the HRC observed in *Lansmänn and Others* v. *Finland*, the interests of broader society must be taken into account.[25] In other decisions, such as *Hopu and Bessert* v. *France*,[26] the HRC explained

---

[21] *Àngela Poma Poma* v. *Peru*, HRC, Comm. No. 1457/2006, 27 March 2009, UN Doc. CCPR/C/95/D/1457/2006 (2009) ¶ 7.6. 159 IACtHR.

[22] *Kitok* v. *Sweden*, Comm. No. 197/1985, Supplement No. 40 (A/43/40), 221–30, 27 July 1986; CCPR/C/33/D/197/1985.

[23] *Ominayak, Chief of Lubicon Lake Band* v. *Canada*, Comm. No. 267/1984. Report of the HRC, UN GOAR, 45th Sess., Supp. No. 2 at 1.

[24] S. James Anaya, 'International Human Rights and Indigenous Peoples: The Move Toward the Multicultural State', *Arizona Journal of International and Comparative Law* 21 (2004), 9–34, 29.

[25] *Lansmänn and Others* v. *Finland*, Comm. No. 511/1992, HRC, UN Doc. CCPR/C/52/D/511/1992 (8 November 1994).

[26] *Hopu and Bessert* v. *France*, Comm. No. 549/1993, HRC, UN Doc. CCPR/C60/D/549/1993/Rev.1 (29 December 1997).

that the cultural rights of indigenous peoples are derived not only from Article 27 of the ICCPR but also from its other Articles, such as Articles 17 and 23, dealing with the right to privacy and family life.

The cultural rights and the recognition of traditional knowledge were confirmed by several other international instruments relating to environmental protection, such as Rio+20, which stated that:

> We recognize that the traditional knowledge, innovations and practices of indigenous peoples and local communities make an important contribution to the conservation and sustainable use of biodiversity, and their wider application can support social well-being and sustainable livelihoods.[27]

Provisions concerning indigenous peoples are also contained in, for example, the 1992 Convention on Biological Diversity (Articles 8j and 15) and Principle 22 of the 1992 Rio Declaration on Environment and Development.

From the general state of human rights law and the practice of human rights bodies concerning the right to culture (and also in general multiculturalism), it would appear that indigenous peoples enjoy the right to whaling so long as it is a *bona fide* expression of their traditional way of life and their traditional use of natural resources. According to Kymlicka, in the case of indigenous peoples, however, there has been a trend towards a greater recognition of customary law and self-governing rights, without any retreat or backlash. This trend culminated in the adoption of the 2007 UNDRIP. Nonetheless, certain indigenous practices have been viewed as culturally conservative and restricting upon individual freedoms due to their overly communitarian and/or traditionalist character,[28] and as expressing a desire for cultural isolationism.[29] Some argue that, inadvertently, social conservatism, traditionalism and isolationism are elevated to 'sacred obligations' in order to silence, manage or otherwise 'delegitimise' group members who want to change such practices.[30] After all, indigenous groups are not immune from inevitable social change within their own communities, and a regime of collective rights – while unquestionably progressive given that it safeguards the cultural

---

[27] Report of the United Nations Conference on Sustainable Development (2012), A/CONF.216/16, Annex, para. 39.

[28] Will Kymlicka, *Multicultural Odysseys: Navigating the New International Politics of Diversity* (Oxford University Press, 2007), p. 149.

[29] Will Kymlicka, *Multiculturalism and Citizenship* (Oxford University Press, 2001), p. 103.

[30] Ibid. Kymlicka, above n. 28, p. 149.

identity and relative autonomy of groups surrounded by outsider dominant cultures – should not lend itself to intra-community oppression when its principal overall purpose is to resist domination and oppression from forces extraneous to the group, such as the State and the dominant culture that envelops such ethnic groups. In contrast, other views emphasise that, unlike Western attitudes towards nature (recognised as self-destructive and unsustainable), indigenous peoples and their practices may, in the same context, often offer inspiration and guidance.[31] An apposite illustration of the contentious nature of the issue of indigenous (aboriginal) whaling and of the lack of clarity as to what defines 'aboriginal cultural whaling' is the case study of the Makah Indians (State of Washington, USA).[32]

The next sensitive question is how aboriginal whaling conforms to the philosophical theories dealing with the rights of animals. As was noted in Chapter 5, there is no one prevailing theory that satisfies every theorist, and all of them have certain drawbacks. The rights-based theory would not be suitable to the present case, given that it would involve the conflicting rights of whales to life and those of indigenous peoples to hunt whales, which cannot be reconciled. The same would apply to the theory propounded by Regan, according to which all (humans and animals) enjoy equal intrinsic value (with certain exceptions). The question may be posed whether aboriginal whaling would amount to such an exception. Other authors have argued that the fact that the legal status of indigenous peoples has been widely recognised by the international community somehow gives rise to the 'responsibility' on the part of such peoples to uphold the rule of international law.[33] It would appear that the animal welfare theorists might be permissive of indigenous whaling; for example, they might support Inuit small-scale whaling as ecologically sound, given that they kill only the bare minimum necessary for their subsistence.[34]

---

[31] Ibid. Will Kymlicka, *Multicultural Citizenship: A Liberal Theory of Minority Rights* (Oxford University Press, 1995), p. 121. See also Alexandra Xanthaki, 'Multiculturalism and International Law: Discussing Universal Standards', *Human Rights Quarterly* 32 (2010), 21–48.

[32] On the Makah tribe's whale hunting, see Section 7.5.1 of this chapter.

[33] Russel Lawrence Barsh, 'Indigenous Peoples', in Daniel Bodansky, Jutta Brunnée and Ellen Hey (eds.), *The Oxford Handbook of International Environmental Law* (Oxford University Press, 2007), p. 850.

[34] Leena Heinämäki, 'Protecting the Rights of Indigenous Peoples – Promoting the Sustainability of the Global Environment?' *International Community Law Review* 11 (2009), 3–68, 66.

Views have been expressed that some claims concerning aboriginal whaling were somewhat weak, such as those of St Vincent and the Grenadines. They have made claims for aboriginal subsistence whaling on behalf of people who are not pre-colonial inhabitants, but descendants of slaves introduced into the Caribbean in the early stages of colonisation. This claim goes back about 150 years. When asked about this relatively recent tradition, the answer was that the question was out of bounds and that reminding Caribbean countries about their history of slavery and colonialism should be cautioned against.[35]

Doubleday expressed the view that indigenous peoples must take part in any discussion that impacts on their aboriginal subsistence rights, and that they ought not to be made to pay for the overexploitation of whales during the nineteenth and twentieth centuries by the whaling industry of the dominant culture that surrounds them.[36] D'Amato and Chopra acknowledged that indigenous peoples have rights to hunt whales only if those rights do not interfere with the rights of whales. However, sudden abandoning of whaling might result in considerable hardship for some indigenous peoples, and they propose that they be offered temporary assistance by States which earlier engaged in commercial whaling.[37]

The right to self-determination, when extended to indigenous peoples, means that indigenous peoples should be free to decide on the development of their culture. This should not, however, under any circumstances mean that indigenous peoples are free to engage in environmentally dangerous practices. If they are to be subjects of international law, they must necessarily be bound by the same environmental principles – such as the sustainability requirement – as States.[38]

It was pointed out that indigenous peoples' commitment to ecologically sustainable living is not a trade-off in return for self-determination, but a necessary requirement for their own future well-being.[39] It may be said that, in general, indigenous peoples have a well-known sustainable

---

[35] Alexander Gillespie, *International Environmental Law, Policy, and Ethics* (2nd edn, Oxford University Press, 2014), p. 90.

[36] Nancy C. Doubleday, 'Aboriginal Subsistence Whaling: The Right of Inuit to Hunt Whales and Implications for International Environmental Law', *Denv. J. Int'l L. & Pol.* 17 (1988–9), 373–94.

[37] Anthony D'Amato and Sudhir K. Chopra, 'Whales: Their Emerging Right to Life', AJIL 85 (1991), 21–62, 60.

[38] Heinämäki, above n. 34, 66.

[39] Benjamin J. Richardson, 'Indigenous Peoples, International Law and Sustainability', RECIEL 10 (2001), 1–12, 3.

relationship with nature, and depict themselves as its guardians.[40] It must be stressed, however, that indigenous whaling should in principle conform, if not to animal rights approaches, at least to animal welfare approaches, that is to say, to ensure that pain and suffering is minimised. There are no inherent guarantees that indigenous whaling would not be exploited by commercial interests. As Gillespie persuasively argues:

> many historical records and contemporary practices have combined to show specific indigenous cultures as being the antithesis of environmental sustainability. This has become increasingly apparent as certain indigenous cultures have apparently exchanged their supposed belief system for financial rewards ... Certain commentators have taken this even further than questions of political economy, and have challenged the idea of indigenous communities as suitable examples of livelihoods overall ... This is *not* to suggest that no indigenous communities are exemplars of environmental sustainability. Rather, the point is that no generic claims can be based suggesting that all indigenous cultures are environmentally benign.[41]

According to some views, exempting aboriginal (Inuit) peoples from the trade ban on seal hunting and, at the same time, presumably from the requirements of animal welfare, is demeaning to them and even racist, as it depicts them as 'noble savages', in contrast to more developed non-indigenous seal-hunting communities, to which the ban and animal welfare requirements apply.[42]

Donaldson and Kymlicka condone the killing of animals only in cases of necessity, and, in their view, this is 'arguably closer to traditional indigenous attitudes than to the mainstream attitudes of Western societies for these past few centuries'.[43] As has already been noted, the 1931 Geneva Whaling Convention contained a technology criterion in its definition of aboriginal whaling which is missing in the ICRW.

There have been a number of cases in which the HRC has clarified the rights of indigenous peoples regarding Article 27 of the ICCPR,[44]

---

[40] Heinämäki, above n. 34, 67–8.

[41] Alexander Gillespie, 'The Ethical Question in the Whaling Debate', *Georgetown Int'l Env'l Law Review* 9 (1997), 355–87, 363.

[42] Nikolas Sellheim, 'Policies and Influence. Tracing and Locating the EU Seal Product Trade Regulation', *International Community Law Review* 17 (2015), 3–36, 33.

[43] Sue Donaldson and Will Kymlicka, *Zoopolis: A Political Theory of Animal Rights* (Oxford University Press, 2011), p. 47.

[44] See e.g. HRC, *Ilmari Länsman et al.* v. *Finland*, Views adopted on 26 October 1994, Comm. No. 511/1992, UN Doc. CCPR/C/57/1, 75–85; *Jouni E. Länsman et al.* v. Finland, Views adopted on 30 October 1996, Comm. No. 671/1995, UN Doc. CCPR/C/58/D/671/1995.

addressing, in particular, the issue of the use of modern technology within traditional indigenous hunting activities. Thus, in the 1994 *Länsman* case, the HRC stated that modern practices adopted by indigenous peoples did not prevent them from invoking Article 27 of the ICCPR.[45] This was confirmed in the *Apirana Mahuika* case, where it was stated that the right to enjoy one's culture cannot be determined in abstract, but has to be placed in context. In particular, Article 27 of the ICCPR not only protects traditional means of livelihood of minorities, but also allows for adaptation of those means to the modern way of life and its ensuing technology.[46]

The use of traditional methods of killing whales by indigenous peoples is a very sensitive issue and of great concern. In traditional practices, pain and suffering are often inflicted despite good intentions. Deaths on average take between 30 and 60 minutes. In 2003, in Greenland, the average time for a minke whale to die was 14 minutes and the average time for a fin whale was 114 minutes. The worst case was 740 minutes. The same concerns were expressed regarding primary killing of small cetaceans.[47] In 1977, the IWC adopted a Resolution which urged aboriginal subsistence whalers to reduce suffering of whales. This request mainly originated from Japan, stemming from a desire for equity in the IWC.[48] According to Harrop, 'there is a clash of moral interests in this area'.[49] On the one hand, there is the desire to rectify past injustices and the view that indigenous peoples' cultural life should be respected; on the other hand, there is moral pressure to secure humane killing.[50]

The cruellest method was the use of the so-called 'cold harpoon' on smaller whales such as minke whales. Alaskan Inuit presently use penthrite projectiles (small grenades). But, as Stoett observes,

> an intense ethical question arises regarding the aboriginal hunts: The more traditional-style hunts were almost certainly agonizing affairs for the whales involved, involving hours of bleeding. Today's aboriginal whaler has recourse to shotguns and other technically expeditious devices,

[45] *Jouni E. Länsman et al.* v. *Finland*, para. 9.3.
[46] *Apirana Mahuika et al.* v. *New Zealand*, Views adopted on 27 October 2000, Comm. No. 447/1993, UN Doc. CCPR/C/70/D/547/1993, para. 9.4.
[47] Gillespie, above n. 35, p. 92.
[48] Stuart R. Harrop, 'From Cartel to Conservation and on to Compassion: Animal Welfare and the International Whaling Commission', *Journal of International Wildlife Law and Policy* 6 (2003), 79–104, 95.
[49] Ibid., 95.   [50] Ibid., 95.

minimizing the pain and suffering of the captured whale; yet again when does a traditional hunt end and a modern one begin?[51]

The contemporary approach of the IWC to the use of technology follows the stand adopted by the HRC, one of the reasons being that the modern means of killing are more humane (even though, it must be noted, many also cause an increase in depletion of whale stocks).[52] However, this is not a uniformly accepted position, as the HRC acknowledgement of the evolving lifestyle of indigenous peoples and also their permissible use of modern technology is seen by certain States as a contentious issue within the IWC:

> [i]ncreased use of technology is another potential issue. Improved technology makes whaling safer, more efficient and more humane, but it may be seen by some to compromise aboriginal authenticity. The world has undoubtedly changed since 1946 when the Convention was written, but for some this may be difficult to accept in the context of indigenous whaling, even when the result of technological advance is a quicker and more humane killing method. For others, use of the more traditional technology is seen as a problem for the opposite reasons.[53]

Therefore, as the practice of the IWC indicates, what it understands by culture and the method of aboriginal (subsistence) whaling is not entirely clear and perhaps not always in line with the jurisprudence of the HRC. The difficulties of placing whaling within the culture of indigenous peoples also result partly from general confusion as to what is understood by culture.

7.2   Early regulation of aboriginal whaling

International recognition of aboriginal subsistence whaling is by no means new. The special position of whaling rights of aboriginal communities was

---

[51] Peter Stoett, 'Of Whales and People: Normative Theory, Symbolism and the IWC', *Journal of International Wildlife Law and Policy* 8 (2005), 151–75, 170.

[52] Report of the Panel Meeting of Experts on Aboriginal/Subsistence Whaling, reprinted in: International Whaling Commission, 'Aboriginal/Subsistence Whaling (with special reference to the Alaska and Greenland fisheries)', *Reports of the International Whaling Commission – Special Issue* 4 (1982), 7–9, available at: http://iwcoffice.org/cache/down loads/7h78clbatfggcw8gg00w8wo4o/RIWC-SI4-ppl-33.pdf, last accessed 31 December 2014. See also Randall R. Reeves, 'The Origins and Character of "Aboriginal Subsistence" Whaling: A Global Review', *Mammal Review* 32 (2002), 71–106, 98.

[53] International Whaling Commission, http://iwc.int/aboriginal, last accessed 14 January 2015.

already recognised and included in the 1931 Geneva Whaling Convention (Article 3),[54] which stated that it did not apply to aborigines dwelling on the coasts of the Parties, provided that:

(1) they only use canoes, pirogues or other exclusively native craft propelled by oars or sails;
(2) they do not carry firearms;
(3) they are not in the employment of persons other than aborigines;
(4) they are not under contract to deliver the products of their whaling to any third person.

However, no equivalent provision was included in either the 1937 London Agreement or the 1938 Protocol amending the 1937 London Agreement.[55]

7.3 Aboriginal whaling within the jurisdiction of the IWC

7.3.1 Aboriginal subsistence whaling: the historical background and the general outline

While the 1946 ICRW does not itself include any special provision regulating aboriginal subsistence whaling, the Schedule to the ICRW recognises its special position by excluding it from the definition of, and the provisions relating to, commercial whaling. When the ICRW was originally concluded, the second paragraph of the Schedule prohibited the taking and killing of grey whales and right whales due to their fragile status. This prohibition did not apply where the whaling of such species was conducted for local consumption of meat and other products by indigenous peoples. The second paragraph of the Schedule stated that: '[i]t is forbidden to take or kill grey whales or right whales, except when the meat and products of such whales are to be used exclusively for local consumption by the aborigines'.[56] Thus, it appears to be clear that even when conducted by indigenous whalers, the whaling of grey whales or right whales either for commercial purposes or when

---

[54] Convention for the Regulation of Whaling, 24 September 1931, 155 LNTS 349.
[55] Protocol amending the International Agreement of 8 June 1937 for the Regulation of Whaling, 24 June 1938, 196 LNTS 131.
[56] See Hisashi Hamaguchi, 'Aboriginal Subsistence Whaling Revisited', in Nobuhiro Kishigami, Hisashi Hamaguchi and James M. Savelle (eds.), Senri Ethnological Studies, No. 84, Anthropological Studies of Whaling (Osaka: National Museum of Ethnology, 2013), pp. 81–99, 82.

the meat or products were to be distributed extensively outside the communities of those indigenous peoples was prohibited.[57] The definition of 'subsistence whaling' has since evolved. In brief, there are two fundamental requirements for the allocation of quotas for aboriginal whaling: ensuring that hunts do not seriously increase risks of extinction and that hunted whale populations are then maintained at healthy, relatively high levels; and enabling native people to hunt whales at levels appropriate to cultural and nutritional requirements (known as 'cultural and nutritional needs'). National governments provide the IWC with evidence of the needs of their indigenous people. This is presented in the form of a 'Needs Statement' that details the cultural, subsistence and nutritional aspects of the hunt, products and distribution. The Scientific Committee provides advice on the sustainability of proposed hunts and safe catch limits.[58]

In 1979, the IWC Anthropology Panel adopted an unofficial definition of 'subsistence whaling' as comprising:

(1) the personal consumption of whale products for food, fuel, shelter, clothing, tools or transportation by participants in the whale harvest;
(2) the barter, trade or sharing of whale products in their harvested form with relatives of the participants in the harvest, with others in the local community or with persons in locations other than the local community with whom local residents share familial, social, cultural or economic ties. A generalised currency is involved in this barter and trade, but the predominant portion of the products from each whale is ordinarily directly consumed or utilised in their harvested form within the local community; and
(3) the making and selling of handicraft articles from whale products, when the whale is harvested for the purposes of (1) and (2) above.

Aboriginal subsistence whaling was again defined in 1981, this time by the IWC's Technical Committee Working Group on Development of Management Principles and Guidelines for Subsistence Catches of Whales by Indigenous (Aboriginal) Peoples as comprising whaling conducted for 'purposes of local aboriginal consumption, carried out by or on behalf of aboriginal, indigenous or native people who share strong community, familial, social and cultural ties related to a continuing

---

[57] Hamaguchi, above n. 56, p. 82.
[58] International Whaling Commission, http://iwc.int/aboriginal, last accessed 13 January 2015.

traditional dependence on whaling and on the use of whales'.[59] These definitions could give rise to more questions than those they were designed to settle. For instance, the interchangeable use of the terms 'aboriginal', 'native' and 'indigenous' is confusing, as in many indigenous communities this leads to different meanings.[60] For example, there has been discussion as to whether whaling in Greenland can qualify as aboriginal. The 1979 definition of 'subsistence use of whale products', coined by cultural anthropologists, is more restrictive as to the area in which the distribution of whale products is permitted; and it does not recognise the distribution of whale products that involve monetary exchanges, as in aboriginal subsistence whaling.[61]

It may also be noted that the report proposing the definitions was perhaps inconsistent as it states that, in some cases, products are distributed to, and used by, communities away from the coastal areas where whaling is actually conducted; and in some areas, the practice of trading to meet subsistence needs has emerged. Further, the IWC ad hoc Working Group stated that it was arguable whether there is a difference in principle between the sale of whale products in order to buy essential goods and the direct exchange of whale products for such goods. According to Hamaguchi, this is indicative of the fact that even the ad hoc Working Group's definition did not completely deny for all cases the extensive distribution of whale products or the distribution involving monetary exchanges for whale-related goods.[62]

At the outset, therefore, it appears that confusion arose due to the lack of any conclusive definition of what constitutes 'commercial' whaling, which, at times, makes the distinction between 'aboriginal' and 'commercial' whaling challenging, despite the efforts of the ad hoc Working Group to distinguish between them. These two forms are considered to be different due to their different objectives, which also include the management and catching. The main objective of the management of aboriginal subsistence whaling was to maintain individual stocks at the highest possible level, and the main purpose of catching whales was to fulfil the nutritional and cultural needs of the indigenous peoples

---

[59] Report of the Cultural Anthropology Panel, reprinted in: International Whaling Commission, 'Aboriginal/Subsistence Whaling (with special reference to the Alaska and Greenland fisheries)', *Reports of the International Whaling Commission – Special Issue* 4 (1982), 35–50, available at www.iwcoffice.org/cache/downloads/ebvrl7xp4e80w40804cssc4s8/RIWC-SI4-pp34-73.pdf, last accessed 24 October 2014.

[60] Reeves, above n. 52, 77.   [61] Hamaguchi, above n. 56, p. 86.   [62] Ibid., p. 86.

contemplated by the relevant agreements. The main objective of commercial whaling was to maximise yields from individual stocks and to ensure the longevity of the respective whaling industries of the State Parties to the ICRW, and the main purpose of catching whales was to sell their products. Hamaguchi observes that 'these differences indicate that aboriginal subsistence whaling prioritizes quality (the cultural aspect) and commercial whaling prioritizes quantity (the economic aspect)'.[63] However, as Reeves postulates, the distinction between commercial and subsistence whaling still remains crude and ambiguous.[64]

The Aboriginal Subsistence Whaling Sub-Committee (ASWS) was established in order to consider documentation on needs relating to aboriginal whaling and to advise the IWC Technical Committee on the setting up of proper management measures. The field of aboriginal subsistence whaling was, consequently, subdivided into the following: (1) subsistence whaling; (2) nutritional whaling; (3) cultural whaling. Thus, as Gillespie has noted, the definitions of aboriginal whaling set out above indicate that aboriginal whaling should be local and non-commercial in nature. However, this conflicts to some extent with the definition of 'consumption' which allows the sale of by-products.[65] Heinämäki correctly criticises this sub-division, observing that 'in practice ... the "subsistence requirement" seems to be a kind of main category, including "food" by definition, whereas nutritional and cultural needs are subcategories to "Aboriginal Subsistence Whaling", which are closely connected to each other'.[66] Apart from this, however, there are a number of problems relating to the definition of the three categories themselves and to their interrelationship. Indeed, the practice of States indicates that the submission of the required evidence proving 'nutritional and cultural need', which is a fundamental requirement for allocation of quotas for aboriginal peoples, has frequently been very difficult to achieve.[67] But,

---

[63] Ibid., p. 86.   [64] Reeves, above n. 52, 77.

[65] Alexander Gillespie, 'Aboriginal Subsistence Whaling: A Critique of the Inter-relationship between International Law and the IWC', *Colorado J. Int. Env'l Law & Policy* 12 (2001), 77–139.

[66] Heinämäki, above n. 34, 45.

[67] Ibid., 44. 'On occasion, the Commission's assessment of "need" has proved difficult and controversial, and there are a number of possible reasons for this. Firstly, there is no definition of key terminology, not just in the 1946 International Convention for the Regulation of Whaling, but in international law more generally. It has never been possible to pin down the concept of "aboriginal" to one rigid and measurable definition. The same is true of "subsistence" and indeed of "need". In addition, each hunt is unique, and different factors are more relevant to different communities. The strength or importance of a whaling tradition in

crucially, Heinämäki also points out that the distinction sought to be made by the IWC between subsistence and nutritional needs conflicts with the interpretation of the HRC, which interpreted traditional liveli-hoods and means of subsistence (including traditional diet) as an integral part of indigenous culture under Article 27 of the ICCPR. Additionally, the HRC allows the inclusion of some commercial elements within the definition of 'aboriginal subsistence' and, indeed, stresses the economic viability of a livelihood as a material criterion of the fulfilment of the provisions of Article 27 of the ICCPR.[68]

Hamaguchi is of the view that the imposition of the Moratorium on commercial whaling has impacted also on aspects of aboriginal subsist-ence whaling due to extensive revision to paragraph 13 of the Schedule, which followed the setting up of the Moratorium.[69] As it stands now, paragraph 13 of the Schedule establishes an ample set of conditions for setting quotas for aboriginal subsistence whaling.[70] For example, changes were made to whaling in Greenland. Due to the revision of paragraph 13 (b) of the Schedule, 'catch limits were only granted for aboriginal sub-sistence whaling, which meant that only the indigenous people in Green-land were allowed to be involved in whaling',[71] whereas before the Moratorium all inhabitants of Greenland were permitted to hunt whales.

---

the country, remoteness, availability of local foodstuffs, health, climate, entitlement to local food security, and the familial or artisanal nature of the hunt, are some of the many factors that may be considered important. The methods of hunting and means of distribution also vary widely. Put simply, no two indigenous communities are the same and nor are their Needs Statements. This can make assessment difficult.' Doubleday is of the view that the aboriginal whaling requires reconsideration, such as is troublesome at times proving of needs, as well as the prohibition against trade of edible products: Nancy Doubleday, 'Arctic Whales: Sustaining Indigenous Peoples and Conserving Arctic Resources', in Milton M. R. Freeman and Urs Kreuter (eds.), *Elephants and Whales. Resources for Whom?* (Basle: Gordon and Breach Science Publishers, 1994), 241–61, 254; International Whaling Commission, http://iwc.int/aboriginal, last accessed 14 January 2015.

[68] Heinämäki, above n. 34, 45.   [69] Hamaguchi, above n. 56, p. 87.

[70] Para. 13 of the Schedule establishes two sets of conditions for ASW. Para 13(a) establishes the first set of conditions, which generally apply to ASW quotas for any stock, which are permitted, according to para 13(b), notwithstanding para. 10 (which imposes the Mora-torium on commercial whaling). Para. 13(a) introduces the three conditions of allocating aboriginal quotas: (1) satisfying the aboriginal subsistence 'need'; (2) for each whaling season; and (3) in accordance with principles. These principles regard the conservation of the stock; the prohibition against striking or killing calves or suckling calves; and the need for national legislation, and are in accordance with para. 13. Para. 13(b) provides a specific set of conditions relating to specific stocks and also establishes specific quotas for each and every stock.

[71] Hamaguchi, above n. 56, p. 87.

7.3.2   Commercial and aboriginal whaling

Greenland's aboriginal whaling is a good example of the great difficulties in drawing a clear division between commercial and aboriginal whaling. As stated in the previous sub-section, the ad hoc Working Group also considered the difference between aboriginal subsistence whaling and commercial whaling. These two forms were different as to two aspects: management and catching (see Section 7.3.1).[72] Several writers argued that the approximation of hunting and fishing activities with waged employment has contributed to a blurring of the distinction between commercial and non-commercial activities. The confusion is compounded by the unclear and inconsistent drafting of paragraph 13 of the Schedule.[73] A substantial part of the *mattak* (the skin and adhering blubber) from belugas and narwhals is sold by hunters and marketed in shops in Greenland. The same applies to narwhal tusks that are sold either to visitors or in shops in Greenland (with a view to exporting them). It has been suggested that 'whaling had become more commodity-based and commercialised as a result of the high monetary value of mattak in particular, and that as a result policy makers in Greenland have become engaged in "redefining" of subsistence hunting'.[74] However, others are of the view that sharing, gift-giving and household consumption of whale products in Greenland still predominate, and that cash transactions have more of an incidental than a central character.[75] According to Hamaguchi:

> the establishment of aboriginal whaling as aboriginal subsistence whaling would result in this being treated as a practice devoid of commercial elements, at least in ideological terms. However, it is difficult for an outsider to comprehend the concept of the distribution of whale products involving cash that is not meant for profit-making purposes; it was here that the misfortunes of aboriginal subsistence whaling began.[76]

The complex nature of aboriginal hunting is also reflected by the two WTO cases regarding the import of seal products.[77] In very general

---

[72] Ibid., p. 86.

[73] See, in detail, Chris Wold and Michael S. Kearney, 'The Legal Effects of Greenland's Unilateral Aboriginal Subsistence Whale Hunt', *American University International Law Review* 30 (2015), 561–609, 580–1.

[74] Reeves, above n. 52, 79.   [75] Ibid., 79.   [76] Hamaguchi, above n. 56, p. 88.

[77] Panel Reports, *European Communities – Measures Prohibiting the Importation and Marketing of Seal Products*, WT/DS400/R and WT/DS401/R (25 November 2013) (hereinafter *EC – Seal Products*), www.wto.org/english/tratop_e/dispu_e/400_401abr_e.pdf, last accessed 30 December 2014. See Ludwig Krämer, 'Case Note: Seal Killing, the Inuit

terms, the dispute arose from complaints by Canada and Norway against a legislative scheme adopted by the EU in 2009 prohibiting the importation into and marketing of seal products in the EU.[78] The issue of the ban proved to be very emotive, as, in the context of indigenous culture in Canada, subsistence seal hunting plays an important role, but such hunting was fiercely opposed by animal welfare organisations.[79] On 24 January 2014, Canada and Norway filed an appeal against the earlier panel's decision, which resulted in the report of the WTO Appellate Body (AB). Under the EU Seal Regime, there was one exception from the overall import ban, namely, for products of traditional indigenous hunting ('the indigenous communities (IC) exception'). Canada and Norway challenged the EU Seal Regime at the WTO. According to these States, this regime was discriminatory against their whaling industries, as indigenous sealers comprise a very small proportion of the seal industry in Canada. Hunting of seals is carried out mainly by non-indigenous fishermen on Canada's east coast and in Newfoundland, whereas in Greenland the sealing industry is almost entirely conducted by the Inuit peoples. According to Canada and Norway, the EU Seal Regime entails de facto discrimination, 'as the seal products made by hunters in Greenland can more easily enter the EU's market, given the higher percentage of

---

and European Union Law', RECIEL 21 (2012), 291–6. According to Krämer, the Canadian government's quota of seals has been increased beyond 250,000 each year. The protests against these quotas also concerned the alleged inhumane methods of killing and suffering caused to seals. See also Dorothée Cambou, 'The Impact of the Ban on Seal Products on the Rights of Indigenous Peoples: A European Issue', *Yearbook of Polar Law* 5 (2013), 389–416; Nikolas Sellheim, 'The Neglected Tradition? The Genesis of the EU Seal Products Trade Ban and Commercial Sealing', *Yearbook of Polar Law* 5 (2013), 417–50. Rob Howse, Joanna Langille and Katie Sykes, 'Animal Welfare, Public Morals and Trade: The WTO Panel Report in *EC – Seal Products*', *ASIL Insights*, 29 January 2014, www.asil.org/insights/volume/18/issue/2/animal-welfare-public-morals-and-trade-wto-panel-report-ec-%E2%80%93-seal, last accessed 30 December 2014; Sellheim, above n. 41. Appellate Body Report, *European Communities – Measures Prohibiting the Importation and Marketing of Seal Products*, WT/DS400/AB/R and WT/DS401/AB/R (22 May 2014) (hereinafter *EC – Seal Products*), https://docs.wto.org/dol2fe/Pages/FE_Search/FE_S_S006.aspx?Query=(@Symbol=%20wt/ds400/ab/r*%20not%20rw*)&Language=ENGLISH&Context=FomerScriptedSearch&languageUIChanged=true#, last accessed 30 December 2014; Rob Howse, Joanna Langille and Katie Sykes, 'Sealing the Deal: The WTO's Appellate Body Report in *EC – Seal Products*', *ASIL Insights*, 4 June 2014, www.asil.org/insights/volume/18/issue/12/sealing-deal-wto%E2%80%99s-appellate-body-report-ec-%E2%80%93-seal-products, last accessed 30 December 2014.

[78] Regulation (EC) No. 1007/2009 of the European Parliament and of the Council of 16 September 2009 on Trade in Seal Products, 2009 OJ (L286), 36.

[79] Sellheim, above n. 42, 9.

indigenous hunters as compared to that of Canada or Norway vis-à-vis their seal industries'.[80] The AB upheld the Panel's conclusion that the EU Seal Regime may be justified under the general exceptions to WTO rules (as per GATT Article XX given that the offending measure (the EU Seal Regime) may be necessary to protect public morals regarding seal welfare, as per Article XX(a) GATT).[81] However, in the event, the AB decided that the EU Seal Regime does not meet the requirements of the chapeau to Article XX GATT 1994 because the IC exception operates in a way that amounts to 'arbitrary or unjustifiable discrimination'.[82] Furthermore, the AB stated that the EU had not done enough to facilitate access of Canadian Inuit seal products to the exception.[83] It was said that some steps could be taken to encourage improved welfare standards in IC hunts and to facilitate Canadian Inuit hunters' access to the EU market under the IC exception.[84]

7.3.3 Aboriginal subsistence whaling under the IWC at present

As referred to in Section 7.3.1, according to the IWC, the objectives of aboriginal subsistence whaling are as follows:

(1) to ensure that the risk of extinction is not seriously increased (the objective with the highest priority);
(2) to enable harvests in perpetuity appropriate to cultural and nutritional requirements; and
(3) to maintain stocks at the highest net recruitment level, and, if they fall below that, to ensure they move towards it.[85]

In general, the IWC has identified four specific whaling operations as qualifying for the status of aboriginal subsistence whaling:

(1) minke and fin whales (formerly also humpback whales) in Greenland;
(2) humpback whales in the Lesser Antilles (specifically at the island of Bequia, St Vincent and the Grenadines);

---

[80] Howse et al., above n. 77.   [81] *EC – Seal Products*, above n. 77, para. 5.167.
[82] Ibid., para. 5.328.   [83] Ibid., para. 5.337; Howse et al., above n. 77.
[84] Howse et al., above n. 77.
[85] See: International Whaling Commission, http://iwcoffice.org/aboriginal, last accessed 24 October 2012. The total number of whales caught for aboriginal (subsistence) whaling in the period 1985–2012 was 9,391 (fin: 335; humpback: 83; sei: 3; minke: 4,309; grey: 3,291; bowhead: 1,370), IWC, http://iwc.int/table_aboriginal, last accessed 29 December 2014.

(3) bowhead whales (and formerly also grey whales) in the USA; and grey whales in Russia (Chukotka); and

(4) bowhead and grey whales in the USA (Alaska).[86]

On the basis of the above objectives and criteria, aboriginal subsistence whaling is allowed at present for the following countries:

(1) Denmark (in relation to the Inuit peoples of Greenland), fin and minke whales;

(2) Russian Federation (Siberia), grey and bowhead whales;

(3) St Vincent and the Grenadines (Bequia), humpback whales; and

(4) USA (Alaska and Makah indigenous peoples), bowhead and grey whales.

It should be recalled that it is the responsibility of national governments to provide the IWC with evidence of the cultural and subsistence 'needs' of their aboriginal peoples, while the Scientific Committee provides scientific advice on safe catch limits for such stocks, as two necessary requirements for the allocation of quotas.[87]

The IWC has for many years been developing the Aboriginal Whaling Management Scheme (AWMS), which is intended to include two elements:

(1) the quota-setting mechanism (which is already in place); and

(2) a supervision and control scheme in order to establish the future management of aboriginal subsistence whaling.

At present, aboriginal subsistence quotas under the quota-setting mechanism are adopted for a period of five years.[88] Under the IWC, there is a marked limitation in the number of species of whales that have been

---

[86] Ibid.   [87] Ibid.

[88] There are the following types of whales in aboriginal whaling: United States (on behalf of the Inupiat in Alaska: bowhead whales and Makah: grey whales); Russia (on behalf of the Chukchi people: grey and bowhead whales); St Vincent and the Grenadines (Bequia: humpback); and Denmark (on behalf of the Inuit in Greenland: fin, bowhead, humpback and minke whales). Catch limits for these stocks were agreed at the 2007 IWC Annual Meeting, with the exception of the catch of West Greenland humpback whales, which was agreed at the 2010 Annual Meeting. This allowed for up to 280 bowhead whales to be landed in the period 2008–12, with no more than 67 whales struck in any year (and up to 15 unused strikes may be carried over each year). Eastern North Pacific grey whales (taken by native people of Chukotka and Washington State): a total catch of 620 whales was allowed for 2008–12, with a maximum of 140 in any one year. East Greenland common minke whales (taken by Greenlanders): an annual strike limit of 12 whales was allowed for 2008–12, with any unused quota available to be carried forward to subsequent years provided that no more than three strikes were added to the quota for any one year.

singled out as eligible for aboriginal hunting, as indicated by the inclusion of bowhead whales in the Moratorium. This measure was objected to by the Inupiat peoples of the North Slope (Alaska). There has been a notable discrepancy between the figures that the Inupiat people and the IWC put forward regarding the existing whale stock in question. The IWC Technology Committee has confirmed the assertions of the Inupiat peoples.[89]

West Greenland bowhead whales (taken by Greenlanders): an annual strike limit of 2 whales was allowed for 2008–12, with an annual review by the Scientific Committee. Any unused quota could be carried forward to subsequent years so long as not more than two strikes were added to the quota for any one year. West Greenland fin whales (taken by Greenlanders): an annual strike limit of 16 whales was allowed for 2010–12. However, at the 2010 IWC Meeting, Denmark and Greenland agreed to voluntarily further reduce the catch limit for the West Greenland stock of fin whales from 16 to 10 each for 2010, 2011 and 2012. West Greenland common minke whales (taken by Greenlanders): an annual strike limit of 178 whales was allowed for 2010–12, with an annual review by the IWC Scientific Committee. Any unused quota could be carried forward, so long as no more than 15 strikes were added to the quota for any one year. West Greenland humpback whales (taken by Greenlanders): an annual strike limit of 9 whales was allowed for 2010–12, with an annual review by the Scientific Committee. Any unused quota could be carried forward so long as not more than two strikes were added to the quota for any one year. Humpback whales (taken by St Vincent and the Grenadines): for the seasons 2013–18 the number of humpback whales to be taken were not to exceed 24. All this information is available at: International Whaling Commission, http://iwcoffice.org/con servation/catches.htm, last accessed 3 March 2012. The subject of the allocation of quotas for indigenous whaling in Greenland was very contentious at the Panama City meeting of the IWC in 2012, during which the IWC rejected a request from Denmark for an increase in the whaling quota for Greenland to 1,300 whales over the next six years. The IWC voted 34 to 25 to reject the request. This proposal got 43% support, which was far short of the three-fourths majority needed according to the IWC rules. The USA supported Greenland and aboriginal whaling, and the EU expressed sympathy for the aboriginal peoples, but it is claimed that Greenland's whaling has been exposed as a commercial enterprise given that whale meat was sold in restaurants and grocery stores and not necessarily distributed to aboriginal people; available at: www.savethewhales.org/STW% 20E-Newsletters/8-12%20E-News.html, last accessed 28 December 2014. With the rejection, Greenland did not have the right to hunt whales after the end of 2012. Representatives from Denmark and Greenland are considering challenging the Commission's decision. See: www.terradaily.com/reports/EU_votes_ down_Greenland_ whaling_999. html, last accessed 24 October 2014.

[89] Scientific surveys indicated that the Beaufort Sea bowhead whale population was very much depleted, with only about 800 whales surviving in 1977. Local hunters stated that the whale population was about 7,000. Using the new census methods, the 1991 bowhead population was conservatively estimated to be in excess of 8,000 whales, despite an annual harvest of between 20 and 40 whales over the past decade. The findings tended to confirm the Inuit 1977 population assessment of about 7,000 animals. Milton M. R. Freeman, 'The Nature and Utility of Traditional Ecological Knowledge: The Northern Perspective' 20

Eventually, the Aboriginal Whaling Management Scheme (including the Aboriginal Whaling Management Procedure (AWMP), once it becomes fully operational) will provide guidelines and will set requirements for surveys and data as well as case-specific elements. It is also likely to cover certain scientific, logistical and regulatory aspects of aboriginal whaling, including the inspection/observation of catches. The IWC Plan for 2012 was a system of block quotas with internal allocations. Provisions included a quota of 289 bowhead whales landed (by agreement, the Alaska Inupiat may take up to 255 whales, with 125 allocated to Russian aboriginal bowhead whalers). In each year, the number of bowhead struck may not exceed sixty-seven whales; and up to fifteen unused strikes may be carried forward to the next year.[90] The Inupiat people have a history of about 200 years of whaling. In contemporary Inupiat society, whaling is very important culturally, socially, spiritually, politically and nutritionally. Whaling is one of the factors defining their community identity. It appears that whaling is absolutely fundamental for Inupiat cultural and social continuation of them as a people given that members of that society hold it to be a defining aspect of their cultural identity.[91]

At the 2002 meeting, the IWC Scientific Committee completed its work with respect to the Bering–Chukchi–Beaufort Seas stock of bowhead whales.[92] It agreed a Strike Limit Algorithm (SLA) for this stock of whales and the scientific aspects of the scheme (that is to say, how many bowheads can be taken in a sustainable manner). The SLA system was adopted by the IWC in 2004. However, the situation of Greenland's whaling for fin and minke whales has proved to be more complicated and at present requires more scientific research to be conducted in cooperation with Greenland's scientists.

Discussions regarding aboriginal whaling quotas can be highly divisive in the IWC. An example of this is the 2009 meeting, where the primary

(1991), available at: www.carc.org/index.php?option=com_wrapper&view=wrapper&Ite mid=174, last accessed 24 October 2014.

[90] See: https://alaskafisheries.noaa.gov/protectedresources/whales/bowhead/bowheadbrochure 1208.pdf, last accessed 24 October 2014.

[91] See Nobuhiro Kishigami, 'Aboriginal Subsistence Whaling in Barrow, Alaska', in *Senri Ethnological Studies*, above n. 56, pp. 101–20, 116.

[92] The Chukchi are an indigenous people living in the circumpolar Arctic of north-eastern Russia. There are two types of Chukchi: 'the Reindeer Chukchi' (who tend reindeer herds) and the 'coastal dwellers' (whose subsistence is based primarily on sea mammals; they hunt with a rifle, a harpoon with a whale line, a harpoon with a drogue, as well as a boat with an outboard motor).

issue was a discussion regarding a request for a catch of ten humpback whales for Greenland. The debate focused on the statement from the IWC Scientific Committee as to whether such a catch would not harm the stock of these whales, and whether Denmark (on behalf of Greenland) had adequately made the case for the 'needs' of Inuit peoples for humpback whales, both of which are necessary conditions for the allocation of quotas for aboriginal subsistence whaling. In the event, Denmark's request was unsuccessful. It may be added that there are also voices that support the view that there are insufficient quotas assigned to Russia's Chukchi people. It appears to be a general trend in relation to indigenous peoples that they will try to argue for higher allocations than those awarded to them.

St Vincent and the Grenadines have whaling quotas allocated for Bequia, a small island (whose population does not appear to be more than 5,000) which is a part of St Vincent and the Grenadines.[93] The total catch of whales from 1991 to 2010 was twenty-two whales, that is to say, on average one whale per year. There have been two whaling boats in operation since 2002.[94] The principal whaling method in Bequia seems rather primitive; whales are weakened by thrusting harpoons into their bodies followed by the use of lances.[95]

At present, there are chiefly four contentious issues that arise with regard to aboriginal (subsistence) whaling, namely:

(1) ongoing hunts that were traditionally considered to be 'aboriginal subsistence' but are at present undergoing an evaluation;
(2) small-scale shore-based hunts (which avoided international scrutiny but have been recently discovered and analysed);
(3) defunct or suspended whaling operations by aboriginal peoples that have resumed (or are expected to resume in the near future);[96] and
(4) the question of so-called small cetaceans (such as the narwhal, contested by many States as outside the jurisdiction of the IWC).

Aboriginal whaling is not the only aboriginal hunting permitted under the relevant treaties in similar regions of the world. In 2000, the US–Russian Bilateral Agreement for the Conservation and Management of the Alaska/Chukotka Polar Bear Population was concluded.[97] This

---

[93] See facts about Bequia at the Tourism Association's website: www.bequiatourism.com/facts.htm.
[94] Hamaguchi, above n. 56, p. 141.   [95] Ibid., p. 141.   [96] Reeves, above n. 52, 73.
[97] Text of the Agreement: http://pbsg.npolar.no/en/agreements/US-Russia.html, last accessed 30 December 2014.

Agreement is linked with the 1973 Agreement on the Conservation of Polar Bears (*Ursus maritimus*)[98] through its enforcement provisions. The purpose of the 2000 Agreement is to facilitate long-term conservation of the Chukchi/Bering polar bear population through the development of a conservation programme, to be implemented and enforced by the United States and Russia.[99] Indigenous polar bear hunting is subject to certain conditions, and its purpose is subsistence.[100]

[98] Text of the Agreement: http://pbsg.npolar.no/en/agreements/agreement1973.html, last accessed 31 December 2014. Parties are: Canada, Denmark, Norway, the United States and the USSR (with Russia being the current successor to this Agreement). See, on both Agreements, Catherine Redgwell, 'Polar Regions', in Michael Bowman, Peter Davies and Catherine Redgwell, *Lyster's International Wildlife Law* (2nd edn, Cambridge University Press, 2010), pp. 351–5.

[99] See Article II: 'The Contracting Parties shall cooperate with the goal of ensuring the conservation of the Alaska-Chukotka polar bear population, the conservation of its habitat, and the regulation of its use for subsistence purposes by native people.' The main purposes of the Agreement are defined as follows: 'Recognition of the right of subsistence use of polar bears from the Alaska-Chukotka population by native people of Alaska and Chukotka (Russia); inclusion of a definition of sustainable harvest level reflecting a clear obligation to conserve the population; establishment of a joint management mechanism, in the form of a bilateral commission, that can establish binding quotas to ensure that subsistence take of polar bears from the Alaska-Chukotka population is consistent with maintenance of that population at sustainable population levels; in the implementation of the Agreement, including a provision that each party will include in its national section in the commission a representative of its native people (as well as a representative of the national government); and additional studies and research relating to the conservation and management of the Alaska-Chukotka polar bear population, including collection of data necessary for regular and accurate population assessment and harvest monitoring.' US Department of State Archives, http://2001-2009. state.gov/g/oes/rls/rm/7168.htm, last accessed 30 December 2014. On the 1973 Agreement on the Conservation of Polar Bears (*Ursus maritimus*), see Tore Henriksen, 'Agreement on the Conservation of Polar Bears', to be published by Edward Elgar Publishing, *The Encyclopaedia of Multilateral Environmental Agreements* (on file with the author). There are also other multilateral environmental agreements (dealing with endangered species) which recognise indigenous whaling under certain conditions: such as the CMS and the Bern Convention. However, the main conditions are that taking animals by indigenous peoples must not be detrimental to animals and must be sustainable.

[100] 2000 Bilateral Agreement on Conservation and Management of the Alaska/Chukotka Polar Bear Population, Article VI: 'Native people may take polar bears of the Alaska-Chukotka population for subsistence purposes, provided that: (a) the take is consistent with Article III(1)(d) of the 1973 Agreement; (b) the taking of females with cubs, cubs less than one year of age, and bears in dens, including bears preparing to enter dens or who have just left dens, is prohibited; (c) the use of aircraft, large motorized vessels and large motorized vehicles for the purpose of taking polar bears is prohibited; and (d) the use of poisons, traps or snares for the purpose of taking polar bears is prohibited.'

The difference with aboriginal whaling is that the indigenous peoples concerned in the 2000 Agreement may use only traditional methods of killing.[101] The Agreement provides for advanced harvest quotas regulation based on sustainable yield. The most prominent feature of the Agreement is the key role played by indigenous groups in its conclusion, implementation and enforcement.[102] Wold and Kearney, having applied the rule of interpretation in the 1969 Vienna Convention on the Law of Treaties, drew several important conclusions on the principles of setting aboriginal subsistence whaling quotas, the most pertinent being that the requirement to adopt national legislation (para. 13(a)(5) of the Schedule) does not indicate that these quotas may be unilaterally adopted.[103]

According to the present author, this lack of legal clarity and consistency in the drafting of paragraph 13 and in State practice makes the politicisation of aboriginal whaling inevitable. By gaining a three-quarters majority in the IWC, any form of whaling that possesses some elements of aboriginal subsistence could potentially be considered and thus endorsed by the IWC (via the three-quarters majority) as aboriginal subsistence whaling. Conversely, such whaling, which seems to have all the hallmarks of aboriginal subsistence whaling, would not be endorsed by the IWC if, say, marginally more than a quarter of IWC members vote against it. Hamaguchi concludes that aboriginal subsistence whaling should be approved only on condition that there is a cultural, nutritional and economic need for it, and that the whales being harvested are not threatened with extinction.[104] Presumably, if the IWC members feel strongly about this lack of legal certainty and can form some majority to push for this, they could adopt some clarificatory statement or declaration to shed more light on what is ICRW-compliant aboriginal subsistence whaling. Such a development could address the seeming inconsistency in the IWC and thus enhance the integrity of the regime in the minds of all its members.

---

[101] Article III: '1. Subject to the provisions of Articles II and IV any Contracting Party may allow the taking of polar bears when such taking is carried out: ... (d) by local people using traditional methods in the exercise of their traditional rights and in accordance with the laws of that Party'.

[102] Redgwell, above n. 98, p. 353.

[103] Wold and Kearney, above n. 73, 591–2. In support of this, these authors cite two US court cases: *Hopson* v. *Krebs* and *Adams* v. *Vance*, in which the US federal courts stated, *inter alia*, that the United States acted consistently with its legal obligations under the ICRW by promulgating regulation halting ASW hunts (at 601–3).

[104] Hamaguchi, above n. 56, p. 96.

7.4   Aboriginal whaling outside the IWC context

A considerable amount of aboriginal whaling takes place outside the purview of the IWC, in States that are not party to the ICRW, such as Equatorial Guinea, Indonesia, Canada and the Philippines, in which there are no quotas allocated by the IWC for aboriginal whaling. These examples illustrate the difficulties in assessing the impact of aboriginal whaling on the whale population, due to the lack of correct data. It should be noted that such States regulate aboriginal whaling unilaterally, thus outside the coordinated and multilateral efforts of the IWC. The Philippines no longer permit such whaling; however, it has been listed below given that there are concerns that it may still be occurring under cover.

7.4.1   Equatorial Guinea

In Equatorial Guinea, commercial humpback whaling started in the eighteenth century and continued until 1959. Aboriginal whaling was well established at Pagalu (also known as Pigalu or Annobon), an island south of São Tomé. There is no available data as to the numbers taken since 1975, but it was presumed that some aboriginal whaling was conducted from small rowing boats, with two rowers and a harpooner. Only small whales could be taken, such as Bryde's whale. The hunt took place in the dry season (July and August). Whales were hunted for consumption and no oil was extracted. Cows were attacked with lances in order to separate them from calves, which were then chased and secured. There is no data as to injury to cows, or as to the percentage of calves struck but lost.[105]

7.4.2   Indonesia

Aboriginal hunting has existed in Indonesia for centuries, in particular for sperm whales, but also for other species (such as baleen whales by the people of Lembata). Fishing, including the hunting of cetaceans, is the main source of subsistence for a large segment of the population of

---

[105] Aboriginal whaling activity still persists in Pagalu until the present time, dedicated mainly to the capture of humpback whale calves, but no recent surveys have been conducted. Reeves, above n. 52, 86; see also Cristina Brito, Cristina Pinco and Inez Carlvaho, 'Small Cetaceans off São Tomé (São Tomé and Príncipe, Gulf of Guinea, West Africa): Species, Sightings and Abundance, Local Human Activities and Conservation', www.researchgate. net/.../242579596_Small_cetaceans_off_So_Tom, last accessed 13 January 2015; and Alex Aguilar, 'Aboriginal Whaling Off Pagalu (Equatorial Guinea)', *Rep. Int. Whale Comm.* 35 (1985), 386.

Lamalera, which is situated on the southern coast of Lamabata Island in East Indonesia.[106] The villagers hunt sperm whales, devil rays and other sea products from a *peledang* (a type of wooden sailing boat) using hand-thrown harpoons.[107] They have a barter system, exchanging sea products for agricultural products. However, at present the villagers use motor boats, rather than wooden boats, and harpoons and net fishing. The use of motor boats appears to have increased the efficiency of whaling given the increases in the final number of hunted whales (in 2010 there were twenty-nine motor boats in service).[108] Harvest records of sperm whales have been kept in Lamalera since 1960 (but are incomplete). They show, however, that 900 whales were caught between 1970 and 2010.[109]

7.4.3   The Philippines

In the Philippines, the origins of some whaling seem to be more recent. For instance, in Selinog Island what were originally accidental catches of whales and dolphins became a deliberate practice that continues to this day. Whaling for Bryde's and Pygmy Bryde's whales is carried out in the Pamilacan Island of the Philippines. The method applied in hunting is that of large hooks fixed onto the whale's back by men jumping from the boat. Different whaling methods are used by the peoples of three villages on Camiguin Island, where whales are taken with a grommet harpoon and motor vessels. Hunting in this region seems to be largely opportunistic, and has been practised there for at least three generations. The last documented catch of Bryde's whales in the Philippines was in 1966. National law has rendered whaling in the Philippines illegal since 1997 (Fisheries Administrative Order 185) when the provisions of the national law which were initially aimed at the prohibition of the killing of dolphins were extended to all cetaceans. In this area, the exact nature of the cultural dimension of aboriginal whaling has not been well documented.[110] As a means of appeasing the natives of Pamilacan Island, who relied on whale and dolphin killing, the government has allowed the commercial exploitation of whale and dolphin watching.

---

[106] Reeves, above n. 52, 87. See also Tomoko Egami and Kotaro Kojima, 'Traditional Whaling Culture and Social Change in Lamalera, Indonesia: An Analysis of the Catch Record of Whaling 1994–2010', in *Senri Ethnological Studies*, above n. 56, pp. 155–77.
[107] Egami and Kojima, above n. 106, p. 155.   [108] Ibid., p. 164.   [109] Ibid., p. 168.
[110] All information: ibid., pp. 86–9.

7.4.4   Canada

Canada is not a party to the ICRW, having withdrawn from it in 1982.[111] However, Canada has continued aboriginal whaling since its departure and has shown reluctance to provide any statistics regarding whaling.[112] Since Canada's withdrawal, whaling in Canada is regulated by national law. Aboriginal whale hunting is only permitted for the Inuit peoples (in the eastern Arctic) and for the Inuvialuit (in the western Arctic). In the eastern Arctic whale hunting (for bowheads) occurs in the Nunavut Settlement Area, which is a self-governing Inuit territory within Canada. Quotas are set by the Nunavut Wildlife Management Board (NWMB) under the 1993 Nunavut Land Claims Act, by the Committee on the Status of Endangered Life in Canada. The NWMB has a mandate to adopt all decisions about the management of wildlife in Nunavut. The Board consists of four representatives of the Inuit peoples and four government representatives, plus a Chairperson. Canada's Department of Fisheries and Oceans (DFO), the Hunters and Trappers Organisation (HTO) and the Regional Wildlife organisations are co-management partners. The DFO acts only in an advisory capacity to the NWMB and to the hunting communities, advising on sustainable hunting levels.

The quotas for hunting whales used to be set on the basis of the Marine Mammals Protection Act by the DFO. However, a new decentral-ised system was put in place, taking the form of 'community-based management'. Under the new system, the quota system has been lifted and the local HTOs manage the hunt. They have placed harvest limits on communities using a set of rules or by-laws which are developed by the local HTO. This set of rules or by-laws addresses the conservation and management of the whale population, the reduction of waste, hunter education and safety. The HTOs are commissioned to collect informa-tion on the number of whales wounded, killed and not landed. Inuit whaling relies on heavier bore rifles to kill the whales after a number of floats have been attached by harpoons. However, animal welfare, governed in Canada by Section 446 of the Criminal Code, does not provide for routine inspections of animal care or enforcement of main-tenance standards. To fill these gaps, an addition has been proposed to the Marine Mammal Regulations.[113] As Reeves notes:

---

[111] On Canada, see Milton M. R. Freeman et al., *Inuit, Whaling, and Sustainability (Con-temporary Native American Communities)* (Lanham, Md.: Altamira Press, 1998), p. 62.
[112] Reeves, above n. 52, 90.   [113] Ibid., 79.

[t]he legal status of whaling by Inuit in Canada was ambiguous. It was
implicitly understood, at least by some Inuits and some bureaucrats, that
a licence to hunt from the federal government was required, yet the
documented killing and wounding of Bowheads in eastern Canada
through the 1970s ... and 1980s ... remained outside any formal management context.[114]

In the western Arctic Inuvialuit have an ancient tradition of hunting
bowheads. The management strategy was created by the 1984 Inuvialuit
land management agreement and developed jointly by the Canadian
Department of Fisheries and Oceans, the Fisheries Joint Management
Committee and the Aklvik Hunters and Trappers Committee. It relies on
IWC data. Reeves described the aboriginal whaling of bowheads situation
as follows: '[i]n effect, Canada was intent upon unilateral management of
the Bowhead hunt while at the same time depending upon data, analysis
and management advice generated within the IWC (primarily owing to
the research programme of the North Slope Borough in Alaska)'.[115]

7.4.5   Conclusions on aboriginal whaling outside the IWC

It is reasonable to assume that aboriginal whaling, whilst not without
controversy, seems more acceptable to many than commercial whaling,
given that the former involves strong arguments in relation to the
cultural rights of social groups such as indigenous peoples. However, as
we have seen, the fact that aboriginal whaling may be less opposed than
commercial whaling does not mean that there are fewer contentious
points present. A detailed analysis of aboriginal whaling leads to the
conclusion that it is equally problematic and involves its fair share of
contentious issues that are questions of law and issues of ethics. The lack
of agreement as to the definitive content of the term 'aboriginal whaling'
and the ongoing disputes regarding the number of whale stocks open to
aboriginal whaling result in the inability of the IWC to manage and
regulate aboriginal whaling effectively and consistently. This is further
compounded by the fact that aboriginal whaling is also taking place
outside the remit of the IWC, and, with regard to such whaling, the real
dearth, in many cases, of statistical data, along with the unilateral regulation on the part of other States, significantly undermine the chances for
effective multilateral regulation of this type of whaling.

---

[114] Ibid., 90.   [115] Ibid., 90.

7.5   The complexity of aboriginal whaling illustrated by selected case studies

The case studies concerning the Makah peoples in the United States and Inuit peoples in Greenland have been included here to illustrate the complex issues that arise with regard to aboriginal whaling (internationally, within the IWC, and nationally within the United States) and to illustrate how the definition of aboriginal cultural needs can be very divisive.

7.5.1   The USA: case study of the Makah peoples (State of Washington)

Whaling by the Makah peoples is one of the most controversial cases of aboriginal whaling.[116] It has been the subject of much discussion at the IWC and was also the subject of much legislative regulation and legal debate within the United States, and it remains controversial in ways that include the following:

(1) it is an instance of a claim (there are others) to resume aboriginal whaling after a period during which, for different reasons, whaling had been abandoned; in this case, a claim by the Makah peoples to resume whaling after a hiatus of several decades;

(2) there was also doubt whether their whaling was purely aboriginal subsistence whaling or whether a commercial dimension was also present;

(3) the claim raised ethical concerns regarding the resumption of aboriginal whaling; and

(4) it also raised the issue as to whether aboriginal whaling constitutes a cultural exemption.[117]

The USA governs aboriginal whaling by Alaskan natives via the Marine Mammal Protection Act (MMPA) and the Endangered Species Act (ESA). Whaling by aboriginal peoples is allowed under national law to the extent that it is approved by the IWC.[118] The ICRW limits how many

---

[116] For an in-depth discussion, see J. Firestone and J. Lilley, 'Aboriginal Subsistence Whaling and the Right to Practice and Revitalize Cultural Traditions and Customs', *Journal of International Wildlife Law and Policy* 8 (2005), 177–219. See also an analysis of Elizabeth M. Bakalar, 'Subsistence Whaling in the Native Village of Barrow: Bringing Autonomy to Native Alaskans Outside the International Whaling Commission', *Brook. J. Int'l L.* 30 (2005), 602–39.

[117] Heinämäki, above n. 34, 46–52.   [118] Firestone and Lilley, above n. 116, 197–200.

bowhead or grey whales aboriginal groups may harvest. However, no domestic law restricts harvest numbers except specific regulations under the ESA or the MMPA (provided the harvest is for non-wasteful subsistence use).[119] The Makah is the only indigenous peoples group in the United States with reserved whaling rights affirmed in a treaty between it and the United States government. According to the US Supreme Court ruling in *US* v. *Dion*, a treaty right cannot be extinguished by the absence of the exercise of that right.[120] For the Makah peoples, the inclusion of this right in a treaty, even if no whales are taken, means that this right remains enforceable (providing that the treaty is in force, the right has not been abrogated, or no other legally significant event capable of extinguishing this right has taken place).

The Makah indigenous peoples live in the State of Washington and have traditionally hunted grey whales for centuries (commencing 1,500 years ago).[121] They ceded certain lands to the USA on the basis of the 1855 Treaty of Neah Bay between the Makah and the US government. This Treaty also guaranteed their rights to hunt for seals and whales and to fish in a reservation to which they were relocated. Around the turn of the twentieth century, the Makah peoples voluntarily ceased hunting for grey whales due to the depletion of their stocks, caused mainly by commercial hunting. The absence of hunting for whales had an adverse impact on the economy of the Makah peoples. When the eastern Pacific grey whale was removed from the endangered species list in 1994, the Makah peoples began preparations to resume hunting, as they alleged in consultation with the National Marine Fisheries Service, for nutritional and cultural reasons.[122] They also claimed that the resumption of whaling would enable them 'to instil in the tribe the values traditionally associated with whaling'.[123] However, the plan to resume this activity after a seventy-year hiatus was met with fierce opposition in the IWC and in the United States Congress; and also by some members of the Makah peoples themselves (acting as observers at the meeting of the IWC), who argued that the resumption of whaling had not been supported by all

---

[119] Ibid.

[120] US Supreme Court, *US* v. *Dion*, 476 US 734 (1986), cited in: Jennifer Sepez, 'Treaty Rights and the Right to Culture: Native American Subsistence Issues in US Law', *Cultural Dynamics* 14 (2002), 143–59, 150, www.sagepub.com/healeystudy5/articles/Ch7/Treatyrights.pdf, last accessed 30 December 2014.

[121] Joanna Brown, 'It's in Our Treaty: The Right to Whale', http://nativecases.evergreen.edu/docs/Makah_Case_Study_rev7_25_08.doc, last accessed 13 November 2014.

[122] Sepez, above n. 120, 149.   [123] Firestone and Lilley, above n. 116, 185.

members of the Makah peoples. Furthermore, due to the change in the IWC policy (following the bowhead crisis), it was open to the United States government to determine what might be the needs of the Makah peoples.[124] From the general exemption for aboriginal subsistence to the policy based on the requirement of 'needs', the Makah peoples' rights to aboriginal whaling were not automatically granted by the IWC.[125] As a result, the IWC decided that the Makah's request did not fulfil the requisite conditions (that is to say, those relating to subsistence needs and continuing traditional dependence) for aboriginal subsistence whaling.

In 1997, the United States resubmitted the request on behalf of the Makah peoples before the IWC. This time, however, the United States submitted a joint request together with the Russian Federation (which was acting on behalf of the Chukchi people). It was in fact a trade-off between the United States and the Russian Federation. The United States argued the case for the resumption of Makah whaling on the basis of the rights granted by the 1855 Treaty of Neah Bay. The IWC agreed to this renewed request and set a limit of 620 catches for the period 1998–2002. The resumption of hunting by the Makah peoples, however, was strongly objected to by environmental NGOs, which contended that after the resumption of hunting for whales, the Makah peoples would be likely to engage in commercial activities, such as selling meat to Japan

---

[124] It may be noted that the issue of bowhead hunting is not new. The status of these whales was uncertain and, as early as 1977, the IWC actually banned all bowhead hunting by aboriginal people, recognising this species as the most endangered. It was a 'drastic measure', as Gambell says. Later this decision was reversed: Ray Gambell, 'International Management of Whales and Whaling: An Historical Review of the Regulation of Commercial and Aboriginal Subsistence Whaling', *Arctic* 46 (1993), 97–107, 101. At the height of the bowhead crisis, the IWC adopted the following resolution concerning the United States' request for bowhead hunting for the Makah Indians: '[The Commission intends] that the needs of the aboriginals of the United States shall be determined by the Government of the United States of America. This need shall be documented annually to the Technical Committee, and shall be based upon the following factors: 1. importance of the bowhead in the traditional diet, 2. possible adverse effects of shifts to non-native foods, 3. availability and acceptability of other food sources, 4. historical take, 5. the integrative functions of the bowhead hunt in contemporary Eskimo society, and the risk to the community identity from an imposed restriction of the bowhead, and 6. to the extent possible, ecological considerations': as cited in Greg Donovan (IWC Secretariat), 'Some thoughts on facilitating the process to agree catch limits for aboriginal subsistence whaling (ASW)', available at: International Whaling Commission, www.iwcoffice.org/cache/downloads/7iqx580699wcswck4sw08oc80/63T3.pdf, last accessed 13 November 2014.

[125] Sepez, above n. 120, 140.

(allegations that were strongly denied by the Makah peoples).[126] The opponents of the resumption of whaling further argued that whaling was not necessary for subsistence of the Makah, noting that they had lived for a long period of time without whale meat. Again, the Makah opposed this contention, insisting that whale meat was a necessary part of their subsistence, despite a break of almost 100 years.[127] There was also opposition to the argument that the resumption of whale hunting would contribute to the cultural revitalisation of the Makah peoples.[128] Opponents also felt that if the Makah's claims were accepted, other claims would be made on the same basis. Additionally, some argued that such whaling would give a boost to Norwegian and Japanese claims for support of their own whaling traditions.

Opposition to the Makah resumption of whaling was also based on environmental grounds. For example, two NGOs[129] wrote to the US Department of Commerce (DOC) and to the National Oceanic and Atmospheric Administration (NOAA), stating that their Departments had breached the National Environmental Policy Act (NEPA) because they authorised Makah whaling without first applying the NEPA or making an Environment Impact Statement (EIS) and Environmental Assessment (EA). In response, a draft EA was issued and a new agreement between the NOAA and the Makah was entered into. The NOAA issued a final EA indicating a finding of no significant impact with regard to the resumption of aboriginal whaling.[130]

The coalition opposed to the resumption of Makah whaling was led by the Sea Shepherd Society. In total, approximately 250 animal welfare organisations and twenty-seven conservation organisations have opposed the resumption. Some of these organisations filed a suit in the courts of the United States, resulting in a court finding that the EA was made too late in the decision-making process, but that whale hunting was already authorised by a treaty.[131] The NOAA had to abandon the agreement with the Makah peoples in light of that decision. In 2001, a new draft EA

[126] Matthew Weinbaum, 'Makah Native Americans vs. Animal Rights Activists', www. umich.edu/~snre492/Jones/makah.htm, last accessed 28 December 2014.
[127] Firestone and Lilley, above n. 116, 186.   [128] Ibid., 185.
[129] Australians for Animals and BEACH Marine Protection.
[130] Firestone and Lilley, above n. 116, 198.
[131] Lawsuit No. 1: Ninth Circuit Court of Appeals, Metcalf v. Daley 214 F.3d 1135, 1143 (9th Cir. 2000); Lawsuit No. 2: Ninth Circuit Court of Appeals, Anderson v. Evans 314 F.3d 1006 (9th Cir. 2002); Lawsuit No. 3: Ninth Circuit Court of Appeals, Anderson v. Evans 371 F.3d 475 (9th Cir. 2004).

was issued; and the same year the NOAA established a quota of five landings of grey whales for 2001 and 2002. This decision was again challenged by the anti-whaling lobby. A national court[132] admitted that the Makah hunt would affect the overall California grey whale population. The dispute in essence was over the localised effect on the whale population in the area of the hunt. The (national) appeal court required a full application of the EIS protocol in light of the ambiguity and uncertainty regarding the failure of the EIS to address fully the effect of the whaling permit on other Native Americans that might wish to hunt, and also of the effect on the other IWC members. According to other national court decisions, the situation concerning the Makah peoples' whaling rights has not yet been resolved.[133]

The claim of the Makah peoples was supported by some scholars,[134] who were of the view that the Makah should not be deprived of their right to hunt whales. The latest decision of the United States government is to scrap a seven-year-old draft environmental study on the impact of Makah tribal whaling and write a new impact statement in light of substantial new scientific information. The latest information is that the grey whales the tribe wants to hunt off the Washington coast may need to be managed separately from the overall population. About 20,000 grey whales migrate up and down the West Coast.[135] Arguably, one of the causes of the unresolved situation concerning the Makah peoples' right to hunt grey whales is concern over environmental issues; and, indeed, in this case environmental considerations (the preservation of grey whale stocks) had to be balanced with the Makah peoples' reserved whaling rights and their rights with regard to cultural diversity. It would, however, be both imprudent and simplistic to attempt to draw general conclusions based on this single case.

---

[132] Ninth Circuit Court of Appeals, *Anderson v. Evans* 371 F.3d 475 (9th Cir. 2004).

[133] Firestone and Lilley, above n. 116, 201–7.

[134] Sepez, above n. 120, 143–59; and Reeves, above n. 52, 71–106.

[135] This decision is based on a study by Canadian scientists Tim Frazier and Jim Darling, who state that a separate, genetically distinct Pacific Coast Feeding Group of about 200 whales regularly feeds in areas that include waters between northern California and south-eastern Alaska during the summer and autumn. According to NOAA spokesman Brian Gorman, additions also will include information from a separate, ongoing NOAA review of grey whale behaviour resulting from the Canadian study. Paul Gottlieb, 'Restart of Whaling Study Disappoints Makah Chairman', *Peninsula News*, available at www.peninsuladailynews.com/article/20120525/news/305259989/restart-of-whaling-study-disappoints-makah-chairman, last accessed 28 December 2014.

According to the national courts' (of the United States) decisions, it appears, however, that the fact that environmental obligations were not fully implemented may have trumped the rights of the Makah peoples in this instance. In other words, the tension between cultural rights, treaty rights and environmental protection objectives was not properly resolved by the courts, given that the issue was determined first and foremost on the basis of a legal technicality (the failure to correctly apply the EA). The question thus arises, what would be the outcome of this case had the application of the EA been properly followed? It is possible that, if there had been a favourable result concerning the application of the EA, Makah hunting for grey whales would have been allowed, due to the fact that there would be no technicality preventing the Makah from exercising their reserved whaling rights, whilst the United States government would attempt to placate the opposition in the IWC.

7.5.2   The case of Greenland

In 1999, Greenland began to draft its own regulations on the protection of beluga and narwhal whales. Hunts were to establish annual and regional quotas, prohibit the killing of females and calves, prohibit hunting using nets, and set trading quotas for meat and blubber (though no mention was made of narwhal tusks, which are the most sought-after part of the narwhal whale). However, up to 2004, the catches of both types of whale were not regulated by any legal act. In 2004, Greenland, under its system of self-government, adopted an Executive Order regarding quotas (the Greenland Home Rule Executive Order No. 2 of 12 February 2004). In June 2004, local quotas were set as from 2005. No hunting quotas were set for East Greenland, which is the part of the island where professional leisure hunters may hunt for narwhals. The Executive Order stated that the total harvest for narwhals in 2004–8 should not exceed 748 narwhals annually. There are no closed seasons, but calves and accompanying females are protected. However, the hunting quotas for 2004 were three times higher than that recommended by marine biologists. The same applies to the hunting of beluga whales. For example, the estimated catch for the 1998 and 1999 harvests was to reach 700 a year; but in 1998 the catch actually reached 744.

As Sejersen said:

> [t]hese large annual harvests, combined with the alarming scientific population estimates, have also caused the Greenlandic and Canadian Joint Commission on the Conservation and Management of Narwhal and

Beluga to define the Greenlandic hunt as non-sustainable, and the Joint Commission has urged the Home Rule [i.e., Greenland's] government to intervene immediately.[136]

Greenland's government attempted to intervene and regulate this hunt; but due to the cultural and economic importance of beluga, this was not completely successful. However, one of the reasons given by Greenland to hunt larger than recommended quotas was the right of the Inuit peoples to cultural diversity.

In relation to whaling by Greenland's Inuit within the remit of quotas set by the IWC, in 2012 Denmark requested on behalf of the Inuit an increase in whale quotas. This request has been met with opposition from certain IWC members, causing additional tensions. One of the reasons for the rejection of this request was because some of the IWC's members were of the view that the proposed quota included an element of commercialisation and was higher than just to meet subsistence needs.[137] However, Greenland has set unilateral quotas for the season 2013–14 (198 whales), much to the concern of other IWC members. This action of Greenland was treated as an infraction by some States, which made a statement to the Infractions Sub-Committee. Denmark opposed a qualification of Greenland's action as an 'infraction'. This dispute was not resolved, partly due to the lack of a clear definition of what constitutes an infraction.[138]

Jones' observations confirm the conflicting nature of aboriginal whale hunting and cultural diversity issues:

Aboriginal hunts of marine mammals are a highly complex ethical issue. It is true that the Inuit and their cousins have traditionally thrived on what they call natural food, caribou, seal, beluga, whales, and other marine mammals. They do not have much money with which to draw food from the cash economy, and they do not fare well on the kind of food eaten by Europeans and Americans. But it turns out that Greenland's hunt for whales is as much about profits as it is about aboriginal rights. I discovered in Nuuk that Greenlanders are not observing the terms of the IWC quota that permits the hunt [to] be conducted solely for aboriginal subsistence purposes.[139]

---

[136] Frank Sejeresen, 'Hunting and Management of Beluga Whales (*Delphinapterus leucas*) in Greenland: Changing Strategies to Cope with New National and Local Interests', *Arctic* 54 (2001), 431–4.

[137] Wold and Kearney, above n. 73, 603–8.   [138] Ibid.

[139] Hardy Jones, 'Greenland Begins Humpback Whale Hunt', www.huffingtonpost.com/hardy-jones/greenland-begins-humpback_b_693054.html, last accessed 29 December 2014.

It must be said that aboriginal whaling is more often than not a thorny issue. A good example is the small island of Bequia (discussed earlier in the present chapter), whose aboriginal whaling also caused some concern at the meetings of the IWC. For example, in 2002, when St Vincent and the Grenadines submitted at the IWC a 'Needs Statement' for the increased quota of whales, New Zealand, Australia and the United Kingdom advocated that a precautionary approach be adopted, given the uncertainty of the scientific evidence of the stock, and thus the request should be turned down. The United Kingdom also suggested that after the retirement of the remaining sixty-nine-year-old harpooner, whaling in Bequia should cease altogether, as assured by St Vincent and the Grenadines. New Zealand and Monaco too, for example, suggested that the whaling in Bequia was really colonial (undertaken by descendants of Scottish and French settlers), therefore not of a subsistence character. However, at present, whaling at Bequia has stabilised, and despite the above-mentioned concerns, it has become 'a symbol of the culture of the Island and a symbol of the collective identity of the islanders'.[140]

Concluding remarks

It may be noted that the recognition by the IWC of the cultural value of subsistence whaling indicates that modern international law acknowledges as being well established the status of the traditional livelihood of indigenous peoples.[141] Heinämäki suggests that, from a legal point of view, indigenous whaling should be treated as lawful if it complies with IWC measures and guidelines. However, she observes that growing environmental pressures (such as climate change) may eventually force aboriginal peoples to abandon their whale hunting altogether.[142]

The controversial approach to aboriginal whaling was very visible during the sixty-fifth Meeting of the IWC in 2014.[143] The meeting started with a vote (of 46 votes for, 11 against, 3 abstentions) regarding Denmark's proposal (which was supported by the EU and the United States) to raise Greenland's quotas per year from 2015 to 2018 for: 19 fin whales, 2 bowhead whales, 10 humpback whales and 176 minke

---

[140] Hamaguchi, above n. 56, p. 152.   [141] Heinämäki, above n. 34, 45.   [142] Ibid., 57.
[143] http://iwc.int/iwc65docs, last accessed 30 December 2014.

whales (12 from the common minke whale stock and 164 from the West Greenland stock).[144] This proposal, which was defeated in 2012, gained approval in 2014, notwithstanding strong opposition within the IWC. Many States, such as Monaco, questioned the methods used to calculate 'need'. The Latin American group of countries known as the Buenos Aires Group, including Argentina, Chile and Uruguay, questioned Denmark over not reporting Greenland's catches taken since the last meeting as infractions. Counter arguments were voiced by Guinea, Japan, Antigua and Barbuda, Norway and Iceland.[145] The Whale and Dolphin Conservation Society (WDCS), a non-governmental organisation, which also spoke on behalf of the Animal Welfare Institute, have challenged the tonnage of whale meat that Greenland seeks because it is significantly more than all the marine protein currently being consumed by Greenlandic people, from whales, seals and small cetaceans put together. Iceland and Norway were strongly criticised at the same meeting for continuation of commercial whaling. Thus, the divisive approaches within the IWC relate to all types of whaling, also including aboriginal whaling. It may be noted that in relation to this type of whaling, there is a persistent question of discontent regarding the lack of any uniform approach to what constitutes 'needs' (this problem was discussed in Section 7.3.1).

There are also continuing discussions regarding the dividing line between commercial and aboriginal whaling. In this respect, there are views expressed that the IWC has a 'money fetish' that results in an approach that all whaling that brings money must be by nature

---

[144] 'More than 800 whales were condemned today just in the Greenland vote', Wendy Higgins of the Humane Society International (HSI) told Agence France Press (AFP) on the first day of the controversy-laden gathering in Slovenia. 'We are concerned that the new IWC quota will give Greenland more whale meat than its native people need for nutritional subsistence and that the surplus will continue to be sold commercially, including to tourists', said the Animal Welfare Institute (AWI). Celine Serrat, 'Whaling: Greenland Hunt Gets Okay, Iceland Blasted', http://news.yahoo.com/whale-huddle-braces-clash-over-japanese-hunting-004713474.html, last accessed 24 April 2015.

[145] Animal Welfare Institute: 'When the non-governmental organizations were allowed to speak, the chair called on Whale and Dolphin Conservation, which spoke on behalf of itself and AWI and challenged the tonnage of whale meat that Greenland seeks because it is significantly more than all the marine protein currently being consumed by Greenlandic people, from whales, seals and small cetaceans put together', https://awionline.org/content/2014-iwc-65-meeting-slovenia, last accessed 13 January 2015.

unsustainable.[146] As Freeman aptly notes, aboriginal whalers can be tolerated because they are poor; they do not have opportunities; and are isolated from the mainstream. On the other hand, non-aboriginal whalers and their customers are intolerable, as they hold a privileged position in the mainstream.[147] Therefore, we can say that the whaling debate (involving aboriginal whaling) has also 'been clouded with fuzzy indictments of money and capitalism, wrapped up in capricious notions about noble savages'.[148] According to Stone, the main problems with aboriginal whaling are the special rules dealing with it, as the application of the aboriginal exception to the Moratorium has been very uneven and inconsistent.[149] Stone asks whether, in light of questionable aboriginal quotas, it is just to deprive non-aboriginal groups such as the Faroese and Norwegians of whale meat in such an arbitrary fashion, an issue which was discussed in Chapter 4 of this publication.[150]

Various views on this type of whaling vary from rather adverse to aboriginal whaling (or at least its current regulation by the IWC), to overly enthusiastic (professing that aboriginal whaling trumps whale welfare). Therefore, the question of aboriginal whaling, without doubt, also contributes to misunderstandings, the tense atmosphere, and at times unproductive work at the IWC. Hossain suggested that the full decision-making power should be vested in indigenous peoples not in States regarding the questions of aboriginal hunting (whales and polar bears).[151] Such a solution appears to be unrealistic under present circumstances. However, some participation of indigenous peoples in allocation of aboriginal quotas would appear to be of merit, and perhaps even helpful in breaking the impasse in the IWC. It would also provide

---

[146] Milton M. R. Freeman, 'Is Money the Root of the Problem? Cultural Conflicts in the IWC', in Robert L. Friedheim (ed.), *Towards a Sustainable Whaling Regime* (Seattle: Washington University Press, 2001), pp. 129–32.

[147] Ibid., p. 130.

[148] Christopher D. Stone, 'Summing Up. Whaling and Its Critics', in Friedheim, above n. 146, p. 180.

[149] Ibid., p. 180. He says that the system of allocation of quotas for aboriginal whaling leads to unexpected results, such as the Chukchi people feeding farmed foxes with allocated grey whale. He also presents a very interesting analysis of the Makah peoples' resumption of whaling, asking if it is really a good idea to step backwards: p. 283.

[150] Ibid., p. 281.

[151] Kamrul Hossain, 'Hunting by Indigenous Peoples of Charismatic Mega-Fauna: Does the Human Rights Approach Challenge the Way Hunting by Indigenous Peoples is Regulated?', *International Community Law Review* 10 (2008), 295–318, 318.

indigenous peoples with the opportunity to voice their points of view, which might contribute to achieving more understanding and coherence in the regulation of aboriginal whaling.[152]

[152] See thoughtful comments of Rupa Gupta, 'The challenge that faces the international community is to articulate a conceptual framework that acknowledges the history of indigenous discrimination, discards the goal of assimilation, and constructs an inclusive regime giving dignity and control to indigenous people. This Note emphasizes the necessity of including the Inuit people in existing and future international organizations that regulate whaling, such as the conceptualization of whale hunting. The international community, which currently views environmental conservation as a struggle between animal species and indigenous communities, will come to recognize that the conservation movement is a holistic continuum of the concerns of the physical world.' 'Indigenous Peoples and International Environmental Community: Accommodating Claims through a Cooperative Legal Process', *New York University Law Review* 74 (1999), 1741–85, 1785.

A case study of the protection of the narwhal whale

Introduction

This chapter analyses the law concerning the protection of the narwhal whale in the Arctic region. It is based on the premise that a great (and steadily growing) number of existing multilateral and bilateral agreements (be they regional or of broader geographical or thematic scope), paradoxically, do not provide sufficient protection for some species such as the narwhal, as they either fall into the loopholes of the Conventions, or the provisions of these Conventions are not sufficiently implemented by State Parties.

8.1 Setting the scene (the narwhal)

The narwhal (*Monodon monoceros*) is a small (sometimes referred to as medium-sized) cetacean exclusively populating the Arctic waters. Not only does the species lack a dorsal fin, but the male narwhal has a distinguishing feature unique in the world of whales: a tooth that grows into a long, spiral tusk, about one and a half to three metres long, for which they are mainly hunted. Narwhals have a cylindrical body, with a blunt head and a small mouth. Males average about five metres long, females about four metres. Mature males usually weigh up to about 1,600 kg, females are somewhat lighter, around 1,000 kg. There is no data available as to their exact number but the estimated population of narwhals ranges between 10,000 and 20,000. In 1996, the International Union for the Conservation of Nature (IUCN) concluded that the threat of extinction could not be adequately assessed due to the lack of precise data, and listed narwhal in the data deficient (DD) category in the 2000 IUCN Red List of Threatened Species.[1] According to the

---

[1] Committee on the Status of Endangered Wildlife in Canada (COSEWIC), 'COSEWIC Assessment and Update Status Report on the Narwhal *Monodon monoceros* in Canada',

1999 Report of the IWC Scientific Committee, which was reinforced by previous findings by Hay and Mansfield in 1989[2] and Strong in 1988,[3] the most recent population surveys were carried out in 1984 and yielded 18,000 narwhals in the four major summering areas.[4]

Narwhals have been heavily exploited for their skin, meat and tusks. In the Davis Strait and Baffin Bay, they are a shared stock under the monitoring of the Canada–Greenland Joint Commission on Conservation and Management of Narwhal and Beluga. The narwhal is discontinuously circumpolar in the Arctic. It is observed only very infrequently south of 65°N in Greenland. However, during spring, when distributional ranges may overlap north of Greenland, its range may become circumpolar. The main part of the population is to be found in the eastern Canadian Arctic and West Greenland. On Svalbard narwhals concentrate in the north-west area of Spitzbergen. In the eastern Canadian Arctic, the species extends mainly from Lancaster Sound and Kane Basin, south through Baffin Bay and Davis Strait as far as Cumberland Sound on Baffin Island and Disko off Western Greenland. Narwhals roam south to the coast of Labrador, rare to accidental south to Iceland, the Norwegian Sea, the North Sea (south to the British Isles, the Netherlands and

Depository Services Program of the Government of Canada, 34, http://dsp-psd.pwgsc.gc.ca/ Collection/CW69-14-420-2005E.pdf, last accessed 1 January 2015. In more detail: Populations: Inglefield Bredning Stock (GL) – Estimate: c. 1,500 – Trend: Declining; Melville Bay Stock (GL) – Estimate: Unknown – Trend: Unknown; Uummannaq aggregation (GL) – Estimate: Unknown – Trend: Unknown; Disco Bay aggregation (GL) – Estimate c. 15,000 – Trend: Declining; Somerset Island Stock (CA) – Estimate: c. 45,000 – Trend: Not threatened; Eclipse Sound Stock (CA) – Estimate: c. 15,000 – Trend: Not threatened; Eclipse Sound Stock (CA) – Estimate: c. 3,200 – Trend: Uncertain; Smith Sound Stock (CA) – Estimate: >1,500 – Trend: Unknown; Jones Sound Stock (CA) – Estimate: Unknown – Trend: Unknown; Parry Island Stock (CA) – Estimate: Unknown – Trend: Unknown; East Baffin Small Stock (CA) – Estimate: Unknown – Trend: Unknown; and Cumberland Sound Stock (CA) – Estimate: Unknown – Trend: Unknown. These sets of data are based on the IWC and the CNB/NAMMCO Reports. WWF, 'The Big Four – a WWF update on Greenland's efforts with regard to species conservation and nature protection – April 2005', WWF Denmark, 41, http://assets.panda.org/downloads/thebigfour.pdf, last accessed 1 January 2015.

[2] K. A. Hay and A. W. Mansfield, 'Narwhal – Monodon monoceros Linneaus, 1758', in S. H. Ridgway and S. R. Harrison (eds.), Handbook of Marine Mammals, vol. IV: River Dolphins and the Larger Toothed Mammals (London: Academic Press, 1989), pp. 145–76.

[3] J. T. Strong, 'Status of the Narwhal Monodon monoceros in Canada', Canadian Field Nat. 102 (1988), 391–8.

[4] Convention on Migratory Species (CMS), 'Monodon monoceros (Linnaeus, 1756)', CMS, 2, www.cms.int/reports/small_cetaceans/data/M_monoceros/m_monoceros.PDF, last accessed 1 January 2015.

Germany), the White Sea and the Arctic coast of mainland Eurasia, and east into the Chukchi Sea and the Bering Sea, as far south as Komandorskiye Ostrova and the north side of the Alaska peninsula.

8.2 Canada, Greenland and the narwhal

8.2.1 Canada

Notwithstanding that Canada was one of the signatory States of the ICRW, in 1981 the Canadian Secretary of State for External Affairs notified of Canada's withdrawal from the ICRW effective as of 30 June 1982. The possibility of Canada rejoining the IWC (and the ICRW) was met with rather strong objections from Canada's Inuit peoples and Canadian officials themselves. According to the 1994 *High North News*, Ms Rosemari Kupanat, President of the Canadian Inuit Council, wrote to the Canadian government. The news report stated that

> Kupanat warned ... against the IWC's attempt to widen its mandate by the inclusion of small and medium sized cetaceans and refers to the fact that 'fortunately there are alternatives', such as the establishment of the Inuit Circumpolar Conference (the 'ICC') which had established the ICC Whaling Commission and the North Atlantic Marine Mammal Commission. The latter organisation was viewed by Ms Kupanat as an organisation which can address the regional management of whale stocks.[5]

The above approach to the participation of Canada in the ICRW was confirmed in a 1996 interview by Mr W. Doubleday, the Director General of Fisheries and Oceans Science for the Federal Government of Canada, and J. Barker, United States Commissioner to the IWC. In reply to the United States government's request for Canada to rejoin the IWC, Mr Doubleday responded on behalf of the Canadian government in the following way: '[w]e have no intention of joining the International Whaling Commission and further, Canadian aboriginal people are strongly opposed to joining the International Whaling Commission, and don't consider that their interest would be properly taken into account by that Commission'.[6]

---

[5] 'Canadian Inuits Say No to IWC', *High North News*, www.highnorth.no/Library/Management_Regimes/IWC/ca-in-sa.htm, last accessed 1 January 2015.

[6] William Doubleday, '[Canada has] No Intention of Joining the International Whaling Commission', High North Alliance, www.animaladvocates.com/watchdog.pl?md=read;id=13528, last accessed 1 January 2015.

The Canadian argument for not returning to the IWC fold was also found in the interpretation of Article 65 of UNCLOS, which was analysed in Chapters 3 and 6. Canada, for its part, argued that it was not obligated to join the IWC or to acknowledge an organisation of which it is not a member as possessing powers to regulate Canadian whaling. What is more, the use of the plural form – that is to say, 'organisations' – in Article 65, according to Canada, clearly indicates that the IWC is not necessarily the only relevant organisation. Furthermore, Canadian scientists continue to participate in IWC Scientific Committee meetings, and provide timely information on whale populations in the waters of Canada. In general, Canada is very critical of the approach to whaling in the IWC, from the point of view of the interests of the Inuits, and the IWC's ban on all commercial whaling, even when it is sustainable. A Resolution passed by the Legislative Assembly of the (Canadian) Northwest Territories in 1992 claimed that the IWC is dominated by member nations that exhibit irrational protectionism (towards whales) rather than manage sustainably the whale stocks.[7]

Protection for narwhal in Canada is focused only on measures administering the hunt, live capture and movement of narwhal products. Arctic marine parks or protected areas that protect narwhals in Canadian waters from hunting or other activities have not been established. The only protection offered to narwhals is in protected marine areas within the Nunavut National Parks, although they are not National Marine Conservation Areas. There is no protection outside the parks, and no protected area (terrestrial or marine) prevents harvest by Inuit in the Nunavut Settlement Area. These restrictions and quotas are set by the Nunavut Wildlife Management Board under the 1993 Nunavut Land Claims Act.[8]

Narwhal hunting in Canada is managed by the Nunavut Wildlife Management Board (NWMB). Canadian legislation allows the NWMB to adopt all decisions about wildlife management in Nunavut. The Board consists of four Inuit and four government representatives, plus a Chairperson. Canada's Department of Fisheries and Oceans (DFO), the Hunters and Trappers organisations (HTOs) and the Regional Wildlife organisations are co-management partners. The DFO acts in an advisory capacity to the NWMB and hunting communities on sustainable hunting levels. This information is used to manage community hunts.[9] Only Inuit

---

[7] Milton M. R. Freeman et al., *Inuit, Whaling, and Sustainability* (Lanham, Md.: Altamira Press, 1998), p. 131.
[8] COSEWIC, above n. 1.   [9] Ibid.

peoples may hunt narwhals, and there is a quota on the number of animals that can be harvested by each community, according to Canada's 1985 Fisheries Act and the Marine Mammal Protection Regulations by the DFO. This legislation also sets the quotas, which were originally set through negotiation with the communities and based on historic harvesting levels. It also set up the new system of community-based management. Under the new regime quotas have been lifted and the local HTOs manage the hunt and have imposed harvest limits for communities, using a set of rules or by-laws which are developed by the local HTO and address the conservation and management of the narwhal population, the reduction of waste, hunter education and safety. The HTOs have also agreed to collect information on the number of narwhals wounded, killed and not landed. The protection of live-captured narwhals is not promoted or regulated by legislation, unlike narwhal whaling and trade in narwhal-derived products, which are controlled by laws and conventions. In that respect, the protection of live-captured narwhals is approached on moral rather than legal grounds.

The NWMB has the mandate to consider applications for live captures. Under the 1985 Marine Mammal Protection Regulations of the Fisheries Act, the DFO has the authority to issue live capture permits. However, in practice, the Department has not issued such permits since 1987. The DFO can attach conditions to live-capture permits but it does not have enforcement authority for animals maintained in captivity. Animal welfare, governed in Canada under Section 446 of the Criminal Code, does not provide for routine inspections of animal care or enforcement of maintenance standards. To fill these gaps, additions have been proposed to the Marine Mammal Regulations.[10] The Canadian Wildlife Service is responsible for issuing import permits, and the governments of Canada's Provinces and Territories are, in general, responsible for issuing the relevant export permits. CITES entered into force in Canada in 1975. For the most part, Canada's international obligations in relation to trade in wild plants and animals stem from CITES, and presently are implemented through the 1991 Wild Animal and Plant Protection and Regulation of Interprovincial Trade Act (entered into force in 1996) together with the set of Regulations – the Wild Animal and Plant Trade Regulations. These Regulations were amended in 2000. Importantly, the terms 'plants' and 'animals' are defined as specimens of species listed in the relevant CITES Appendices in

---

[10] Ibid., 33.

the form of a rolling definition as 'amended from time to time'. The definition also includes the possibility for States to file a reservation to a new listing, which then would not be binding on them.[11]

In 2010, a quota of about 700 narwhals was set for Inuit hunting. Legal and illegal trade in narwhal tusks is a matter of concern in Canada. There is also an ongoing disagreement as to quotas. In 2012, the DFO suggested a new quota for narwhals of about 1,200. However, this suggestion was subject to objections from some Nunavut groups on the basis that it imposed undue restriction on hunting of narwhal stocks.[12]

8.2.2   Greenland

Greenland falls within the ambit of the IWC through the participation of Denmark, which is responsible for Greenland's external affairs. Denmark submitted its instrument of ratification in 1950. However, the regulation of narwhal hunting is, as has already been discussed, perceived by some States as outside the remit of the IWC, and is entirely regulated within Greenland's system of self-government. By law, hunters are required to provide a hunting report documenting the number and sex of narwhals killed, and the hunting gear and type of vessel used, as well as details about the hunter, including their address and social security number. In 1996, however, Greenland acknowledged in its communications with CITES its difficulties in obtaining full and accurate data on narwhal hunts, citing logistical issues (namely, that each Wildlife Inspector had, on average, to cover 50,000 km^2 of coastal areas).

Tusks are bought from hunters by Pilersuisoq, a Greenland State-owned company that buys non-food hunting by-products from the hunters for resale purposes. In 1999, Greenland began drafting new regulations for the beluga and narwhal hunts to establish annual and regional quotas, prohibit the killing of females and juveniles, prohibit hunting using nets, and set trading quotas for meat and blubber, though there was no mention of tusks.[13]

---

[11] Nigel Bankes, 'International Wildlife Law: Canadian Wildlife Law Project', Paper No. 1 (Calgary: Canadian Institute of Resources Law, 2006) (on file with the author).

[12] Randy Boswell, Postmedia News, 'Alleged narwhal-tusk smuggling operation smashed in joint Canada–US effort', 2 January 2013, http://news.nationalpost.com/news/alleged-narwhal-tusk-smugling-operation-smashed-in-joint-canada-u-s-effort, last accessed 17 July 2015.

[13] Whale and Dolphin Conservation Society (WDCS), 'The Review of Significant Trade in the Narwhal (*Monodon monoceros*) – A briefing by the WDCS for the 20th meeting of CITES Animals Committee', CITES (29 March–2 April 2004), 3.

Until 2004, catches of narwhal had not been regulated by any quotas. Some regulation was introduced by Greenland in 2004 when it adopted quotas for narwhals (by way of the Greenland Home Rule Executive Order No. 2 of 12 February 2004 on the Protection and Hunting of Beluga and Narwhals) for more than 11,000 licensed professional and leisure hunters. In June 2004, local quotas were set for 2005. However, no hunting quotas were set for East Greenland, which is a part where professional and leisure hunters may hunt narwhals. The legislation stated that the total harvest between 2004 and 2008 might not exceed 748 narwhals annually. There are no closed seasons but juveniles and accompanying females are protected.[14] However, the hunting quotas for 2004 were three times higher than those recommended by marine biologists.[15] In West Greenland, the quotas and harvest are monitored by the municipal authorities and by the Fisheries, Hunting and Agriculture Agency, through a licence and reporting system. Management advice is given by the (Canada and Greenland) Joint Commission on Conservation and Management of Narwhal and Beluga (JCNB) and scientific advice for the JCNB on harvest sustainability is provided by a Joint Working Group (JWG) of the Scientific Working Group of the JCNB and a Working Group from the Scientific Committee of NAMMCO. Quotas are based on the JCNB management recommendations on quotas and on advice from the Hunting Council, which includes representatives from the Organisation of Fishermen and Hunters (KNAPK), the Organisation of Leisure Hunters (TPAK) and the Greenland Association of Municipalities (KANUKOKA). Quotas are adopted by the Cabinet based on a proposal by the Department of Fisheries, Hunting and Agriculture. Quotas are distributed by the municipal authorities among the different settlements and individual hunters. The municipal authority is responsible for ending the harvest once the quota has been reached. Any excess catches and illegal captures are subtracted from the municipal quota for the following year. Calves, and females accompanied by calves, are protected. All usable meat and skin should be utilised. Failure to comply with the legislation may result in the confiscation of the catch and of the equipment, and in a fine. However, narwhals found in ice-entrapments are not included in the quota and can, following approval by the Department of Fisheries, Hunting and Agriculture, be hunted without regulations.

---

[14] WWF, 'The Big Four' above n. 1, 46.   [15] Ibid.

In West Greenland, it is local authorities that provide licences for hunters before they set out to hunt narwhals. After the hunt, hunters are obliged to report their catch by filling in a form for each narwhal taken which must contain biological information, and information about the licence and about the hunter. Hunters have to deliver catch reports to the municipal authorities in order to sell the products of their hunt, and to obtain a new licence. Additionally, once a year, all hunters have to report monthly catches of most species, including narwhals. These annual reports are mandatory in order to renew the hunting permits. However, on the basis of the numbers of catch reports received, the system works better in West Greenland than in East Greenland. This is an additional disparity in what emerges as an inconsistent regulatory patchwork for narwhal whaling across Greenland's territories.

Hunting methods vary according to local rules and traditions. Narwhals are hunted with hand harpoons from kayaks, with high-powered rifles from open boats or with nets placed at strategic points. Narwhals are hunted during summer in the east and north-west, and during winter in the west.[16]

8.3   The IWC and small cetaceans

As was discussed at various points in the earlier parts of the present publication, the mandate of the IWC regarding the management of small cetaceans is contested.[17] There are definitional problems relating to the classification of cetaceans. A rough classification of whales into baleen (great whales) and toothed (small and medium) whales does not reflect

---

[16] Lars Witting, Fernando Ugarte and Mads Peter Heide-Jørgensen, 'Greenland, Narwhal (*Monodon monoceros*)', NDF Workshop Case Studies, WG 5 – Mammals, Case Study 7, *Monodon monoceros*, Country – Greenland, 4. See www.conabio.gob.mx/institucion/cooperacion_internacional/TallerNDF/Links-Documentos/WG-CS/WG5-Mammals/WG5-CS7%20Monodon/WG5-CS7.pdf, last accessed 30 December 2014.

[17] See, in depth, Alexander Gillespie, 'Small Cetaceans, International Law and the International Whaling Commission', *Melbourne Journal of International Law* 2 (2001), 257–303; Alexander Gillespie, *Whaling Diplomacy: Defining Issues in International Environmental Law* (Cheltenham: Edward Elgar Publishing, 2005). See also Patricia Birnie, 'Small Cetaceans and the International Whaling Commission', *Georgetown International Environmental Law Review* 10 (1997), 1–27; Patricia Birnie, 'Are Twentieth-Century Marine Conservation Conventions Adaptable to Twenty-First-Century Goals and Principles?', *International Journal of Marine and Estuarine (Coastal) Law* 12 (1997), Part I, 307–39; Part II, 488–532; Steven Freeland and Julie Drysdale, 'Co-operation or Chaos? Article 65 of the United Nations Convention on the Law of the Sea and the Future of the International Whaling Commission', MqJICEL 2 (2005), 1–36.

reality, which is far more complex, and there are many exceptions. The population of cetaceans is divided into two groups: large and small. However, there is difficulty in achieving a consistent classification of species within each category, as there are no accepted definitions that would combine the biological aspects and the political interests at play so as to arrive at a single classification acceptable to all IWC members.[18] The original nomenclature attached to the ICRW did not follow the dividing line between the toothed and baleen whales. However, the Schedule to the ICRW, which is amended over time, is based on the assumption that baleen whales and toothed whales are different subcategories.[19] In the intervening years the ongoing debate in the IWC as to the cetaceans under its mandate has become even more political than scientific. As Gillespie aptly observes, '[w]ithin this broader debate, the answer whether a species is "small" or not, and the interlinking question of whether that grants the IWC jurisdiction over them, will often depend on which side of the jurisdictional debate the protagonist falls'.[20] Gillespie, citing the views of Burns, states that the classification of whether a species is large or small within the context of the IWC turns on the debate whether the whale species in question has been traditionally exploited by the commercial whaling industry.[21] In the early 1970s, the IWC Scientific Committee strongly recommended that the IWC review the issues concerning small cetaceans, and a special Sub-committee on small cetaceans was established.

The debate on the IWC mandate over the management of small cetaceans is not settled. The fundamental issues of the IWC's jurisdiction were defined with more precision at the thirty-second meeting of the IWC in 1982, and included such questions as: whether the ICRW bestows competence upon the IWC to manage small cetaceans; the possible conflict with coastal States' jurisdiction as an aspect of their reserved sovereign prerogatives; and the role of regional organisations in the administration of small cetaceans.[22]

The first issue commands the interpretation of the text of the ICRW and the related documents. The ICRW refers to 'whales' in general terms

---

[18] Gillespie, *Whaling Diplomacy*, above n. 17, p. 277.   [19] Ibid., p. 278.   [20] Ibid.
[21] Ibid. Gillespie, *Whaling Diplomacy*, above n. 17, p. 307, wherein Gillespie cites William C. G. Burns, 'The International Whaling Commission and the Regulation of the Consumptive and Non-Consumptive Uses of Small Cetaceans: The Critical Agenda for the 1990s', *Wisconsin International Law Journal* 13 (1994), 105–44.
[22] Gillespie, *Whaling Diplomacy*, above n. 17, pp. 282–9.

(without the distinction between large and small cetaceans), such as in the Preamble to the Convention and Article V, where it refers to 'whales', as a generic term; this creates confusion given that the term 'whales' could sensibly be interpreted broadly to include such cetaceans that are directly associated with notions of 'whale' (that is to say, to exclude dolphins and porpoises), or more narrowly, to include only such whale species as were historically of interest to the whaling industries up to the point of the ICRW being negotiated. Again, these are just a few – out of a great many – considerations that may feature in interpretative jurisprudential inquiries into the meaning of the term.

The objections of States to the management by the IWC of small cetaceans were based on the lack of the inclusion of small cetaceans in the original nomenclature. However, documents with regard to the nomenclature are treated as a guide, not as an exhaustive listing; what is more, any such guide is something capable of evolving, as was noted by Conference of the Parties (COP) 10 in 2010. Some States suggested that if the whale name was not listed originally, it was placed outside the jurisdiction of the ICRW, unless there was agreement of all IWC members regarding its inclusion.[23] The list of whales was adopted unanimously and any changes to it which would extend the mandate of the IWC to additional species should be effected only through unanimous agreement among all the State Parties to the ICRW. The result of the adoption of such an interpretation of the jurisdiction of the IWC would lead to its jurisdiction being exercised only in relation to the species named in the original Annex. Many States, however, were of the view that the original nomenclature could not be used as an obstacle to extending the jurisdiction of the IWC. Among such States was the United Kingdom, which in principle did not object to the 'creeping jurisdiction' of the IWC. However, many other States, such as Mexico and Russia, strongly objected to it, and Norway expressed its preference to cooperate on the issue of small cetaceans through NAMMCO and ASCOBANS. At the end of the day, Gillespie argues that the answer to whether a species is within the jurisdiction of the IWC depends on whether it is placed in the Schedule in accordance with the three-quarters majority procedure of the IWC.[24]

In 1975–6, pursuant to the work of the IWC Scientific Committee, the ICRW Schedule was amended so as not to require the transmission to the IWC of information on all small cetaceans, but only to require, for

---

[23] Ibid., p. 288.   [24] Ibid., p. 289.

the record, submission particulars of whales taken in 'small whaling operations' (as in 'small-scale' rather than 'relating to small cetaceans'), that is to say, 'catching operations using powered vessels with mounted harpoon guns hunting extensively for minke, bottle-nose, pilot and killer whales'.[25] In 1976, the United Nations Environment Programme (UNEP) adopted a Resolution from its Governing Council to set up its control, and expressed its concern about the conservation of whales as a global resource. The 1972 Stockholm Conference on the Human Environment prompted the suggestion that the ICRW should be amended to extend to all types of cetaceans. The IWC Scientific Committee was of the view that there was a need for a new organisation to deal with the stocks of cetaceans not covered in the ICRW Schedule.[26]

The second issue regarding the jurisdiction of the IWC over small cetaceans is any overlap with the UNCLOS jurisdiction in the coastal zones within the direct jurisdiction of coastal States. This is an important question, due to the highly coastal nature of small cetaceans.[27] In several Resolutions adopted by the IWC members, they objected to the establishment of the IWC jurisdiction in such zones, and treated any IWC actions addressing the management of species in these zones as being *ultra vires* and an encroachment on their sovereignty. However, the rights of coastal States in their territorial seas and in their EEZs are different, ranging from full sovereignty over their territorial seas to sovereign rights and jurisdiction over their EEZs.

The ICRW, following the example of the 1937 International Agreement for the Regulation of Whaling, stated in Article 1(2) that it applies 'to all waters in which whaling is prosecuted by such factory ships, land stations, and whale catchers' (note that 'prosecuted' here has the meaning of 'being carried out'); this would suggest over all maritime areas in which whaling is conducted. The question thus arises whether the regime of UNCLOS takes precedence over that of the ICRW. Gillespie poses two questions regarding the IWC and UNCLOS: do the signatories agree to cede their sovereignty to the IWC on such issues; and is the ICRW compatible with UNCLOS? These issues derive from the application of Article 311 of UNCLOS.[28] Relevant to this debate is Article 65 of

---

[25] 27th Report of the Commission (1975/1976), Item 10, as cited in Birnie (Part II), above n. 17, 503.

[26] Ibid., 503.   [27] Gillespie, *Whaling Diplomacy*, above n. 17, pp. 289–97.

[28] Ibid., p. 292. Article 311 of UNCLOS reads as follows: '[t]he Convention shall not alter rights and obligations of State Parties which arise from other agreements compatible with

UNCLOS. Gillespie interprets this provision as making the IWC 'the central and uppermost international authority for cetaceans'.[29] However (as discussed earlier in the present chapter with regard to Canada), there is merit in the Canadian approach to this provision, which denies an exclusive leading role to the IWC, and focuses on the plural form of the formulation 'organisations' in Article 65 which admits the possibility that other organisations may be competent and duly involved in marine mammal related issues.

Gillespie further argues that his views are supported by Article 120 of UNCLOS, which refers to Article 65 also in relation to conservation and management of marine mammals in the high seas, and by Section 17 of Agenda 21, which not only reiterates Article 65 of UNCLOS, but also explicitly refers to the IWC as studying larger whales as well as other cetaceans and working with other organisations (such as ASCOBANS and the Bonn Convention) 'in the conservation, management and study of cetaceans and other marine mammals' (Section 17.61). Gillespie also analyses two provisions of UNCLOS that may limit the jurisdiction of the coastal States that are parties to UNCLOS: Articles 64[30] and 63.[31] Annex

---

this convention and which do not affect the enjoyment by other States Parties of their rights or the performance of their obligations under this Convention'.

[29] Gillespie, *Whaling Diplomacy*, above n. 17, p. 292.

[30] Article 64 ('Highly Migratory Species') reads as follows: '1. The coastal State and other States whose nationals fish in the region for the highly migratory species listed in Annex I shall co-operate directly or through appropriate international organizations with a view to ensuring conservation and promoting the objective of optimum utilization of such species throughout the region, both within and beyond the exclusive economic zone. In regions for which no appropriate international organization exists, the coastal State and other States whose nationals harvest these species in the region shall co-operate to establish such an organization and participate in its work. 2. The provisions of paragraph 1 apply in addition to the other provisions of this Part.' Gillespie, *Whaling Diplomacy*, above n. 17, p. 294.

[31] Article 63 ('Stocks Occurring within the Exclusive Economic Zones of two or More Coastal States or Both within the Exclusive Economic Zone and in an Area Beyond or Adjacent to it') reads as follows: '1. Where the same stock or stocks of associated species occur within the exclusive economic zones of two or more coastal States, these States shall seek, either directly or through appropriate sub regional or regional organizations, to agree upon the measures necessary to co-ordinate and ensure the conservation and development of such stocks without prejudice to the other provisions of this Part. 2. Where the same stock or stocks of associated species occur both within the exclusive economic zone and in an area beyond and adjacent to the zone, the coastal State and the States fishing for such stocks in the adjacent area shall seek, either directly or through appropriate sub regional or regional organisations, to agree upon the measures necessary for the conservation of these stocks in the adjacent area.'

I of UNCLOS lists highly migratory species, and, in addition to large cetaceans, also includes the families of small to medium cetaceans, including *Monodontidae*, to which beluga and narwhal whales belong. Gillespie also noted that in the case of Article 64 of UNCLOS, States must seek the cooperation of an international organisation, and in the case of Article 63 of UNCLOS, that of a regional or sub-regional one.[32]

8.3.1 The IWC and the narwhal

The IWC Scientific Committee reviewed the status of narwhals in 1992 and expressed continuing concern about the sustainability of harvests from the Baffin Bay stock (Canada). It conducted another review in 1999, and reiterated its Recommendations from 1992 concerning the importance of studies to identify stocks, and the efforts to improve catch reporting and estimation of hunting losses.

It was noted earlier in this chapter that Canada withdrew from the IWC in 1982 and that Greenland (through its Danish representation) has consistently rejected IWC competence over small cetaceans, including the narwhal. Consequently, this has to a considerable extent undermined the IWC's importance in such matters, particularly, in the absence of strong textual support, for its competence regarding small cetaceans. Consequently, the two countries' contributions to the IWC Scientific Committee's review in 1999 were very limited. In June 2003, the IWC Scientific Committee again considered the status of the narwhal, and reiterated its previous Recommendations concerning the desirability of better information on stock identity and catch reporting. The IWC asked Greenland to provide information to the next annual meeting, but Greenland's representative stated that it would not do so.[33] As referred to above, Greenland has introduced an improved reporting system, but purely for its own regulation of narwhal management.

In 1996, the Director General of Canada's Fisheries and Oceans Science Department wrote to the IWC Secretary General stating that:

> It is the Government of Canada's view that the International Whaling Commission does not have legal competence for the management of small cetaceans. As members of the Commission will also be aware, the status of stocks of narwhal and beluga in Canadian waters are subject to a peer review process on a regular basis similar to that followed for fish

---

[32] Gillespie, *Whaling Diplomacy*, above n. 17, p. 294.   [33] See WDCS, above n. 13, 6.

stocks. In addition, the assessment of the status of stocks of narwhal and beluga which migrate between Canadian and Greenland waters is undertaken by the Scientific Working Group of the Canada/Greenland Joint Commission on Narwhal and Beluga. Status reports resulting from these assessments are available to the public. It is the view of the Government of Canada that since peer reviewed stock assessment and the provision of scientific advice on stocks of narwhal and beluga in Canadian waters is already being provided, there is no need for the IWC's Scientific Committee to conduct a review of these stocks. Should the IWC's Scientific Committee decide to proceed with such a review in 1998, it is unlikely that Canada would send scientists to such a meeting.[34]

In 2010, according to the IWC, the NAMMCO/JCNB annual catch statistics in Canada substantially underestimated the total numbers of narwhals killed due primarily to the incomplete reporting of whales that are struck and killed but lost.[35]

---

[34] William Doubleday, 'The IWC Does Not Have Legal Competence for the Management of Small Cetaceans', High North Alliance, www.highnorth.no/Library/Policies/National/th-iw-do.htm, last accessed 26 October 2014. ICTMN Staff, *Indian Country*, 'Summer Narwhal Hunt Confirmed for 2013'. In 2013, the Canadian Government (Fisheries and Oceans Canada) made the following (controversial) statement: 'We are pleased to confirm that the majority of Inuit hunters will be able to continue to sell narwhal by-products resulting from their subsistence hunt on international markets'; 'This decision was made based on the best available scientific information and in consultation with partners including Nunavut Tunngavik Inc., the Government of Nunavut, the Nunavut Wildlife Management Board, hunters and trappers organizations, and northern communities to ensure the long-term sustainability of the traditional narwhal hunt.' 'The consultation was done in recognition of "the importance of the traditional narwhal hunt to many Nunavut communities", said the statement released jointly by Fisheries and Oceans Minister Keith Ashfield, Environment Minister Peter Kent and Health Minister Leona Aglukkaq, who also serves as minister of the Canadian Northern Economic Development and is the Member of Parliament for Nunavut.' Further it was stated that: 'After evaluating the narwhal hunt for its impact on the endangered species, Fisheries and Oceans Canada announced on June 14 that Inuit of Nunavut could continue harvesting the animals and selling their by-products internationally. The agency conducted its evaluation in light of the Convention on International Trade in Endangered Species of Wild Fauna and Flora (CITES).' '"At times, the development of the plan was very difficult, but in the end, Inuit now have a management plan in place that we feel meets our needs and respects our harvesting rights", said James Eetoolook, Acting President of Nunavut Tunngavik Inc., in a statement after the management plan was announced in January. Under the management plan, the narwhal limit for the community of Grise Fiord harvesting from Jones Sound was raised from 20 to 50.'
[35] 'Narwhal: Unicorns of the Sea', www.strangeanimals.info/2010/12/narwhal.html, last accessed 25 April 2015.

8.3.2   Conclusions on the IWC and narwhal management

The role of the IWC in the sustainable management of the narwhal stocks is negligible, and lacks practical effects in influencing the behaviour of States. This is the result of many factors. There is an ongoing debate whether the IWC possesses the competence to deal with the issue of small cetaceans, which is a matter that seems unlikely to be resolved in the near future. Greenland refuses to enter into any discussion on the subject, citing the needs of its indigenous peoples. Canada, no longer a party to the ICRW, is entirely outside the purview of the IWC. Accordingly, Canada may ignore all decisions of the IWC.

8.4   The 1973 Convention on International Trade in Endangered Species of Wild Fauna and Flora

8.4.1   CITES and the trade in narwhals

The narwhal was added to CITES Appendix III, the lowest level of conservation concern, in 1975, by Canada, and in 1977, by Greenland. Narwhals were uplisted (that is to say, shifted from a lower risk list to a higher risk list) in 1979 to CITES Appendix II. This means that Canada and Denmark (on account of whaling taking place in Greenland) are required to make science-based 'non-detrimental' findings before allowing any exports. These findings are made up according to each country, mostly based on population surveys, which were difficult to obtain. Between 1992 and 2002, Denmark imported 1,124 tusks and 3,793 carvings from Greenland. It re-exported 356 tusks, 1,109 carvings and 500 unidentified 'specimens'. Between 1992 and 2002, at least twenty-six countries imported narwhal products from Greenland.[36]

A Review of Significant Trade (RST) in the products of the narwhal was conducted by the CITES Animals Committee in 1995/1996. The Committee made a series of Recommendations to both Canada and Greenland, such as to conduct surveys. In 2004, the Committee was not satisfied with the compliance with its Recommendations, and set a new deadline. The review was concluded in October 2004, when Recommendations had been complied with. As a result of the 1995 RST, the reviewers concluded that:

---

[36] WDCS, above n. 13, 4.

Despite the long history of exploitation, there are insufficient data to determine whether narwhal populations have declined and to assess reliably whether current exploitation is sustainable. Further research ... is required in order to better assess the impact of current take on narwhal populations. While there is clearly an international market for narwhal tusks, there is insufficient trade information to determine ... whether international trade *per se* is affecting the conservation status of the species. A greater understanding of the domestic and international market for narwhal products will be central to any efforts to ensure that take does not threaten individual populations of this species. Standardization of terms (tusks, teeth) when reporting trade to CITES is also required to identify the number of animals represented by this trade.[37]

The Animals Committee responded to this Review with the Primary and Secondary Recommendations that were sent to the Parties concerned. The Primary Recommendations were as follows: the responsible authorities of Canada and Greenland should inform the Secretariat of the basis for their non-detrimental findings in accordance with Article IV(2)(a) of the Convention. The Secondary Recommendations were as follows: the responsible authorities of Canada and Greenland should initiate a scientifically based survey programme for the Baffin Bay stock, if one was not already in operation, which should form the basis of an improved population monitoring programme. At the seventeenth meeting of the Animals Committee, the observer from Canada explained that Canada 'was having some difficulties with surveying its Narwhal populations and that consultations with Greenland and Denmark were taking time'. He claimed that 'current levels of harvest were sustainable and that he would make the necessary data available to the Committee'. The action agreed was for 'the Management Authority of Canada to provide the Committee with survey results that demonstrate sustainability of present harvest levels'.[38] The results of this survey have not been submitted.

The legal framework for CITES implementation in Greenland is fragmentary and spread over a number of Regulations, but is principally provided for in Greenland legislation (under its system of self-government), namely, in Regulation No. 14 of 10 December 1981.[39]

---

[37] Ibid., 6.   [38] Ibid., 7.

[39] However, the obsolescence of the regulation is illustrated by Article 3 of the regulation document: 'Article 3. Permits [for export from Greenland] are issued by the Danish Ministry for Greenlandic Affairs on behalf of the Greenland Home Rule.' The Danish Ministry concerned was closed many years ago as it was redundant, since when Greenland has issued its own CITES permits. Thor Hjarsen, 'CITES in Greenland', *TRAFFIC*

In fulfilment of the requirements of CITES, according to the domestic law of Greenland, the export of parts and/or derivatives requires a prior permit.[40] However, the rules had significant flaws in that no legal sanctions were provided for breaches, and there was no indication as to the kind of permit that is required. In 2001, Greenland introduced a new system for the management of CITES permits. CITES permits were pre-issued and submitted in large numbers to souvenir shops. A shop may receive around twenty to forty pre-printed CITES export permits for narwhal without any consideration of sustainability of this trade. The WWF Denmark submitted that the number of CITES permits used for tourist export has risen tenfold since the pre-2001 period.[41] Permits to trade Appendix 2 species are issued by the Ministry of Domestic Affairs, Environment and Nature. To obtain a permit, a positive declaration of sustainability is required.

Until 2004, Greenland lacked its own Scientific Authority to evaluate exports of species and products listed in CITES Appendices I and II. In 2005, this Authority could not establish that the export of narwhals was non-detrimental for the survival of species; therefore, Greenland imposed a temporary ban on exports of narwhal products, which will be lifted once the export is pronounced as non-detrimental.[42] However, the recently established Scientific Authority in Greenland announced that, based on the current gaps in the management of the narwhal, and due to excessive hunting, it is impossible to declare the export and trade as non-detrimental to the survival of the species in the wild.[43]

Until 2005, trade with the CITES permit souvenirs in Greenland was significant; according to Greenland's own estimate, the value of this trade

---

Bulletin 20 (2000), 17, at 17, www.traffic.org/traffic-bulletin/traffic_pub_bulletin_20_1. pdf, last accessed 30 December 2014.

[40] §15 of Reg. No. 30 of 11 October 1995. Thor Hjarsen, 'Greenland's International Obligations', WWF Denmark, p. 20, http://assets.panda.org/downloads/greenlandfinalre port.pdf, last accessed 30 December 2014.

[41] Ibid., p. 23.

[42] Helena Berends and Jonathan Pearse, 'Overseas Countries and Territories Environmental Profile', European Commission, p. 14, http://ec.europa.eu/development/center/reposi tory/ environmental_profile_north_atlantic_en.pdf, last accessed 1 January 2015.

[43] It said as follows: '[I]t cannot be concluded that the current export of Narwhal products from Greenland is non-detrimental as, with the current catches, it might be detrimental to Narwhal in West Greenland.' Cited in: Ecoadvise & Communication, 'Narwhal Quota Increase 2005–2006 in Greenland', www.ecoadvise.dk/news_narwhal.html, last accessed 30 December 2014.

to tourists reached around 20 million DKK. In 2005, CITES considered imposing an international trade ban on the sale of narwhal tusks and items made from narwhal ivory. A report tabled at a recent CITES meeting claimed that the hunting of narwhal in Canada and Greenland had increased since 1995 to unsustainable levels, and the 'international trade in narwhal products has also increased and changed in focus, from whole tusks to a high volume of carvings and pieces of tusk', thus 'making it harder to assess the real impact of the trade on the species'.[44]

The EU's Representative at CITES recommended that CITES undertake a trade review of narwhal product sales, claiming that narwhal hunting has increased in West Greenland and Canada since the last CITES trade review in 1995, and that hunting is carried out at an unsustainable level in both countries. The report notes that Greenland adopted its first narwhal-hunt regulations in 2004, yet its legal quota of 300 narwhals that year was still above the limit of 135 recommended by marine biologists. It must be mentioned, as well, that there are no quotas set for East Greenland, since there is no available data as to its narwhal population.[45] However, Greenland objected to all these observations. In its response to the recommendation calling for a review of the narwhal trade, Greenland argued that international trade is not the main incentive for narwhal hunting, and that banning international trade is unlikely to have any effect on the level of exploitation, because the trade in tusks and carvings is not the most important objective of the hunt, and no export permits are given to fish plants to export narwhal meat, blubber or *mattak* (that is to say, a foodstuff containing whale skin and blubber). Therefore, according to Greenland, CITES was exceeding its mandate, due to the fact that it was supposed to control trade only when species are threatened by the trade itself. The narwhal hunt in Greenland is mainly a subsistence hunt, with the tusk being a surplus product, and the only part occasionally traded internationally. The rest of the animal is used domestically for human and animal sustenance.

Greenland argues that its hunting of narwhals has not increased, but rather that it has decreased. However, while there is a decline in the

---

[44] International Network for Whaling Research (INWR), 'CITES Eyes Narwhal Ivory', INWR, www.wcu.edu/inwr/digest/digest32.html#CITES, last accessed 30 December 2014.
[45] Ecoadvise & Communication, 'Greenland Announce New Narwhal Quota – 20/09/2006', www.ecoadvise.dk/news_narwhal.html, last accessed 30 December 2014.

narwhal population, necessary measures have already been adopted to conserve the stock. Greenland further states that it will improve its export system for narwhal. Further, Greenland argues the following: that even the selling of tusks makes the hunt more sustainable, because it encourages hunters to kill tusk-bearing males rather than females; that an import–export ban might lead to the hunting of more females and a depletion of the stock; that craft products can be made either from old parts of narwhals, such as bones found on beaches, or from animal parts made and exported years after the whale was killed; that trade appears to be increasing because it is now easier for people in Greenland to get export permits; and, finally, that there is continuing confusion between items made from narwhal teeth and tusks.[46]

In 2005, the EU imposed a ban on all commercial trade in narwhal products, but not on items bought by tourists. However, until 2005, exemption was granted for the products of cetaceans that were taken by the people of Greenland under licence granted by the competent authority of Greenland or Denmark, notwithstanding that all cetacean species are listed in Annex A (equivalent to CITES Appendix I) of the European Regulations that implement CITES. In 2006, Greenland temporarily imposed a ban on export of narwhal products, which prevented a Review of Significant Trade by CITES being performed. The export is now prohibited, but export permits can be issued to Greenland residents who take up residence in another country and own narwhal products as part of their household items. In the view of the present author, this temporary ban is a positive step forward. However, there are some examples of individuals taking advantage of this loophole, transporting several narwhal tusks to their new homes in Denmark. There are also no statistics about narwhal products smuggled out of Greenland. But given the lack of systematic control in harbours and airports, it is not impossible that a number of narwhal items leave the island unnoticed.[47]

---

[46] All information is from: Jane George, 'As Narwhal Exports Increase, CITES Threatens to Ban International Trade', *Nunatsiaq News*, news/nunavut/50610_09.html, last accessed 1 January 2015. See also a proposal of the EU at the CITES in 2005 for a significant review of the narwhal trade: Katalin Rodics (as the European representative of the Animals Committee), 'The Need for a New Review of Significant Trade in the Narwhal', CITES AC21 Inf. 1 (Rev 1), www.cites.org/common/com/ac/21/E21i-01.pdf, last accessed 30 December 2014.

[47] Witting, Ugarte and Heide-Jørgensen, above n. 16.

The Whale and Dolphin Conservation Society (WDCS) remains concerned that narwhal hunting continues at unsustainable levels, and that tusks will simply be stockpiled until the trade resumes.[48] Hopefully, the draft of Greenland's new set of CITES-related Regulations will fulfil all requirements in CITES, most importantly those relating to enforcement through customs control, international inspections and confiscations.[49]

Canada permits limited trade of narwhal products. In 1971, after years of unregulated hunting and trade, Canada enacted Narwhal Protection Regulations that established an annual catch quota for individual Inuit hunters. In 1976, this system was replaced by quotas awarded to settlements and enforced by the issuance of tags to be attached to the carcass or tusk of each narwhal taken. However, Canada abandoned the quota scheme. The average reported annual catch by the Baffin Island communities between 1996 and 2000 was 364 narwhals.[50]

The price of narwhal ivory has increased substantially over the past years. Canadian narwhal ivory was traditionally exported to the United Kingdom, then often re-exported. However the EU banned such a trade. New markets have developed in Japan and Switzerland. The international ivory trade is interested in large tusks, and this may have affected the nature and intensity of the hunt. At present, international trade is regulated through CITES, requiring national permits for import and export. Greenland installed a ban on all narwhal product exports in 2006.[51]

8.4.2   Conclusions on CITES and the narwhal

The regulation of trade in narwhal products by CITES is inconsistent and haphazard. There is neither effective policy nor satisfactory legal measures. CITES bodies lack any reliable information as to the state of narwhal stocks, trade quotas and even of the domestic legislation in relation to the implementation of the CITES Regulations and specifically in relation to the narwhal. In the case of Greenland, the fundamental issue is the strengthening of customs control so that CITES can be implemented effectively. Therefore, at present, it may be concluded that CITES, as also seems to be the case for the IWC, fails to some extent effectively to regulate trade in narwhal products and thus fails to some extent effectively to protect the

---

[48]   See WDCS, 'Greenland's Narwhal Hunters off the Hook', 14 July 2006, http://us.whales. org/news/2006/07/greenlands-narwhal-hunters-off-hook-again, last accessed 30 December 2014.

[49]   Hjarsen, above n. 39, 24.   [50]   WDCS, above n. 13, 3.   [51]   Ibid.

species. However, it may be noted that there is some general improvement in the CITES implementation (Greenland).

8.5 The 1979 Bonn Convention on the Conservation of Migratory Species of Wild Animals

8.5.1 The CMS and small cetaceans

The CMS expressed interest in cetaceans in general in 1985, with the listing of a number of large cetaceans in its Appendix I. The CMS Scientific Committee submitted that a number of small cetaceans were threatened, and suggested the inclusion of many of these species in Appendix II by the decision of its COP. Resolution 1.7 was adopted which set up a Committee on Small Cetaceans. At the COP 2 in 1988, the majority of States added seven species of small cetaceans to Appendix II (with Norway and Denmark objecting).[52] In 1991, the list was supplemented by other species. By 1994, twenty-seven species of small cetaceans were included in CMS Appendix II.[53]

8.5.2 The CMS and the narwhal

The narwhal is listed in CMS Appendix II. It was included in 1991 despite objections by Greenland, which argued that the species was already subject to an agreement between Canada and Greenland.[54] In relation to such species, the CMS provides as follows:

> Article IV: Migratory Species to be the Subject of Agreements: Appendix II
>
> 1. Appendix II shall list migratory species which have an unfavourable conservation status and which require international agreements for their conservation and management, as well as those which have a conservation status which would significantly benefit from the international cooperation that could be achieved by an international agreement.
> 2. If the circumstances so warrant, a migratory species may be listed both in Appendix I and Appendix II.

---

[52] After initial reservations to certain whale species, including narwhal, in 2010 Norway repealed the reservations of all species of whales and sharks on CMS Appendix II and the great white shark on Appendix I, including the following species of cetaceans: white-beaked dolphin, Atlantic white-sided dolphin, killer whale, narwhal, pygmy right whale, Antarctic minke whale, Bryde's whale, fin whale, sei whale and sperm whale: www.iisd.ca/cms/cop10/, last accessed 17 July 2015.

[53] Gillespie, *Whaling Diplomacy*, above n. 17, p. 300.   [54] Ibid., pp. 300 and 315.

3. Parties that are Range States of migratory species listed in Appendix II shall endeavour to conclude Agreements where these should benefit the species and should give priority to those species in an unfavourable conservation status.

4. Parties are encouraged to take action with a view to concluding agreements for any population or any geographically separate part of the population of any species or lower taxon of wild animals, members of which periodically cross one or more national jurisdiction boundaries.

5. The Secretariat shall be provided with a copy of each Agreement concluded pursuant to the provisions of this Article.

The CMS prepared a Report on the Narwhal. The comments on the status of the narwhal population in this Report are not encouraging and clearly indicate the escalating depletion of narwhal stocks.[55]

8.5.3   Conclusions on the CMS and narwhal management

The CMS is a framework Convention, which lacks direct regulatory powers. Its function is only to encourage States to enter into agreements on protection of migratory species. The CMS fulfils more of an advisory function as its organs provide scientific data and draw the state of certain species to the attention of the CMS State Parties – as in the case of the narwhal – by listing them in CMS Appendix II, and producing relevant Reports. Thus, without direct cooperation between States on protection of the narwhal, the CMS has no real effect in this respect.

---

[55] The CMS Report states as follows: 'The narwhal has been hunted since the earliest times by the Inuit . . ., with an annual take in the order of 1,000 animals. Recent data confirms that these levels are still maintained today, with annual catch rates at 535 and 433 between 2000–2004 in West Greenland and Canada, respectively . . . However, while male narwhals compose most of the landed catch, annual harvest statistics underestimate total numbers of narwhals killed due primarily to the non-reporting of struck and killed but lost whales. The estimated total kill of narwhals may exceed the reported landed catch by 40%. The North Atlantic Marine Mammal Commission . . . repeatedly expressed grave concern on the apparent decline of stocks in West Greenland, and while commending Greenland for the recent introduction of quotas, there is still serious concern that present takes of narwhals in West Greenland, according to the advice of both the NAMMCO Scientific Committee and the Canada/Greenland Joint Commission on Narwhal and Beluga Scientific Working Group are not sustainable and will lead to further depletion of the stocks. The quota for Greenland was 385 animals in the 2006/2007 season, again well above the recommended level of 135. In East Greenland, around 100 are assumed to be taken annually, without quotas nor harvest sustainability assessment.' www.cms.int/reports/small_cetaceans/data/M_monoceros/m_monoceros.htm, last accessed 26 March 2015.

8.6 Regional cooperation: the Canada–Greenland Joint Commission on the Conservation and Management of Narwhal and Beluga and the 1992 North Atlantic Marine Mammal Commission

8.6.1 The Canada–Greenland Joint Commission

The Canada–Greenland Joint Commission (JCNB) was formed to study common issues concerning the narwhal and beluga species which (although this is not entirely certain) migrate between Canada and Greenland.[56] The JCNB, similarly to NAMMCO, has an advisory capacity. It was established on the basis of the Memorandum of Understanding (MOU) between the Canadian Department of Fisheries and Oceans and Greenland's Department of Fisheries, Hunting and Agriculture. The MOU notes the importance of both beluga and narwhal for the cultures of the Inuit peoples, and pledges their rational management in accordance with UNCLOS.

Each Party has two commissioners, one representing the government and the other the hunting community (such as Greenland Hunters and Fishers Organisation (KNAPK) and the Nunavut Wildlife Management Board). The activities of the JCNB are conducted by the Scientific Working Group (SWG), composed of scientists and biologists. An interesting feature of the JCNB is that Western science is supplemented by traditional ecological knowledge (TEK) during the meetings of the SWG. Both scientists and hunters are frequently in 'an acute' disagreement.[57] At the time of writing in 1998, Freeman stated that the JCNB had no concerns about the state of the narwhal and that, according to its assessment, narwhal stocks appeared to be sustainable. Freeman was of the view that there were several advantages of the Commission, such as employing a regional approach; dealing exclusively with Inuit-hunted small cetaceans; supporting sustainable use; and being sensitive to Inuit culture. However, among its drawbacks, he referred to the limitation of the JCNB in covering only these two species, meaning that the ecology and the general management of natural resources should be approached in a more holistic manner. He therefore suggested the extension of the scope of the JCNB's functions with a meaningful incorporation of the Inuit TEK.[58]

Despite the claims of the JCNB that the state of narwhal stocks is sustainable, there are no absolutely reliable estimates concerning the

---

[56] Freeman et al., above n. 7, p. 141.   [57] Ibid., p. 141.   [58] Ibid., p. 142.

narwhal population. In 2012, the Canadian Science Advisory Secretariat in its Science Advisory Report 2012/021 said as follows:

> Most of the survey estimates used in the analysis are dated, particularly the 1996 Somerset Island stock estimate. In some cases, results have been quite different between surveys conducted more than once in the same areas. This suggests that sampling error may be larger than is indicated . . . but there has been no independent assessment of loss rates in different hunting locations or seasons.[59]

The tenth meeting of the (Canada–Greenland) JCNB was held in Canada in April 2006 and confirmed the above observations that West Greenland narwhals were depleted to approximately one quarter of the historical abundance. To halt the decline of the West Greenland narwhals, the JWG advised that total removal in West Greenland, except Melville Bay, should be reduced to no more than 135 individuals. In Melville Bay, given the lack of scientific evidence, the Commission recommended the precautionary approach to establish harvest levels. The Commission expressed grave concern at the recent conclusion of the JWG regarding the status of the narwhal in West Greenland. The Commission stated that it would like to see a work plan with a timeframe addressing the JWG recommendation aiming at the reduction in total removal. The Commission considered that the short-term management objective for the West Greenland stock should be halted in order to prevent the decline of narwhal stocks.[60]

In 2008, the JCNB strongly advised Greenland to immediately reduce its quotas for narwhal and beluga hunting, or else both Greenland and Canada would suffer the consequences. The JCNB recommended a precautionary approach to the determination of appropriate quotas of beluga. The narwhal population in West Greenland has declined to only 25 per cent of its original size. There may be as few as 1,500 narwhal left, down from a population of about 30,000 not so long ago.[61] However, despite the above concerns, there was an increase of narwhal quotas for West Greenland. Greenland stated on its official webpage that:

> Of these, 15 will be taken in Melville Bay, 75 will be taken from the rest of West Greenland and the remaining 10 will be allocated in the spring, if

---

[59] Advice on Total Allowable Landed Catch for Baffin Bay Narwhal Population, 2012. See Canadian government webpage, http://publications.gc.ca/site/eng/431811/publication. html, last accessed 31 December 2014.

[60] 10th Meeting of the JCNB, held in Canada in April 2006.

[61] See Ecoadvise, 'Greenland Needs to Cut Narwhal Beluga Hunts', www.ecoadvise.dk/ news_narwhal.html, last accessed 31 December 2014.

necessary. The season ends [on] June 31, 2007. The total quota for the whole of West Greenland, including Melville Bay, is 385. However, in the 2005–2006 seasons the quota was exceeded with 68 animals and those have been withdrawn from the 2006 and 2007 quotas. In the season 2005 and 2006 the quota for the West Greenland Stock was exceeded by 54 animals, while the quota for the Melville Bay was exceeded by 15. These animals are withdrawn from the final quotas.[62]

8.6.2   NAMMCO and the narwhal

NAMMCO in its 2002 Report stated that:

[t]he Management Committee noted its previous concerns about the sustained ability of harvest in some areas. Assessments were made of the stocks of narwhals in West Greenland to estimate their current status and the sustainable levels of harvest ... and they considered that, given the rapid decline in numbers suggested by the assessments, the main goal must be to halt the decline in the short term.[63]

8.6.3   A joint meeting of the NAMMCO Scientific Committee Working Group and the JCNB Scientific Working Group (the Joint Working Group)

This body, during its May 2001 meeting, concluded that:

There are no recent reliable survey estimates for narwhal in either the Canadian High Arctic or West Greenland. New information seriously

---

[62] Greenland's justification for raising quotas: 'Hunters considered the previous quotas as being far too restrictive and continuously emphasised that there are enough Narwhals to sustain a higher harvest. The Cabinet decided to raise the Narwhal quota in consideration to the difficult situation of the hunters and taking into account reports of large groups of narwhals seen close to shore. The quota is 385 but 68 whales had already been caught in the previous quota year 2005–6. This excessive hunt has been deducted from the next year's quota, that is to say, the maximum hunt from 1 July 2006 to 30 June 2007 is now 307 narwhals. It should be noted that there are slight discrepancies between available data sets of NAMMCO and Greenland. Also note that in some years no quotas had been fixed.' See 'Increase of Narwhal Quotas for West Greenland', Greenland's Home Rule, www.landstinget.gl/English/Nyheder/_2006_dec_narwhal_quotas.aspx, last accessed 1 January 2015. See also the report from the 16th Meeting of the NAMMCO Scientific Committee: Mads Lunde, 'IWC-Observer Report on the 16th NAMMCO Annual Meeting, Norway, February 2007', IWC, www.iwcoffice.org/_documents/commission/IWC-59docs/59-4.pdf, last accessed 1 January 2015. Ecoadvise & Communication, above n. 43.
[63] NAMMCO in 2002, quoted in WWF, 'The Big Four', above n. 1, 42.

challenges our previous confidence that the hunting has been sustainable. There is a high chance that some stock units are contributing to several hunts annually. There is a risk that at least some stock units may be overharvested.[64]

The Joint Working Group stated that:

the risk assessment conducted by the JWG in 2004 indicated that an annual catch of 150 narwhals in West Greenland implies a risk of extinction near 80 [per cent] after 30 years. The only catch level that appeared to have zero risk of extinction, even after 50 years, is 20 animals.[65]

8.6.4   Conclusions on NAMMCO and the JCNB

NAMMCO and the JCNB operate on an advisory basis with no mandate to set the whaling policy of either Canada or Greenland. Both organisations have expressed grave concern regarding the level of exploitation of narwhal species, and recommend that existing quotas be lowered. These organisations are well equipped to carry out scientific research on narwhals, but lack the powers to enforce their Recommendations.

8.7   The 1991 Agreement on the Conservation of Small Cetaceans of the Baltic, North East Atlantic, Irish and North Seas

8.7.1   Implications of new developments for the narwhal

At present, ASCOBANS does not cover the narwhal.[66] However, at the fifteenth meeting of the ASCOBANS Advisory Committee on 27 March 2008, there had been discussion on the possible inclusion of all cetaceans in the agreement area.[67] The Advisory Committee, having analysed the problem, reached the following conclusions:

---

[64] WDCS, above n. 13, 5.   [65] Rodics, above n. 46, 4.

[66] ASCOBANS covers all species, subspecies or populations of toothed whales in these four seas except for the sperm whale (*Physeter macrocephalus*). The most important of these species are: the harbour porpoise, the bottlenosed dolphin, the common dolphin, the white-beaked dolphin, the Atlantic white-sided dolphin, the striped dolphin, Risso's dolphin, the killer whale, the long-finned pilot whale, the northern bottlenosed whale and other beaked whales. ASCOBANS, 'Small Cetaceans Covered by ASCOBANS', www.ascobans.org/, last accessed 17 July 2015.

[67] Peter G. H. Evans and Mark P. Simmonds, 'Implications for ASCOBANS of Enlarging the Agreement Area and Including all Cetaceans', Doc. AC15/Doc.28(O), www.ascobans.org/sites/default/files/document/AC15_28_SpeciesExtension_1.pdf, last accessed 31 December 2014; see also Daniel Owen, 'The Interaction between the ASCOBANS MOP and the

We see the following advantages to including all cetaceans in the ASCO-BANS Agreement: (1) It facilitates consideration at government level of all conservation issues affecting cetacean species; at present, no other legislative instrument or management body gives equal weight to examining all conservation problems for all cetaceans in the region (thus ensuring that issues like ship strikes, by-catch and sound disturbance affecting large cetaceans remain on the radar screen, and would receive more attention politically). (2) It would provide complementarity with its sister Agreement ACCOBAMS, and be more attractive for potential new Parties such as Spain and Portugal. (3) It would encourage closer co-operation with management authorities such as IWC. (4) It offers a holistic approach to cetacean conservation which makes logical sense. Our recommendation is therefore that parties propose at MOP4 for the inclusion of all cetacean species in the Agreement.[68]

8.7.2   ASCOBANS and the narwhal

This Agreement relies mainly on the cooperation of the Parties to it 'in order to achieve and maintain a favourable conservation status for small cetaceans'.[69]

As Gillespie observes, when ASCOBANS was introduced to the CMS, there was a degree of concern that the Agreement was weak, lacking teeth. A number of the Range States within the context of ASCOBANS have not become parties to it, as is the case with Norway, which has only committed to scientific cooperation, due to its desire to maintain a consistent national policy, and although it supports sustainable use of cetaceans, it wishes to be able to kill them while conducting scientific research. Further, Estonia, Ireland, Latvia, Portugal, Russia and Spain are not parties to ASCOBANS.[70] All these concerns as to the effectiveness of ASCOBANS would also relate to narwhal whaling regulation, were it to be brought within the scope of ASCOBANS.

Gillespie states, however, that despite all its shortcomings, ASCO-BANS developed several plans of action which, in conjunction with the

IWC, NAMMCO and EC', Doc. AC15/Doc.30(O), www.ascobans.org/sites/default/files/document/AC15_30_InstitutionalInteractions_1.pdf, last accessed 31 December 2014.
[68] Evans and Simmonds, above n. 67, 7.
[69] Conservation and Management Plan, annexed to ASCOBANS as amended in 2003, first and fourth paragraphs; text available at www.ascobans.org/es/documents/agreement-text, last accessed 31 December 2014. It may be mentioned that ACCOBAMS (a sister agreement) covers all cetaceans.
[70] Gillespie, *Whaling Diplomacy*, above n. 17, pp. 302–3.

IWC, aim at the study of the effects of the pollution on cetaceans, and the reduction of the offending substances; the reduction of disturbances on cetaceans (including the regulating of whale watching, seismic testing and military activities); the establishment of protected areas; and the control of the problem of bycatch.[71]

8.8   The 1979 Bern Convention on the Conservation of European Wildlife and Natural Habitats

The Bern Convention focuses on the protection of endangered natural habitats and vulnerable species, including migratory ones. Appendix II (titled 'Strictly Protected Fauna Species') covers the narwhal (under its *Monodon monoceros* designation). Denmark is a party to this Convention.[72] Beyond the mere listing of the narwhal, no steps have been taken relating to the narwhal's conservation. In any event, this Convention is also quite weak and it is based on promoting cooperation between States and, thus, its importance in relation to the protection of the narwhal is unlikely to be of any great significance.

8.9   The European Union and its 1992 EEC Habitats Directive

The Habitats Directive (Directive 92/43/EEC), adopted in 1992, establishes a common framework for the conservation of wild animal and plant species and natural habitats of importance to the European Union. It provides for the creation of a network of special areas of conservation within its Natura 2000 scheme, to 'maintain and restore, at favourable conservation status, natural habitats and species of wild fauna and flora of Community interest' (European Commission, 2003).[73] The Habitats Directive sets the goal of establishing an EU-wide network for nature conservation (referred to as its 'Special Areas of Conservation' (SACs)). The 1992 Directive has five Annexes: Annex I relates to natural and

[71] Ibid., p. 303.
[72] Also relevant are the following Bern Convention provisions: Article 4 (the protection of habitats), Article 6 (the obligation to enact necessary legislation by the Parties) and Article 9 (the exceptions to Articles 4–8 of the Convention).
[73] The Natura 2000 Networking Programme on behalf of the EU's Commission was terminated in 2007, www.natura.org/nnp_final_message.pdf, last accessed 31 December 2014. See http://ec.europa.eu/environment/nature/legislation/habitatsdirective/index_en.htm, last accessed 31 December 2014, for background information on the EU's regime with regard to natural habitat preservation.

semi-natural habitat types of EU interest, whose conservation requires the designation of special areas of conservation; Annex II relates to animal and plant species of EU interest, whose conservation requires the designation of special areas of conservation; Annex III relates to criteria for selecting sites eligible for identification as sites of community importance and designation as special areas of conservation; Annex IV relates to animal and plant species of EU interest in need of strict protection; and Annex V relates to animal and plant species of EU interest, the taking of which in the wild and the exploitation of which may be subject to management measures. Narwhal is listed in Annex IV.[74] Similarly to the Bern Convention, the EU, apart from listing, has not taken any steps relating to the narwhal.

Concluding remarks

The present chapter highlights how the protection of certain types of small cetaceans remains patchy and inconsistent between regimes. We have seen how there are broad multilateral regimes – such as that pertaining to CITES – that provide degrees of regulation with regard to the narwhal; however, this is limited to the trade aspects of narwhal-derived products, and to the extent that narwhals are deemed endangered. Other regimes, such as the ICRW, provide, in the final analysis, no protection for this small whale species given the dominant view that its regime does not extend to this type of whale. Other regimes are toothless due to their advisory nature.

The inadequacy of the international regulatory system with regard to the whaling of narwhal is the result of several factors, an important one being the lack of reliable data that could form the basis for a multilateral regime predicated on a sound scientific basis that could encourage broader buy-in on the part of States. Currently, there appears to be a situation by which States seek to exonerate themselves by citing the lack of scientific data. However, the species concerned are largely of a coastal nature, and this makes it difficult for the necessary data to be collated impartially by an independent organisation, as this would require extensive oversight operations in maritime areas within the direct jurisdiction of coastal States. We have seen how States that continue to permit narwhal whaling are not forthcoming with data. Hopefully,

---

[74] Council Directive 92/43/EEC of 21 May 1992 on the Conservation of Natural Habitats and of Wild Fauna and Flora, OJ L 206 (22 July 1992), p. 7.

NAMMCO and the JCNB Joint Working Group[75] on narwhal may eventually help to eliminate the persistent recourse on the part of narwhal whaling States to the 'lack of reliable data' excuse as it no longer needs to act as a stumbling block to narwhal regulation. In this respect the precautionary principle could provide the conceptual foundation for the development of a multilateral policy on narwhal (and other small-sized whale species). Several conventions are based on this principle, which endorses the appropriate action without full scientific certainty (Principle 15 of the Rio Declaration). For example, CITES explicitly adopted this principle in 1994.[76] International agreements, such as CITES, are well equipped to deal with the protection of species through imposing trade restrictions or bans with regard to products derived from certain species. However, some of the CITES State Parties, in particular in the present context in relation to the narwhal of both Canada and Greenland (through Denmark), are reluctant to provide the required information. The legal competence of the IWC in relation to certain types of small cetaceans, including narwhal and beluga, is still (after over sixty-two years of existence) a subject of heated discussion, thus preventing it from functioning effectively. What is more, in relation to Canada, the IWC has no regulatory powers, as Canada is no longer a party to the ICRW. The CMS and the Bern Convention are no more than framework treaties. Thus they have been unable to provide an effective level of protection to narwhal. It should also be noted that, in general, the international agreements lack effective enforcement mechanisms, given that implementation is largely left to national measures.[77]

Both NAMMCO and the JCNB appear to be rather weak in regulatory powers and enforcement mechanisms. They are more akin to associations of Parties with shared interests rather than fully fledged international organisations with certain regulatory powers. It would be inaccurate, however, to deny that they express their concerns as to the level of the narwhal stocks and, within their limited powers, make certain Recommendations. The stern language used by the JCNB in its session in

---

[75] See e.g. a report of a joint meeting, www.nammco.no/webcronize/images/Nammco/766. pdf, last accessed 12 January 2015.

[76] See e.g. Barnabas Dickson, 'The Precautionary Principle in CITES: A Critical Assessment', *Natural Resources Journal* 39 (1999), 211–28.

[77] Ibid.

2008, concerning the limiting of the hunting for narwhal and beluga, indicates that the regional institutions take the current situation very seriously. It has been suggested that it would be advisable to incorporate more traditional knowledge and to find ways to resolve differences between scientists and hunters on beluga and narwhal stock structure; and that it would be advisable to make better estimates of struck and lost rates and to study methods to reduce loss rates.

On a positive note, it ought to be mentioned that Greenland is at present at the forefront of very modern legislation on commercial and research-related use of biological resources. Therefore, it is possible that the areas relating to the preservation of the Arctic biodiversity, including narwhal, will soon be regulated.

Lastly, the question may be posed whether a general Arctic Treaty would be of any assistance in cases of the protection of species, such as the narwhal, the protection of which falls between the cracks of international environmental and trade regulation. In the view of the present author, this is an unlikely solution to this problem, as the whole idea of such a treaty is fraught with difficulties, and it is likely to be more of a framework instrument that does not address the regulation of specific species. A more adequate solution would be to mobilise and strengthen the existing treaties, and to foster more interpretative harmonisation between them, and, as Hans Corell suggested, to support these by engaging 'the general public, business, politicians and governments'.[78] In that regard, it is, clearly, for the mindsets of States to shift more towards regarding the welfare of the most endangered whale stocks as a *res communis* – a common good and a common heritage of humankind – that cannot be meaningfully defended unless it is done multilaterally.[79] At the current juncture, it seems that this is a stage at which States have not uniformly arrived. The protection of the most endangered whale stocks, such as narwhal, should, in the view of the present author, take precedence over other considerations (historical or cultural).

---

[78] Hans Corell, 'Reflections on the Possibilities and Limitations of a Binding Legal Regime', *Environmental Policy and Law* 37 (2007), 321–4, 324.

[79] In this respect, see the *Whaling in the Antarctic* case, which is thought to be an example of the implementation of the *erga omnes partes* concept.

~

Conclusion

Whaling is a commercial, social and cultural practice that has been analysed within the present publication primarily from a legal standpoint, as supplemented by some analysis from ethical and socio-cultural standpoints. The analysis appears to support the following conclusions.

Whaling is a practice that lacks homogeneity in that it takes place for different purposes – commercial, cultural, scientific, and varying combinations of these three – and in relation to different species. As a result, when we examine the question of any regulation in this field, we need to ask in relation to which purpose is whaling being conducted, and over which species. However, whaling raises not only legal questions but also questions that concern cultural diversity and the rights of animals, as well as questions concerning general environmental ethics. All these concerns result in a whole catalogue of contentious issues, given that it juxtaposes sets of rights and obligations against each other. This lack of homogeneity suggests that legal solutions – such as the development of a cohesive multilateral regime – must ensure that they sufficiently accommodate the various considerations at play.

The 2014 ICJ *Whaling in the Antarctic* case has, in the view of the present author, contributed to the solution of these contentious issues only to a limited degree (as of course was expected from the limited nature of the case). In the first place, it only dealt with one aspect of whaling, namely, scientific whaling – and more specifically, Japanese scientific whaling in the Antarctic. The Judgment, however, has shed some light on those obligations of Japan that may also be shared by other States. In order to find a solution to the impasse within the IWC, in the view of the present author, however, whaling needs to be analysed in a comprehensive and holistic manner, as the various types of whaling are not entirely disassociated from one another, and scientific whaling cannot be assessed without an analysis of the commercial dimension that may arise; and this is also the case with aboriginal subsistence whaling within the framework of the IWC.

However, whaling is conducted outside the IWC, and there is also whaling conducted within the remit of NAMMCO. This still does not exhaust all the potential problems: there is also regulation of whaling, or at least its trade aspects (to be more precise) by other multilateral environmental agreements such as CITES. It is a complex picture with no immediately discernible viable solution in sight to resolve all the pending deadlocks that are played out in various international organisations – with the IWC being the most prominent example. As already mentioned, the issues that arise are not necessarily legal; they are also issues of policy in relation to animal welfare and animal rights and human rights, including cultural rights. In that respect, the debates are not settled, and therefore, without any cohesive normative framework to deal with all aspects of whaling, political conflicts are inescapable. In that context, the law cannot resolve what politics has still to decide. Thus, there is no solution at present to such questions as the relationship between animal rights and cultural diversity (in particular when this issue arises outside the context of indigenous peoples) and how to reconcile these two concepts. Is such a claim to cultural diversity justified? What is the character and content of such a right? Does it have any tangible effect?

A whaling regime (of sorts) does emerge, albeit one that is not universal – one that is, rather, a patchwork of regimes that involves different sets of parties with different geographical and thematic scopes.

Despite the current state of play, there are certain feasible steps that could incrementally lead to a more cohesive multilateral system; for instance, the IWC could be better supported by other international organisations (as is the case with CITES).

The intransigence of IWC members makes any degree of internal renewal of the IWC rather unlikely. These fruitless attitudes have been adopted not only in relation to the resumption of commercial whaling and to scientific whaling, but also, recently, with regard to aboriginal subsistence whaling.

The issues concerning the acceptance of the New Management Procedure also contribute to the impasse and to the delay in finding any reasonable solution to the poor functioning of the IWC. There is an unresolved question – coloured by the emotional attitudes of the concerned States that preclude a reasonable discussion – of whether environmental concerns and the protection of biodiversity (which are of course of the foremost importance) do necessarily preclude resumption, in a very limited scope, of commercial whaling. In the view of some States, some commercial whaling could be an acceptable means of management of whale stocks, provided it was conducted entirely in line with disinterested scientific findings, so as only to take place in relation to abundant stocks of whales, the status of which is scientifically well documented. In this respect, it goes without saying, of course, that any discussion of the resumption of commercial whaling – on any scale and at any point in the future – should not under any circumstances be envisaged in relation to endangered species, or species of which the status is not entirely known. In any event, if resumed, such very limited commercial whaling would have to be entirely regulated at the interstate level, given the migratory nature of stocks, and also given the fact that whale stocks amount to a common patronage when they are found in waters outside the jurisdiction or control of coastal States (such as in the high seas). To some States, whaling will always remain an abhorrent activity whether it concerns endangered species or not. Such an attitude is not based on the number of whales and on the concept of the use of marine resources (which in itself is very unclear), but on ethics and possibly the rights of animals.

However, a purely legal question may be posed whether the ongoing IWC Moratorium on whaling (which initially was imposed for a limited period of time, and which as it stands at present appears to have become permanent) is not in accordance with the object and purpose of the 1946 ICRW, even when one assumes that practice and the passage of time may have meant that this instrument could sensibly be seen as having evolved. It is clear that this instrument was adopted with a view, at least in part, to promoting the long-term interests of the respective whaling industries of its Parties; to argue therefore that it ought to be the basis for permanently banning whaling is to entirely change the object and purpose of the ICRW, which, as the ICJ noted, cannot be done by the practice of States (or the IWC). On this basis, for a permanent ban on whaling, however desirable such an end might be, some other multilateral basis would have to be relied upon; not the ICRW per se, particularly given the current deadlock between its Parties (and its original object and purpose). What is more, the concept of sustainable development – including the concept of sustainable use – at least in a traditional sense, allows the exploitation of natural resources the existence of which is not endangered.

In the view of the present author, it seems that there are other concerns that are not often discussed, which may be behind prevailing negative attitudes towards whaling: concerns which accord, perhaps, to whales a symbolic – almost totemic – value as beings which are more than just a natural sea resource, but which are, rather, a symbol of nature and its indomitability, and which, as such, ought, almost religiously, to be protected from any form of human exploitation. However, if we are prepared to allow different values from those commonly adopted in the West to colour our views on whaling, we may find ourselves thinking differently, and making certain concessions towards whaling nations. We also ought to take into consideration that it is not only the Japanese but also Norwegians, Faroese and Icelanders who do not share the dominant Western notions and sensibilities about the whale as a resource that ought not to be subject to human exploitation.

What is more, support for cultural diversity does not preclude support for animal rights or animal welfare. As was explained in earlier parts of the present publication, animal rights theorists do not belong to some monolithic homogenous school of thought – there are shades of opinion that accept that cultural rights, particularly those of indigenous peoples, could at times displace animal rights when there is a conflict between them.

A less frequently discussed issue is a certain lack of consistency in regulating aboriginal subsistence whaling, in relation to which a more uniform system of regulation would be desirable. Again, this is an effect of the lack of an overall regime. For instance, the IWC does not regulate Canada, and therefore its indigenous whaling is outside regulation and normative harmonisation. It is not only Canada's whaling that is outside the purview of the IWC, but, as was discussed, there are other States, like Indonesia, which allow a certain degree of whaling.

As touched upon earlier, at times it is very difficult to distinguish between commercial and aboriginal subsistence whaling. Aboriginal whaling is also a source of constant aggravation and contention due to the demand on the part of States that represent indigenous peoples' interests in such whaling for increases in IWC quotas. Such whaling should be regulated in a clear way with well-defined guidelines, as at present it is subject to rules that are opaque and contradictory. There should be an established cooperation between the human rights bodies (in particular the HRC) and the IWC in the matter of aboriginal rights and whaling, as it appears that there is hardly any at all. As we have seen in earlier parts of this book, there are certain scholars and civil society organisations which do not fully support aboriginal whaling. In particular, there is a certain degree of concern regarding some of the traditional aboriginal methods of killing whales. Such an issue is very sensitive as it relates to the whole question of indigenous rights and rights to culture, and again there is no readily available solution.

It may be said, in fact, that there is no single area of the IWC's functioning that is devoid of contentions, tensions and even hostility. Is there a solution for this state of affairs? In the view of the present author, not under the current interpretation of the ICRW which, by maintaining the Moratorium on whaling, is not entirely faithful to its objects and purposes, particularly given that the stocks of various whale species could allow for some very limited commercial whaling. The ambiguous situation was confirmed by the USA's recent suggestion to remove humpback whale from the US Endangered Species List.

It has to be observed that, unlike many other international organisations which have evolved in intervening years, the IWC has remained mired in the same issues for at least the last thirty years. There is little change from the contentious issues concerning whaling in the 1980s and the 1990s, and the contemporary situation in the IWC was evidenced by the *Whaling in the Antarctic* case, not only by the Judgment but also by the pleadings of the parties to the dispute.

However, the attitudes of States seem unlikely to change; and the functioning of the IWC will continue to be impaired. There are several potential scenarios which in theory might remedy the current situation, but which, however, in the view of the present author, are in practice not viable or possible:

- Japan could leave the IWC and resume whaling outside its remit, though this is very unlikely;
- Japan could leave the ICRW and seek to re-enter (as did Iceland), with a reservation to the Moratorium. However, the negative views expressed by certain States at the time of Iceland's re-accession to the ICRW as to the legality of such a reservation suggest that it would not be an easy task or politically cost-free for Japan to attempt to do so;
- the IWC could approve limited commercial whaling; however, this too seems unlikely given the configuration of States present in the IWC which oppose commercial whaling; and
- Norway and Iceland, disappointed by the continuation of the Moratorium, could leave the IWC, considering that they are already parties to NAMMCO.

Thus, the deadlock seems unlikely to be broken any time soon. The establishment of a new overarching whaling organisation in and of itself, existing alongside the IWC, seems unlikely to solve the persistent sticking points, in the same way that NAMMCO did not, considering that it is, in fact, but a regional organisation with a very limited membership.

It would, however, be a very unsatisfactory and unfortunate outcome were the IWC to stop functioning altogether. This would, of course, be very undesirable and detrimental to the state of multilateral whaling regulation, but considering the present situation, it is rather likely.

The establishment of a new global organisation also seems a remote possibility, given the attitudes of the interested States, which would not immediately change or relent. The more likely scenario would be the creation of several regional organisations that could result in yet further fragmentation of whaling management, with potentially adverse effects. The global management of whaling stocks, even as imperfect as the present one, by one global organisation is perhaps more desirable than a fragmented approach by regional organisations that lack transparency. That said, however, the combination of many organisations at the regional level could, cumulatively, amount to some effective regulation so long as meaningful and consistent efforts appear across the spectrum of regimes. A top-down universal regime in and of itself does not guarantee effectiveness when it is, for instance, weak; whereas a plethora of effective regimes that involve sets of coastal States in their majority (albeit fragmentarily) could go a long way towards the regulation of whaling overall.

Finally, it might be the case that all multilateral cooperation on whaling breaks down, which would be a very discouraging development, particularly if this were to happen after almost seventy years of the IWC's existence, and with it being one of the first organisations in the field of environmental protection. This development would leave whale populations vulnerable and subject to unilateral action by States, without an overall management strategy that aims at addressing a variety of objectives including animal welfare and sustainability, which notion is subject to different interpretations. It may be said that at the international level, outside the realm of the IWC, some global management would be exercised within other multilateral environmental agreements that are based on more modern ecological policies. However, such a suggestion appears to be unworkable at present, as many of these other conventions are of a general and framework character, thus unsuitable in themselves for the protection of one particular species.

It may be said that such a state of affairs will unfortunately continue, as the post-Judgment contentious meeting of the IWC in September 2014 clearly evidenced. It appears to be an unfortunate conclusion that there is no immediate solution to the current deadlock. Perhaps the IWC in its efforts to please many suitors disappoints all – be they preservationist or conservationist States, NGOs, indigenous communities, and so on. Notwithstanding the clear statement contained in the ICJ's Judgment in the *Whaling in the Antarctic* case that the object and purpose of the ICRW has remained unchanged (thus still including the two main objectives of conservation of whales and the orderly development of the whaling industry), the two groups of States will continue to adhere to their inflexible contrasting attitudes. The author of the present book does not envisage in the foreseeable future the lifting of the Moratorium and the resumption of even very limited commercial whaling. As was announced by Japan, its scientific whaling will continue. The ICJ's Judgment no doubt has contributed to scaling down of this type of whaling; but there is no certainty that even these reduced quotas will not result in protestations from the opposing States, leading to further disagreements and/or even international litigation. Finally, due to increasing quotas for aboriginal whaling and its altogether unclear character, it might lead to further polarisation within the IWC and even to certain States leaving the Commission.

Appendix A

Taxonomy of whales: a brief introduction on selected species

1. Introduction to taxonomy of whales

It is extremely difficult, if not impossible, to state the exact figures relating to the entire whale population. This uncertainty results from the current methods of calculation and also historical mistakes – both accidental and deliberate – concerning calculation. Gillespie recommends caution regarding all estimates, and opines that, generally speaking, long-term non-lethal studies of certain whale species, such as the right and humpback whales, result in more reliable population estimates than vessel-based surveys conducted every five years.[1] According to the International Whaling Commission (IWC), threats to cetaceans can be said to include two broad categories. The first are those that result in death in the short term, such as direct hunting and accidental or incidental mortality (e.g. bycatches in fishing gear, ship strikes). The second category of longer-term threats is more difficult to identify and especially to quantify. These threats can be said to affect the 'overall fitness' of the population with respect to reproductive success or survivorship and are generally related to environmental degradation (including such factors as chemical pollution, noise pollution, overexploitation of prey, disturbance, climate change, etc.). Environmental threats can adversely influence populations of all species.[2] Detailed data for whale species may be obtained from papers and reports of the IWC Scientific Committee, marine mammal status reports published by the US (www.nmfs.noaa.gov/pr/sars/) and documents produced

---

[1] Alexander Gillespie, *Whaling Diplomacy: Defining Issues in International Environmental Law* (Cheltenham: Edward Elgar Publishing, 2005), p. 19. See also IWC: http://iwc.int/ cetacea, last accessed 27 December 2014.

[2] http://iwc.int/status, last accessed 27 December 2014. See also Benjamin van Dreimmelen, 'The International Mismanagement of Whaling', *Pacific Basin Journal* 10 (1991), pp. 240–59.

for the IUCN Red List (www.iucnredlist.org/). This Annex is mainly based on the IUCN listing,

Whales are mammals belonging to the order of cetacean. There are about 86 species of whales, dolphins and porpoises. The cetaceans are divided into three major groups: the *Odontoceti* or toothed whales; the *Mysticeti* or baleen (moustache whales); and the *Archeoceti* or ancient whales, which are extinct. The 1946 Whaling Convention does not define the term 'whale'. However, a list of names in a number of languages was annexed to the Final Act of the Convention. Consequently, the jurisdiction of the IWC over the various types of whales is a matter of much controversy and the subject of dispute between various parties. (This is examined in Chapters 3, 6 and 8.)

2.   Species of whales

2.1   *Right whales* (Eubalena spp.)

Right whales[3] acquired their name due to being deemed the 'right' type of whale to hunt.[4] They are listed by the IUCN as 'endangered'. They swim slowly and close to shore, float at the surface when harpooned, and contain large amounts of oil. Consequently, the right whale was unsustainably hunted by commercial whalers and this resulted in the depletion of their stocks.[5] The IWC, as had been the case with its predecessors under the 1931 Geneva Convention and 1937 London Agreement on Whaling, protects the right whale from hunting, as does Canada, which is a not a member of the IWC.[6] Article 4 of the 1931 Convention stated as follows: 'The taking or killing of the Right whales, which shall be deemed to include North Cape whales, Greenland whales, southern Right whales, Pacific Right whales and southern pygmy Right whales, is prohibited.'

In 1972, the IWC imposed a ban on the hunting of right whales, and it recommended for this to be indefinite, which was finally reaffirmed in

---

[3] On right whale taxonomy, see IUCN, www.iucnredlist.org/details/41712/0, last accessed 26 April 2015.

[4] Tønnessen and Johnsen stated that the term 'right whale' has a double meaning, referring both to the family and to the species. See J. N. Tønnessen and A. O. Johnsen, *The History of Modern Whaling*, trans. R. I. Christophersen (Canberra: Australian National University Press, 1982), p. 6.

[5] Kieran Mulvaney, 'Saving Right Whales? There's an App for That', http://news.discovery. com/earth/saving-right-whales-theres-an-app-for-that-120412.html, last accessed 27 December 2014.

[6] Ibid.

1978.[7] Both the USA and Canada strive to decrease right whale deaths and injuries due to ship strikes and entanglements. Both countries developed recovery plans securing collaboration among the various stakeholders.

2.1.1   Southern right whales (protected since the mid 1930s apart from some illegal whaling) (*Eubalaena australis*)

These stocks[8] were severely depleted by pre-twentieth-century whaling; there may once have been around 150,000. The breeding populations of Argentina, Brazil, South Africa and Australia have shown evidence of strong recovery, with annual rates of increase of 7–8 per cent, and together may now total over 16,000, assuming those increase rates to have continued since the 1990s. Other populations (for example, off the west coast of South America) have not shown similar signs of increase and remain small; it is estimated that there are only about 3,000–7,000 southern right whales (down from 60,000).[9] (Listed by the IUCN as 'least concern'.)

2.1.2   North Atlantic right whales (protected since the early 1930s)

The North Atlantic right whale[10] was severely depleted by pre-twentieth-century whaling and (similarly to North Pacific right whales) has shown little sign of recovery. It is one of the most endangered species of large whale. In the eastern North Atlantic sightings are extremely rare. In the western North Atlantic, the population numbers around 300–350, with little sign of significant increase.[11] The majority of right whales of the North Atlantic live at least part of the year in the waters off the north-eastern United States. In these waters there is a substantial degree of fishing and shipping activity which has resulted in the fact that nearly three-quarters of known right whales bear scars from past entanglements in fishing gear, and about 29 per cent of documented post-1970 right whale deaths have been caused by collisions with ships.[12] Based on scarring from fishing gear, it is estimated that at least 72 per cent of the right whale population has been involved in an entanglement event at

---

[7] IWC 24th Report (1974), 28, and IWC 30th Report (1980).

[8] On southern right whale taxonomy, see IUCN, www.iucnredlist.org/details/8153/0, last accessed 26 April 2015.

[9] On right whale taxonomy, see IUCN, www.iucnredlist.org/details/8153/0, last accessed 26 April 2015.

[10] On the North Atlantic right whale taxonomy, see IUCN, www.iucnredlist.org/details/41712/0, last accessed 26 April 2015.

[11] http://iwc.int/status, last accessed 25 December 2014.   [12] Ibid.

some point in their lives, and that between 10 and 20 per cent of the population is entangled each year.[13] The low reproduction rate in the North Atlantic in past years has been thought to be due to genetic factors, poor nutrition, chemical contaminants, bio-toxins and disease. Recently, however, reproduction has increased.[14] (Listed by the IUCN as 'endangered'.)

2.1.3 North Pacific right whales (protected since the early 1930s apart from some illegal whaling) (*Eubalaena japonica*)

The North Pacific right whale[15] was severely depleted by pre-twentieth-century whaling and has shown little sign of recovery. The assessment based on the lower end of the range of the available abundance estimates, which are approximately 400 for the Okhotsk Sea and approximately 100 for the rest of the North Pacific, implies a total of approximately 500, of which about half may be mature.[16] It is one of the most endangered species of large whale. The USA regulations, approved by the International Maritime Organization (IMO), aimed at protecting right whales chiefly relate to modifications to fishing gear and to restrictions on certain types of gear in areas where, and times when, right whales are common. However, as the International Union for Conservation of Nature (IUCN) has observed, there is as yet no indication of a decrease in the rate of human-caused mortality, due to the lack of clarity whether the measures taken to date are sufficient.[17] (Listed by the IUCN as 'endangered'.)

2.1.4 Bowhead whales (*Baleana mysticetus*) (protected since the early 1930s apart from limited subsistence whaling)

The bowhead[18] is one of the categories of right whales. The species is listed by IUCN to be of 'least concern'. There are five traditionally

---

[13] IUCN, above n. 3. See also Randall R. Reeves et al., *Dolphins, Whales, and Porpoises: 2002–2010 Conservation Action Plan for the World's Cetaceans* (IUCN/SSC Cetacean Specialist Group, 2003), pp. 33–4. Gillespie, above n. 1, p. 19.

[14] http://iwc.int/status, last accessed 25 December 2014.

[15] On North Pacific right whale taxonomy, see IUCN, www.iucnredlist.org/details/41711/0, last accessed 26 April 2015.

[16] Gillespie, above n. 1, p. 19.   [17] IUCN, above n. 3.

[18] On the taxonomy of bowheads, see IUCN, www.iucnredlist.org/details/2467/0, last accessed 26 April 2015. All bowhead subpopulations were severely depleted by commercial whaling, which had begun in the north-eastern Atlantic by 1611. Basque whalers took bowheads in the north-west Atlantic (Labrador in Canada) in the sixteenth century, but ambiguities over the species identity of whales taken in early commercial whaling make pre-1600 catch records difficult to interpret. IUCN, www.iucnredlist.org/details/2467/0, last accessed 26 April 2015.

recognised geographical IWC stocks (see below), of which two (Okhotsk Sea and Svalbard–Barents Sea (Spitsbergen)) have separate Red List assessments as subpopulations, on a scale from 'least concern' to 'critically endangered'.[19] The range-wide abundance is not known with precision but numbers over 10,000 individuals, with 10,050 (8,200–13,500) (in 2001) in the Bering–Chukchi–Beaufort Seas, and provisional estimates of 3,633 (1,382–9,550) and 7,300 (3,100–16,900) for parts of the range of the Hudson Bay–Foxe Basin and Baffin Bay– Davis Strait stocks. There are no reliable abundance estimates for the small Okhotsk Sea and Svalbard–Barents Sea (Spitsbergen) stocks.[20]

Since the 1970s there has been concern that disturbance from oil and gas exploration and extraction activities in the Arctic region might affect bowhead whales. As with other right whales, there is also evidence of incidental mortality and serious injury caused by entanglement in fishing gear and ship strikes. Mention must be made as well of the possibility of threats from pollution and disturbance from tourist traffic. Yet another threat might result from climate change, namely, by the melting of ice sheets in the Arctic.[21]

2.2   Grey whales (Eschrichtius robustus) (protected since the 1930s apart from some subsistence whaling)

There are two populations of grey whales,[22] both of which were severely depleted by pre-twentieth-century whaling. Encouragingly, the eastern North Pacific population has now recovered to around its pre-exploitation level (about 20,000 animals). By contrast, the western North Pacific population probably numbers fewer than 130 animals and is critically endangered. Thus the grey whale as a species is in no danger of extinction, but its western population is at a very low level and is extremely vulnerable.[23] This type of whale is listed at the IUCN as being of 'least concern': the size of stocks is above the threshold for a threatened category, and the population has increased over the last three generations. However, the western subpopulation is listed separately as critically endangered due to its geographic and genetic

---

[19] Ibid.   [20] http://iwce.int/estimate#tabl, last accessed 27 December 2014.   [21] Ibid.
[22] On the taxonomy of grey whales, see IUCN, www.iucnredlist.org/details/8097/0, last accessed 26 April 2015.
[23] http://iwce.int/estimate#tabl, above n. 20.

isolation and the fact that there are probably fewer than 100 individuals.[24]

The most recent estimate of the eastern stock is 15,000–22,000 for 2001–2, which indicates some recent decrease in population, for which the reasons are not yet fully understood; environmental conditions might be a contributing factor.[25] The eastern Pacific subpopulation is very small and estimated to number about 100 individuals, of which 20–30 are mature females.[26] The IWC estimate for the eastern North Atlantic is around 26,300 individuals (approximate point estimate).[27]

2.3 Blue whales (including pygmy blue whales) (Aenoptera musculus) (protected worldwide since the 1960s)

Blue whales[28] in the Southern Hemisphere were reduced to only a few percent of their unexploited stock size (which may have been as many as 200,000) by industrial whaling in the Southern Ocean, primarily from the 1920s to the 1940s. The total population has been depleted by at least 70 per cent.

Blue whales in the North Atlantic were also exploited heavily. However, there is no available full assessment of the present status. The available evidence indicates that they are increasing, at least in the area of the central North Atlantic.[29]

---

[24] See the IUCN List of Threatened Species, above n. 3. Historically, the grey whale was once found in the North Atlantic. Sub-fossil remains have been found on the eastern seaboard of North America from Florida to New Jersey and on the coasts of the English Channel and the North and Baltic seas. There are historical accounts of living grey whales from Iceland in the early 1600s and possibly off New England (United States) in the early 1700s. Grey whales have been hunted since prehistoric times, due to their characteristics. Due to unclear causes, the North Atlantic population was extinct by the early 1700s. Over-exploitation was thought to have caused the extinction of the western grey whale in the Soviet Union. The eastern North Pacific subpopulation has now recovered to at or near carrying capacity, its abundance showing some fluctuation in response to environmental conditions. www.iucnredlist.org/details/8097/0, last accessed 26 April 2015. The eastern North Pacific subpopulation is subject to human-caused threats such as entanglements in fishing gear, disturbance by vessels and other noise, collisions, and possibly petroleum-related and other contaminants.

[25] IUCN, above n. 25.   [26] Ibid.

[27] http://iwc.int/status, last accessed 27 December 2014.

[28] On the taxonomy of blue whales, see IUCN, www.iucnredlist.org/details/2477/0, last accessed 26 April 2015.

[29] www.iucnredlist.org/details/2477/0, last accessed 27 April 2015.

Blue whales in the North Pacific were also subject to heavy exploitation. There is insufficient data available to comment on the present
status in most parts of the North Pacific, although there is evidence of an
increase rate of about 3 per cent for the Gulf of California.[30] Blue whales
have been classified as a 'critically endangered' species on the IUCN Red
List, as the population is less than 3 per cent of its level of three
generations ago (at least a 97 per cent decline) (1914–2007).[31]

*2.4   Humpback whales (*Megaptera novaengliae*) (protected worldwide
since the 1960s, although a few individuals are allowed to be caught by
subsistence whalers)*

Humpback whales in the Southern Hemisphere were subject to heavy
exploitation by commercial whaling primarily from the 1920s to the
1950s in both their Southern Ocean feeding grounds and their tropical
breeding grounds. In most areas for which good data is available, humpback whales have shown evidence of strong recovery towards their
unexploited size (which may have been 75,000–100,000 in total). No
specific data is available of the present or past abundance of humpback
whales in the eastern North Atlantic, but numbers are considerably less
than in the western North Atlantic. Humpback whales in the North
Pacific were also heavily exploited and again have shown positive
increase rates in most areas for which there is data.

Humpback whales are listed on the IUCN Red List as being of 'least
concern'.[32] Despite having been severely depleted to a world population in
the low thousands, humpbacks have since recovered strongly, to a world
population that is estimated at over 60,000 animals, and is now increasing.[33]

*2.5   Fin whales (*Balaenoptera physalus*) (protected in the Southern
Ocean and North Pacific since the 1970s and in the North Atlantic by the
Moratorium from 1986; some special permit and commercial whaling
under objection has occurred since)*

Fin whale populations[34] in the Southern Hemisphere were heavily
exploited by commercial whaling in the Southern Ocean (particularly
between the 1930s and the 1960s). (Listed as 'endangered' by the IUCN

---

[30] http://iwc.int/status, last accessed 31 December 2014.   [31] IUCN, above n. 28.
[32] http://iwc.int/status, above n. 30.   [33] Ibid.
[34] On the taxonomy of fin whales, see IUCN, www.iucnredlist.org/details/2478/0, last
accessed 26 April 2015.

(population declined by 70 per cent, 1929–2007).) There is insufficient data available for a full assessment of their present status. There is no evidence that they have recovered to anywhere near unexploited levels (which may have been around 200,000).[35] The existing estimates from the limited parts of the range covered are of the order of several thousand animals. Fin whale populations were exploited throughout the North Atlantic. Present total abundance in the North Atlantic is over 35,000 animals, although not all areas have been surveyed. Assessments of the population status in the central North Atlantic and off West Greenland have shown populations there to be in a healthy state. There is data regarding the status of fin whales in other parts of the North Atlantic. Fin whale populations were exploited throughout the North Pacific.[36] However, partial estimates for the eastern North Pacific reveal around 10,000 animals, with some evidence of annual increase rates of 4–5 per cent.[37] The Mediterranean has probably fewer than 10,000 individuals. No reliable estimates are available for the regions of the Gulf of California and the East China Sea.[38]

2.6   Sperm whales (Physeter macrocephalus)

This type of whale is listed on the IUCN Red List of Endangered Species as 'vulnerable'. The pre-whaling population was estimated at about 1,100,000. It has been reduced due to modern whaling. Despite the ban on sperm whale hunting, their population is threatened by entanglement in fishing gear, particularly gill nets, especially in the Mediterranean Sea.[39] According to Gillespie, an independent global estimate of the number of sperm whales in 2002 was closer to 360,000.[40]

2.7   Sei whales (Balaenoptera borealis) (protected since the mid-1970s apart from in the central North Atlantic where protection came with the Moratorium in 1986; some special permit catches occur)

Sei whale populations[41] in the Southern Ocean were heavily exploited by industrial whaling after the decline in numbers of blue and fin

---

[35] www.iucnredlist.org/details/2478/0, last accessed 26 April 2015.
[36] http://iwc.int/status, above n. 30.
[37] http://iwc.int/status, last accessed 27 December 2014.
[38] www.iucnredlist.org/details/2478/0, last accessed 26 April 2015.   [39] Ibid.
[40] Gillespie, above n. 1, p. 28.
[41] On the taxonomy of sei whales, see IUCN, www.iucnredlist.org/details/2475/1, last accessed 26 April 2015.

whales, primarily from the mid-1960s to the early 1970s. IUCN lists them as 'endangered'. There is insufficient data available to undertake an assessment of their status in the Southern Ocean. Sei whale populations in the North Atlantic were exploited by commercial whaling up until the 1970s. There is insufficient data to undertake an assessment of their present status. Surveys reveal little sign of recovery of sei whales in the north-eastern Atlantic. Exploitation was much less severe in the central North Atlantic. Sei whales were heavily exploited off Canada up until the 1970s but no recent abundance estimates are available. Sei whale populations in the North Pacific were heavily exploited by commercial whaling. There is insufficient data to undertake an assessment of their present status. The only recent abundance estimate (around 7,700 animals in 2006–7) is from a part of their range in the western North Pacific.[42]

2.8   Bryde's whale (Balaenoptera edeni) (protected since the Moratorium apart from some special permit catches in the North Pacific)

Bryde's whales[43] are generally found between around 40°N and 40°S. They have been subject to a shorter and less intensive history of commercial whaling compared to the other baleen whales; and primarily for this reason neither the species itself nor any population is considered endangered. The only region for which sufficient data exists to undertake an assessment is the western North Pacific; the most recent (partial) abundance estimate is around 20,500 for the year 2000. The only other reliable estimate of abundance (around 13,000 in the late 1980s) is for the eastern tropical Pacific.[44] The entry for Bryde's whales on the IUCN Red List refers to this type of whale as being 'data deficient'. There has been difficulty in distinguishing between Bryde's whales and sei whales. In 1970, the IWC Scientific Committee made a distinction between both stocks, but only after the recognition of the sei whale as a protected stock was the Bryde's whale given precise quotas.

[42] http://iwc.int/estimate, last accessed 27 December 2014.
[43] On the taxonomy of Bryde's whales, see IUCN, www.iucnredlist.org/details/2476/0, last accessed 26 April 2015.
[44] http://iwc.int/status, last accessed 27 December 2014.

*2.9   Antarctic Minke whales (*Balaenoptera bonaerensis, *protected
       since the Moratorium apart from special permit catches)*

Minke whales[45] are listed on the IUCN List as being data deficient, owing
to the uncertainties relating to their apparent decline.[46] Despite the lack
of reliable data, the population size is estimated to be in the hundreds of
thousands.[47]

Commercial exploitation of Antarctic minke whales (the smallest of
the large whales)[48] began in the early 1970s, much later than the other
large whale species. However, there has been an appreciable decline
in their estimated abundance between the multi-year circumpolar
surveys.[49]

It is estimated that the North Atlantic minke whale stock has been
reduced in population by 45 to 70 per cent of its pre-exploitation
abundance.[50] Following several discrepancies in the estimates of minke
stocks for the North East Atlantic, in 1977 the IWC stated that there were
no valid estimates for the size of minke whale stocks.[51]

2.9.1   Common minke whales (protected since the
Moratorium apart from commercial catches under objection
and subsistence catches in the North Atlantic and
special permit catches in the North Pacific
(*balaenoptera acutorostrata*))

Apart from the dwarf sub-species, common minke whales[52] are only
found in the Northern Hemisphere. Their status on the IUCN Red List is
of the 'least concern', as their stocks are well above the thresholds for a
threatened category.

---

[45] On the taxonomy of minke whales, see IUCN, www.iucnredlist.org/details/2474/0, last
accessed 26 April 2015.
[46] http://iwc.int/status, last accessed 31 December 2014.   [47] Ibid.
[48] On the taxonomy of Antarctic minke whales, see IUCN, www.iucnredlist.org/details/
2480/0, last accessed 27 April 2015.
[49] http://iwc.int/status, last accessed 27 December 2014.   [50] IWC 43rd Report (1993).
[51] Appendix 6, IWC Resolution 1995–6, 'Resolution on Northeastern Atlantic Minke
Whales', IWC 46th Report (1996), 44.
[52] On the taxonomy of common minke whales, see IUCN, www.iucnredlist.org/details/
2474/0, last accessed 27 April 2015.

Appendix B

1946 International Convention for the Regulation of Whaling

Adopted in Washington, USA on 2 December 1946
(http://iwcoffice.org/commission/convention.htm)

The Governments whose duly authorised representatives have subscribed hereto,

Recognizing the interest of the nations of the world in safeguarding for future generations the great natural resources represented by the whale stocks;

Considering that the history of whaling has seen over-fishing of one area after another and of one species of whale after another to such a degree that it is essential to protect all species of whales from further over-fishing;

Recognizing that the whale stocks are susceptible of natural increases if whaling is properly regulated, and that increases in the size of whale stocks will permit increases in the number of whales which may be captured without endangering these natural resources;

Recognizing that it is in the common interest to achieve the optimum level of whale stocks as rapidly as possible without causing widespread economic and nutritional distress;

Recognizing that in the course of achieving these objectives, whaling operations should be confined to those species best able to sustain exploitation in order to give an interval for recovery to certain species of whales now depleted in numbers;

Desiring to establish a system of international regulation for the whale fisheries to ensure proper and effective conservation and development of whale stocks on the basis of the principles embodied in the provisions of the International Agreement for the Regulation of Whaling, signed in London on 8th June, 1937, and the protocols to that Agreement signed in London on 24th June, 1938, and 26th November, 1945; and

Having decided to conclude a convention to provide for the proper conservation of whale stocks and thus make possible the orderly development of the whaling industry;

Have agreed as follows:

Article I

1. This Convention includes the Schedule attached thereto which forms an integral part thereof. All references to 'Convention' shall be understood as including the said Schedule either in its present terms or as amended in accordance with the provisions of Article V.
2. This Convention applies to factory ships, land stations, and whale catchers under the jurisdiction of the Contracting Governments and to all waters in which whaling is prosecuted by such factory ships, land stations, and whale catchers.

Article II

As used in this Convention:

1. 'Factory ship' means a ship in which or on which whales are treated either wholly or in part;
2. 'Land station' means a factory on the land at which whales are treated whether wholly or in part;
3. 'Whale catcher' means a ship used for the purpose of hunting, taking, towing, holding on to, or scouting for whales;
4. 'Contracting Government' means any Government which has deposited an instrument of ratification or has given notice of adherence to this Convention.

Article III

1. The Contracting Governments agree to establish an International Whaling Commission, hereinafter referred to as the Commission, to be composed of one member from each Contracting Government. Each member shall have one vote and may be accompanied by one or more experts and advisers.
2. The Commission shall elect from its own members a Chairman and Vice-Chairman and shall determine its own Rules of Procedure. Decisions of the Commission shall be taken by a simple majority of

those members voting except that a three-fourths majority of those members voting shall be required for action in pursuance of Article V. The Rules of Procedure may provide for decisions otherwise than at meetings of the Commission.

3. The Commission may appoint its own Secretary and staff.
4. The Commission may set up, from among its own members and experts or advisers, such committees as it considers desirable to perform such functions as it may authorize.
5. The expenses of each member of the Commission and of his experts and advisers shall be determined and paid by his own Government.
6. Recognizing that specialized agencies related to the United Nations will be concerned with the conservation and development of whale fisheries and the products arising therefrom and desiring to avoid duplication of functions, the Contracting Governments will consult among themselves within two years after the coming into force of this Convention to decide whether the Commission shall be brought within the framework of a specialized agency related to the United Nations.
7. In the meantime the Government of the United Kingdom of Great Britain and Northern Ireland shall arrange, in consultation with the other Contracting Governments, to convene the first meeting of the Commission, and shall initiate the consultation referred to in paragraph 6 above.
8. Subsequent meetings of the Commission shall be convened as the Commission may determine.

Article IV

1. The Commission may either in collaboration with or through independent agencies of the Contracting Governments or other public or private agencies, establishments, or organizations, or independently
   (a) encourage, recommend, or if necessary, organize studies and investigations relating to whales and whaling;
   (b) collect and analyse statistical information concerning the current condition and trend of the whale stocks and the effects of whaling activities thereon;
   (c) study, appraise, and disseminate information concerning methods of maintaining and increasing the populations of whale stocks.
2. The Commission shall arrange for the publication of reports of its activities, and it may publish independently or in collaboration with

the International Bureau for Whaling Statistics at Sandefjord in Norway and other organizations and agencies such reports as it deems appropriate, as well as statistical, scientific, and other pertinent information relating to whales and whaling.

Article V

1. The Commission may amend from time to time the provisions of the Schedule by adopting regulations with respect to the conservation and utilization of whale resources, fixing
   (a) protected and unprotected species;
   (b) open and closed seasons;
   (c) open and closed waters, including the designation of sanctuary areas;
   (d) size limits for each species;
   (e) time, methods, and intensity of whaling (including the maximum catch of whales to be taken in any one season);
   (f) types and specifications of gear and apparatus and appliances which may be used;
   (g) methods of measurement; and
   (h) catch returns and other statistical and biological records.
2. These amendments of the Schedule
   (a) shall be such as are necessary to carry out the objectives and purposes of this Convention and to provide for the conservation, development, and optimum utilization of the whale resources;
   (b) shall be based on scientific findings;
   (c) shall not involve restrictions on the number or nationality of factory ships or land stations, nor allocate specific quotas to any factory ship or land station or to any group of factory ships or land stations; and
   (d) shall take into consideration the interests of the consumers of whale products and the whaling industry.
3. Each of such amendments shall become effective with respect to the Contracting Governments ninety days following notification of the amendment by the Commission to each of the Contracting Governments, except that
   (a) if any Government presents to the Commission objection to any amendment prior to the expiration of this ninety-day period, the amendment shall not become effective with respect to any of the Governments for an additional ninety days;

(b) thereupon, any other Contracting Government may present objection to the amendment at any time prior to the expiration of the additional ninety-day period, or before the expiration of thirty days from the date of receipt of the last objection received during such additional ninety-day period, whichever date shall be the later; and

(c) thereafter, the amendment shall become effective with respect to all Contracting Governments which have not presented objection but shall not become effective with respect to any Government which has so objected until such date as the objection is withdrawn. The Commission shall notify each Contracting Government immediately upon receipt of each objection and withdrawal and each Contracting Government shall acknowledge receipt of all notifications of amendments, objections, and withdrawals.

4. No amendments shall become effective before 1st July, 1949.

Article VI

The Commission may from time to time make recommendations to any or all Contracting Governments on any matters which relate to whales or whaling and to the objectives and purposes of this Convention.

Article VII

The Contracting Government shall ensure prompt transmission to the International Bureau for Whaling Statistics at Sandefjord in Norway, or to such other body as the Commission may designate, of notifications and statistical and other information required by this Convention in such form and manner as may be prescribed by the Commission.

Article VIII

1. Notwithstanding anything contained in this Convention any Contracting Government may grant to any of its nationals a special permit authorizing that national to kill, take and treat whales for purposes of scientific research subject to such restrictions as to number and subject to such other conditions as the Contracting Government thinks fit, and the killing, taking, and treating of whales in accordance

with the provisions of this Article shall be exempt from the operation of this Convention. Each Contracting Government shall report at once to the Commission all such authorizations which it has granted. Each Contracting Government may at any time revoke any such special permit which it has granted.

2. Any whales taken under these special permits shall so far as practicable be processed and the proceeds shall be dealt with in accordance with directions issued by the Government by which the permit was granted.

3. Each Contracting Government shall transmit to such body as may be designated by the Commission, in so far as practicable, and at intervals of not more than one year, scientific information available to that Government with respect to whales and whaling, including the results of research conducted pursuant to paragraph 1 of this Article and to Article IV.

4. Recognizing that continuous collection and analysis of biological data in connection with the operations of factory ships and land stations are indispensable to sound and constructive management of the whale fisheries, the Contracting Governments will take all practicable measures to obtain such data.

Article IX

1. Each Contracting Government shall take appropriate measures to ensure the application of the provisions of this Convention and the punishment of infractions against the said provisions in operations carried out by persons or by vessels under its jurisdiction.

2. No bonus or other remuneration calculated with relation to the results of their work shall be paid to the gunners and crews of whale catchers in respect of any whales the taking of which is forbidden by this Convention.

3. Prosecution for infractions against or contraventions of this Convention shall be instituted by the Government having jurisdiction over the offence.

4. Each Contracting Government shall transmit to the Commission full details of each infraction of the provisions of this Convention by persons or vessels under the jurisdiction of that Government as reported by its inspectors. This information shall include a statement of measures taken for dealing with the infraction and of penalties imposed.

Article X

1. This Convention shall be ratified and the instruments of ratifications shall be deposited with the Government of the United States of America.
2. Any Government which has not signed this Convention may adhere thereto after it enters into force by a notification in writing to the Government of the United States of America.
3. The Government of the United States of America shall inform all other signatory Governments and all adhering Governments of all ratifications deposited and adherences received.
4. This Convention shall, when instruments of ratification have been deposited by at least six signatory Governments, which shall include the Governments of the Netherlands, Norway, the Union of Soviet Socialist Republics, the United Kingdom of Great Britain and Northern Ireland, and the United States of America, enter into force with respect to those Governments and shall enter into force with respect to each Government which subsequently ratifies or adheres on the date of the deposit of its instrument of ratification or the receipt of its notification of adherence.
5. The provisions of the Schedule shall not apply prior to 1st July, 1948. Amendments to the Schedule adopted pursuant to Article V shall not apply prior to 1st July, 1949.

Article XI

Any Contracting Government may withdraw from this Convention on 30th June, of any year by giving notice on or before 1st January, of the same year to the depository Government, which upon receipt of such a notice shall at once communicate it to the other Contracting Governments. Any other Contracting Government may, in like manner, within one month of the receipt of a copy of such a notice from the depository Government give notice of withdrawal, so that the Convention shall cease to be in force on 30th June, of the same year with respect to the Government giving such notice of withdrawal.

The Convention shall bear the date on which it is opened for signature and shall remain open for signature for a period of fourteen days thereafter.

In witness whereof the undersigned, being duly authorized, have signed this Convention.

Done in Washington this second day of December, 1946, in the English language, the original of which shall be deposited in the archives of the Government of the United States of America. The Government of the United States of America shall transmit certified copies thereof to all the other signatory and adhering Governments.

Protocol to the International Convention for the Regulation of Whaling, signed at Washington under date of 2 December 1946

Adopted in Washington, USA on 19 November 1956
(http://iwcoffice.org/commission/convention.htm)

The Contracting Governments to the International Convention for the Regulation of Whaling signed at Washington under date of 2nd December, 1946 which Convention is hereinafter referred to as the 1946 Whaling Convention, desiring to extend the application of that Convention to helicopters and other aircraft and to include provisions on methods of inspection among those Schedule provisions which may be amended by the Commission, agree as follows:

Article I

Subparagraph 3 of the Article II of the 1946 Whaling Convention shall be amended to read as follows: '3. "whale catcher" means a helicopter, or other aircraft, or a ship, used for the purpose of hunting, taking, killing, towing, holding on to, or scouting for whales.'

Article II

Paragraph 1 of Article V of the 1946 Whaling Convention shall be amended by deleting the word 'and' preceding clause (h), substituting a semicolon for the period at the end of the paragraph, and adding the following language: 'and (i) methods of inspection'.

Article III

1. This Protocol shall be open for signature and ratification or for adherence on behalf of any Contracting Government to the 1946 Whaling Convention.
2. This Protocol shall enter into force on the date upon which instruments of ratification have been deposited with, or written notifications of adherence have been received by, the Government of the United

States of America on behalf of all the Contracting Governments to the 1946 Whaling Convention.

3. The Government of the United States of America shall inform all Governments signatory or adhering to the 1946 Whaling Convention of all ratifications deposited and adherences received.

4. This Protocol shall bear the date on which it is opened for signature and shall remain open for signature for a period of fourteen days thereafter, following which period it shall be open for adherence.

IN WITNESS WHEREOF the undersigned, being duly authorized, have signed this Protocol.

DONE in Washington this nineteenth day of November, 1956, in the English Language, the original of which shall be deposited in the archives of the Government of the United States of America. The Government of the United States of America shall transmit certified copies thereof to all Governments signatory or adhering to the 1946 Whaling Convention.

Schedule

Explanatory notes

The Schedule printed on the following pages contains the amendments made by the Commission at its 61st Annual Meeting in June 2009. The amendments, which are shown in *italic bold* type, came into effect on 2 January 2010.

In Tables 1, 2 and 3 unclassified stocks are indicated by a dash. Other positions in the Tables have been filled with a dot to aid legibility.

Numbered footnotes are integral parts of the Schedule formally adopted by the Commission. Other footnotes are editorial.

The Commission was informed in June 1992 by the ambassador in London that the membership of the Union of Soviet Socialist Republics in the International Convention for the Regulation of Whaling from 1948 is continued by the Russian Federation.

The Commission recorded at its 39th (1987) meeting the fact that references to names of native inhabitants in Schedule paragraph 13(*b*)(4) would be for geographical purposes alone, so as not to be in contravention of Article V.2(c) of the Convention (*Rep. int. Whal. Commn* 38:21).

I. Interpretation

1. The following expressions have the meanings respectively assigned to them, that is to say:

Table 1 *Baleen whale stock classifications and catch limits*[+] *(excluding Bryde's whales)*

	Sei		Minke		Fin		Blue		Right, Bowhead, Humpback		Pygmy Right		Grey	
	Classi-fication	Catch limit	Classi-fication	Catch limit	Classi-fication	Catch limit	Classi-fication	Catch limit	Classi-fication	Catch limit	Classi-fication	Catch limit	Classi-fication	Catch limit
Southern Hemisphere – 2009/2010 pelagic season and 2010 coastal season ▲														
Area														
I 120°W–60°W	PS	0	–	0	PS	0	PS	0	PS	0	•	0	•	•
II 60°W–0°	PS	0	–	0	PS	0	PS	0	PS	0	•	0	•	•
III 0°–70°E	PS	0	–	0	PS	0	PS	0	PS	0	•	0	•	•
IV 70°E–130°E	PS	0	–	0	PS	0	PS	0	PS	0	•	0	•	•
V 130°E–170°E	PS	0	–	0	PS	0	PS	0	PS	0	•	0	•	•
VI 170°W–120°W	PS	0	–	0	PS	0	PS	0	PS	0	•	0	•	•
Total catch not to exceed:		0				0		0		0		0		
Northern Hemisphere – 2010 season ▲														
ARCTIC	•	•	•	•	•	•	•	•	PS	•	•	0	•	•
NORTH PACIFIC														
Whole region	PS	0	•	•	PS	0	PS	0	PS	0	•	0	•	•
Okhotsk Sea–West Pacific Stock	•	•	–	0	•	•	•	•	PS	•	•	•	•	•
Sea of Japan–Yellow Sea–East China Sea Stock	•	•	PS	0	•	•	•	•	•	•	•	•	•	•
Remainder	•	•	IMS	0	•	•	•	•	•	•	•	•	•	•
Eastern Stock	•	•	•	•	•	•	•	•	•	•	•	•	SMS	[1]
Western Stock	•	•	•	•	•	•	•	•	•	•	•	•	PS	0
NORTH ATLANTIC														
Whole region	•	•	PS	•	PS	•	PS	•	PS	•	•	•	•	•
West Greenland Stock	PS	0	–	0	PS	19[2]	PS	0	PS	0	•	•	•	•
Newfoundland–Labrador Stock	•	•	–	•	–	0	•	•	•	•	•	•	•	•
Canadian East Coast Stock	•	•	–	0	•	•	•	•	•	•	•	•	•	•

Table 1 (*cont.*)

Stock	Sei Classification	Sei Catch limit	Minke Classification	Minke Catch limit	Fin Classification	Fin Catch limit	Blue Classification	Blue Catch limit	Right, Bowhead, Humpback Classification	Right, Bowhead, Humpback Catch limit	Pygmy Right Classification	Pygmy Right Catch limit	Grey Classification	Grey Catch limit
Nova Scotia Stock	PS	0	•	•	PS	0	•	•	•	•	•	•	•	•
Central Stock	•	•	–	•	•	•	•	•	•	•	•	•	•	•
East Greenland–Iceland Stock	•	0	SMS	•	•	0	•	•	•	•	•	•	•	•
Iceland–Denmark Strait Stock	–	•	•	•	•	•	•	•	•	•	•	•	•	•
Spain–Portugal–British Isles Stock	•	•	–	0	–	0	•	•	•	•	•	•	•	•
Northeastern Stock	•	•	PS*	0	•	•	•	•	•	•	•	•	•	•
West Norway–Faroe Islands Stock	•	•	PS	•	PS	0	•	•	•	•	•	•	•	•
North Norway Stock	•	•	–	0	–	0	•	•	•	•	•	•	•	•
Eastern Stock	-	0	•	•	•	•	•	•	•	•	•	0	•	•
NORTHERN INDIAN OCEAN	•	•	IMS	0	PS	•	PS	0	PS	0	•	0	•	•

[1] Available to be taken by aborigines or a Contracting Government on behalf of aborigines pursuant to paragraph 13(b)2.

[2] Available to be struck by aborigines pursuant to paragraph 13(b)3. Catch limit for each of the years 2008, 2009, 2010, 2011 and 2012.

+The catch limits of zero introduced into Table 1 as editorial amendments as a result of the coming into effect of paragraph 10(e) are not binding upon the governments of the countries which lodged and have not withdrawn objections to the said paragraph.

*The Government of Norway presented objection to the classification of the Northeastern Atlantic stock of minke whales as a Protection Stock within the prescribed period. This classification came into force on 30 January 1986 but is not binding on the Government of Norway.

▲ *The Government of the Czech Republic lodged an objection within the prescribed period to the amendments to the Schedule arising from the 61st Annual Meeting of the Commission, i.e. changes to the dates of the pelagic and coastal whaling seasons given in paragraphs 11 and 12 and Tables 1, 2 and 3. For all other Contracting Governments, these dates came into force on 2 January 2010. The Czech Republic lodged a similar objection to Schedule amendments arising from the 60th Annual Meeting of the Commission. This objection has not been withdrawn.*

Table 2 *Bryde's whale stock classifications and catch limits.*[+]

	Classification	Catch limit
Southern Hemisphere–*2009/2010* pelagic season and *2010* coastal season▲		
South Atlantic Stock	–	0
Southern Indian Ocean Stock	IMS	0
South African Inshore Stock	–	0
Solomon Islands Stock	IMS	0
Western South Pacific Stock	IMS	0
Eastern South Pacific Stock	IMS	0
Peruvian Stock	–	0
NORTH PACIFIC–*2010* season▲		
Eastern Stock	IMS	0
Western Stock	IMS	0
East China Sea Stock	PS	0
NORTH ATLANTIC–*2010* season▲	IMS	0
NORTHERN INDIAN OCEAN–*2010* season▲	–	0

[+]The catch limits of zero introduced in Table 2 as editorial amendments as a result of the coming into effect of paragraph 10*(e)* are not binding upon the governments of the countries which lodged and have not withdrawn objections to the said paragraph.
▲ *See footnote to Table 1.*

A.   Baleen whales

'baleen whale' means any whale which has baleen or whale bone in the mouth, i.e. any whale other than a toothed whale.

'blue whale' (*Balaenoptera musculus*) means any whale known as blue whale, Sibbald's rorqual, or sulphur bottom, and including pygmy blue whale.

'bowhead whale' (*Balaena mysticetus*) means any whale known as bowhead, Arctic right whale, great polar whale, Greenland right whale, Greenland whale.

'Bryde's whale' (*Balaenoptera edeni, B. brydei*) means any whale known as Bryde's whale.

'fin whale' (*Balaenoptera physalus*) means any whale known as common finback, common rorqual, fin whale, herring whale, or true fin whale.

'grey whale' (*Eschrichtius robustus*) means any whale known as grey whale, California grey, devil fish, hard head, mussel digger, grey back, or rip sack.

Table 3 *Toothed whale stock classifications and catch limits.*[+]

SOUTHERN HEMISPHERE – *2009/2010* pelagic season and *2010* coastal season[▲]

Division	Longitudes	SPERM Classification	Catch limit
1	60°W–30°W	–	0
2	30°W–20°E	–	0
3	20°E–60°E	–	0
4	60°E–90°E	–	0
5	90°E–130°E	–	0
6	130°E–160°E	–	0
7	160°E–170°W	–	0
8	170°W–100°W	–	0
9	100°W–60°W	–	0
NORTHERN HEMISPHERE– *2010* season[▲]			
NORTH PACIFIC			
Western Division		PS	0[1]
Eastern Division		–	0
NORTH ATLANTIC		–	0
NORTHERN INDIAN OCEAN		–	0
		BOTTLENOSE	
NORTH ATLANTIC		PS	0

[1]No whales may be taken from this stock until catch limits including any limitations on size and sex are established by the Commission.

[+]The catch limits of zero introduced in Table 3 as editorial amendments as a result of the coming into effect of paragraph 10*(e)* are not binding upon the governments of the countries which lodged and have not withdrawn objections to the said paragraph.

[▲]*See footnote to Table 1.*

'humpback whale' (*Megaptera novaeangliae*) means any whale known as
    bunch, humpback, humpback whale, humpbacked whale, hump whale
    or hunchbacked whale.
'minke whale' (*Balaenoptera acutorostrata, B. bonaerensis*) means any
    whale known as lesser rorqual, little piked whale, minke whale, pike-
    headed whale or sharp headed finner.
'pygmy right whale' (*Caperea marginata*) means any whale known as
    southern pygmy right whale or pygmy right whale.

'right whale' (*Eubalaena glacialis, E. australis*) means any whale known as Atlantic right whale, Arctic right whale, Biscayan right whale, Nordkaper, North Atlantic right whale, North Cape whale, Pacific right whale, or southern right whale.

'sei whale' (*Balaenoptera borealis*) means any whale known as sei whale, Rudolphi's rorqual, pollack whale, or coalfish whale.

B.   Toothed whales

'toothed whale' means any whale which has teeth in the jaws.

'beaked whale' means any whale belonging to the genus Mesoplodon, or any whale known as Cuvier's beaked whale (*Ziphius cavirostris*), or Shepherd's beaked whale (*Tasmacetus shepherdi*).

'bottlenose whale' means any whale known as Baird's beaked whale (*Berardius bairdii*), Arnoux's whale (*Berardius arnuxii*), southern bottlenose whale (*Hyperoodon planifrons*), or northern bottlenose whale (*Hyperoodon ampullatus*).

'killer whale' (*Orcinus orca*) means any whale known as killer whale or orca.

'pilot whale' means any whale known as long-finned pilot whale (*Globicephala melaena*) or short-finned pilot whale (*G. macrorhynchus*).

'sperm whale' (*Physeter macrocephalus*) means any whale known as sperm whale, spermacet whale, cachalot or pot whale.

C.   General

'strike' means to penetrate with a weapon used for whaling.

'land' means to retrieve to a factory ship, land station, or other place where a whale can be treated.

'take' means to flag, buoy or make fast to a whale catcher.

'lose' means to either strike or take but not to land.

'dauhval' means any unclaimed dead whale found floating.

'lactating whale' means (a) with respect to baleen whales – a female which has any milk present in a mammary gland, (b) with respect to sperm whales – a female which has milk present in a mammary gland the maximum thickness (depth) of which is 10cm or more. This measurement shall be at the mid ventral point of the mammary gland perpendicular to the body axis, and shall be logged to the nearest centimetre; that is to say, any gland between 9.5cm and 10.5cm shall be logged as 10cm. The measurement of any gland which falls on an exact 0.5 centimetre shall be logged at the next 0.5 centimetre, e.g. 10.5cm shall be logged as 11.0cm. However, notwithstanding these criteria, a whale shall not be considered a lactating whale if scientific (histological or other biological) evidence is presented to the appropriate national authority establishing that the whale could not at that point in its physical cycle have had a calf dependent on it for milk.

'small-type whaling' means catching operations using powered vessels with mounted harpoon guns hunting exclusively for minke, bottlenose, beaked, pilot or killer whales.

II. Seasons

Factory ship operations

2. (a) It is forbidden to use a factory ship or whale catcher attached thereto for the purpose of taking or treating baleen whales except minke whales, in any waters south of 40° South Latitude except during the period from 12th December to 7th April following, both days inclusive.

(b) It is forbidden to use a factory ship or whale catcher attached thereto for the purpose of taking or treating sperm or minke whales, except as permitted by the Contracting Governments in accordance with subparagraphs (c) and (d) of this paragraph, and paragraph 5.

(c) Each Contracting Government shall declare for all factory ships and whale catchers attached thereto under its jurisdiction, an open season or seasons not to exceed eight months out of any period of twelve months during which the taking or killing of sperm whales by whale catchers may be permitted; provided that a separate open season may be declared for each factory ship and the whale catchers attached thereto.

(d) Each Contracting Government shall declare for all factory ships and whale catchers attached thereto under its jurisdiction one continuous open season not to exceed six months out of any period of twelve months during which the taking or killing of minke whales by the whale catchers may be permitted provided that:

(1) a separate open season may be declared for each factory ship and the whale catchers attached thereto;

(2) the open season need not necessarily include the whole or any part of the period declared for other baleen whales pursuant to subparagraph (a) of this paragraph.

3. It is forbidden to use a factory ship which has been used during a season in any waters south of 40° South Latitude for the purpose of treating baleen whales, except minke whales, in any other area except the North Pacific Ocean and its dependent waters north of the Equator for the same purpose within a period of one year from the termination of that season; provided that catch limits in the North Pacific Ocean and dependent waters are established as provided in paragraphs 12 and 16 of this Schedule and provided that this paragraph shall not apply to a ship which has been used during the season solely for freezing or salting the meat and entrails of whales intended for human food or feeding animals.

Land station operations

4. (a) It is forbidden to use a whale catcher attached to a land station for the purpose of killing or attempting to kill baleen and sperm whales except as permitted by the Contracting Government in accordance with sub-paragraphs (b), (c) and (d) of this paragraph.

(b) Each Contracting Government shall declare for all land stations under its jurisdiction, and whale catchers attached to such land stations, one open season during which the taking or killing of baleen whales, except minke whales, by the whale catchers shall be permitted. Such open season shall be for a period of not more than six consecutive months in any period of twelve months and shall apply to all land stations under the jurisdiction of the Contracting Government: provided that a separate open season may be declared for any land station used for the taking or treating of baleen whales, except minke whales, which is more than 1,000 miles from the nearest land station used for the taking or treating of baleen whales, except minke whales, under the jurisdiction of the same Contracting Government.

(c) Each Contracting Government shall declare for all land stations under its jurisdiction and for whale catchers attached to such land stations, one open season not to exceed eight continuous months in any one period of twelve months, during which the taking or killing of sperm whales by the whale catchers shall be permitted, provided that a separate open season may be declared for any land station used for the taking or treating of sperm whales which is more than 1,000 miles from the nearest land station used for the taking or treating of sperm whales under the jurisdiction of the same Contracting Government.

(d) Each Contracting Government shall declare for all land stations under its jurisdiction and for whale catchers attached to such land stations one open season not to exceed six continuous months in any period of twelve months during which the taking or killing of minke whales by the whale catchers shall be permitted (such period not being necessarily concurrent with the period declared for other baleen whales, as provided for in sub-paragraph (b) of this paragraph); provided that a separate open season may be declared for any land station used for the taking or treating of minke whales which is more than 1,000 miles from the nearest land station used for the taking or treating of minke whales under the jurisdiction of the same Contracting Government. Except that a separate open season may be declared for any land station used for the taking or treating of minke whales which is located in an area having oceanographic conditions clearly distinguishable from those of the area in which are located the other land stations used for the taking or treating of minke whales under the jurisdiction of the same Contracting Government; but the declaration of a separate open season by virtue of the provisions of this sub-paragraph shall not cause thereby the period of time covering the open seasons declared by the same Contracting Government to exceed nine continuous months of any twelve months.

(e) The prohibitions contained in this paragraph shall apply to all land stations as defined in Article II of the Whaling Convention of 1946.

Other operations

5. Each Contracting Government shall declare for all whale catchers under its jurisdiction not operating in conjunction with a factory ship or land station one continuous open season not to exceed six months out of any period of twelve months during which the taking or killing of minke whales by such whale catchers may be permitted. Notwithstanding this paragraph one continuous open season not to exceed nine months may be implemented so far as Greenland is concerned.

III. Capture

6. The killing for commercial purposes of whales, except minke whales using the cold grenade harpoon shall be forbidden from the beginning of

the 1980/81 pelagic and 1981 coastal seasons. The killing for commercial purposes of minke whales using the cold grenade harpoon shall be forbidden from the beginning of the 1982/83 pelagic and the 1983 coastal seasons.*

7. (a) In accordance with Article V(1)(c) of the Convention, commercial whaling, whether by pelagic operations or from land stations, is prohibited in a region designated as the Indian Ocean Sanctuary. This comprises the waters of the Northern Hemisphere from the coast of Africa to 100°E, including the Red and Arabian Seas and the Gulf of Oman; and the waters of the Southern Hemisphere in the sector from 20°E to 130°E, with the Southern boundary set at 55°S. This prohibition applies irrespective of such catch limits for baleen or toothed whales as may from time to time be determined by the Commission. This prohibition shall be reviewed by the Commission at its Annual Meeting in 2002.☼

(b) In accordance with Article V(1)(c) of the Convention, commercial whaling, whether by pelagic operations or from land stations, is prohibited in a region designated as the Southern Ocean Sanctuary. This Sanctuary comprises the waters of the Southern Hemisphere southwards of the following line: starting from 40 degrees S, 50 degrees W; thence due east to 20 degrees E; thence due south to 55 degrees S; thence due east to 130 degrees E; thence due north to 40 degrees S; thence due east to 130 degrees W; thence due south to 60 degrees S; thence due east to 50 degrees W; thence due north to the point of beginning. This prohibition applies irrespective of the conservation status of baleen and toothed whale stocks in this Sanctuary, as may from time to time be determined by the Commission. However, this prohibition shall be reviewed ten years after its initial adoption and at succeeding ten year intervals, and could be revised at such times by the Commission.

---

* The Governments of Brazil, Iceland, Japan, Norway and the Union of Soviet Socialist Republics lodged objections to the second sentence of paragraph 6 within the prescribed period. For all other Contracting Governments this sentence came into force on 8 March 1982. Norway withdrew its objection on 9 July 1985 and Brazil on 8 January 1992. Iceland withdrew from the Convention with effect from 30 June 1992. The objections of Japan and the Russian Federation not having been withdrawn, this sentence is not binding upon these governments.

☼ At its 54th Annual Meeting in 2002, the Commission agreed to continue this prohibition but did not discuss whether or not it should set a time when it should be reviewed again.

Nothing in this sub-paragraph is intended to prejudice the special legal and political status of Antarctica.***+

Area limits for factory ships

8. It is forbidden to use a factory ship or whale catcher attached thereto, for the purpose of taking or treating baleen whales, except minke whales, in any of the following areas:

  (a) in the waters north of 66°N, except that from 150°E eastwards as far as 140°W, the taking or killing of baleen whales by a factory ship or whale catcher shall be permitted between 66°N and 72°N;
  (b) in the Atlantic Ocean and its dependent waters north of 40°S;
  (c) in the Pacific Ocean and its dependent waters east of 150°W between 40°S and 35°N;
  (d) in the Pacific Ocean and its dependent waters west of 150°W between 40°S and 20°N;
  (e) in the Indian Ocean and its dependent waters north of 40°S.

Classification of Areas and Divisions

9. (a) *Classification of Areas*
       Areas relating to Southern Hemisphere baleen whales except Bryde's whales are those waters between the ice-edge and the Equator and between the meridians of longitude listed in Table 1.
   (b) *Classification of Divisions*
       Divisions relating to Southern Hemisphere sperm whales are those waters between the ice-edge and the Equator and between the meridians of longitude listed in Table 3.
   (c) *Geographical boundaries in the North Atlantic*
       The geographical boundaries for the fin, minke and sei whale stocks in the North Atlantic are:

** The Government of Japan lodged an objection within the prescribed period to paragraph 7(b) to the extent that it applies to the Antarctic minke whale stocks. The Government of the Russian Federation also lodged an objection to paragraph 7(b) within the prescribed period but withdrew it on 26 October 1994. For all Contracting Governments except Japan paragraph 7(b) came into force on 6 December 1994.

+ Paragraph 7(b) contains a provision for review of the Southern Ocean Sanctuary 'ten years after its initial adoption'. Paragraph 7(b) was adopted at the 46th (1994) Annual Meeting. Therefore, the first review is due in 2004.

Fin whale stocks   Nova Scotia
South and West of a line through:
47°N 54°W, 46°N 54°30′W,
46°N 42°W, 20°N 42°W.

Newfoundland–Labrador
West of a line through:
75°N 73°30′W, 69°N 59°W, 61°N 59°W,
52°20′N 42°W, 46°N 42°W and
North of a line through:
46°N 42°W, 46°N 54°30′W, 47°N 54°W.

West Greenland
East of a line through:
75°N 73°30′W, 69°N 59°W,
61°N 59°W, 52°20′N 42°W,
and West of a line through
52°20′N 42°W, 59°N 42°W,
59°N 44°W, Kap Farvel.

East Greenland–Iceland
East of a line through:
Kap Farvel (South Greenland),
59°N 44°W, 59°N 42°W, 20°N 42°W,
and West of a line through:
20°N 18°W, 60°N 18°W, 68°N 3°E,
74°N 3°E, and South of 74°N.

North Norway
North and East of a line through:
74°N 22°W, 74°N 3°E, 68°N 3°E,
67°N 0°, 67°N 14°E.

West Norway–Faroe Islands
South of a line through:
67°N 14°E, 67°N 0°, 60°N 18°W,
and North of a line through:
61°N 16°W, 61°N 0°, Thyborøn
(Western entrance to Limfjorden, Denmark).

Spain-Portugal-British Isles
South of a line through:
Thyborøn (Denmark), 61°N 0°, 61°N 16°W,
and East of a line through:
63°N 11°W, 60°N 18°W, 22°N 18°W.

Minke whale stocks   Canadian East Coast
West of a line through:
75°N 73°30'W, 69°N 59°W, 61°N 59°W,
52°20'N 42°W, 20°N 42°W.

Central
East of a line through:
Kap Farvel (South Greenland),
59°N 44°W, 59°N 42°W, 20°N 42°W,
and West of a line through:
20°N 18°W, 60°N 18°W, 68°N 3°E,
74°N 3°E, and South of 74°N.

West Greenland
East of a line through:
75°N 73°30'W, 69°N 59°W, 61°N 59°W,
52°20'N 42°W, and
West of a line through:
52°20'N 42°W, 59°N 42°W,
59°N 44°W, Kap Farvel.

Northeastern
East of a line through:
20°N 18°W, 60°N 18°W, 68°N 3°E, 74°N 3°E,
and North of a line through:
74°N 3°E, 74°N 22°W.

Sei whale stocks   Nova Scotia
South and West of a line through:
47°N 54°W, 46°N 54°30'W, 46°N 42°W,
20°N 42°W.

Iceland-Denmark Strait
East of a line through:

Kap Farvel (South Greenland),
59°N 44°W, 59°N 42°W, 20°N 42°W,
and West of a line through:
20°N 18°W, 60°N 18°W, 68°N 3°E,
74°N 3°E, and South of 74°N.

Eastern
East of a line through:
20°N 18°W, 60°N 18°W, 68°N 3°E, 74°N 3°E,
and North of a line through:
74°N 3°E, 74°N 22°W

> (d) *Geographical boundaries in the North Pacific*
> The geographical boundaries for the sperm, Bryde's and minke whale stocks in the North Pacific are:

Sperm whale stocks   Western Division
West of a line from the ice-edge south along the 180° meridian of longitude to 180°, 50°N, then east along the 50°N parallel of latitude to 160°W, 50°N, then south along the 160°W meridian of longitude to 160°W, 40°N, then east along the 40°N parallel of latitude to 150°W, 40°N, then south along the 150°W meridian of longitude to the Equator.

Eastern Division
East of the line described above.

Bryde's whale stocks   East China Sea
West of the Ryukyu Island chain.

Eastern
East of 160°W (excluding the Peruvian stock area).

Western
West of 160°W (excluding the East China Sea stock area).

Minke whale stocks   Sea of Japan–Yellow Sea–East China Sea
West of a line through the Philippine Islands, Taiwan, Ryukyu Islands, Kyushu, Honshu, Hokkaido and Sakhalin Island, north of the Equator.

Okhotsk Sea–West Pacific
East of the Sea of Japan–Yellow Sea–East China Sea stock and west of
   180°, north of the Equator.

Remainder
East of the Okhotsk Sea–West Pacific stock, north of the Equator.
(e) *Geographical boundaries for Bryde's whale stocks in the Southern
   Hemisphere*

Southern Indian Ocean
20°E to 130°E,
South of the Equator.

Solomon Islands
150°E to 170°E,
20°S to the Equator.

Peruvian
110°W to the South American coast,
10°S to 10°N.

Eastern South Pacific
150°W to 70°W,
South of the Equator (excluding the Peruvian stock area).

Western South Pacific
130°E to 150°W,
South of the Equator (excluding the Solomon Islands stock area).

South Atlantic
70°W to 20°E,
South of the Equator (excluding the South African inshore stock area).

South African Inshore
South African coast west of 27°E and out to the 200 metre isobath.

Classification of stocks

   10. All stocks of whales shall be classified in one of three categories
according to the advice of the Scientific Committee as follows:

(a) A Sustained Management Stock (SMS) is a stock which is not more than 10 per cent of Maximum Sustainable Yield (hereinafter referred to as MSY) stock level below MSY stock level, and not more than 20 per cent above that level; MSY being determined on the basis of the number of whales.

When a stock has remained at a stable level for a considerable period under a regime of approximately constant catches, it shall be classified as a Sustained Management Stock in the absence of any positive evidence that it should be otherwise classified.

Commercial whaling shall be permitted on Sustained Management Stocks according to the advice of the Scientific Committee. These stocks are listed in Tables 1, 2 and 3 of this Schedule.

For stocks at or above the MSY stock level, the permitted catch shall not exceed 90 per cent of the MSY. For stocks between the MSY stock level and 10 per cent below that level, the permitted catch shall not exceed the number of whales obtained by taking 90 per cent of the MSY and reducing that number by 10 per cent for every 1 per cent by which the stock falls short of the MSY stock level.

(b) An Initial Management Stock (IMS) is a stock more than 20 per cent of MSY stock level above MSY stock level. Commercial whaling shall be permitted on Initial Management Stocks according to the advice of the Scientific Committee as to measures necessary to bring the stocks to the MSY stock level and then optimum level in an efficient manner and without risk of reducing them below this level. The permitted catch for such stocks will not be more than 90 per cent of MSY as far as this is known, or, where it will be more appropriate, catching effort shall be limited to that which will take 90 per cent of MSY in a stock at MSY stock level. In the absence of any positive evidence that a continuing higher percentage will not reduce the stock below the MSY stock level no more than 5 per cent of the estimated initial exploitable stock shall be taken in any one year. Exploitation should not commence until an estimate of stock size has been obtained which is satisfactory in the view of the Scientific Committee. Stocks classified as Initial Management Stock are listed in Tables 1, 2 and 3 of this Schedule.

(c) A Protection Stock (PS) is a stock which is below 10 per cent of MSY stock level below MSY stock level. There shall be no commercial whaling on Protection Stocks. Stocks so classified are listed in Tables 1, 2 and 3 of this Schedule.

(d) Notwithstanding the other provisions of paragraph 10 there shall be a moratorium on the taking, killing or treating of whales, except minke whales, by factory ships or whale catchers attached to factory ships. This moratorium applies to sperm whales, killer whales and baleen whales, except minke whales.

(e) Notwithstanding the other provisions of paragraph 10, catch limits for the killing for commercial purposes of whales from all stocks for the 1986 coastal and the 1985/86 pelagic seasons and thereafter shall be zero. This provision will be kept under review, based upon the best scientific advice, and by 1990 at the latest the Commission will undertake a comprehensive assessment of the effects of this decision on whale stocks and consider modification of this provision and the establishment of other catch limits.*•#

---

* The Governments of Japan, Norway, Peru and the Union of Soviet Socialist Republics lodged objection to paragraph 10(e) within the prescribed period. For all other Contracting Governments this paragraph came into force on 3 February 1983. Peru withdrew its objection on 22 July 1983. The Government of Japan withdrew its objections with effect from 1 May 1987 with respect to commercial pelagic whaling; from 1 October 1987 with respect to commercial coastal whaling for minke and Bryde's whales; and from 1 April 1988 with respect to commercial coastal sperm whaling. The objections of Norway and the Russian Federation not having been withdrawn, the paragraph is not binding upon these Governments.

• Iceland's instrument of adherence to the International Convention for the Regulation of Whaling and the Protocol to the Convention deposited on 10 October 2002 states that Iceland 'adheres to the aforesaid Convention and Protocol with a reservation with respect to paragraph 10(e) of the Schedule attached to the Convention'. The instrument further states the following:

'Notwithstanding this, the Government of Iceland will not authorise whaling for commercial purposes by Icelandic vessels before 2006 and, thereafter, will not authorise such whaling while progress is being made in negotiations within the IWC on the RMS. This does not apply, however, in case of the so-called moratorium on whaling for commercial purposes, contained in paragraph 10(e) of the Schedule not being lifted within a reasonable time after the completion of the RMS. Under no circumstances will whaling for commercial purposes be authorised without a sound scientific basis and an effective management and enforcement scheme.'

The Governments of Argentina, Australia, Brazil, Chile, Finland, France, Germany, Italy, Mexico, Monaco, the Netherlands, New Zealand, Peru, San Marino, Spain, Sweden, UK and the USA have lodged objections to Iceland's reservation to paragraph 10(e).

Baleen whale catch limits

11. The number of baleen whales taken in the Southern Hemisphere in the *2009/2010* pelagic season and the *2009* coastal season shall not exceed the limits shown in Tables 1 and 2.▲

12. The number of baleen whales taken in the North Pacific Ocean and dependent waters in *2010* and in the North Atlantic Ocean in *2010* shall not exceed the limits shown in Tables 1 and 2.▲

13. (a) Notwithstanding the provisions of paragraph 10, catch limits for aboriginal subsistence whaling to satisfy aboriginal subsistence need for the 1984 whaling season and each whaling season thereafter shall be established in accordance with the following principles:

   (1) For stocks at or above MSY level, aboriginal subsistence catches shall be permitted so long as total removals do not exceed 90 per cent of MSY.

   (2) For stocks below the MSY level but above a certain minimum level, aboriginal subsistence catches shall be permitted so long as they are set at levels which will allow whale stocks to move to the MSY level.[1]

   (3) The above provisions will be kept under review, based upon the best scientific advice, and by 1990 at the latest the Commission will undertake a comprehensive assessment of the effects of these provisions on whale stocks and consider modification.

   (4) For aboriginal whaling conducted under subparagraphs (b)(1), (b)(2), and (b)(3) of this paragraph, it is forbidden to strike, take or kill calves or any whale accompanied by a calf. For aboriginal whaling conducted under subparagraphs (b)(4) of this paragraph, it is forbidden to strike, take or kill suckling calves or female whales accompanied by calves.

   (5) All aboriginal whaling shall be conducted under national legislation that accords with this paragraph.

▲ *See footnote to Table 1.*   ▲ *See footnote to Table 1.*

[1] The Commission, on advice of the Scientific Committee, shall establish as far as possible (a) a minimum stock level for each stock below which whales shall not be taken, and (b) a rate of increase towards the MSY level for each stock. The Scientific Committee shall advise on a minimum stock level and on a range of rates of increase towards the MSY level under different catch regimes.

(b) Catch limits for aboriginal subsistence whaling are as follows:
  (1) The taking of bowhead whales from the Bering–Chukchi–Beaufort Seas stock by aborigines is permitted, but only when the meat and products of such whales are to be used exclusively for local consumption by the aborigines and further provided that:
    (i) For the years 2008, 2009, 2010, 2011 and 2012, the number of bowhead whales landed shall not exceed 280. For each of these years the number of bowhead whales struck shall not exceed 67, except that any unused portion of a strike quota from any year (including 15 unused strikes from the 2003–2007 quota) shall be carried forward and added to the strike quotas of any subsequent years, provided that no more than 15 strikes shall be added to the strike quota for any one year.
    (ii) This provision shall be reviewed annually by the Commission in light of the advice of the Scientific Committee.
  (2) The taking of grey whales from the Eastern stock in the North Pacific is permitted, but only by aborigines or a Contracting Government on behalf of aborigines, and then only when the meat and products of such whales are to be used exclusively for local consumption by the aborigines.
    (i) For the years 2008, 2009, 2010, 2011 and 2012, the number of grey whales taken in accordance with this sub-paragraph shall not exceed 620, provided that the number of grey whales taken in any one of the years 2008, 2009, 2010, 2011 and 2012 shall not exceed 140.
    (ii) This provision shall be reviewed annually by the Commission in light of the advice of the Scientific Committee.
  (3) The taking by aborigines of minke whales from the West Greenland and Central stocks and fin whales from the West Greenland stock and bowhead whales from the West Greenland feeding aggregation is permitted and then only when the meat and products are to be used exclusively for local consumption.
    (i) The number of fin whales struck from the West Greenland stock in accordance with this sub-paragraph shall

not exceed 19 in each of the years 2008, 2009, 2010, 2011 and 2012.

(ii) The number of minke whales struck from the Central stock in accordance with this sub-paragraph shall not exceed 12 in each of the years 2008, 2009, 2010, 2011 and 2012, except that any unused portion of the quota for each year shall be carried forward from that year and added to the quota of any subsequent years, provided that no more than 3 shall be added to the quota for any one year.

(iii) The number of minke whales struck from the West Greenland stock shall not exceed 200 in each of the years 2008, 2009, 2010, 2011 and 2012, except that any unused portion of the quota for each year shall be carried forward from that year and added to the strike quota of any of the subsequent years, provided that no more than 15 strikes shall be added to the strike quota for any one year. This provision will be reviewed annually by the Commission, according to the findings and recommendations by the Scientific Committee, which shall be binding.

(iv) The number of bowhead whales struck off West Greenland in accordance with this sub-paragraph shall not exceed 2 in each of the years 2008, 2009, 2010, 2011 and 2012, except that any unused portion of the quota for each year shall be carried forward from that year and added to the quota of any subsequent years, provided that no more than 2 shall be added to the quota for any one year. Furthermore, the quota for each year shall only become operative when the Commission has received advice from the Scientific Committee that the strikes are unlikely to endanger the stock.

(4) For the seasons 2008–2012 the number of humpback whales to be taken by the Bequians of St Vincent and The Grenadines shall not exceed 20. The meat and products of such whales are to be used exclusively for local consumption in St Vincent and The Grenadines.

14. It is forbidden to take or kill suckling calves or female whales accompanied by calves.

Baleen whale size limits

15. (a) It is forbidden to take or kill any sei or Bryde's whales below 40 feet (12.2 metres) in length except that sei and Bryde's whales of not less than 35 feet (10.7 metres) may be taken for delivery to land stations, provided that the meat of such whales is to be used for local consumption as human or animal food.

    (b) It is forbidden to take or kill any fin whales below 57 feet (17.4 metres) in length in the Southern Hemisphere, and it is forbidden to take or kill fin whales below 55 feet (16.8 metres) in the Northern Hemisphere; except that fin whales of not less than 55 feet (16.8 metres) may be taken in the Southern Hemisphere for delivery to land stations and fin whales of not less than 50 feet (15.2 metres) may be taken in the Northern Hemisphere for delivery to land stations, provided that, in each case the meat of such whales is to be used for local consumption as human or animal food.

Sperm whale catch limits

16. Catch limits for sperm whales of both sexes shall be set at zero in the Southern Hemisphere for the 1981/82 pelagic season and 1982 coastal seasons and following seasons, and at zero in the Northern Hemisphere for the 1982 and following coastal seasons; except that the catch limits for the 1982 coastal season and following seasons in the Western Division of the North Pacific shall remain undetermined and subject to decision by the Commission following special or annual meetings of the Scientific Committee. These limits shall remain in force until such time as the Commission, on the basis of the scientific information which will be reviewed annually, decides otherwise in accordance with the procedures followed at that time by the Commission.

17. It is forbidden to take or kill suckling calves or female whales accompanied by calves.

Sperm whale size limits

18. (a) It is forbidden to take or kill any sperm whales below 30 feet (9.2 metres) in length except in the North Atlantic Ocean where it is forbidden to take or kill any sperm whales below 35 feet (10.7 metres).

(b) It is forbidden to take or kill any sperm whale over 45 feet (13.7 metres) in length in the Southern Hemisphere north of 40° South Latitude during the months of October to January inclusive.

(c) It is forbidden to take or kill any sperm whale over 45 feet (13.7 metres) in length in the North Pacific Ocean and dependent waters south of 40° North Latitude during the months of March to June inclusive.

IV.   Treatment

19. (a) It is forbidden to use a factory ship or a land station for the purpose of treating any whales which are classified as Protection Stocks in paragraph 10 or are taken in contravention of paragraphs 2, 3, 4, 5, 6, 7, 8, 11, 12, 14, 16 and 17 of this Schedule, whether or not taken by whale catchers under the jurisdiction of a Contracting Government.

(b) All other whales taken, except minke whales, shall be delivered to the factory ship or land station and all parts of such whales shall be processed by boiling or otherwise, except the internal organs, whale bone and flippers of all whales, the meat of sperm whales and parts of whales intended for human food or feeding animals. A Contracting Government may in less developed regions exceptionally permit treating of whales without use of land stations, provided that such whales are fully utilised in accordance with this paragraph.

(c) Complete treatment of the carcases of 'dauhval' and of whales used as fenders will not be required in cases where the meat or bone of such whales is in bad condition.

20. (a) The taking of whales for treatment by a factory ship shall be so regulated or restricted by the master or person in charge of the factory ship that no whale carcase (except of a whale used as a fender, which shall be processed as soon as is reasonably practicable) shall remain in the sea for a longer period than thirty-three hours from the time of killing to the time when it is hauled up for treatment.

(b) Whales taken by all whale catchers, whether for factory ships or land stations, shall be clearly marked so as to identify the catcher and to indicate the order of catching.

V. Supervision and control

21. (a) There shall be maintained on each factory ship at least two inspectors of whaling for the purpose of maintaining twenty-four hour inspection provided that at least one such inspector shall be maintained on each catcher functioning as a factory ship. These inspectors shall be appointed and paid by the Government having jurisdiction over the factory ship; provided that inspectors need not be appointed to ships which, apart from the storage of products, are used during the season solely for freezing or salting the meat and entrails of whales intended for human food or feeding animals.

    (b) Adequate inspection shall be maintained at each land station. The inspectors serving at each land station shall be appointed and paid by the Government having jurisdiction over the land station.

    (c) There shall be received such observers as the member countries may arrange to place on factory ships and land stations or groups of land stations of other member countries. The observers shall be appointed by the Commission acting through its Secretary and paid by the Government nominating them.

22. Gunners and crews of factory ships, land stations, and whale catchers, shall be engaged on such terms that their remuneration shall depend to a considerable extent upon such factors as the species, size and yield of whales and not merely upon the number of the whales taken. No bonus or other remuneration shall be paid to the gunners or crews of whale catchers in respect of the taking of lactating whales.

23. Whales must be measured when at rest on deck or platform after the hauling out wire and grasping device have been released, by means of a tape-measure made of a non-stretching material. The zero end of the tape-measure shall be attached to a spike or stable device to be positioned on the deck or platform abreast of one end of the whale. Alternatively the spike may be stuck into the tail fluke abreast of the apex of the notch. The tape-measure shall be held taut in a straight line parallel to the deck and the whale's body, and other than in exceptional circumstances along the whale's back, and read abreast of the other end of the whale. The ends of the whale for measurement purposes shall be the tip of the upper jaw, or in sperm whales the most forward part of the head, and the apex of the notch between the tail flukes.

Measurements shall be logged to the nearest foot or 0.1 metre. That is to say, any whale between 75 feet 6 inches and 76 feet 6 inches shall be logged as 76 feet, and any whale between 76 feet 6 inches and 77 feet 6 inches shall be logged as 77 feet. Similarly, any whale between 10.15 metres and 10.25 metres shall be logged as 10.2 metres, and any whale between 10.25 metres and 10.35 metres shall be logged as 10.3 metres. The measurement of any whale which falls on an exact half foot or 0.05 metre shall be logged at the next half foot or 0.05 metre, e.g. 76 feet 6 inches precisely shall be logged as 77 feet and 10.25 metres precisely shall be logged as 10.3 metres.

VI. Information required

24. (a) All whale catchers operating in conjunction with a factory ship shall report by radio to the factory ship:
    (1) the time when each whale is taken
    (2) its species, and
    (3) its marking effected pursuant to paragraph 20(b).
   (b) The information specified in sub-paragraph (a) of this paragraph shall be entered immediately by a factory ship in a permanent record which shall be available at all times for examination by the whaling inspectors; and in addition there shall be entered in such permanent record the following information as soon as it becomes available:
    (1) time of hauling up for treatment
    (2) length, measured pursuant to paragraph 23
    (3) sex
    (4) if female, whether lactating
    (5) length and sex of foetus, if present, and
    (6) a full explanation of each infraction.
   (c) A record similar to that described in sub-paragraph (b) of this paragraph shall be maintained by land stations, and all of the information mentioned in the said sub-paragraph shall be entered therein as soon as available.
   (d) A record similar to that described in sub-paragraph (b) of this paragraph shall be maintained by 'small-type whaling' operations conducted from shore or by pelagic fleets, and all of this information mentioned in the said sub-paragraph shall be entered therein as soon as available.

25. (a) All Contracting Governments shall report to the Commission for all whale catchers operating in conjunction with factory ships and land stations the following information:
    (1) methods used to kill each whale, other than a harpoon, and in particular compressed air;
    (2) number of whales struck but lost.

(b) A record similar to that described in sub-paragraph (a) of this paragraph shall be maintained by vessels engaged in 'small-type whaling' operations and by native peoples taking species listed in paragraph 1, and all the information mentioned in the said sub-paragraph shall be entered therein as soon as available, and forwarded by Contracting Governments to the Commission.

26. (a) Notification shall be given in accordance with the provisions of Article VII of the Convention, within two days after the end of each calendar week, of data on the number of baleen whales by species taken in any waters south of 40° South Latitude by all factory ships or whale catchers attached thereto under the jurisdiction of each Contracting Government, provided that when the number of each of these species taken is deemed by the Secretary to the International Whaling Commission to have reached 85 per cent of whatever total catch limit is imposed by the Commission notification shall be given as aforesaid at the end of each day of data on the number of each of these species taken.

(b) If it appears that the maximum catches of whales permitted by paragraph 11 may be reached before 7 April of any year, the Secretary to the International Whaling Commission shall determine, on the basis of the data provided, the date on which the maximum catch of each of these species shall be deemed to have been reached and shall notify the master of each factory ship and each Contracting Government of that date not less than four days in advance thereof. The taking or attempting to take baleen whales, so notified, by factory ships or whale catchers attached thereto shall be illegal in any waters south of 40° South Latitude after midnight of the date so determined.

(c) Notification shall be given in accordance with the provisions of Article VII of the Convention of each factory ship intending to engage in whaling operations in any waters south of 40° South Latitude.

27. Notification shall be given in accordance with the provisions of Article VII of the Convention with regard to all factory ships and catcher ships of the following statistical information:

    (a) concerning the number of whales of each species taken, the number thereof lost, and the number treated at each factory ship or land station, and

    (b) as to the aggregate amounts of oil of each grade and quantities of meal, fertiliser (guano), and other products derived from them, together with

    (c) particulars with respect to each whale treated in the factory ship, land station or 'small-type whaling' operations as to the date and approximate latitude and longitude of taking, the species and sex of the whale, its length and, if it contains a foetus, the length and sex, if ascertainable, of the foetus. The data referred to in (a) and (c) above shall be verified at the time of the tally and there shall also be notification to the Commission of any information which may be collected or obtained concerning the calving grounds and migration of whales.

28. (a) Notification shall be given in accordance with the provisions of Article VII of the Convention with regard to all factory ships and catcher ships of the following statistical information:

        (1) the name and gross tonnage of each factory ship,

        (2) for each catcher ship attached to a factory ship or land station:

            (i) the dates on which each is commissioned and ceases whaling for the season,

            (ii) the number of days on which each is at sea on the whaling grounds each season,

            (iii) the gross tonnage, horsepower, length and other characteristics of each; vessels used only as tow boats should be specified.

        (3) A list of the land stations which were in operation during the period concerned, and the number of miles searched per day by aircraft, if any.

(b) The information required under paragraph (a)(2)(iii) should also be recorded together with the following information, in the logbook format shown in Appendix A, and forwarded to the Commission:

(1) where possible the time spent each day on different components of the catching operation,

(2) any modifications of the measures in paragraphs (a)(2)(i)–(iii) or (b)(1) or data from other suitable indicators of fishing effort for 'small-type whaling' operations.

29. (a) Where possible all factory ships and land stations shall collect from each whale taken and report on:

   (1) both ovaries or the combined weight of both testes,

   (2) at least one ear plug, or one tooth (preferably first mandibular).

(b) Where possible similar collections to those described in sub-paragraph (a) of this paragraph shall be undertaken and reported by 'small-type whaling' operations conducted from shore or by pelagic fleets.

(c) All specimens collected under sub-paragraphs (a) and (b) shall be properly labelled with platform or other identification number of the whale and be appropriately preserved.

(d) Contracting Governments shall arrange for the analysis as soon as possible of the tissue samples and specimens collected under sub-paragraphs (a) and (b) and report to the Commission on the results of such analyses.

30. A Contracting Government shall provide the Secretary to the International Whaling Commission with proposed scientific permits before they are issued and in sufficient time to allow the Scientific Committee to review and comment on them. The proposed permits should specify:

(a) objectives of the research;

(b) number, sex, size and stock of the animals to be taken;

(c) opportunities for participation in the research by scientists of other nations; and

(d) possible effect on conservation of stock.

Proposed permits shall be reviewed and commented on by the Scientific Committee at Annual Meetings when possible. When permits would be granted prior to the next Annual Meeting, the Secretary shall send the proposed permits to members of the Scientific Committee by mail for their comment and review. Preliminary results of any research resulting from the permits should be made available at the next Annual Meeting of the Scientific Committee.

31. A Contracting Government shall transmit to the Commission copies of all its official laws and regulations relating to whales and whaling and changes in such laws and regulations.

International Convention for the Regulation of Whaling, 1946, Schedule Appendix A

Title Page
(one logbook per catcher per season)

Catcher name .... Year built ....

Attached to expedition/land station ....

Season ....

Overall length .... Wooden/steel hull ....

Gross tonnage ....

Type of engine .... H.P.............................

Maximum speed .... Average searching speed ....

Asdic set, make and model no..

Date of installation ....

Make and size of cannon ....

Type of first harpoon used ....explosive/electric/non-explosive

Type of killer harpoon used ....

Length and type of forerunner ....

Type of whaleline ....

Height of barrel above sea level ....

Speedboat used, Yes/No

Name of Captain ....

Number of years experience ....

Name of gunner ....

Number of years experience ....

Number of crew ....

International Convention for the Regulation of Whaling, 1946

DAILY RECORD SHEET	Table 1

Date......	Catcher name.................	Sheet No........................

Searching:	Time started (or resumed) searching	....
	*Time whales seen or reported to catcher	....
	Whale species	....
	Number seen and no. of groups	....
	Position found	....
	Name of catcher that found whales	....
Chasing:	Time started chasing (or confirmed whales)	....
	Time whale shot or chasing discontinued	....
	Asdic used (Yes/No)	....
Handling:	Time whale flagged or alongside for towing	....
	Serial No. of catch	....
Towing:	Time started picking up	....
	Time finished picking up or started towing	....
	Date and time delivered to factory	....
Resting:	Time stopped (for drifting or resting)	....
	Time finished drifting/resting	....
	Time ceased operations	....

WEATHER CONDITIONS

Total searching time
Total chasing time

	Time	Sea state	Wind force and direction	Visibility
A) with asdic				
B) without asdic	....	....	....	....
Total handling time				
Total towing time	....	....	....	....
Total resting time				
Other time (e.g.	....	....	....	....
bunkering, in port)				

Whales Seen (No. and No. of schools)

Blue	Bryde's
Fin	Minke
Humpback	Sperm
Right	Others (specify)
Sei	
Signed	

*Time whales reported to catcher means the time when the catcher is told of the position of a school and starts to move towards it to chase it.

Schedule Appendix A

Schooling Report

Table 2

To be completed by pelagic expedition or coastal station for each sperm whale school chased. A separate form to be used each day.

Name of expedition or coastal station

Date.................................... Noon position of factory ship...

Time School Found..

Total Number of Whales in School..

Number of Takeable Whales in School...

Number of Whales Caught from School by each Catcher..

Name of Catcher..

Name of Catcher..

Name of Catcher..

Name of Catcher..

Total Number Caught from School...

Remarks:

Explanatory notes

A. Fill in one column for each school chased with number of whales caught by each catcher taking part in the chase; if catchers chase the school but do not catch from it, enter 0; for catchers in fleet which do not chase that school enter X.

B. A school on this form means a group of whales which are sufficiently close together that a catcher having completed handling one whale can start chasing another whale almost immediately without spending time searching. A solitary whale should be entered as a school of 1 whale.

C. A takeable whale is a whale of a size or kind which the catchers would take if possible. It does not necessarily include all whales above legal size, e.g. if catchers are concentrating on large whales only these would be counted as takeable.

D. Information about catchers from other expeditions or companies operating on the same school should be recorded under Remarks.

BIBLIOGRAPHY

Aguilar, Alex, 'Aboriginal Whaling Off Pagalu (Equatorial Guinea)', *Reports of the International Whaling Commission* 35 (1985), 386

Akamine, Jun, 'Intangible Food Heritage: Dynamics of Whale Foodways in the Age of Whale Meat Rarity', in Nobuhiro Kishigami, Hisashi Hamaguchi and James M. Savelle (eds.), *Senri Ethnological Studies, No. 84, Anthropological Studies on Whaling* (Osaka: National Museum of Ethnology, 2013), p. 214

Altherr, Sandra and Londsale, Jennifer, 'Breaking Ranks: Denmark Goes Alone on Whaling Policy', www.hsi.org/assets/pdfs/breaking_ranks_may_2012.pdf

Anaya, S. James, 'International Human Rights and Indigenous Peoples: The Move Toward the Multicultural State', *Arizona Journal of International and Comparative Law* 21 (2004), 9

Andresen, Steinar, 'The International Whaling Regime: Order at the Turn of the Century?' in D. Vidas and W. Oestreng (eds.), *Order for the Oceans at the Turn of the Century* (Lysaker: Nansen Institute, 1999), p. 215

'The Role of Scientific Expertise in Multilateral Environmental Agreements: Influence and Effectiveness', in Monika Ambrus, Karin Arts, Ellen Hey and Helena Raulus (eds.), *The Role of 'Experts' in International and European Decision-Making Processes. Advisors, Decision Makers or Irrelevant Actors?* (Cambridge University Press, 2014), p. 115

Andresen, Steinar, Walløe, Lars and Rosendal, G. Kristin, 'The Precautionary Principle: Knowledge Counts but Power Decides', in Rosie Cooney and Barney Dickson (eds.), *Biodiversity and the Precautionary Principle: Risk and Uncertainty in Conservation and Sustainable Use* (London: Earthscan, 2005), p. 39

Anton, Donald K., Makgill, Robert A. and Payne, Cymie R., 'Advisory Opinion on *Responsibility and Liability for International Seabed Mining* (ITLOS Case No. 17): International Environmental Law in the Seabed Disputes Chamber', http://ssrn.com/AuthorID=371838

Arato, Julian, 'Subsequent Practice in the Whaling Case, and What the ICJ Implies about Treaty Interpretation in International Organizations', *EJIL: Talk!* www.ejiltalk.org/subsequent-practice-in-the-whaling-case-and-what-the-icj-implies-about-treaty-interpretation-in-international-organizations/

'Constitutional Transformation in the ECtHR: Strasbourg's Expansive Recourse to International Rules of International Law', *Brooklyn Journal of International Law* 37 (2012), 349

Aron, William, Burke, William T. and Freeman, Milton, M. R., 'Scientists versus Whaling: Science, Advocacy, and Errors of Judgment', *Bioscience* 12 (2002), 1137

'Science and Advocacy: A Cautionary Tale from the International Whaling Debate', in William C. G. Burns and Alexander Gillespie (eds.), *The Future of Cetaceans in a Changing World* (Ardsley, NY: Transnational Publishers, 2003), p. 89

Babcock, Hope M., 'Putting a Price on Whales to Save Them: What Do Morals Have to Do with It?', *Environmental Law* 43 (2013), 1

Backer, I. L., Fauchald, O. K. and Voigt, C. (eds.), *Pro Natura – Festskrift til Hans Christian Bugge* (Oslo: Universitetsforlaget, 2012)

Bailey, Jennifer L., 'Arrested Development: The Fight to End Commercial Whaling as a Case of a Failed Norm Change', *European Journal of International Relations* 14 (2008), 289

Bakalar, Elizabeth M., 'Subsistence Whaling in the Native Village of Barrow: Bringing Autonomy to Native Alaskans Outside the International Whaling Commission', *Brooklyn Journal of International Law* 30 (2005), 602

Bankes, Nigel, 'International Wildlife Law: Canadian Wildlife Law Project', Paper No. 1 (Calgary: Canadian Institute of Resources Law', 2006) (text unpublished)

Barratt, Amanda and Afadameh-Adeyemi, Ashimizo, 'Indigenous Peoples and the Right to Culture: The Potential Significance for African Indigenous Communities of the Committee on Economic, Social and Cultural Rights: General Comment 21', *African Human Rights Journal* 11 (2011), 560

Barsh, Russel Lawrence, 'Indigenous Peoples', in Daniel Bodansky, Jutta Brunnée and Ellen Hey (eds.), *The Oxford Handbook of International Environmental Law* (Oxford University Press, 2007), p. 850

Bentham, Jeremy, *The Principles of Morals and Legislation* (Amherst, NY: Prometheus Books, 1988)

Berends, Helena and Pearse, Jonathan, 'Overseas Countries and Territories' Environmental Profile', European Commission, http://ec.europa.eu/development/center/repository/ environmental_profile_north_atlantic_en.pdf

Bestor, Theodore C., 'Socio-Economic Implications of Zero Catch Limit on Distribution Channels and Related Activities in Hokkaido and Myiagi Prefectures, Japan', *IWC/41/ SE1*. 77 (1989)

Beyer Broch, Harald, 'North Norwegian Whalers' Conceptualization of Current Whale Management Conflicts', in Milton M. R. Freeman and Urs Kreuter (eds.), *Elephants and Whales. Resources for Whom?* (Basle: Gordon and Breach Science Publishers, 1994), p. 203

Birnie, Patricia W. W., 'Opinion on the Legality of the Development of the Southern Ocean Whale Sanctuary by the International Whaling Commission' (High North Alliance, 1995)

'Are Twentieth-Century Marine Conservation Conventions Adaptable to Twenty-First-Century Goals and Principles?' *International Journal of Marine and Estuarine (Coastal) Law* 12 (1997), Part I, 307; Part II, 488

'Small Cetaceans and the International Whaling Commission', *Georgetown International Environmental Law Review* 10 (1997), 1

'Framework for Cooperation', in William C. G. Burns and Alexander Gillespie (eds.), *The Future of Cetaceans in a Changing World* (Ardsley, NY: Transnational Publishers, 2003), p. 101

Black, Richard, 'Petition calls for whaling moratorium to remain', BBC News, 22 June 2010, www.bbc.co.uk/news/19384336

Bodansky, Daniel, Brunnée, Jutta and Hey, Ellen (eds.), *The Oxford Handbook of International Environmental Law* (Oxford University Press, 2007)

Borg, Simone, 'The Influence of International Case Law on Aspects of International Law Relating to Conservation of Living Marine Resources beyond National Jurisdiction', *Yearbook of International Environmental Law*, 23 (2012), 44

Borgen, Christopher J., 'Resolving Treaty Conflicts', *George Washington International Law Review* 37 (2005), 573

Bowman, Michael, 'The Protection of Animals under International Law', *Connecticut Journal of International Law* 4 (1989), 487

'The Philosophical Foundations of International Wildlife', in Michael Bowman, Peter Davies and Catherine Redgwell, *Lyster's International Wildlife Law* (2nd edn, Cambridge University Press, 2010), p. 62

'Wildlife and Welfare', in Michael Bowman, Peter Davies and Catherine Redgwell, *Lyster's International Wildlife Law* (2nd edn, Cambridge University Press, 2010), p. 672

Bowman, Michael, Davies, Peter and Redgwell, Catherine, *Lyster's International Wildlife Law* (Cambridge University Press, 2010)

Boyle, Alan, 'Codification of International Environmental Law and the International Law Commission: Injurious Consequences Revisited', in Alan Boyle and David Freestone (eds.), *International Law and Sustainable Development* (Oxford University Press, 1999), p. 61

Boyle, Alan and Anderson, Michael, *Human Rights Approaches to Environmental Protection* (Oxford University Press, 1998)

Brimheim, Elin, 'Why we should let Faroe islanders hunt whales', http://elinbrim heimheinesen.blogspot.co.uk/2012/05/10-arguments-against-pilot-whaling-and.html

Brighton, Claire, 'Unraveling Reasonableness: A Question of Treaty Interpretation', *AYBIL* 32 (2015), 125.

Brito, Cristina, Pinco, Cristina and Carlvaho, Inez, 'Small Cetaceans Off São Tomé (São Tomé and Príncipe, Gulf of Guinea, West Africa): Species, Sightings and Abundance, Local Human Activities and Conservation', www.research gate.net/.../242579596_Small_cetaceans_off_So_Tom

Brown, Alexander, *Ronald Dworkin's Theory of Equality. Domestic and Global Perspective* (Basingstoke: Palgrave Macmillan, 2009)

Brown, Joanna 'It's in Our Treaty: The Right to Whale', http://nativecases.ever green.edu/docs/Makah_Case_Study_rev7_25_08.doc

Brown Weiss, Edith, *In Fairness to Future Generations* (Ardsley, NY: Transnational Publishers, 1989)
    'Implementing Intergenerational Equity', in Malgosia Fitzmaurice, David Ong and Panos Merkouris (eds.), *Research Handbook on International Environmental Law* (Cheltenham: Edward Elgar Publishing, 2011), p. 100

Brydon, Anne, 'In the Eye of the Guest: Icelandic Nationalist Discourse and the Whaling Issue', http://digitool.library.mcgill.ca/view/action/singleViewer. do?dvs=1374935032269~27&locale=en_GB&show_metadata=false&VIE WER_URL=/view/action/singleViewer.do?&DELIVERY_RULE_ID=6&ad jacency=N&application=DIGITOOL-3&frameId=1&usePid1=true&use Pid2=true

Burke, William T., 'Legal Aspects of the IWC Decision on the Southern Ocean Sanctuary', *Ocean Development and International Law* 28 (1997), 313
    'A New Whaling Agreement and International Law', in Robert L. Friedheim (ed.), *Toward a Sustainable Whaling Regime* (Washington University Press, 2001), p. 51

Burnett, Graham, *The Sounding of a Whale. Science and Cetaceans in the Twentieth Century* (University of Chicago Press, 2012)

Burns, William C. G., 'The International Whaling Commission and the Regulation of the Consumptive and Non-Consumptive Uses of Small Cetaceans: The Critical Agenda for the 1990s', *Wisconsin International Law Journal* 13 (1994), 105
    'The International Whaling Commission and the Future of Cetaceans', *Colorado Journal of International Environmental Law and Policy* 8 (1997), 31

Burns, William C. G. and Gillespie, Alexander (eds.), *The Future of Cetaceans in a Changing World* (Ardsley, NY: Transnational Publishers, 2003)

Burns, William C. G. and Wandesforde-Smith, Geoffrey, 'The International Whaling Commission and the Future of Cetaceans in a Changing World', *Review of European Community and International Environmental Law* 11 (2002), 199

Butterworth, Doug S., 'Why a Management Procedure Approach? Some Positives and Negatives', *ICES Journal of Marine Science* 63 (2006), 613

Caddell, Richard, 'Science Fiction: Antarctic Research Whaling and the International Court of Justice', *Journal of International Law* 26 (2014), 331

Calabresi, Guido and Melamed, David, 'Property Rules, Liability Rules and Inalienability: One View of the Cathedral', *Harvard Law Review* 85 (1972), 1089

Cambou, Dorothée, 'The Impact of the Ban on Seal Products on the Rights of Indigenous Peoples: A European Issue', *Yearbook of Polar Law* 5 (2013), 387

Cannizzaro, Enzo (ed.), *The Law of Treaties Beyond the Vienna Convention* (Oxford University Press, 2011)

Caron, David D., 'The International Whaling Commission and the North Atlantic Marine Mammal Commission: The Institutional Risks of Coercion for Consensual Structures', *American Journal of International Law* 89 (1995), 154

Casal, Paula, 'Is Multiculturalism Bad for Animals?' *Journal of Political Philosophy* 11 (2003), 1

Cavallieri, Paola, *The Animal Question: Why Non-Human Animals Deserve Human Rights* (Oxford University Press, 1992)

Charlesworth, Hilary, 'Human Rights and the UNESCO Memory of the World Programme', in Michele Langfield, William Logan and Máiréd Craith (eds.), *Cultural Diversity, Heritage and Human Rights* (New York: Routledge, 2010), p. 21

Churchill, Robin, 'The Agreement on the Conservation of Small Cetaceans of the Baltic and North Seas', in William C. G. Burns and Alexander Gillespie (eds.), *The Future of Cetaceans in a Changing World* (Ardsley, NY: Transnational Publishers, 2003), p. 283

Clapham, Philip, 'Japan's Whaling Following the International Court of Justice Ruling: Brave New World or Business as Usual?', *Marine Policy* 51 (2014), 238

ClientEarth (2010), 'The Proposed Reform of the International Whaling Convention and EU Voting Rules', www.clientearth.org/reports/100520-marine-protection-eu-voting-and-iwc-f.pdf

Connolly, Peggy, Cox-White, Becky, Keller David R. and Lever, Martin G. (eds.), *Ethics in Action: A Case-Based Approach* (Malden, Mass.: Wiley-Blackwell, 2009)

Cooney, Rosie, 'The Precautionary Principle in Biodiversity Conservation and Natural Resource Management. An issues paper for policy-makers, researchers and practitioners' (Cambridge: International Union for Conservation of Nature, 2004)

Cooney, Rosie and Dickson, Barney (eds.), *Biodiversity and the Precautionary Principle* (London: Earthscan, 2005)

Corell, Hans, 'Reflections on the Possibilities and Limitations of a Binding Legal Regime', *Environmental Policy and Law* 37 (2007), 321

Couzens, Ed, *Whales and Elephants in International Conservation Law and Politics: A Comparative Study* (Abingdon: Routledge, 2014)

Coyle, Sean and Morrow, Karin, *The Philosophical Foundations of Environmental Law, Property Rights and Nature* (Oxford: Hart Publishing, 2004)

Crawford, James, 'Chance, Order, Change: The Course of International Law', *General Course on Public International Law/Recueil des Cours de Droit International*, 365 (2013), 9

'Responsibilities for Breaches of Communitarian Norms: An Appraisal of Article 48 of the ILC Articles on Responsibility of States for Wrongful Acts', in Ulrich Fastenrath et al. (eds.), *From Bilateralism to Community Interest. Essays in Honour of Bruno Simma* (Oxford University Press, 2013), p. 362

State Responsibility: The General Part (Cambridge University Press, 2013)

Crawford, James and Nevill, Penelope, 'Relations between International Courts and Tribunals: The "Regime Problem"', in Margaret Young (ed.), *Regime Interaction in International Law: Facing Fragmentation* (Cambridge University Press, 2012), p. 235

Culik, Boris M., 'Review of Small Cetaceans. Distribution, Behaviour, Migration and Threats', Marine Mammal Action Plan/Regional Seas Reports and Studies no. 17, UNEP/CMS Regional Seas, www.unep.org/regionalseas/publications/reports/RSRS/pdfs/rsrs177.pdf

Currie, Duncan, 'Whales, Sustainability and International Environmental Governance', *Review of European Community and International Environmental Law* 16 (2007), 45

Dahl, K. N., 'The Application of Successive Treaties Dealing with the Same Subject-matter', *Indian Journal of International Affairs* 17 (1974), 279

D'Amato, Anthony and Chopra, Sudhir K., 'Whales: Their Emerging Right to Life', *American Journal of International Law* 85 (1991), 21

Davies, Peter, 'Cetaceans', in Michael Bowman, Peter Davies and Catherine Redgwell, *Lyster's International Wildlife Law* (2nd edn, Cambridge University Press, 2010), p. 150

De Grazia, David, *Taking Animal Rights Seriously* (Cambridge University Press, 1996)

de la Mare, William, Gales, Nick and Mangel, Marc, 'Applying Scientific Principles in International Law on Whaling', *Science and Law* 345 (2014), 1125

del Castillo, Lilian, 'Some Comments on the Whaling in the Antarctic Judgment', in Lilian del Castillo (ed.), *Law of the Sea, from Grotius to the International Tribunal for the Law of the Sea: Liber Amicorum Judge Hugo Caminos* (Leiden: Brill–Nijhoff, 2015), p. 175

Descartes, René, *Discourse on Method and Meditation on First Philosophy*, trans. John Cottingham, Robert Stoothoff and Dugald Murdoch (Cambridge University Press, 1991)

Desierto, Diane, 'Evidence in Environmental/Scientific Exceptions: Some Contrasts between the WTO Panel Report in *China–Rare Earths* and the ICJ Judgment in *Whaling in the Antarctic*', EJIL: Talk! www.ejiltalk.org/evidence-in-environmentalscientific-exceptions-some-contrasts-between-the-wto-panel-report-in-china-rare-earths-and-the-icj-Judgment-in-whaling-in-the-antarctic/

Dickson, Barnabas, 'The Precautionary Principle in CITES: A Critical Assessment', *Natural Resources Journal* 39 (1999), 211

Donaldson, Sue and Kymlicka, Will, *Zoopolis: A Political Theory of Animal Rights* (Oxford University Press, 2011)

Dorsey, Kurkpatrick, *Whales and Nations: Environmental Diplomacy on the High Seas* (University of Washington Press, 2014)

Doubleday, Nancy C., 'Aboriginal Subsistence Whaling: The Right of Inuit to Hunt Whales and Implications for International Environmental Law', *Denver Journal of International Law and Policy* 17 (1988–9), 373

'Arctic Whales: Sustaining Indigenous Peoples and Conserving Arctic Resources', in Milton M. R. Freeman and Urs Kreuter (eds.), *Elephants and Whales. Resources for Whom?* (Basle: Gordon and Breach Science Publishers, 1994), p. 241

Doubleday, William, '[Canada has] No Intention of Joining the International Whaling Commission', High North Alliance, www.animaladvocates.com/watchdog.pl?md=read;id=13528

'The IWC Does Not Have Legal Competence for the Management of Small Cetaceans', High North Alliance, www.highnorth.no/Library/Policies/national/th-iw-do.htm

Dreimmelen, Benjamin van, 'The International Mismanagement of Whaling', *Pacific Basin Journal* 10 (1991), p. 240

Dworkin, Ronald, *Taking Rights Seriously* (London: Duckworth, 1977)

Is Democracy Possible Here? Principles for a New Political Debate (Princeton University Press, 2006)

Ecoadvise & Communication, 'Greenland Announce New Narwhal Quota – 20/09/2006', www.ecoadvise.dk/news_narwhal.html

'Greenland Needs to Cut Narwhal Beluga Hunts', www.ecoadvise.dk/news_narwhal.html

'Narwhal Quota Increase 2005–2006 in Greenland', www.ecoadvise.dk/news_narwhal.html

Ecott, Tim, 'Why We Should Let Faroe Islanders Hunt Whales', *Spectator*, 1 February 2014

EFTEC, 'Norwegian Use of Whales: Past, Present and Future Trends', Final Report for the Society for the Protection of Animals (WSPA), 2011, www.wspa.org.au/Images/Whaling_Full_report_tcm30-21294.pdf

Egami, Tomoko and Kojima, Kotaro, 'Traditional Whaling Culture and Social Change in Lamalera, Indonesia: An Analysis of the Catch Record of Whaling 1994–2010', in Nobuhiro Kishigami, Hisashi Hamaguchi and James M. Savelle (eds.), *Senri Ethnological Studies, No. 84, Anthropological Studies on Whaling* (Osaka: National Museum of Ethnology, 2013), p. 155

Einarsson, Niels, *Culture, Conflict and Crises in the Icelandic Fisheries*, Uppsala Studies in Cultural Anthropology 48 (Uppsala Universitet, 2011)

Elliot, Robert and Gare, Arran E. (eds.), *Environmental Philosophy* (University Park: Penn. State University Press, 1983)

Ellis, Richard, *Men and Whales* (New York: Knopf, 1991)

Epstein, Charlotte, *The Power of Words in International Relations. Birth of an Anti-Whaling Discourse* (Cambridge, Mass.: MIT Press, 2008)

Evans, Peter G. H. and Simmonds, Mark P., 'Implications for ASCOBANS of Enlarging the Agreement Area and Including all Cetaceans', Doc. AC15/Doc.28(O), www.ascobans.org/sites/default/files/document/AC15_28_Species Extension_1.pdf

Fabra, A. and Gascón, V., 'The Convention on the Conservation of Antarctic Marine Living Resources (CCAMLR) and the Ecosystem Approach', *International Journal of Marine and Coastal Law* 23 (2008), 567

Firestone, J. and Lilley, J., 'Aboriginal Subsistence Whaling and the Right to Practice and Revitalize Cultural Traditions and Customs', *Journal of International Wildlife Law and Policy* 8 (2005), 177

Fitzmaurice, Malgosia, 'The International Court of Justice and International Environmental Law', in Christian Tams and James Sloan (eds.), *The Development of International Law by the International Court of Justice* (Cambridge University Press, 2013), p. 353

'The Whaling Case and Thorny Issues of Interpretation', in Malgosia Fitzmaurice and Dai Tamada (eds.), *Whaling in the Antarctic: The Judgment and its Implications* (Leiden: Brill–Njihoff, 2016)

Fitzmaurice, Malgosia and Elias, Olufemi, *Contemporary Issues in the Law of Treaties* (Utrecht: Eleven International Publishing, 2005)

Fitzmaurice, Malgosia, Ong, David and Merkouris, Panos (eds.), *Research Handbook on International Environmental Law* (Cheltenham: Edward Elgar Publishing, 2011)

Fitzmaurice, Malgosia and Tamada, Dai, *Whaling in the Antarctic: The Judgment and its Implications* (Leiden: Brill–Nijhoff, 2016)

Foster, Caroline E., *Science and the Precautionary Principle in International Courts and Tribunals. Expert Evidence, Burden of Proof and Finality* (Cambridge University Press, 2011)

'Motivations and Methodologies. Was Japan's Whaling Programme for Purposes of Scientific Research?', chapter to be published in Malgosia Fitzmaurice and Dai Tamada (eds.), *Whaling in the Antarctic: The Judgment and its Implications* (Leiden: Brill–Nijhoff, 2016)

Francione, Gary, *Animals as Persons: Essays on Abolition of Animal Exploitation* (New York: Columbia University Press, 2008)

Franckx, Erick, 'The Protection of Biodiversity and Fisheries Management: Issues Raised by Relationship between CITES and LOSC', in David Freestone, Richard Barnes and David Ong (eds.), *The Law of the Sea: Progress and Prospects* (Oxford University Press, 2006), p. 210

Freeland, Steven and Drysdale, Julie, 'Co-operation or Chaos? Article 65 of the United Nations Convention on the Law of the Sea and the Future of the

International Whaling Commission', *Macquarie Journal of International and Comparative Environmental Law* 2 (2005), 1

Freeman, Milton M. R., 'The Nature and Utility of Traditional Ecological Knowledge: The Northern Perspective' (1991), available at: www.carc.org/index. php?option=com_wrapper&view=wrapper&Itemid=174

'Science and Trans-Science in the Whaling Debate', in Milton M. R. Freeman and Urs Kreuter (eds.), *Elephants and Whales. Resources for Whom?* (Basle: Gordon and Breach Science Publishers, 1994), p. 143

'Is Money the Root of the Problem? Cultural Conflicts in the IWC', in Robert L. Friedheim (ed.), *Toward a Sustainable Whaling Regime* (Seattle: Washington University Press, 2001), p. 123

'Culture-Based Conflict in the International Whaling Commission: The Case of Japanese Small-Type Whaling', in William C. G. Burns and Alexander Gillespie (eds.), *The Future of Cetaceans in a Changing World* (Ardsley, NY: Transnational Publishers, 2003), p. 33

Freeman, Milton M. R., Bogoslovskaya, Lyudmila, Caulfield, Richard A., Egede, Ingmar, Krupnik, Igor I. and Stevenson, Marc G., *Inuit, Whaling, and Sustainability (Contemporary Native American Communities)* (Lanham, Md.: Altamira Press, 1998)

Freeman, Milton M. R. and Kreuter, Urs P. (eds.), *Elephants and Whales. Resources for Whom?* (Basle: Gordon and Breach Science Publishers, 1994)

Freestone, David, Barnes, Richard and Ong, David (eds.), *The Law of the Sea: Progress and Prospects* (Oxford University Press, 2006)

Freestone, David and Hey, Ellen (eds.), *The Precautionary Principle: The Challenge of Implementation* (The Hague: Kluwer Law International, 1996)

French, Duncan, *International Law and Policy of Sustainable Development* (Manchester University Press, 2005)

Friedheim, Robert L., 'Moderation in the Pursuit: Explaining Japan's Failure in the International Whaling Negotiations', *Ocean Development and International Law* 27(1996), 349

'Introduction: The IWC as a Contested Regime', in Robert L. Friedheim (ed.), *Toward a Sustainable Whaling Regime* (Seattle: Washington University Press, 2001), p. 36

(ed.), *Toward a Sustainable Whaling Regime* (Seattle: Washington University Press, 2001)

Fuentes, Alejandro, 'Cultural Diversity and Indigenous Peoples' Land Claims. Argumentative Dynamics and Jurisprudential Approach in the Americas', PhD dissertation, http://rwi.lu.se/wp-content/uploads/2012/08/Alejandro-Fuentes-doctoral-thesis.pdf

Gaja, Giorgio, 'The Protection of General Interests in the International Community', *General Course of Public International Law/Recueil des Cours de Droit International* 364 (2011), 171

Gambell, Ray, 'World Whale Stocks', *Mammal Review* 6 (1976), 41

'International Management of Whales and Whaling: An Historical Review of the Regulation of Commercial and Aboriginal Subsistence Whaling', *Arctic* 46(1993), 97

'The International Whaling Commission Today', in Gudrun Pertursdottir (ed.), *Whaling in the North Atlantic: Economic and Political Perspectives* (Reykjavik: University of Iceland Press, 1997)

'The International Whaling Commission and the Contemporary Whaling Debate', in John R. Twiss Jr and Randall R. Reeves (eds.), *Conservation and Management of Marine Mammals* (Washington: Smithsonian Institution Press, 1999), p. 179

Gellecum, Hans van, 'Environmental Law in the Context of Article 31(3)(c) of the Vienna Convention on the Law of Treaties: Reconciling Treaty Interpretation and Progressive Environmental Norms: The *Pulp Mills* Case and Beyond', Social Science Research Network, http://papers.ssrn.com/sol3/papers.cfm?abstract_id=1989468

Ghouri, Ahmad Ali, 'Determining Hierarchy Between Conflicting Treaties: Are Vertical Rules in the Horizontal System?' *Asian Journal of International Law* 2 (2012), 235

Gillespie, Alexander, 'The Precautionary Principle and the 21st Century: A Case Study of Noise Pollution in the Ocean', http://workspace.ascobans.org/sites/ascobans/files/the%20precautionary%20principle%20and%20noise%20pollution2.pdf

'The Ethical Question in the Whaling Debate', *Georgetown International Environmental Law Review* 9 (1997), 355

International Environmental Law, Policy and Ethics (Oxford University Press, 1997)

'Aboriginal Subsistence Whaling: A Critique of the Inter-relationship Between International Law and the International Whaling Commission', *Colorado Journal of International Environmental Law and Policy* 12 (2001), 77

'Small Cetaceans, International Law and the International Whaling Commission', *Melbourne Journal of International Law* 2 (2001), 257

'Humane Killing: A Recognition of Universal Common Sense in International Law', *Journal of International Wildlife Law and Policy* 6 (2003), 1–29

'Iceland's Reservation at the International Whaling Commission', *European Journal of International Law* 14 (2003), 977

Whaling Diplomacy: Defining Issues in International Environmental Law (Cheltenham: Edward Elgar Publishing, 2005)

'Science, Value and People: The Three Factors that Will Define the Next Generation of International Conservation Agreements', *Transnational Environmental Law* 1 (2012), 169

International Environmental Law, Politics, and Ethics (2nd edn, Oxford University Press, 2014)

Goodman, Dan, 'Japanese Whaling and International Politics', in Nobuhiro Kishigami, Hisashi Hamaguchi and James M. Savelle (eds.), *Senri Ethnological Studies, No. 84, Anthropological Studies on Whaling* (Osaka: National Museum of Ethnology, 2013), p. 327

Gottlieb, Paul, 'Restart of Whaling Study Disappoints Makah Chairman', *Peninsula News*, www.peninsuladailynews.com/article/20120525/news/305259989/ restart-of-whaling-study-disappoints-makah-chairman

Grendstad, Gunnar, Selle, Per, Strømsnes, Kristin and Bortne, Øystein, *Unique Environmentalism. A Comparative Perspective* (New York: Springer, 2006)

Gupta, Rupa, 'Indigenous Peoples and International Environmental Community: Accommodating Claims through a Cooperative Legal Process', *New York University Law Review* 74 (1999), 1741

Hamaguchi, Hisashi, 'Aboriginal Subsistence Whaling Revisited', in Nobuhiro Kishigami, Hisashi Hamaguchi and James M. Savelle (eds.), *Senri Ethnological Studies, No. 84, Anthropological Studies of Whaling* (Osaka: National Museum of Ethnology, 2013), p. 81

Hamamoto, Shotaro, 'Procedural Questions in the Whaling Judgment: Admissibility, Intervention and the Use of Experts', Japanese Society of International Law (19–21 September 2014), The Honourable Shigeru Oda Commemorative Lectures, 'ICJ Judgment on Whaling in the Antarctic: Its Significance and Implications', www.jsil.jp/annual_documents/2014/2014manuscript_hamamoto.pdf

Hankins, Stephen M., 'The United States' Abuse of the Aboriginal Whaling Exception: A Contradiction in United States Policy and a Dangerous Precedent for the Whale', *University of California-Davis Law Review* 24 (1990), 489

Hardy, Brettny, 'A Regional Approach to Whaling: How the North Atlantic Marine Mammal Commission is Shifting the Tides for Whale Management', *Duke Journal of Comparative and International Law* 17 (2006), 169

Harris, A. W., 'The Best Scientific Evidence Available: The Whaling Moratorium and Divergent Interpretations of Science', *William & Mary Environmental Law and Policy Review* 29 (2005), 375

Harrop, Stuart R., 'From Cartel to Conservation and on to Compassion: Animal Welfare and the International Whaling Commission', *Journal of International Wildlife Law and Policy* 6 (2003), 79

Hay, K. A. and Mansfield, A. W., 'Narwhal – *Monodon monoceros Linneaus*, 1758', in S. H. Ridgway and S. R. Harrison (eds.), *Handbook of Marine Mammals*, vol. IV: *River Dolphins and the Larger Toothed Mammals* (London: Academic Press, 1989), p. 145

Heazle, Michael, *Scientific Uncertainty and the Politics of Whaling* (London and Seattle: University of Washington Press, 2006)

Heinämäki, Leena, 'Protecting the Rights of Indigenous Peoples – Promoting the Sustainability of the Global Environment?', *International Community Law Review* 11 (2009), 3

Helmersen, Torp, 'Evolutive Treaty Interpretation: Legality, Semantics and Distinctions', *European Journal of Legal Studies* 6 (2013), 127

Henriksen, Tore, 'North Atlantic Marine Mammal Commission (NAMMCO)' and 'Agreement on the Conservation of Polar Bears' (to be published in *The Encyclopaedia of Multilateral Environmental Agreements* (Cheltenham: Edward Elgar Publishing, 2016))

Hirata, Keiko, 'Why Japan Supports Whaling', *Journal of International Wildlife Law and Policy* 8 (2005), 129

Hjarsen, Thor, 'Greenland's International Obligations', WWF Denmark, http://assets.panda.org/downloads/greenlandfinalreport.pdf

'CITES in Greenland', *TRAFFIC Bulletin* 20 (2000), 17, www.traffic.org/traffic-bulletin/traffic_pub_bulletin_20_1.pdf

Hossain, Kamrul, 'Hunting by Indigenous Peoples of Charismatic Mega-Fauna: Does the Human Rights Approach Challenge the Way Hunting by Indigenous Peoples is Regulated?', *International Community Law Review* 10 (2008), 295

Hovelsrud-Broda, Grete, 'NAMMCO – Regional Cooperation, Sustainable Use, Sustainable Communities', in William C. G. Burns and Alexander Gillespie (eds.), *The Future of Cetaceans in a Changing World* (Ardsley, NY: Transnational Publishers, 2003), p. 144

Howse, Rob, Langille, Joanna and Sykes, Katie, 'Animal Welfare, Public Morals and Trade: The WTO Panel Report in *EC – Seal Products*', *ASIL Insights*, 29 January 2014, www.asil.org/insights/volume/18/issue/2/animal-welfare-public-morals-and-trade-wto-panel-report-ec-%E2%80%93-seal

'Sealing the Deal: The WTO's Appellate Body Report in *EC – Seal Products*', *ASIL Insights*, 4 June 2014, www.asil.org/insights/volume/18/issue/12/sealing-deal-wto%E2%80%99s-appellate-body-report-ec-%E2%80%93-seal-products

Iino, Yasuo and Goodman, Dan, 'Japan's Position in the International Whaling Commission', in William C. G. Burns and Alexander Gillespie (eds.), *The Future of Cetaceans in a Changing World* (Ardsley, NY: Transnational Publishers, 2003), p. 3

Ivashchenko, Yulia, 'Soviet Whaling: Past History and Present Impacts', PhD, Southern Cross University e Publications@SC, 2013

Ivashchenko, Yulia V. and Clapham, Philip J., 'Too Much Is Never Enough: The Cautionary Tale of Soviet Illegal Whaling', *Marine Fisheries Review* 76 (2014), 1

Jamieson, Dale, *Ethics and the Environment. An Introduction* (Cambridge University Press, 2008)

Jessup, Philip, 'L'exploitation des richesses de la mer', *Recueil des Cours de Droit International* 29 (1929), 401

Johnson, Michael, 'Whaling in the Antarctic – The ICJ Decision and its Consequences for Future Special Permit Whaling', *AYBIL* 32 (2015), 87

Jones, Hardy, 'Greenland Begins Humpback Whale Hunt', www.huffingtonpost.
com/hardy-jones/greenland-begins-humpback_b_693054.html

Jordan, Tara, 'Revising the International Convention on the Regulation of
Whaling: A Proposal to End Stalemate within the International Whaling
Commission', *Wisconsin International Law Journal* 29 (2012), 833

Kalland, Arne, 'Whose Whale Is That? Diverting the Commodity Path', in Milton
M. R. Freeman and Urs Kreuter (eds.), *Elephants and Whales. Resources for
Whom?* (Basle: Gordon and Breach Science Publishers, 1994), p. 159
Unveiling the Whale: Discourses on Whales and Whaling (New York: Berghahn
Books, 2009)

Kalland, Arne and Moeran, Brian, *Japanese Whaling, End of an Area* (New York:
Routledge, 1993)

Kant, Immanuel, *Lectures on Ethics*, ed. and trans. Peter Heath, ed. J. B. Schneewind (Cambridge University Press, 1997)

Keller, David R. and Goodman, Dan, 'Straights of Strife: Japanese Whaling,
Cultural Relativism, and International Politics', in Peggy Connolly, Becky
Cox-White, David R. Keller and Martin G. Leever (eds.), *Ethics in Action:
A Case-Based Approach* (Malden, Mass.: Wiley-Blackwell, 2009)

Kellogg, R., 'What is Known of the Migration of Some of the Whalebone Whales',
Annual Report of the Smithsonian Institution (1928), 467

Kishigami, Nobuhiro, 'Aboriginal Subsistence Whaling in Barrow, Alaska', in
Nobuhiro Kishigami, Hisashi Hamaguchi and James M. Savelle (eds.), *Senri
Ethnological Studies, No. 84, Anthropological Studies on Whaling* (Osaka:
National Museum of Ethnology, 2013), p. 101

Klabbers, Jan, 'Beyond the Vienna Convention: Conflicting Treaty Provisions', in
Enzo Cannizzaro (ed.), *The Law of Treaties Beyond the Vienna Convention*
(Oxford University Press, 2011), p. 192

Kobayashi, Lisa, 'Lifting the International Whaling Commission's Moratorium on
Commercial Whaling as the Most Effective Global Regulation of Whaling',
Environs 29 (2006), 177

Kolb, Robert, 'Short Reflections on the ICJ's Whaling Case and the Review by International Courts and Tribunals of "Discretionary Powers"', *AYBIL* 32 (2015), 135

Komatsu, M. and Misaki, S., *Whales and the Japanese: How We Have Come to Live
in Harmony with the Bounty of the Sea* (Tokyo: Institute of Cetacean
Research, 2003)

Krämer, Ludwig, 'Negotiating and Voting on Whale Protection within the IWC.
Analysis for the International Fund for Animal Welfare', http://opinion-
former-resources.politics.co.uk/microsites2/364355/graphics/ifawlegalpaper
iwc.pdf (2010)

'Case Note: Seal Killing, the Inuit and European Union Law', *Review of European Community and International Environmental Law* 21 (2012), 291

Kymlicka, Will, *Multicultural Citizenship: A Liberal Theory of Minority Rights* (Oxford University Press, 1995)

Multiculturalism and Citizenship (Oxford University Press, 2001)

Politics in the Vernacular: Nationalism, Multiculturalism and Citizenship (Oxford University Press, 2001)

Multicultural Odysseys: Navigating the New International Politics of Diversity (Oxford University Press, 2007)

Langfield, Michele, Logan, William and Craith, Máiréd (eds.), *Cultural Diversity, Heritage and Human Rights* (New York: Routledge, 2010)

League of Nations, *Committee of Experts on the Progressive Codification of International Law (1925–1928)*, 2 vols. (1972)

Conference on the Codification of International Law (1930), 4 vols. (1975)

Leahy, Michael P. T., *Against Liberation. Putting Animals in Perspective* (Abingdon: Routledge, 1993)

Lenzerini, Frederico, 'Cultural Rights and Cultural Heritage', 2012 ILA Final Report of the Group on Indigenous Rights, 1–31, www.ila-hq.org/download

Leonard, L. Larry, 'Recent Negotiations Toward the International Regulation of Whaling', *American Journal of International Law* 35 (1941), 90

Leslie, Jeff and Sunstein, Cass R., 'Animals Rights Without Controversy', John M. Olin Law and Economics Working Paper No. 283 (2D Series), Public Law and Legal Theory Working Paper No. 120, 2006, www.law.uchicago.edu/academics/publiclaw/.index/html

Lévi-Strauss, Claude, *The Savage Mind* (Chicago University Press, 1968)

Light, Andrew and Katz, Eric (eds.), *Environmental Pragmatism* (London: Routledge, 1996)

Lowe, Vaughan, 'Sustainable Development and Unsustainable Argument', in Alan Boyle and David Freestone (eds.), *International Law and Sustainable Development* (Oxford University Press, 1999), p. 19

Maffei, Maria C., 'The International Convention for the Regulation of Whaling', *International Journal of Marine and Estuarine (Coastal Law)* 12 (1997), 287

Manning, Aubrey and Serpell, James, *Animals and Human Society* (Abingdon: Routledge, 1994)

Matz-Lück, Nele, 'Norm Interpretation Across International Regimes', in Margaret Young (ed.), *Regime Interaction in International Law. Facing Fragmentation* (Cambridge University Press, 2012), p. 206

Matz-Lück, Nele and Fuchs, Johannes, 'Marine Living Resources', in Donald R. Rothwell, Alex G. Oude Elferink, Karen N. Scott and Tim Stephens (eds.), *The Oxford Handbook on the Law of the Sea* (Oxford University Press, 2015), p. 491

McLachlan, Campbell, 'The Principle of Systemic Integration and Article 31(3)(c) of the Vienna Convention', *International and Comparative Law Quarterly* 54 (2005), 279

'The Evolution of Treaty Obligations in International Law', in Georg Nolte (ed.), *Treaties and Subsequent Practice* (Oxford University Press, 2014), p. 69

Mence, David, 'The Cetacean Right to Life', *International Journal in Context* 11 (2015), 17

Merkouris, Panos, 'Case Concerning Pulp Mills on the River Uruguay (Argentina v. Uruguay): Of Environmental Impact Assessments and "Phantom Experts"', www.haguejusticeportal.net/index.php?id=11878

'Debating the *Ouroboros* of International Law: The Drafting History of Article 31(3)(c)', *International Community Law Review* 9 (2007), 1

Article 31(3)(c) VCLT and the Principle of Systemic Integration: Normative Shadows in Plato's Cave (Boston and Leiden: Nijhoff Brill, 2015)

Milanovic, Marko, 'ICJ Decides in the *Antarctic Case*: Australia Wins', *EJIL: Talk!* www.ejiltalk.org/icj-decides-the-whaling-in-the-antarctic-case-australia-wins/

Millar, Nicole, 'Polar Pirates: Friend or Foe? Should the Definition of Piracy Be Altered to Exclude the Activities of Sea Shepherd in the Southern Ocean?' dissertation, University of Otago, October 2013, www.otago.ac.nz/law/research/journals/otago065270.pdf

Moeran, Brian, 'The Cultural Construction of Value. "Subsistence", "Commercial" and Other Terms in the Debate about Whaling', *MAST (Maritime Anthropological Studies)* 5 (1992), 1

Morishita, Joji, 'The Truth about the Commercial Whaling Moratorium', in Nobuhiro Kishigami, Hisashi Hamaguchi and James M. Savelle (eds.), *Senri Ethnological Studies, No. 84, Anthropological Studies on Whaling* (Osaka: National Museum of Ethnology, 2013), p. 327

'IWC and the ICJ Judgment', chapter to be published in Malgosia Fitzmaurice and Dai Tamada (eds.), *Whaling in the Antarctic: The Judgment and its Implications* (Leiden: Brill–Nijhoff , 2016)

Morishita, Joji and Goodman, Dan, 'Role and Problems of the Scientific Committee of the International Whaling Commission in Terms of Conservation and Sustainable Utilization of Whale Stocks', *Global Environmental Research* 9 (2005), 157

Mulvaney, Kieran, 'Saving Right Whales? There's an App for That', http://news.discovery.com/earth/saving-right-whales-theres-an-app-for-that-120412.html

Murphy, Sean P., 'US Sanctions Against Japan for Whaling', *American Journal of International Law* 95 (2001), 151

Mus, J. B., 'Conflicts between Treaties in International Law', *Netherlands International Law Review* 45 (1998), 208

Nagtzaam, Gerry J., *The Making of International Environmental Treaties. Neoliberal and Constructivist Analyses of Normative Evolution* (Cheltenham: Edward Elgar Publishing, 2009)

'The International Whaling Commission and the Elusive Great White Whale of Preservationism', http://works.bepress.com/gerry_nagtzaam/2

'Righting the Ship? Australia, New Zealand and Japan at the ICJ and the Barbed Issue of "Scientific Whaling"', *Australian Journal of Environmental Law* 1 (2014), 71

Nash, Roderick Frazier, *The Rights of Nature. A History of Environmental Ethics* (Madison, Wis.: Wisconsin University Press, 1989)

Næss, Arne, 'The Shallow and the Deep. Long Range Ecology Movement', *Inquiry* 16 (1973), 95

Nollkaemper, Andre, 'International Adjudication of Global Public Goods: The Intersection of Substance and Procedure', SHARES Research Paper 9/2012, 2

Nolte, Georg (ed.), *Treaties and Subsequent Practice* (Oxford University Press, 2014)

Nurse, Angus, *Animal Harm. Perspectives on Why People Harm and Kill Animals* (Farnham: Ashgate, 2013)

Oberthür, Sebastian, 'The International Convention for the Regulation of Whaling: From Over-Exploitation to Total Prohibition', *Yearbook of International Co-operation on Environment and Development* (1998–9), 29

Orellana Zabalza, Gabriel, *The Principle of Systemic Integration: Towards a Coherent International Legal Order* (Münster: LIT, 2012)

Owen, Daniel, 'The Interaction between the ASCOBANS MOP and the IWC, NAMMCO and EC', Doc. AC15/Doc.30(O), www.ascobans.org/sites/default/files/document/AC15_30_InstitutionalInteractions_1.pdf

Palmer, Sir Geoffrey, 'A Victory for Whales: Sir Geoffrey Palmer QC Explains Aspects of the ICJ Decision', *New Zealand Law Journal* (2014), 124, http://papers.ssrn.com/sol3/papers.cfm?abstract_id=2477544

Papanicolopulu, Irini and Scovazzi, Tullio, 'The Implications of the Extending of the Scope of ASCOBANS to All Cetaceans. Legal Aspects', 2008, www.ascobans.org/pdf/ac15/ac15-29.pdf

Pauwelyn, Joost, *Conflict of Norms in Public International Law: How WTO Law Relates to Other Rules of International Law* (Cambridge University Press, 2003)

Payne, Cymie R., '*Australia v. Japan*: ICJ Halts Antarctic Whaling', *ASIL Insights*, www.asil.org/insights/volume/18/issue/9/australia-v-japan-icj-halts-antarctic-whaling

Peat, Daniel, 'The Use of the Court-Appointed Experts by the International Court of Justice', *British Yearbook of International Law* 84 (2013), 271

Peel, Jacqueline, *Science and Risk Regulation in International Law* (Cambridge University Press, 2010)

Pertursdottir, Gudrun (ed.), *Whaling in the North Atlantic: Economic and Political Perspectives* (Reykjavik: University of Iceland Press, 1997)

Peterson, Anna L., *Being Animal. Beasts and Boundaries in Nature Ethics* (New York: Columbia University Press, 2013)

Peterson, Dale, *Moral Lives of Animals* (London: Bloomsbury Press, 2011)

Plakokefalos, Ilias, 'Seabed Disputes Chamber of the International Tribunal for the Law of the Sea, *Responsibilities and Obligations of States Sponsoring Persons and Entities with Respect to Activities in the Area* (Advisory Opinion)', *Journal of Environmental Law* 24 (2012), 1

Prost, Mario, *The Concept of Unity in Public International Law* (Oxford: Hart Publishing, 2014)

Pulkowski, Dirk, *The International Law and Politics of International Conflict* (Oxford University Press, 2014)

Punt, André E. and Donovan, Greg P., 'Developing Management Procedures that are Robust to Uncertainty: Lessons from the International Whaling Commission', *ICES Journal of Marine Science* 64 (2007), 603

Raestad, Arnold, 'La chasse à la baleine en mer libre', *Revue de Droit International* 2 (1928), 595

Rahman, Mohammad Rubaiyat, 'Battle for Whales in The Hague: Analysis of Judgment in *Australia* v. *Japan*', http://papers.ssrn.com/sol3/papers.cfm?abstract_id=2418817

Ranganathan, Surabhi, *Strategically Created Treaty Conflicts and the Politics of International Law* (Cambridge University Press, 2015)

Rawls, John, *The Law of Peoples* (Cambridge, Mass.: Harvard University Press, 1999)

Redgwell, Catherine, 'Life, the Universe and Everything: A Critique of Anthropocentric Rights', in Alan Boyle and Michael Anderson (eds.), *Human Approaches to Environmental Protection* (Oxford University Press, 1996), p. 1

  'The Biodiversity Convention and Biosafety Protocol', in Michael Bowman, Peter Davies and Catherine Redgwell, *Lyster's International Wildlife Law* (2nd edn, Cambridge University Press, 2010), p. 587

  'Polar Regions', in Michael Bowman, Peter Davies and Catherine Redgwell, *Lyster's International Wildlife Law* (2nd edn, Cambridge University Press, 2010), p. 353

Reeves, Randall R., 'The Origins and Character of "Aboriginal Subsistence" Whaling: A Global Review', *Mammal Review* 32 (2002), 71

Reeves, Randall R., et al., *Dolphins, Whales, and Porpoises: 2002–2010 Conservation Action Plan for the World's Cetaceans* (IUCN/SSC Cetacean Specialist Group, 2003)

Regan, Tom, *The Case for Animals Rights* (Berkeley: University of California Press, 1983)

Richardson, Benjamin J., 'Indigenous Peoples, International Law and Sustainability', *Review of European Community and International Environmental Law* 10 (2001), 1

Ridgway, S. H. and Harrison, S. R. (eds.), *Handbook of Marine Mammals*, vol. IV: *River Dolphins and the Larger Toothed Mammals* (London: Academic Press, 1989)

Ridings, Penelope, 'The Intervention Procedure in Whaling in the Antarctic: A Threat to Bilateralism', *AYBIL* 32 (2015), 97

Rodics, Katalin, 'The Need for a New Review of Significant Trade in the Narwhal', CITES AC21 Inf. 1 (Rev 1), p. 4, www.cites.org/common/com/ac/21/E21i-01.pdf

Rose, Gregory and Paleokrassis, George, 'Compliance with International Environmental Obligations: A Case Study of the International Whaling Commission', in James Cameron, Jacob Werksman and Peter Roderick (eds.), *Improving Compliance with International Environmental Law* (London: Earthscan, 1996), p. 147

Rosenne, Shabtai (ed.), *The Law of Treaties: A Guide to the Legislative History of the Vienna Convention* (A. W. Sijthoff, 1970)

Rothenberg, David, 'Love of Nature vs. Love of Respect. Non-Violence in Practice in Norway', in Andrew Light and Eric Katz (eds.), *Environmental Pragmatism* (London: Routledge, 1996)

Rothwell, Donald R., 'The *Whaling Case*: International Law Perspectives', *Law Council Review* 10 (April–July 2014), www.lawcouncil.asn.au/lawcouncil/images/LawCouncilReview/Issue%2010%20Web.pdf

Rothwell, Donald R., Oude Elferink, Alex G., Scott, Karen N. and Stephens, Tim (eds.), *The Oxford Handbook on the Law of the Sea* (Oxford University Press, 2015)

Sadat-Akhavi, Seyed Ali, *Methods of Resolving Conflict between Treaties* (Leiden: Brill Academic Publishers, 2003)

Safrin, Sabrina, 'Treaties in Collision? The Biosafety Protocol and the World Trade Organization Agreements', *American Journal of International Law* 96 (2002), 606

Sage-Fuller, Bénédicte, *The Precautionary Principle in Marine Environmental Law. With Special Reference to High Risk Vessels* (Abingdon: Routledge, 2013)

Sakai, Hironobu, 'After the *Whaling Case*: Its Lessons from a Japanese Perspective', chapter to be published in Malgosia Fitzmaurice and Dai Tamada (eds.), *Whaling in the Antarctic: The Judgment and its Implications* (Leiden: Brill–Nijhoff, 2016)

Sand, Peter H., 'Japan's "Research Whaling" in the Antarctic Southern Ocean and in the North Pacific Ocean in the Face of the Endangered Species Convention (CITES)', *Review of European Community and International Environmental Law* 17 (2008), 56

Sanderson, Kate, '*Grind* – Ambiguity and Pressure to Conform – Faroese Whaling and the Anti-Whaling Protest', in Milton M. R. Freeman and Urs P. Kreuter (eds.), *Elephants and Whales. Resources for Whom?* (Basle: Gordon and Breach Science Publishers, 1994), p. 187

Sands, Philippe, 'Treaty, Custom and Cross-Fertilization of International Law', *Yale Human Rights and Development Journal* 1 (1998), 85

Savelle, James M. and Kishigami, Nobuhiro, 'Anthropological Research on Whaling: Prehistoric, Historic and Current Contexts', in Nobuhiro Kishigami, Hisashi Hamaguchi and James M. Savelle (eds.), *Senri Ethnological Studies, No. 84, Anthropological Studies on Whaling* (Osaka: National Museum of Ethnology, 2013), p. 1

Schiffman, Howard S., 'The Competence of Pro-Consumptive International Organisations to Regulate Cetacean Resources', in C. G. Burns and Alexander Gillespie (eds.), *The Future of Cetaceans in a Changing World* (Ardsley, NY: Transnational Publishers, 2003)

Scott, Shirley V. and Oriana, Lucia, 'International Convention for the Regulation of Whaling/International Court of Justice', *International Journal of Marine and Coastal Law* 29 (2014), 547

Scruton, Roger, *Animals Rights and Wrongs* (London: Metro, 2000)

Scully, Mathew, *Dominion: The Power of Man, the Suffering of Animals, and the Call to Mercy* (New York: St Martin's Press, 2003)

Sejeresen, Frank, 'Hunting and Management of Beluga Whales (*Delphinapterus leucas*) in Greenland: Changing Strategies to Cope with New National and Local Interests', *Arctic* 54 (2001), 431

Sellheim, Nikolas, 'The Neglected Tradition? The Genesis of the EU Seal Products Trade Ban and Commercial Sealing', *Yearbook of Polar Law* 5 (2013), 417

'Policies and Influence. Tracing and Locating the EU Seal Product Trade Regulation', *International Community Law Review* 17 (2015), 3

Sepez, Jennifer, 'Treaty Rights and the Right to Culture: Native American Subsistence Issues in US Law', *Cultural Dynamics* 14 (2002), 143

Shoham, S. and Lamay, N., 'Commission for Future Generations', in Joerg Chet Tremmel (ed.), *Handbook of Intergenerational Justice* (Cheltenham: Edward Elgar Publishing, 2006)

Simma, Bruno, and Pulkowski, Dirk, 'Of Planets and the Universe: Self Contained Regimes in International Law', *European Journal of International Law* 16 (2006), 483

Singer, Peter, *Animal Liberation* (New York: Harper Perennial, 2001)

'Animal Liberation at 30', *New York Review of Books*, 15 May 2003

Singer, Peter and Regan, Tom (eds.), *Animal Rights and Human Obligations* (Englewood Cliffs, NJ: Prentice Hall, 1976)

Smith, Jeffrey J., 'Evolving Conservation? The International Court's Decision in the *Australia/Japan* Case', *Ocean Development and International Law*, 45 (2014), 301

Stephens, Tim, 'Law of the Sea Symposium – Comment', http://opiniojuris.org/2013/05/27/law-of-thesea-symposium/

Stoett, Peter J., *The International Politics of Whaling* (Vancouver: UBC Press, 1997)

'Of Whales and People: Normative Theory, Symbolism and the IWC', *Journal of International Wildlife Law and Policy* 8 (2005), 151

Stone, Christopher D., 'Summing Up. Whaling and Its Critics', in Robert L. Friedheim (ed.), *Toward a Sustainable Whaling Regime* (Seattle: Washington University Press, 2001), p. 180

Strong, J. T., 'Status of the Narwhal *Monodon monoceros* in Canada', *Canadian Field Naturalist* 102 (1988), 391

Suarez, M. José, 'Exploitation of the Products of the Sea', Report to the Council of the League of Nations on the Questions Which Appear Ripe for Codification, League of Nations Doc. 196.M.70.1927.V, 122

Sunstein, Cass R., 'The Rights of Animals: A Very Short Primer', University of Chicago, John M. Olin Law and Economics Working Paper No. 157 (2D Series) Public Law and Legal Theory Working Paper No. 20, 2006, www.law.uchicago.edu/academics/publiclaw/uindex.html

Sykes, Katie, 'The Appeal of Science and the Formation of Global Animal Law', *EJIL* (forthcoming, 2015), SSRN: http//SSTN.com/abstract=2632812

Tamada, Dai, 'On the Way to Definitive Settlement of Dispute: Lessons from the *Whaling Case*', *Australian Yearbook of International Law* 32 (2015), 113

Tams, Christian, *Enforcing Obligations Erga Omnes in International Law* (rev. edn, Cambridge University Press, 2010)

'Roads Not Taken, Opportunities Missed: Procedural and Jurisdictional Questions Sidestepped in the Whaling Judgment', chapter to be published in Malgosia Fitzmaurice and Dai Tamada (eds.), *Whaling in the Antarctic: The Judgment and its Implications* (Leiden: Brill–Nijhoff, 2016)

Tams, Christian and Sloan, James (eds.), *The Development of International Law by the International Court of Justice* (Cambridge University Press, 2013)

Telesetsky, Anastasia, Anton, Donald K. and Koivurova, Timo, ' ICJ's Decision in *Australia/Japan*: Giving up the Spear or Refining the Scientific Design?' *Ocean Development and International Law*, 45 (2014), 328

Tønnessen, J. N. and Johnsen, A. O., *The History of Modern Whaling* (Canberra: Australian National University Press, 1982)

Torrissen, Ole, Glover, Kevin Alan, Haug, Tore, Misund, Ole Arve, Skaug, Hans Julius and Kaiser, Matthias, 'Food for Thought: Good Ethics or Political and Cultural Censoring in Science?', *ICES Journal of Marine Science* 69 (2012), 3, http://icesjms.oxfordjournals.org/content/early/2012/03/06/icesjms.fss016. full.pdf+html

Tremmel, Joerg Chet, 'Establishing Intergenerational Justice in National Consti- tutions', in Joerg Chet Tremmel (ed.), *Handbook of Intergenerational Justice* (Cheltenham: Edward Elgar Publishing, 2006)

(ed.), *Handbook of Intergenerational Justice* (Cheltenham: Edward Elgar Pub- lishing, 2006)

Trouwborst, A., *Evolution and Status of the Precautionary Principle in Inter- national Law* (The Hague: Kluwer Law International, 2002)

Precautionary Rights and Duties of States (Leiden: Martinus Nijhoff Publishers, 2006)

Twiss Jr, John R. and Reeves, Randall R. (eds.), *Conservation and Management of Marine Mammals* (Washington: Smithsonian Institution Press, 1999)

Urs, Priya, 'Guest Post: Are States Injured by Whaling in the Antarctic?' *Opinio Iuris*, http://opiniojuris.org/2014/08/14/guest-post-states-injured-whaling-antarctic/

Vallance, William Roy, 'The International Convention for Regulation of Whaling and the Act of Congress Giving Effect to its Provisions', *American Journal of International Law* 31 (1937), 112

Voigt, Christina, 'A Precautionary Approach to the Whaling Convention: Will the ICJ Challenge the Legality of Scientific Whaling?', in I. L. Backer, O. K. Fauchald and C. Voigt (eds.), *Pro Natura – Festskrift til Hans Christian Bugge* (Oslo: Universitetsforlaget, 2012), p. 557

Vrdoljak, Ana Filipa (ed.), *The Cultural Dimension of Human Rights. Collected Courses of the Academy of European Law* (Oxford University Press, 2013)

Warren, Mary Anne, 'The Rights of the Non-Human World', in Robert Elliot and Arran E. Gare (eds.), *Environmental Philosophy* (University Park: Penn. State University Press, 1983), p. 109

Watkins, Casey, 'Whaling in the Antarctic: Case Analysis and Suggestions for the Future of Antarctic Whaling and Stock Management', *New York Inter- national Law Review* 25 (2012), 49

Weinbaum, Matthew, 'Makah Native Americans vs. Animal Rights Activists', www.umich.edu/~snre492/Jones/makah.htm

Wiessner, Siegfried, 'Culture and Rights of Indigenous Peoples', in Ana Filipa Vrdoljak (ed.), *The Cultural Dimension of Human Rights. Collected Courses of the Academy of European Law* (Oxford University Press, 2013), p. 117

Wiessner, Siegfried and Battiste, Marie, 'The 2000 Revision of the United Nations Draft Principles and Guidelines on the Protection of the Heritage of Indi- genous People', *St Thomas Law Review* 13 (2000), 383

Witting, Lars, Ugarte, Fernando and Heide-Jørgensen, Mads Peter, 'Greenland, Narwhal (*Mondon monoceros*)', NDF Workshop Case Studies, WG 5 – Mammals, Case Study 7, *Monodon monoceros*, Country – Greenland, 4. See www.conabio.gob.mx/institucion/cooperacion_internacional/TallerNDF/

Links-Documentos/WG-CS/WG5-Mammals/WG5-CS7%20Monodon/WG5-CS7.pdf

Wold, Chris and Kearney, Michael S., 'The Legal Effects of Greenland's Unilateral Aboriginal Subsistence Whale Hunt', *American University International Law Review* 30 (2015), 561

Wolfrum, Rüdiger and Matz, Nele, *Conflicts in International Environmental Law* (Berlin: Springer, 2003)

Wouters, Judith, 'Japan and the IWC: Investigating Japan's Whaling Policy Objectives', Master's Dissertation, University of Leuven, 2008–9, www.scriptie bank.be/sites/default/files/e4c466ef30d18f4c25bfeaeb883f2058.pdf

WWF Denmark, 'The Big Four – a WWF update on Greenland's efforts with regard to species conservation and nature protection – April 2005', 41, http://assets.panda.org/downloads/thebigfour.pdf

Wyatt, Julian, 'Should we Presume that Japan Acted in Good Faith? Reflections on Judge Abraham's Balance of Proof Based Analysis', *AYBIL* 32 (2015), 145

Xanthaki, Alexandra, 'Multiculturalism and International Law: Discussing Universal Standards', *Human Rights Quarterly* 32 (2010), 21

Young, Margaret, *Trading Fish, Saving Fish: The Interactions between Regimes in International Law* (Cambridge University Press, 2011)

   (ed.), *Regime Interaction in International Law. Facing Fragmentation* (Cambridge University Press, 2012)

Young, Oran R., 'Subsistence, Sustainability, and the Sea Mammals: Reconstructing the International Whaling Regime', *Ocean and Coastal Management* 23 (1994), 117

Yupsanis, Athanasios, 'The Meaning of "Culture" in Article 15(1)(a) of the ICESCR – Positive Aspects of the CESCR's General Comment No. 21 for the Safeguarding of Minority Cultures', *German Yearbook of International Law* 55 (2012), 345

   'Article 27 of the ICCPR Revisited: The Right to Culture as a Normative Source for Minority/Indigenous Participatory Claims in the Case Law of the Human Rights Committee', *Hague Yearbook of International Law* 26 (2013), 359

INDEX

Abe, Shinzo 115
Aboriginal Subsistence Whaling Sub-
    Committee (ASWSC) 60, 250
aboriginal whaling 1, 34, 42, 47–9, 84,
    105, 151, 166, 234–75
    and animal rights 242–4
    areas of confusion/inconsistency 242,
        246, 249–50, 260, 272–5, 310
    calls for banning 45–6, 108–9
    case studies 265–75
    categories 250–1
    complexity of issues 234
    contentious issues 258–60, 264
    and cultural diversity 123, 129
    definitions 16, 49, 248–51
    determination of quotas 349
    early regulation 246–7
    exemption from restrictions/
        prohibitions 15–16, 18, 49, 72–3,
        274
    IWC regulation 247–51, 254–60
    killing methods 245–6, 260
    national regulation 43–4
    objectives 254
    outside IWC jurisdiction 261–4
    overlap with commercial whaling
        249–50, 252–4, 273–4, 310
    permitted regions/peoples 255,
        350–1
    permitted species 254–6, 350–1
    quotas 49, 189–90, 216–17, 248, 251,
        255–8, 349–51
    right to 234, 241–6
    sale of by-products 252–4, 267–72
    use of modern technology 244–6
    weak arguments for 243
    welfare requirements 183

Aboriginal Whaling Management
    Scheme/Procedure (AWMS/
    AWMP) 255–7
Abraham, Ronny, Judge 106
Acheson, Dean 29–30
age at sexual maturity, research
    into 118–19
Aglukkaq, Leona 289
Al-Khasawneh, Judge 103, 121
Altherr, Sandra 210
American Cetacean Society (ACS) 143–4
Andresen, Stienar 53–4, 58, 104–5
animal rights 1, 153–83
    Animal Rights Theory 163–4, 182
    changed focus of debate 158–65
    and concept of selfhood 163–4
    and cultural diversity 181–2, 308
    distinguished from animal welfare
        161–5
    distinguished from
        environmentalism 140–1, 143
    diversity of views on 153, 162–5,
        168–70, 182, 310
    in international law 155–7
    metaphysical expression 155
    moral arguments 165–70
    philosophy of 153–65
    restriction to certain species 154–5,
        167
    'strong rights' vs. 'weak rights'
        approach 163
    and whaling 164–8, 242–4
    wild/domesticated animals,
        distinction between 162–4
    see also animal welfare; 'speciesism'
animal welfare, theory of 165
    and aboriginal whaling 242–4

384

expert witnesses, use of 102–4, 121
explosives, first use of 4–6

factory ships 4–5
  geographical restrictions 338–9, 342
  loopholes in law 24
  Moratorium on 69–70
  notification requirements 355–9
  open/closed seasons 338–9
  patenting of slipway for 6
  prohibited uses 353
  record of vessel name/characteristics 357
  regulation 19–23
  supervision 354
family life, right to 241
Faroe Islands 310
  exclusion from international conventions 201, 212–13
  land stations 24–5
  membership of NAMMCO 189–90
Faroe Islands, pilot whale hunt 1, 28, 123, 129–30, 143–7, 189
  arguments for 144–6, 148
  closeness to nature 146
  consumption of products 20
  danger to participants 146
  killing methods 144–5, 169
  regulation 144
  scale of catch 144
fin whales
  aboriginal quotas 257–8
  defined 335
  killing methods/times 245
  level of stocks 13, 320–1
  North Atlantic stocks 342–4
  numbers caught 8
  permitted for aboriginal whaling 254–6
  research quotas 88, 100–1
  reservations concerning 206
  size limits 352
  uncertainty of data 320–1
Finance and Administration Committee 60–1
fish, whales equated with 50, 135
forum shopping 205
Foster, Caroline E. 93, 121

Foyn, Sven 5
fragmentation (in international law) 219–25, 232–3
  proposed solutions 221–2, 225, 231–2
  studies 221–2
France
  contributions to whaling debates 11, 24, 30–1
  Council for the Rights of Future Generations 176–7
  whaling history 4
Francione, Gary 164
Frazier, Tim 268
Freeland, Stephen 38, 40
Freeman, Milton M.R. 53, 62–3, 89, 136–7, 274, 298
Friedheim, Robert L. 77–8
Fuentes, Alejandro 125–6

Gaja, Giorgio 111
Gales, Nick 101–2, 104
Gambell, Ray 79–80, 266–7
Germany
  contributions to whaling debates 11
  national Constitution 176
  whaling history 4–5, 8, 19
Gillespie, Alexander 41–2, 46, 51, 66, 151–2, 163, 168–9, 186, 192, 200–2, 204–5, 208–9, 244, 250, 284–5, 287–8, 302, 314
Goodman, Dan 53, 70–1, 86–7, 133, 136
gray whales
  aboriginal whaling of 255–6, 266–70, 350
  defined 335
  extinct varieties 319
  population levels 318–19
  prohibition on killing 21, 247–8
  quotas 350
Greenland 201, 210
  arguments for narwhal hunt 293–4
  ban on narwhal exports 292
  (claimed) exemption from EU laws 213, 294
  export of narwhal products 290
  fin whale stocks 343
  Hunting Council 282
  hunting methods 283

Lightning Source UK Ltd.
Milton Keynes UK
UKHW022204260719
346914UK00020B/429/P